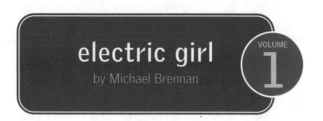

electric girl

by Michael Brennan

VOLUME 1

AiT/PLANETLAR

San Francisco

Electric Girl volume 1
by Michael Brennan

Published by
AiT/Planet Lar
2034 47th Avenue
San Francisco, CA 94116
www.ait-planetlar.com

First Edition December 2000
Third Edition April 2006
10 9 8 7 6 5 4 3

Written and Drawn by Michael Brennan
Cover Design by Christine Gleason
Cover Art by Michael Brennan

ISBN 0-9703555-0-5

Printed and bound in Canada by Lebonfon Printing

Thanks to everyone who helped make this book possible.

the origin of the electric girl

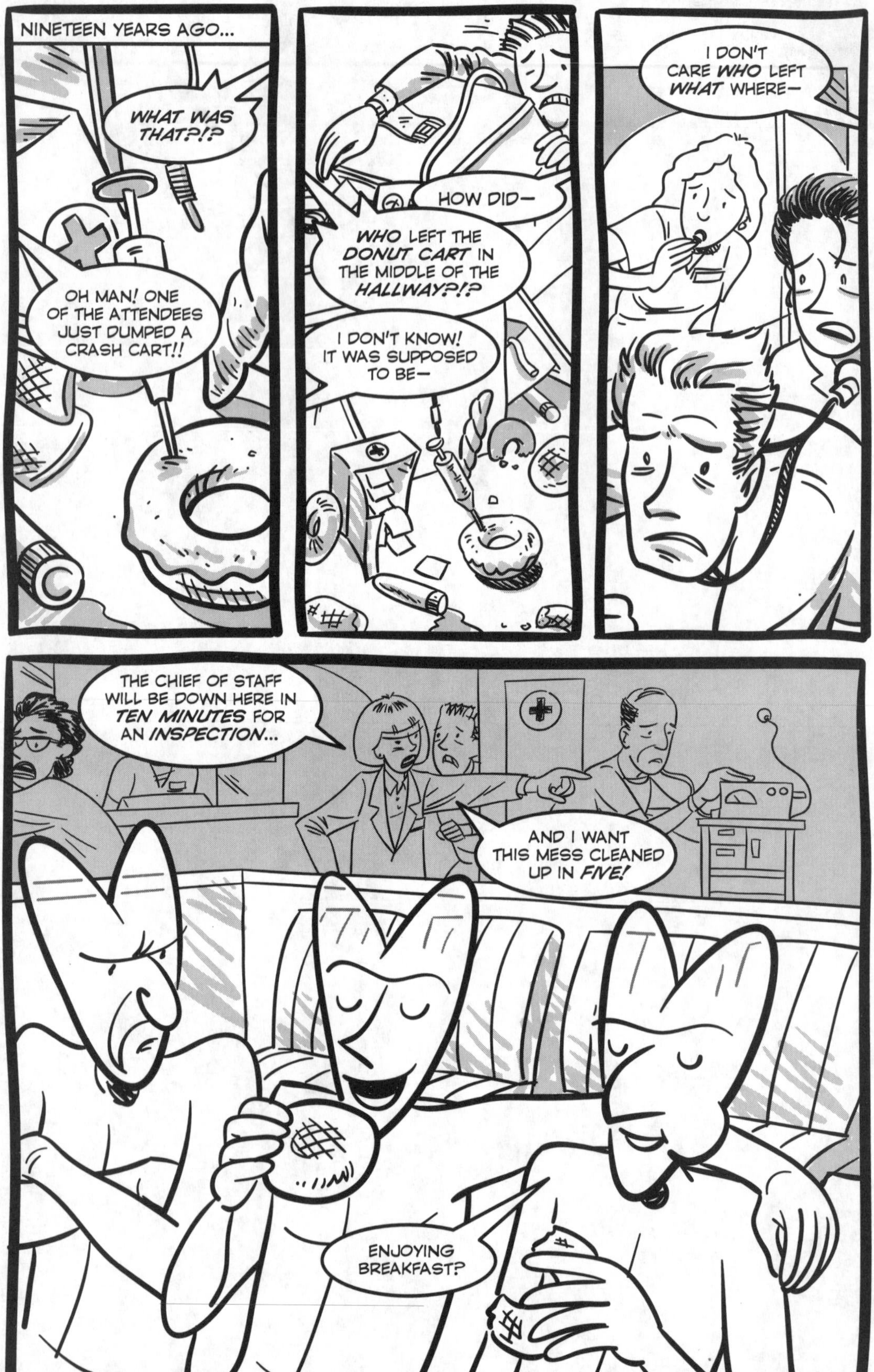
NINETEEN YEARS AGO...
WHAT WAS THAT?!?
OH MAN! ONE OF THE ATTENDEES JUST DUMPED A CRASH CART!!
HOW DID—
WHO LEFT THE DONUT CART IN THE MIDDLE OF THE HALLWAY?!?
I DON'T KNOW! IT WAS SUPPOSED TO BE—
I DON'T CARE WHO LEFT WHAT WHERE—
THE CHIEF OF STAFF WILL BE DOWN HERE IN TEN MINUTES FOR AN INSPECTION...
AND I WANT THIS MESS CLEANED UP IN FIVE!
ENJOYING BREAKFAST?

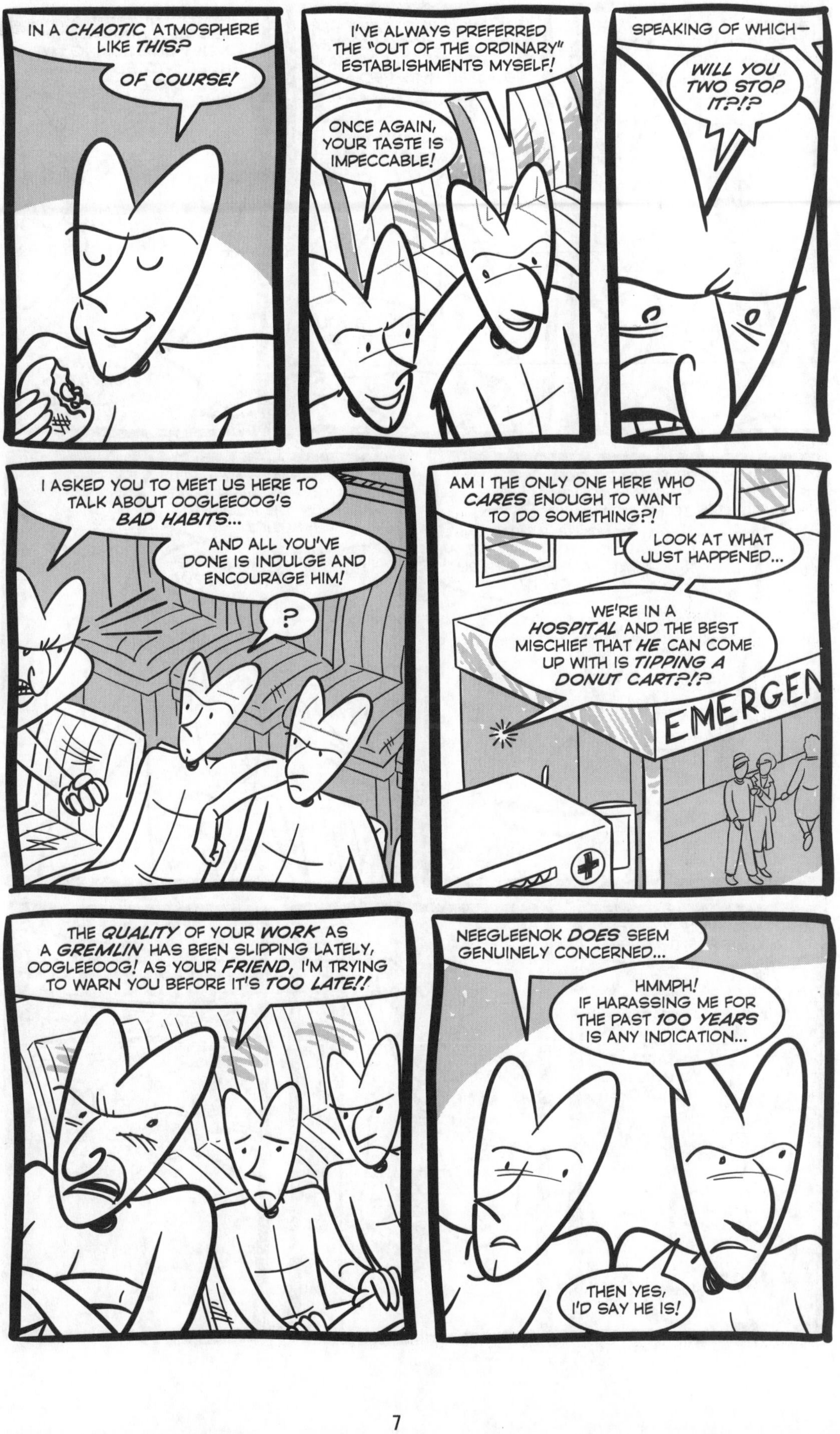
IN A CHAOTIC ATMOSPHERE LIKE THIS?
OF COURSE!
I'VE ALWAYS PREFERRED THE "OUT OF THE ORDINARY" ESTABLISHMENTS MYSELF!
ONCE AGAIN, YOUR TASTE IS IMPECCABLE!
SPEAKING OF WHICH—
WILL YOU TWO STOP IT?!?
I ASKED YOU TO MEET US HERE TO TALK ABOUT OOGLEEOOG'S BAD HABITS...
AND ALL YOU'VE DONE IS INDULGE AND ENCOURAGE HIM!
?
AM I THE ONLY ONE HERE WHO CARES ENOUGH TO WANT TO DO SOMETHING?!
LOOK AT WHAT JUST HAPPENED...
WE'RE IN A HOSPITAL AND THE BEST MISCHIEF THAT HE CAN COME UP WITH IS TIPPING A DONUT CART?!?
EMERGEN
THE QUALITY OF YOUR WORK AS A GREMLIN HAS BEEN SLIPPING LATELY, OOGLEEOOG! AS YOUR FRIEND, I'M TRYING TO WARN YOU BEFORE IT'S TOO LATE!!
NEEGLEENOK DOES SEEM GENUINELY CONCERNED...
HMMPH! IF HARASSING ME FOR THE PAST 100 YEARS IS ANY INDICATION...
THEN YES, I'D SAY HE IS!

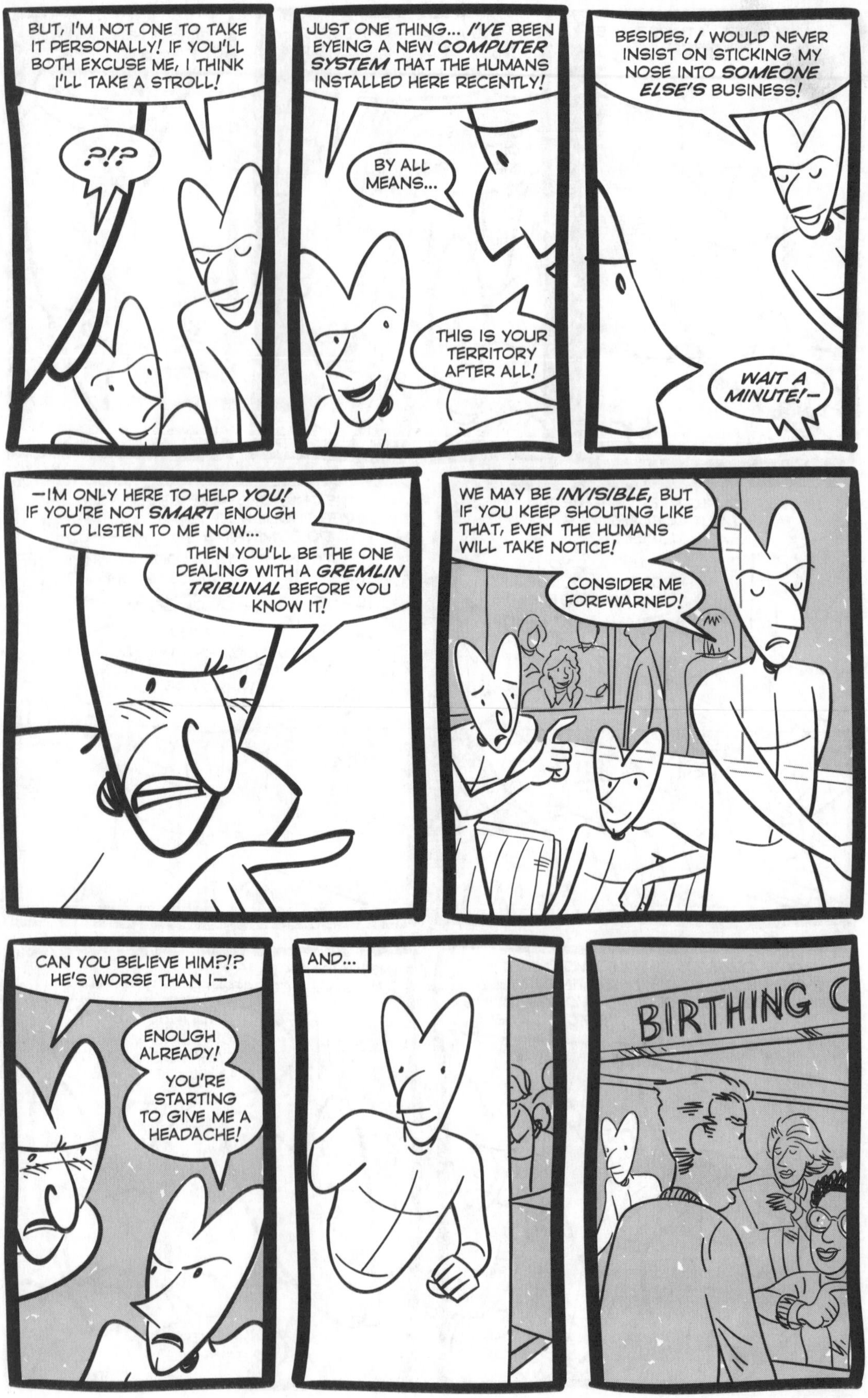
BUT, I'M NOT ONE TO TAKE IT PERSONALLY! IF YOU'LL BOTH EXCUSE ME, I THINK I'LL TAKE A STROLL!
?!?
JUST ONE THING... I'VE BEEN EYEING A NEW COMPUTER SYSTEM THAT THE HUMANS INSTALLED HERE RECENTLY!
BY ALL MEANS...
THIS IS YOUR TERRITORY AFTER ALL!
BESIDES, I WOULD NEVER INSIST ON STICKING MY NOSE INTO SOMEONE ELSE'S BUSINESS!
WAIT A MINUTE!—
—I'M ONLY HERE TO HELP YOU! IF YOU'RE NOT SMART ENOUGH TO LISTEN TO ME NOW...
THEN YOU'LL BE THE ONE DEALING WITH A GREMLIN TRIBUNAL BEFORE YOU KNOW IT!
WE MAY BE INVISIBLE, BUT IF YOU KEEP SHOUTING LIKE THAT, EVEN THE HUMANS WILL TAKE NOTICE!
CONSIDER ME FOREWARNED!
CAN YOU BELIEVE HIM?!? HE'S WORSE THAN I—
ENOUGH ALREADY!
YOU'RE STARTING TO GIVE ME A HEADACHE!
AND...
BIRTHING C

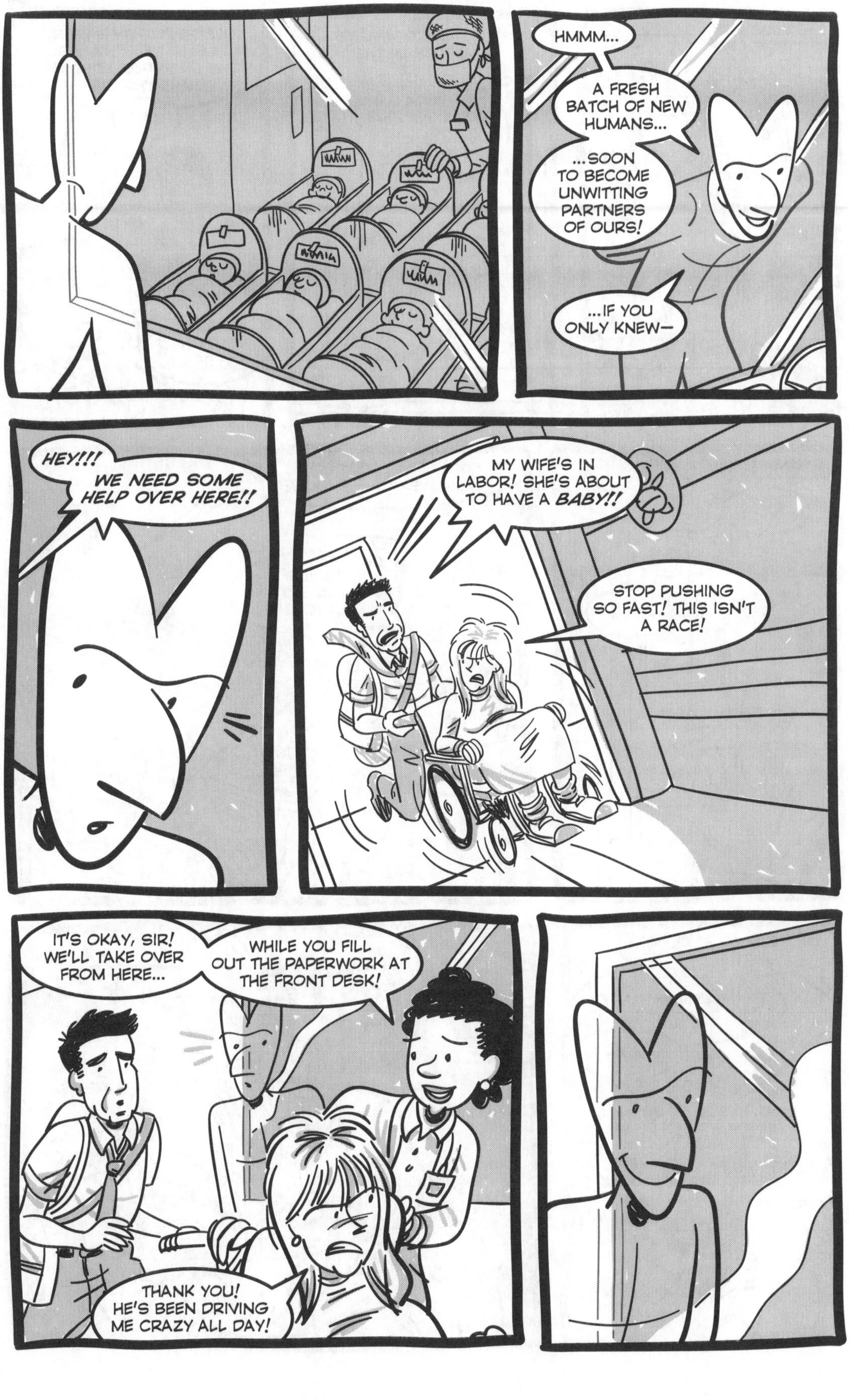
HMMM...
A FRESH BATCH OF NEW HUMANS...
...SOON TO BECOME UNWITTING PARTNERS OF OURS!
...IF YOU ONLY KNEW—
HEY!!! WE NEED SOME HELP OVER HERE!!
MY WIFE'S IN LABOR! SHE'S ABOUT TO HAVE A BABY!!
STOP PUSHING SO FAST! THIS ISN'T A RACE!
IT'S OKAY, SIR! WE'LL TAKE OVER FROM HERE...
WHILE YOU FILL OUT THE PAPERWORK AT THE FRONT DESK!
THANK YOU! HE'S BEEN DRIVING ME CRAZY ALL DAY!

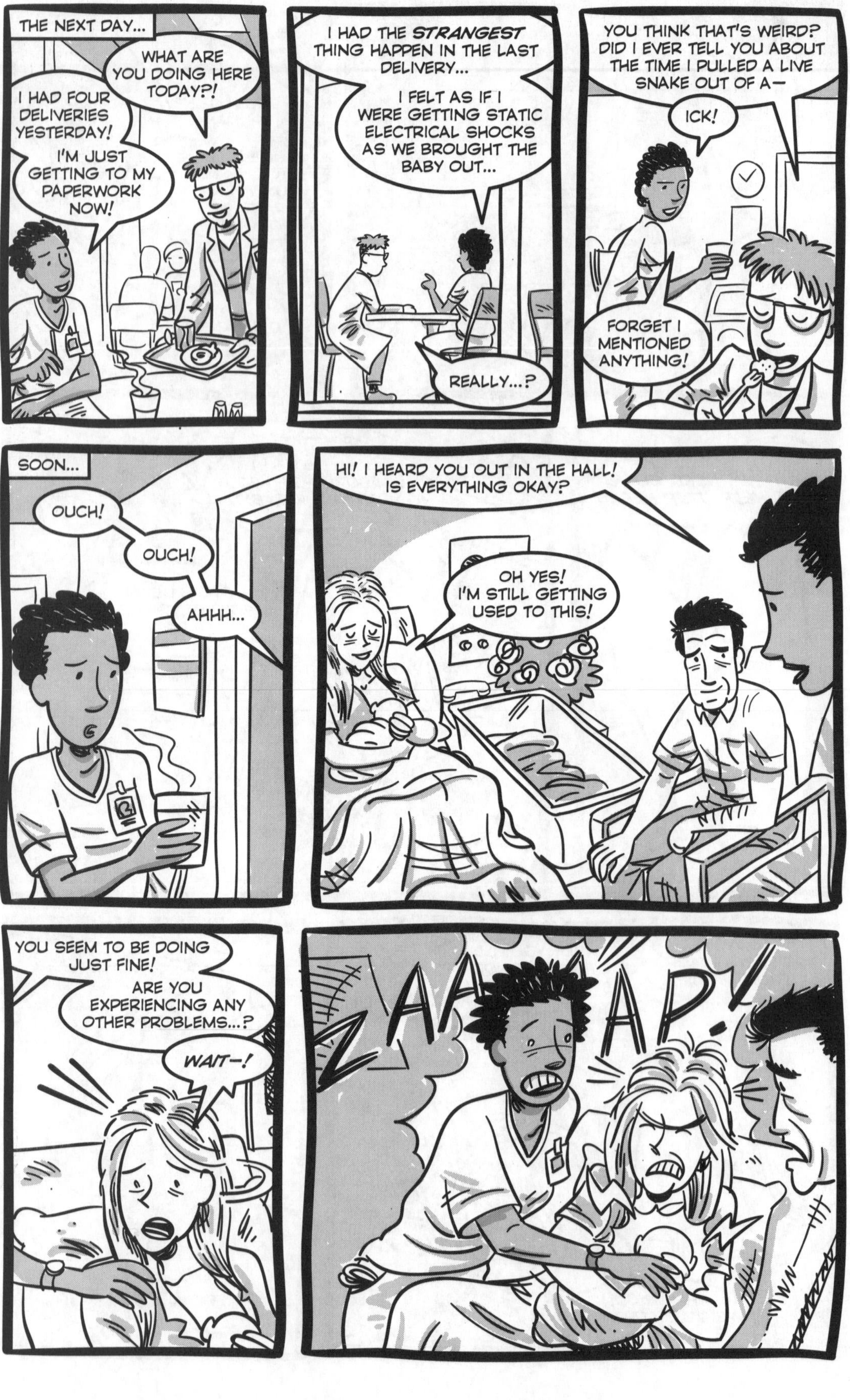
THE NEXT DAY...
WHAT ARE YOU DOING HERE TODAY?!
I HAD FOUR DELIVERIES YESTERDAY!
I'M JUST GETTING TO MY PAPERWORK NOW!
I HAD THE STRANGEST THING HAPPEN IN THE LAST DELIVERY...
I FELT AS IF I WERE GETTING STATIC ELECTRICAL SHOCKS AS WE BROUGHT THE BABY OUT...
REALLY...?
YOU THINK THAT'S WEIRD? DID I EVER TELL YOU ABOUT THE TIME I PULLED A LIVE SNAKE OUT OF A—
ICK!
FORGET I MENTIONED ANYTHING!
SOON...
OUCH!
OUCH!
AHHH...
HI! I HEARD YOU OUT IN THE HALL! IS EVERYTHING OKAY?
OH YES! I'M STILL GETTING USED TO THIS!
YOU SEEM TO BE DOING JUST FINE!
ARE YOU EXPERIENCING ANY OTHER PROBLEMS...?
WAIT—!
ZAAAP!

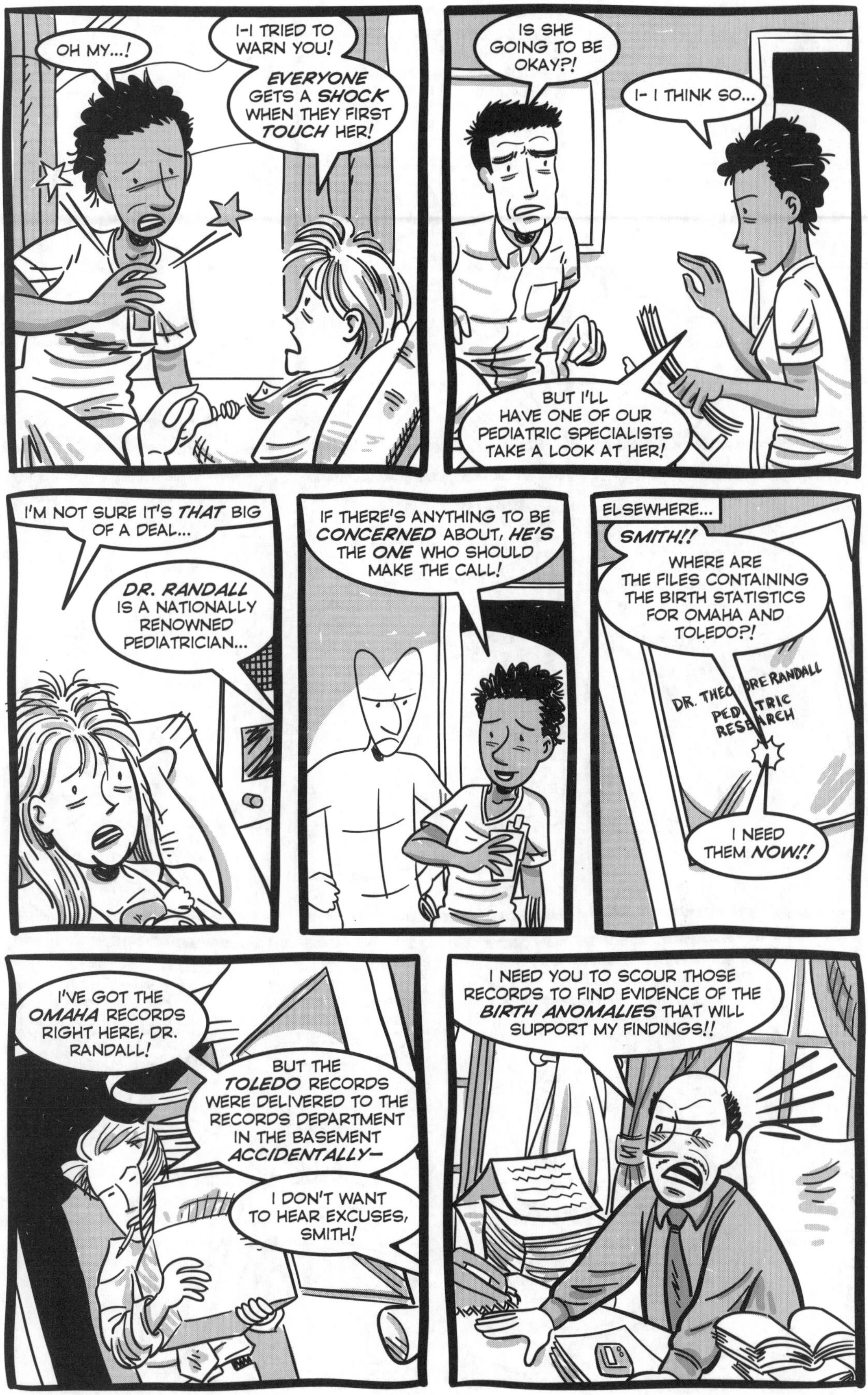
OH MY...!
I-I TRIED TO WARN YOU!
EVERYONE GETS A SHOCK WHEN THEY FIRST TOUCH HER!
IS SHE GOING TO BE OKAY?!
I- I THINK SO...
BUT I'LL HAVE ONE OF OUR PEDIATRIC SPECIALISTS TAKE A LOOK AT HER!
I'M NOT SURE IT'S THAT BIG OF A DEAL...
DR. RANDALL IS A NATIONALLY RENOWNED PEDIATRICIAN...
IF THERE'S ANYTHING TO BE CONCERNED ABOUT, HE'S THE ONE WHO SHOULD MAKE THE CALL!
ELSEWHERE...
SMITH!!
WHERE ARE THE FILES CONTAINING THE BIRTH STATISTICS FOR OMAHA AND TOLEDO?!
I NEED THEM NOW!!
I'VE GOT THE OMAHA RECORDS RIGHT HERE, DR. RANDALL!
BUT THE TOLEDO RECORDS WERE DELIVERED TO THE RECORDS DEPARTMENT IN THE BASEMENT ACCIDENTALLY—
I DON'T WANT TO HEAR EXCUSES, SMITH!
I NEED YOU TO SCOUR THOSE RECORDS TO FIND EVIDENCE OF THE BIRTH ANOMALIES THAT WILL SUPPORT MY FINDINGS!!

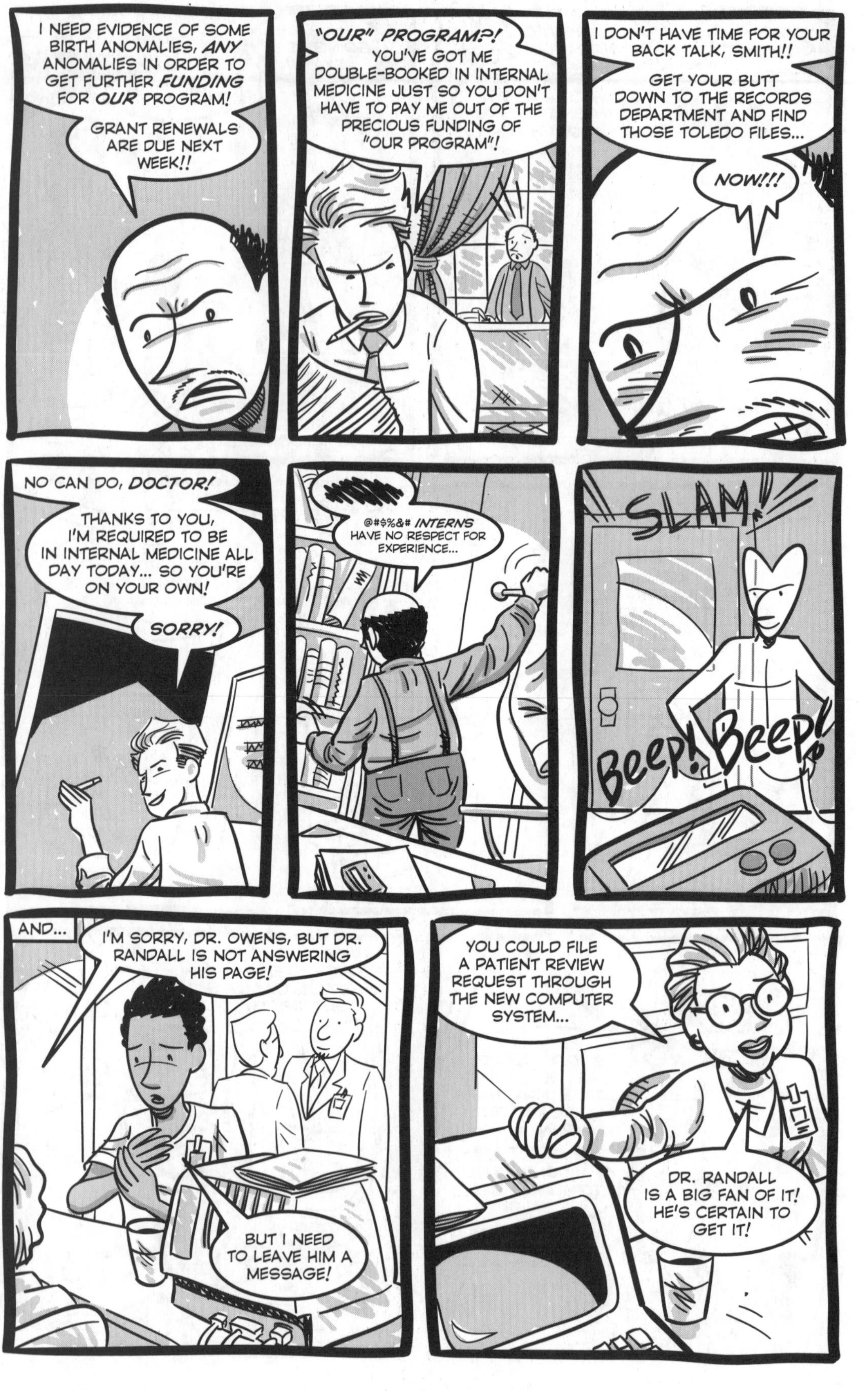

I NEED EVIDENCE OF SOME BIRTH ANOMALIES, ANY ANOMALIES IN ORDER TO GET FURTHER FUNDING FOR OUR PROGRAM!
GRANT RENEWALS ARE DUE NEXT WEEK!!
"OUR" PROGRAM?! YOU'VE GOT ME DOUBLE-BOOKED IN INTERNAL MEDICINE JUST SO YOU DON'T HAVE TO PAY ME OUT OF THE PRECIOUS FUNDING OF "OUR PROGRAM"!
I DON'T HAVE TIME FOR YOUR BACK TALK, SMITH!!
GET YOUR BUTT DOWN TO THE RECORDS DEPARTMENT AND FIND THOSE TOLEDO FILES...
NOW!!!
NO CAN DO, DOCTOR!
THANKS TO YOU, I'M REQUIRED TO BE IN INTERNAL MEDICINE ALL DAY TODAY... SO YOU'RE ON YOUR OWN!
SORRY!
@#$%&# INTERNS HAVE NO RESPECT FOR EXPERIENCE...
SLAM!
Beep! Beep!
AND...
I'M SORRY, DR. OWENS, BUT DR. RANDALL IS NOT ANSWERING HIS PAGE!
BUT I NEED TO LEAVE HIM A MESSAGE!
YOU COULD FILE A PATIENT REVIEW REQUEST THROUGH THE NEW COMPUTER SYSTEM...
DR. RANDALL IS A BIG FAN OF IT! HE'S CERTAIN TO GET IT!

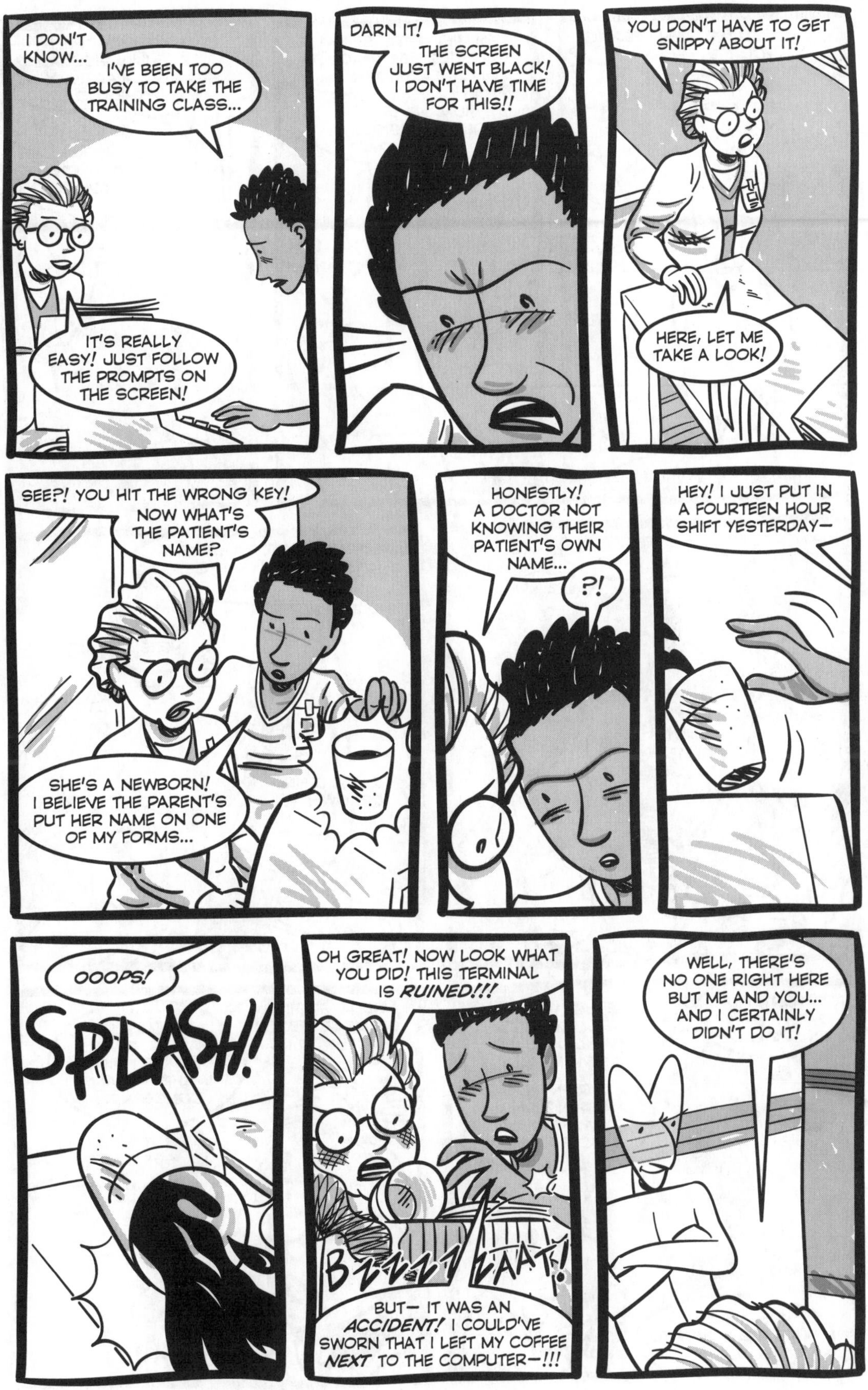

I DON'T KNOW...
I'VE BEEN TOO BUSY TO TAKE THE TRAINING CLASS...
IT'S REALLY EASY! JUST FOLLOW THE PROMPTS ON THE SCREEN!
DARN IT!
THE SCREEN JUST WENT BLACK! I DON'T HAVE TIME FOR THIS!!
YOU DON'T HAVE TO GET SNIPPY ABOUT IT!
HERE, LET ME TAKE A LOOK!
SEE?! YOU HIT THE WRONG KEY!
NOW WHAT'S THE PATIENT'S NAME?
SHE'S A NEWBORN! I BELIEVE THE PARENT'S PUT HER NAME ON ONE OF MY FORMS...
HONESTLY! A DOCTOR NOT KNOWING THEIR PATIENT'S OWN NAME...
?!
HEY! I JUST PUT IN A FOURTEEN HOUR SHIFT YESTERDAY—
OOOPS!
SPLASH!
OH GREAT! NOW LOOK WHAT YOU DID! THIS TERMINAL IS RUINED!!!
BZZZZZAAT!
BUT— IT WAS AN ACCIDENT! I COULD'VE SWORN THAT I LEFT MY COFFEE NEXT TO THE COMPUTER—!!!
WELL, THERE'S NO ONE RIGHT HERE BUT ME AND YOU... AND I CERTAINLY DIDN'T DO IT!

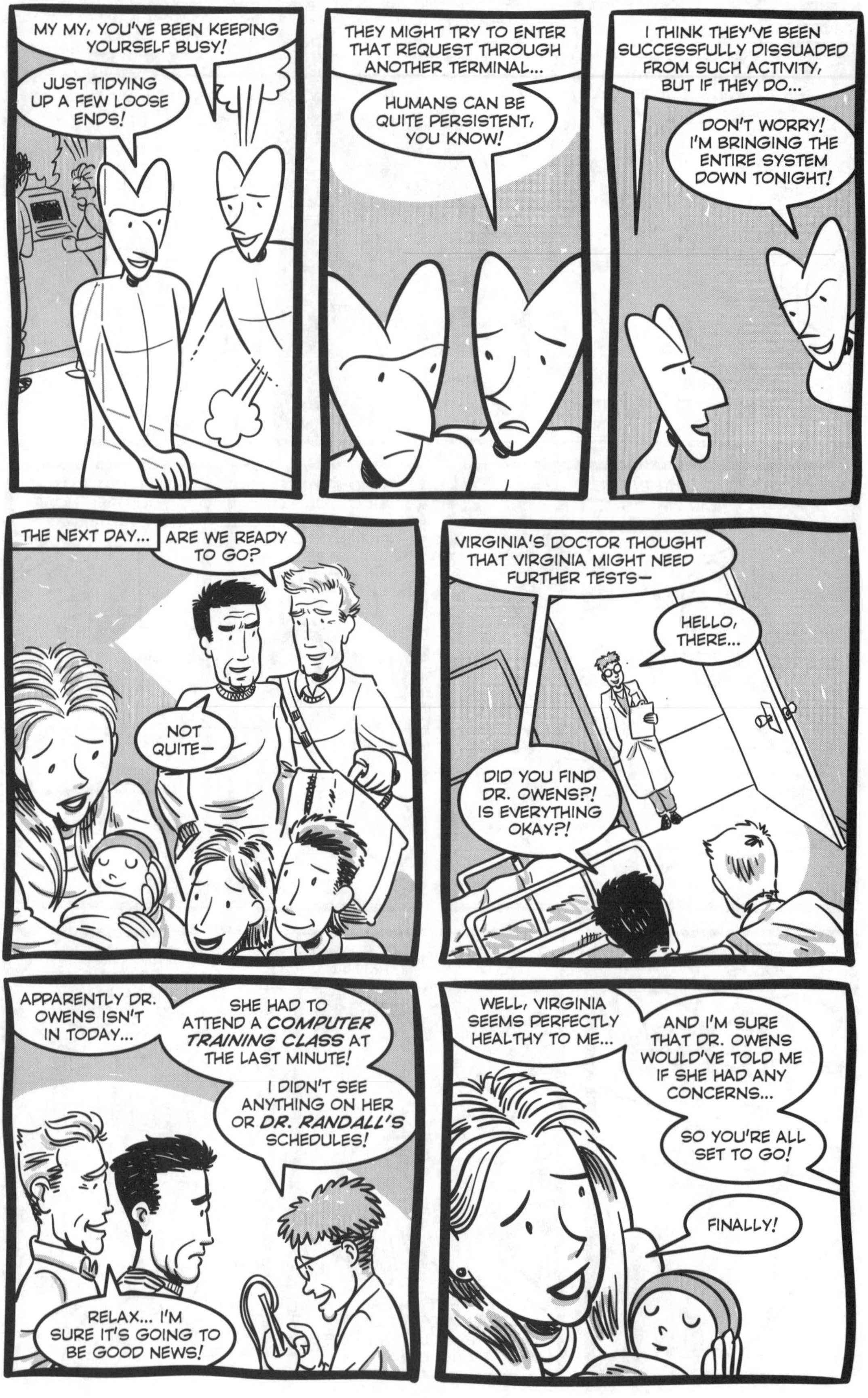

MY MY, YOU'VE BEEN KEEPING YOURSELF BUSY!
JUST TIDYING UP A FEW LOOSE ENDS!
THEY MIGHT TRY TO ENTER THAT REQUEST THROUGH ANOTHER TERMINAL...
HUMANS CAN BE QUITE PERSISTENT, YOU KNOW!
I THINK THEY'VE BEEN SUCCESSFULLY DISSUADED FROM SUCH ACTIVITY, BUT IF THEY DO...
DON'T WORRY! I'M BRINGING THE ENTIRE SYSTEM DOWN TONIGHT!
THE NEXT DAY...
ARE WE READY TO GO?
NOT QUITE—
VIRGINIA'S DOCTOR THOUGHT THAT VIRGINIA MIGHT NEED FURTHER TESTS—
HELLO, THERE...
DID YOU FIND DR. OWENS?! IS EVERYTHING OKAY?!
APPARENTLY DR. OWENS ISN'T IN TODAY...
SHE HAD TO ATTEND A COMPUTER TRAINING CLASS AT THE LAST MINUTE!
I DIDN'T SEE ANYTHING ON HER OR DR. RANDALL'S SCHEDULES!
RELAX... I'M SURE IT'S GOING TO BE GOOD NEWS!
WELL, VIRGINIA SEEMS PERFECTLY HEALTHY TO ME...
AND I'M SURE THAT DR. OWENS WOULD'VE TOLD ME IF SHE HAD ANY CONCERNS...
SO YOU'RE ALL SET TO GO!
FINALLY!

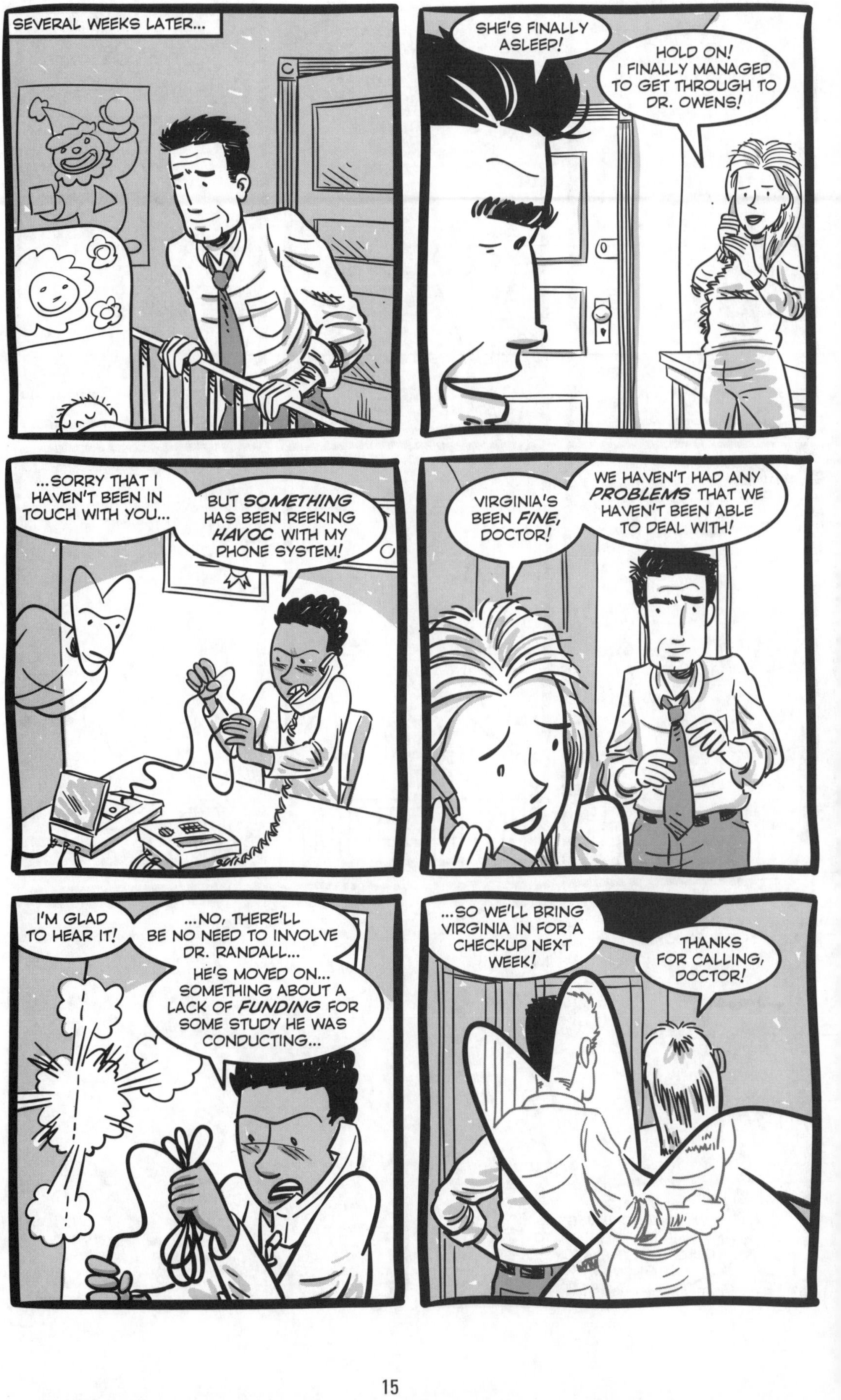
SEVERAL WEEKS LATER...
SHE'S FINALLY ASLEEP!
HOLD ON! I FINALLY MANAGED TO GET THROUGH TO DR. OWENS!
...SORRY THAT I HAVEN'T BEEN IN TOUCH WITH YOU...
BUT SOMETHING HAS BEEN REEKING HAVOC WITH MY PHONE SYSTEM!
VIRGINIA'S BEEN FINE, DOCTOR!
WE HAVEN'T HAD ANY PROBLEMS THAT WE HAVEN'T BEEN ABLE TO DEAL WITH!
I'M GLAD TO HEAR IT!
...NO, THERE'LL BE NO NEED TO INVOLVE DR. RANDALL...
HE'S MOVED ON... SOMETHING ABOUT A LACK OF FUNDING FOR SOME STUDY HE WAS CONDUCTING...
...SO WE'LL BRING VIRGINIA IN FOR A CHECKUP NEXT WEEK!
THANKS FOR CALLING, DOCTOR!

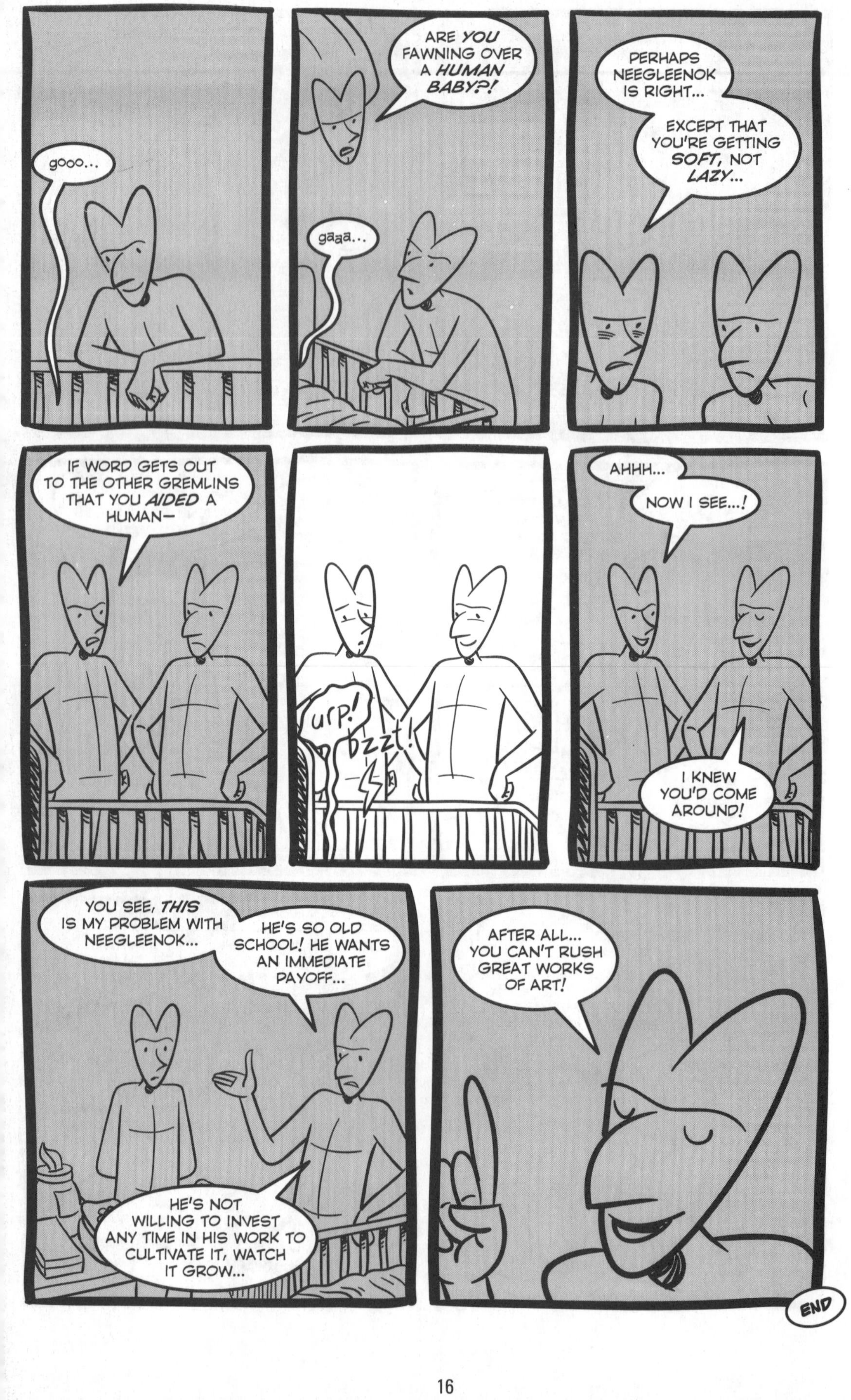
gooo...
ARE YOU FAWNING OVER A HUMAN BABY?!
gaaa...
PERHAPS NEEGLEENOK IS RIGHT...
EXCEPT THAT YOU'RE GETTING SOFT, NOT LAZY...
IF WORD GETS OUT TO THE OTHER GREMLINS THAT YOU AIDED A HUMAN—
urp!
bzzt!
AHHH...
NOW I SEE...!
I KNEW YOU'D COME AROUND!
YOU SEE, THIS IS MY PROBLEM WITH NEEGLEENOK...
HE'S SO OLD SCHOOL! HE WANTS AN IMMEDIATE PAYOFF...
HE'S NOT WILLING TO INVEST ANY TIME IN HIS WORK TO CULTIVATE IT, WATCH IT GROW...
AFTER ALL... YOU CAN'T RUSH GREAT WORKS OF ART!
END

electric girl issue ①

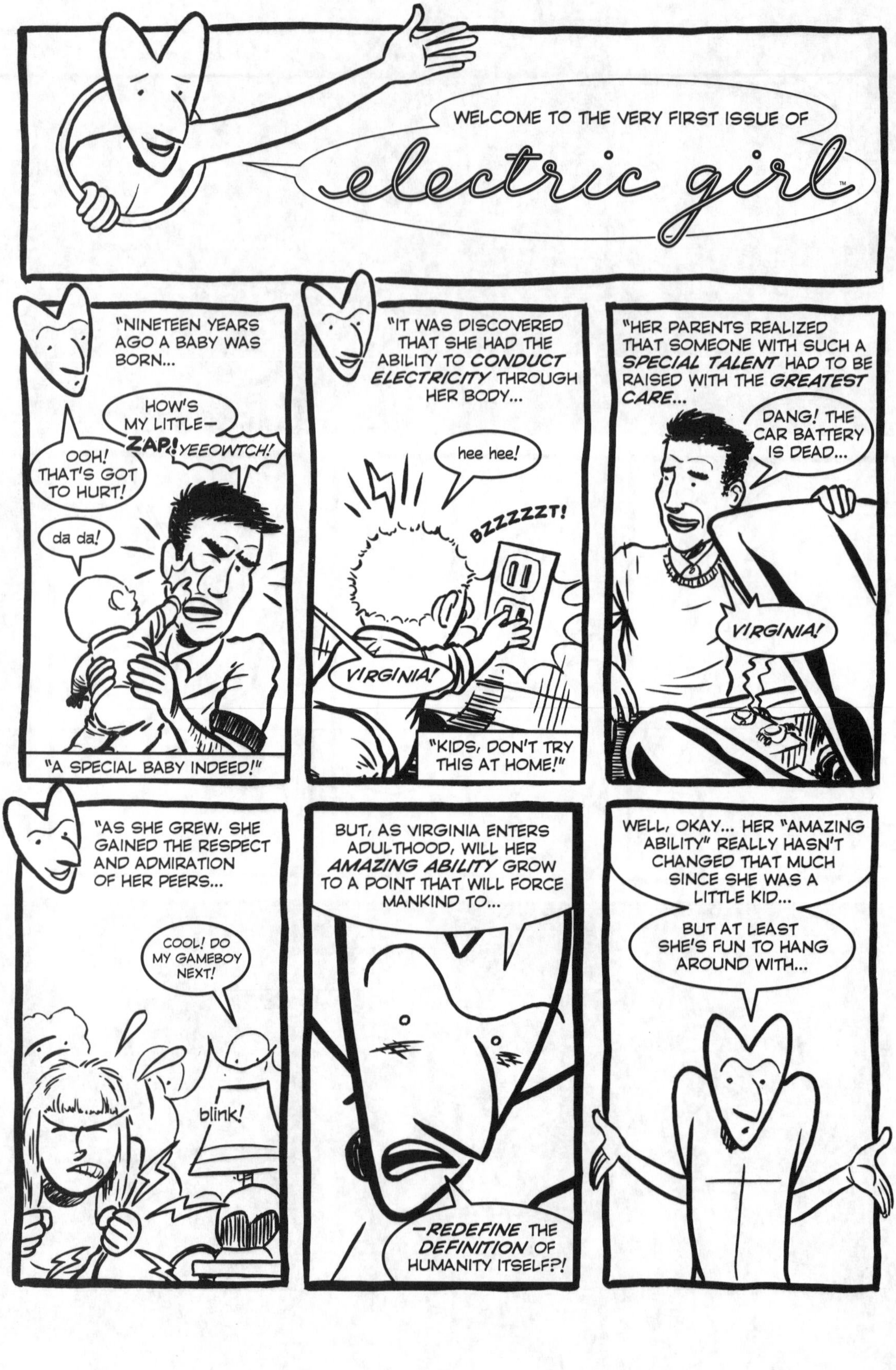
WELCOME TO THE VERY FIRST ISSUE OF
electric girl™
"NINETEEN YEARS AGO A BABY WAS BORN...
HOW'S MY LITTLE—
ZAP!
YEEOWTCH!
OOH! THAT'S GOT TO HURT!
da da!
"A SPECIAL BABY INDEED!"
"IT WAS DISCOVERED THAT SHE HAD THE ABILITY TO CONDUCT ELECTRICITY THROUGH HER BODY...
hee hee!
BZZZZZT!
VIRGINIA!
"KIDS, DON'T TRY THIS AT HOME!"
"HER PARENTS REALIZED THAT SOMEONE WITH SUCH A SPECIAL TALENT HAD TO BE RAISED WITH THE GREATEST CARE...
DANG! THE CAR BATTERY IS DEAD...
VIRGINIA!
"AS SHE GREW, SHE GAINED THE RESPECT AND ADMIRATION OF HER PEERS...
COOL! DO MY GAMEBOY NEXT!
blink!
BUT, AS VIRGINIA ENTERS ADULTHOOD, WILL HER AMAZING ABILITY GROW TO A POINT THAT WILL FORCE MANKIND TO...
—REDEFINE THE DEFINITION OF HUMANITY ITSELF?!
WELL, OKAY... HER "AMAZING ABILITY" REALLY HASN'T CHANGED THAT MUCH SINCE SHE WAS A LITTLE KID...
BUT AT LEAST SHE'S FUN TO HANG AROUND WITH...

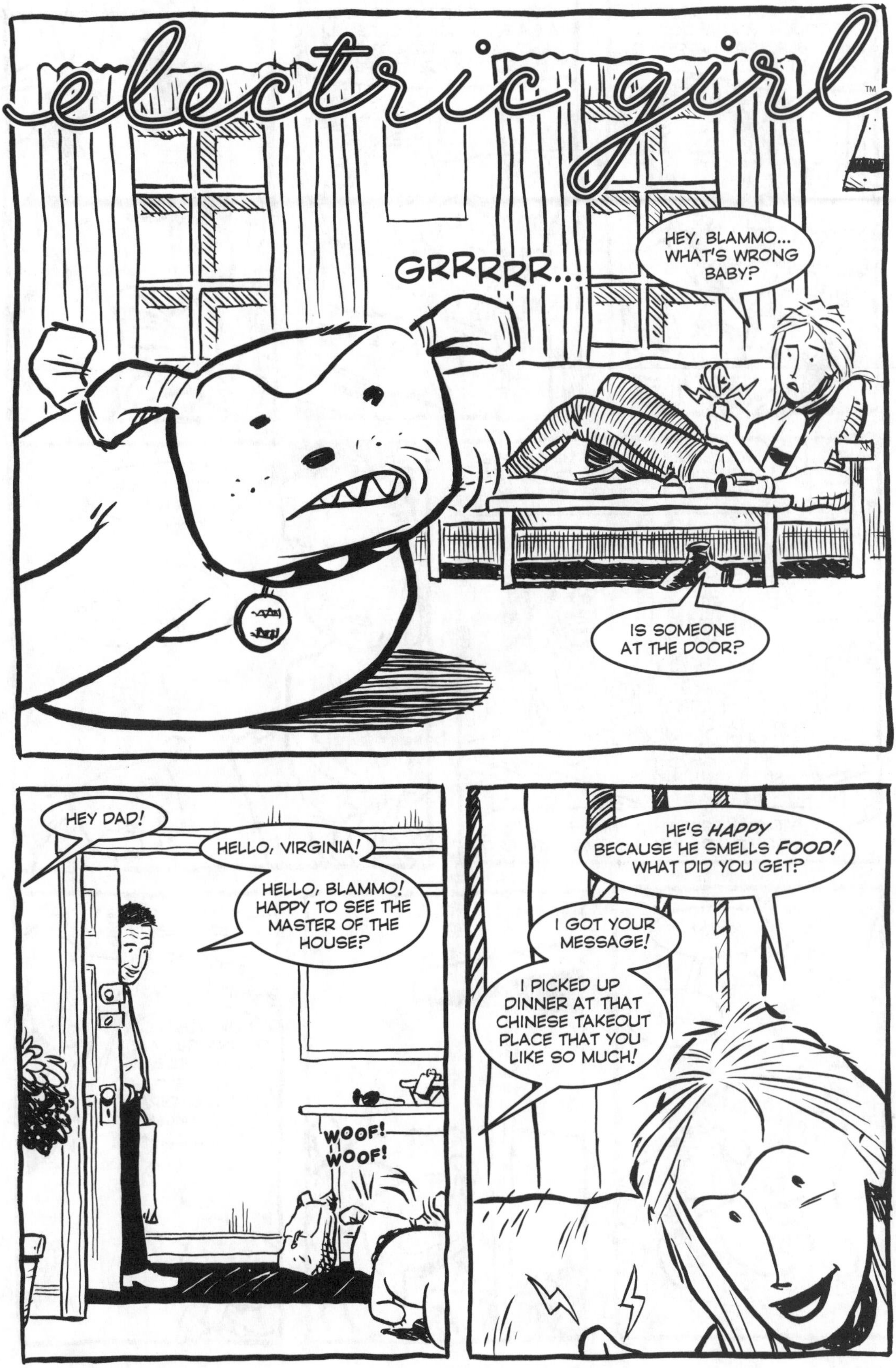
electric girl™
GRRRRR...
HEY, BLAMMO... WHAT'S WRONG BABY?
IS SOMEONE AT THE DOOR?
HEY DAD!
HELLO, VIRGINIA!
HELLO, BLAMMO! HAPPY TO SEE THE MASTER OF THE HOUSE?
WOOF! WOOF!
HE'S *HAPPY* BECAUSE HE SMELLS *FOOD!* WHAT DID YOU GET?
I GOT YOUR MESSAGE!
I PICKED UP DINNER AT THAT CHINESE TAKEOUT PLACE THAT YOU LIKE SO MUCH!

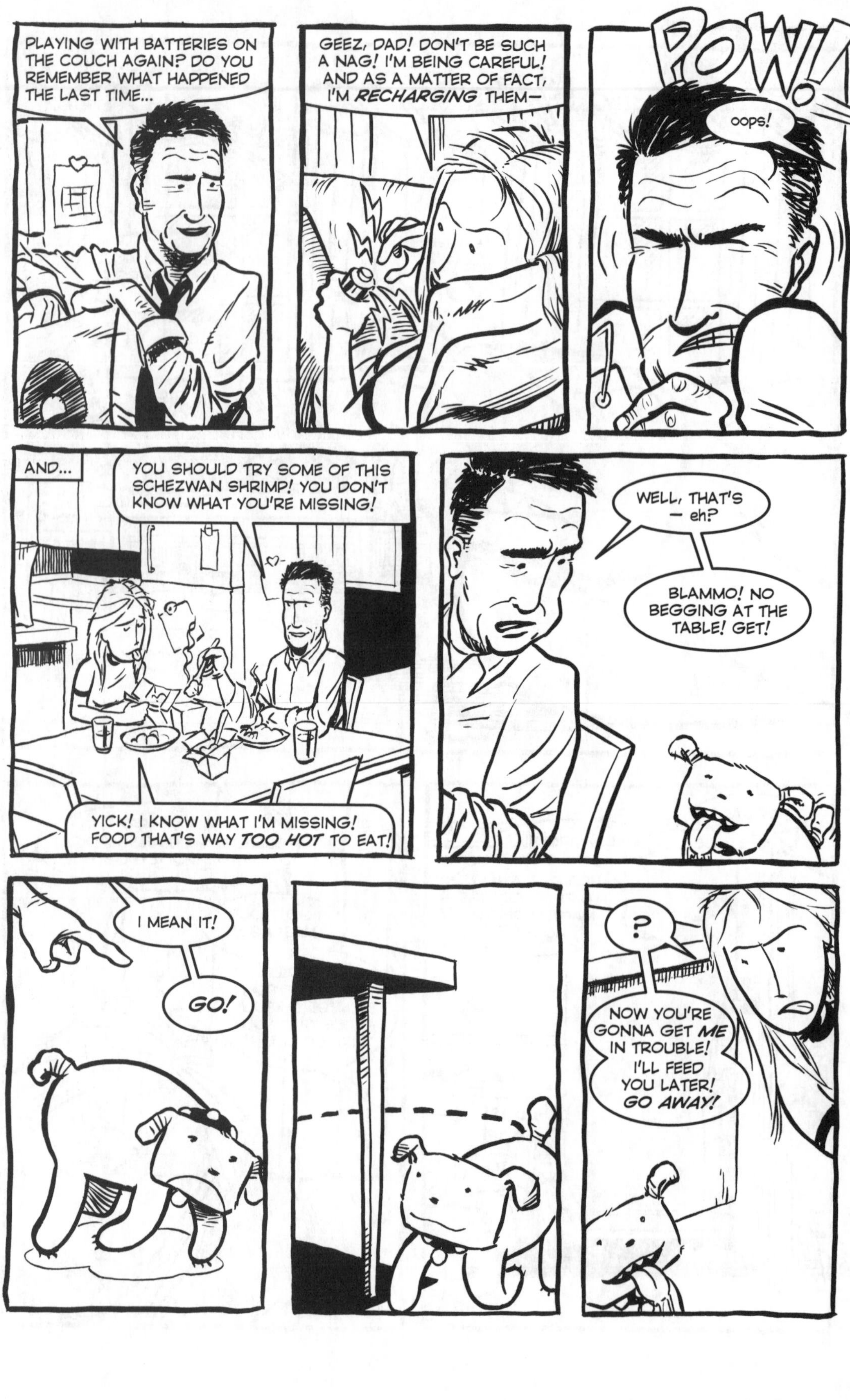
PLAYING WITH BATTERIES ON THE COUCH AGAIN? DO YOU REMEMBER WHAT HAPPENED THE LAST TIME...
GEEZ, DAD! DON'T BE SUCH A NAG! I'M BEING CAREFUL! AND AS A MATTER OF FACT, I'M *RECHARGING* THEM—
POW!
oops!
AND...
YOU SHOULD TRY SOME OF THIS SCHEZWAN SHRIMP! YOU DON'T KNOW WHAT YOU'RE MISSING!
YICK! I KNOW WHAT I'M MISSING! FOOD THAT'S WAY *TOO HOT* TO EAT!
WELL, THAT'S — eh?
BLAMMO! NO BEGGING AT THE TABLE! GET!
I MEAN IT!
GO!
?
NOW YOU'RE GONNA GET *ME* IN TROUBLE!
I'LL FEED YOU LATER! *GO AWAY!*

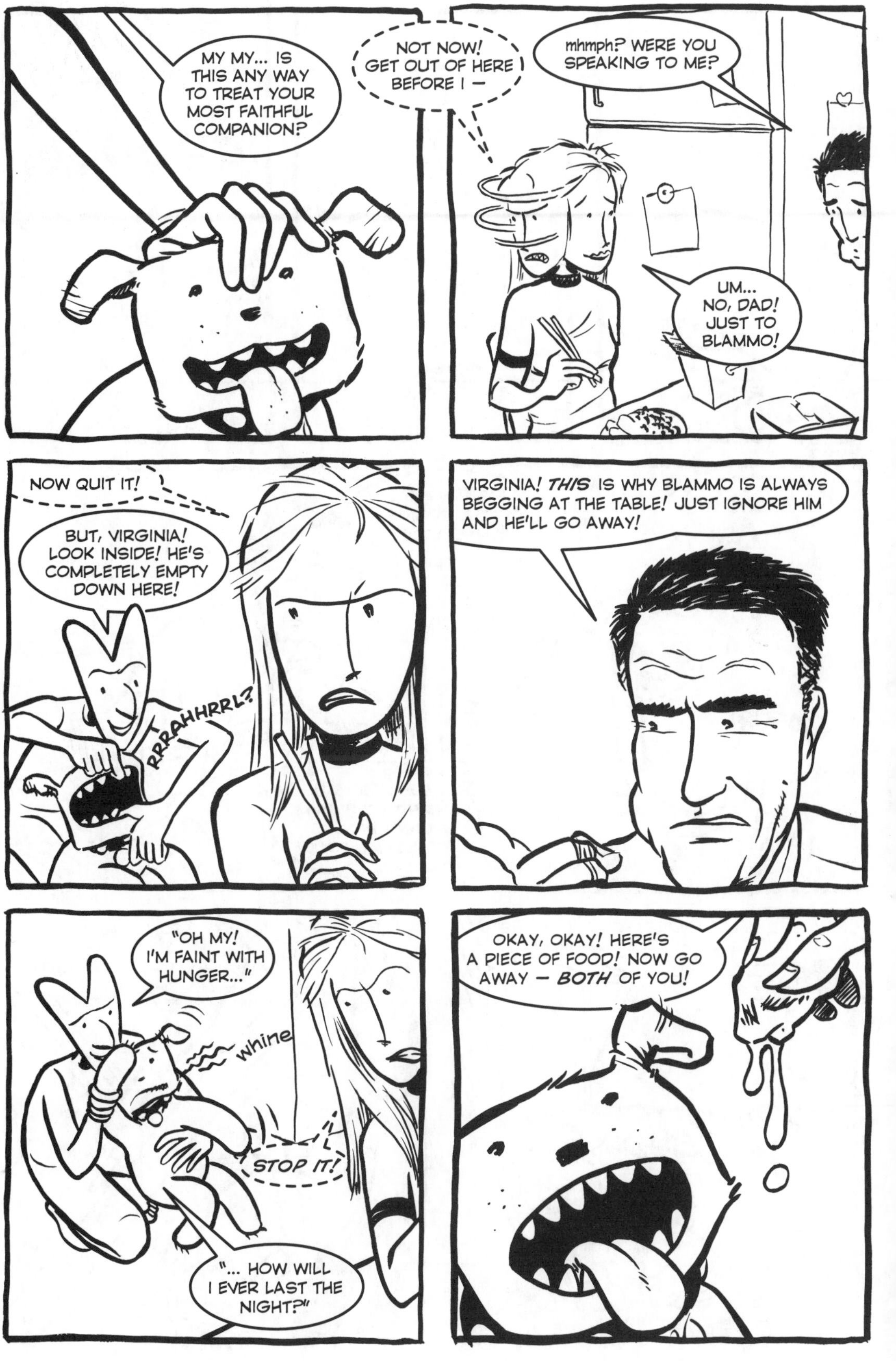
MY MY... IS THIS ANY WAY TO TREAT YOUR MOST FAITHFUL COMPANION?
NOT NOW! GET OUT OF HERE BEFORE I —
mhmph? WERE YOU SPEAKING TO ME?
UM... NO, DAD! JUST TO BLAMMO!
NOW QUIT IT!
BUT, VIRGINIA! LOOK INSIDE! HE'S COMPLETELY EMPTY DOWN HERE!
RRRAHHRRL?
VIRGINIA! THIS IS WHY BLAMMO IS ALWAYS BEGGING AT THE TABLE! JUST IGNORE HIM AND HE'LL GO AWAY!
"OH MY! I'M FAINT WITH HUNGER..."
whine
STOP IT!
"... HOW WILL I EVER LAST THE NIGHT?"
OKAY, OKAY! HERE'S A PIECE OF FOOD! NOW GO AWAY — BOTH OF YOU!

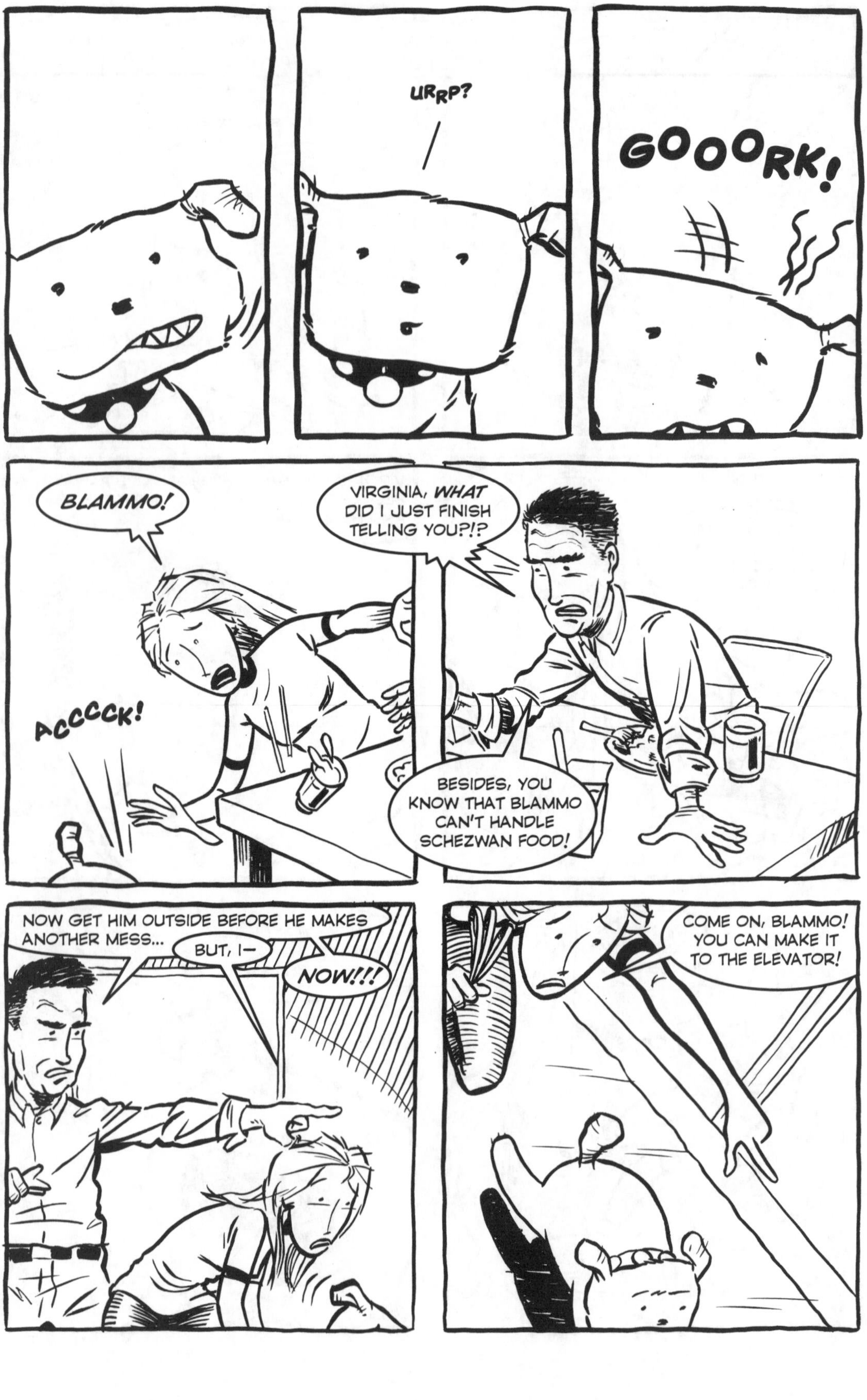
URRP?
GOOORK!
BLAMMO!
VIRGINIA, WHAT DID I JUST FINISH TELLING YOU?!?
ACCCCK!
BESIDES, YOU KNOW THAT BLAMMO CAN'T HANDLE SCHEZWAN FOOD!
NOW GET HIM OUTSIDE BEFORE HE MAKES ANOTHER MESS...
BUT, I—
NOW!!!
COME ON, BLAMMO! YOU CAN MAKE IT TO THE ELEVATOR!

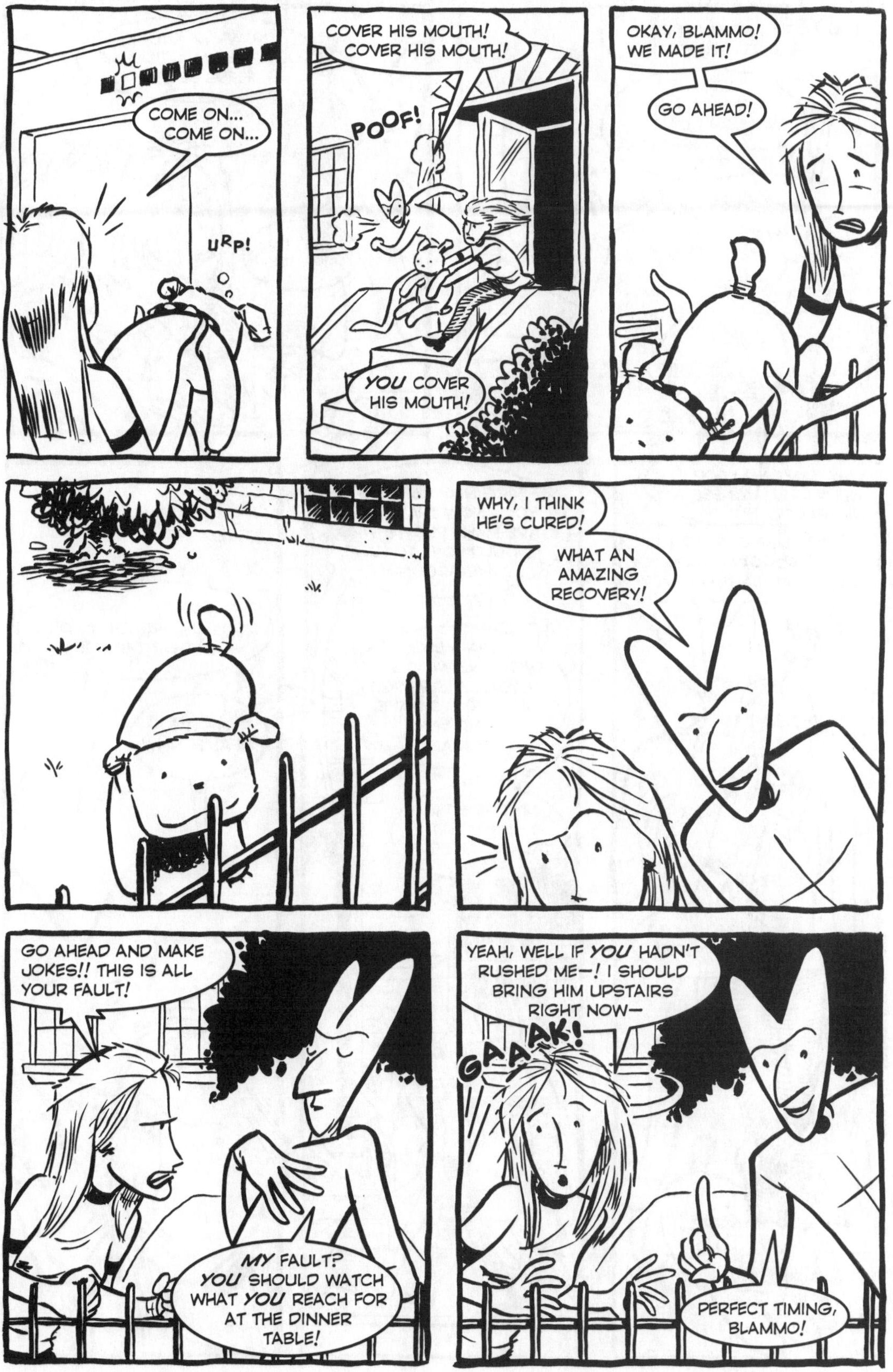
COME ON... COME ON...
URP!
COVER HIS MOUTH! COVER HIS MOUTH!
POOF!
YOU COVER HIS MOUTH!
OKAY, BLAMMO! WE MADE IT!
GO AHEAD!
WHY, I THINK HE'S CURED!
WHAT AN AMAZING RECOVERY!
GO AHEAD AND MAKE JOKES!! THIS IS ALL YOUR FAULT!
MY FAULT? YOU SHOULD WATCH WHAT YOU REACH FOR AT THE DINNER TABLE!
YEAH, WELL IF YOU HADN'T RUSHED ME—! I SHOULD BRING HIM UPSTAIRS RIGHT NOW—
GAAAK!
PERFECT TIMING, BLAMMO!

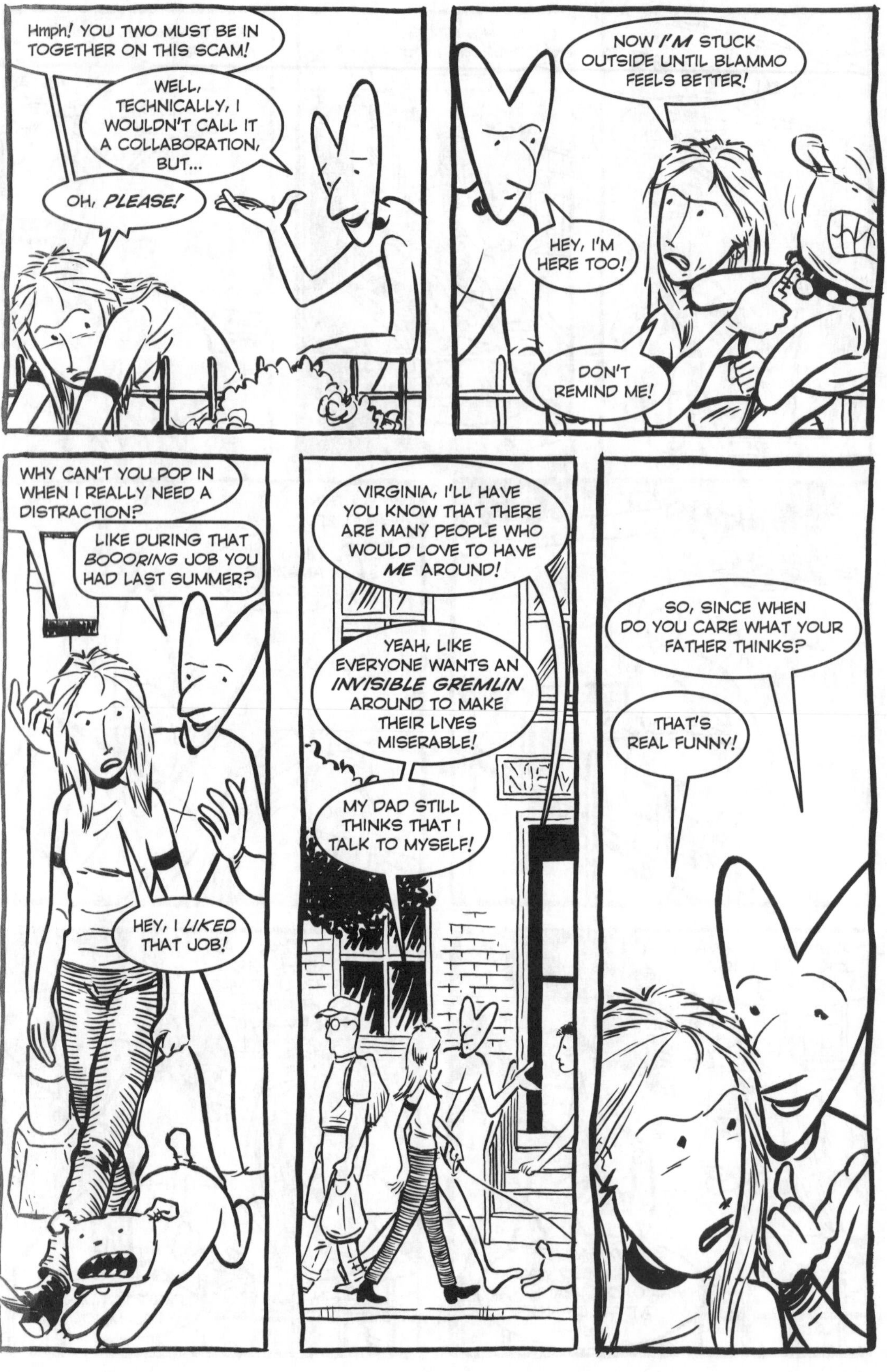
Hmph! YOU TWO MUST BE IN TOGETHER ON THIS SCAM!
WELL, TECHNICALLY, I WOULDN'T CALL IT A COLLABORATION, BUT...
OH, PLEASE!
NOW I'M STUCK OUTSIDE UNTIL BLAMMO FEELS BETTER!
HEY, I'M HERE TOO!
DON'T REMIND ME!
WHY CAN'T YOU POP IN WHEN I REALLY NEED A DISTRACTION?
LIKE DURING THAT BOOORING JOB YOU HAD LAST SUMMER?
HEY, I LIKED THAT JOB!
VIRGINIA, I'LL HAVE YOU KNOW THAT THERE ARE MANY PEOPLE WHO WOULD LOVE TO HAVE ME AROUND!
YEAH, LIKE EVERYONE WANTS AN INVISIBLE GREMLIN AROUND TO MAKE THEIR LIVES MISERABLE!
MY DAD STILL THINKS THAT I TALK TO MYSELF!
SO, SINCE WHEN DO YOU CARE WHAT YOUR FATHER THINKS?
THAT'S REAL FUNNY!

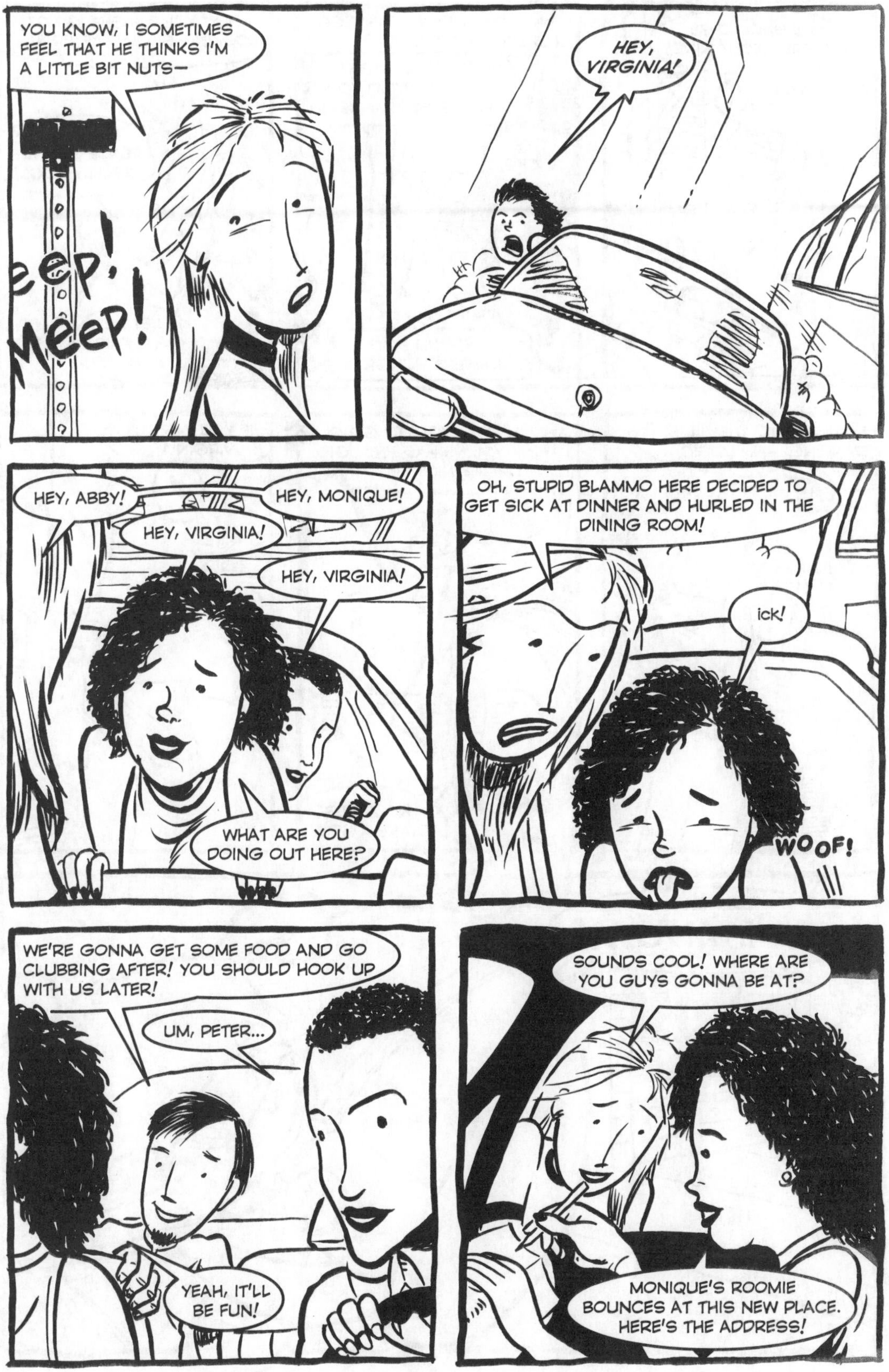
YOU KNOW, I SOMETIMES FEEL THAT HE THINKS I'M A LITTLE BIT NUTS—
eep! Meep!
HEY, VIRGINIA!
HEY, ABBY!
HEY, MONIQUE!
HEY, VIRGINIA!
HEY, VIRGINIA!
WHAT ARE YOU DOING OUT HERE?
OH, STUPID BLAMMO HERE DECIDED TO GET SICK AT DINNER AND HURLED IN THE DINING ROOM!
ick!
WOOF!
WE'RE GONNA GET SOME FOOD AND GO CLUBBING AFTER! YOU SHOULD HOOK UP WITH US LATER!
UM, PETER...
YEAH, IT'LL BE FUN!
SOUNDS COOL! WHERE ARE YOU GUYS GONNA BE AT?
MONIQUE'S ROOMIE BOUNCES AT THIS NEW PLACE. HERE'S THE ADDRESS!

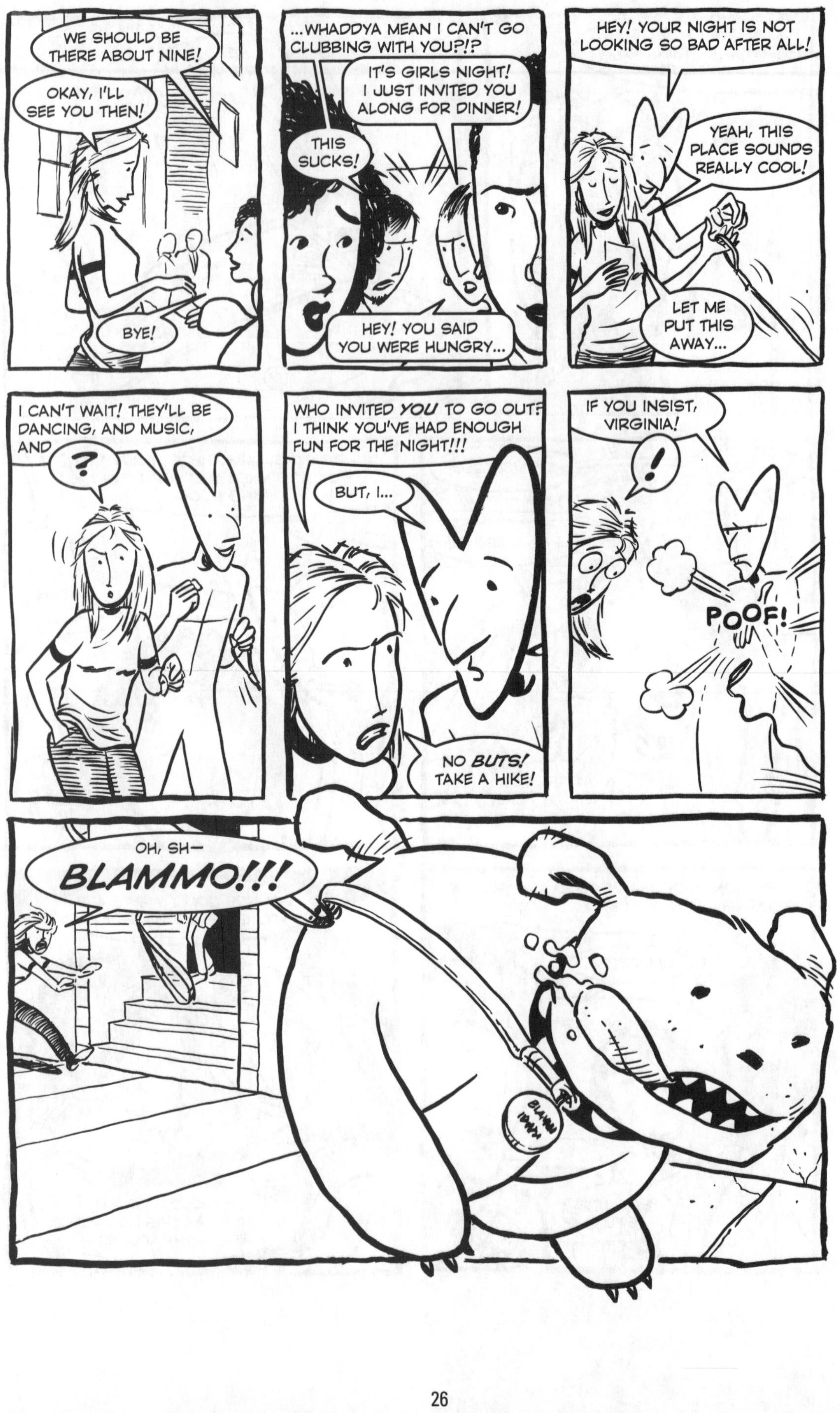
WE SHOULD BE THERE ABOUT NINE!
OKAY, I'LL SEE YOU THEN!
BYE!
...WHADDYA MEAN I CAN'T GO CLUBBING WITH YOU?!?
IT'S GIRLS NIGHT! I JUST INVITED YOU ALONG FOR DINNER!
THIS SUCKS!
HEY! YOU SAID YOU WERE HUNGRY...
HEY! YOUR NIGHT IS NOT LOOKING SO BAD AFTER ALL!
YEAH, THIS PLACE SOUNDS REALLY COOL!
LET ME PUT THIS AWAY...
I CAN'T WAIT! THEY'LL BE DANCING, AND MUSIC, AND
?
WHO INVITED *YOU* TO GO OUT? I THINK YOU'VE HAD ENOUGH FUN FOR THE NIGHT!!!
BUT, I...
NO *BUTS!* TAKE A HIKE!
IF YOU INSIST, VIRGINIA!
!
POOF!
OH, SH—
BLAMMO!!!

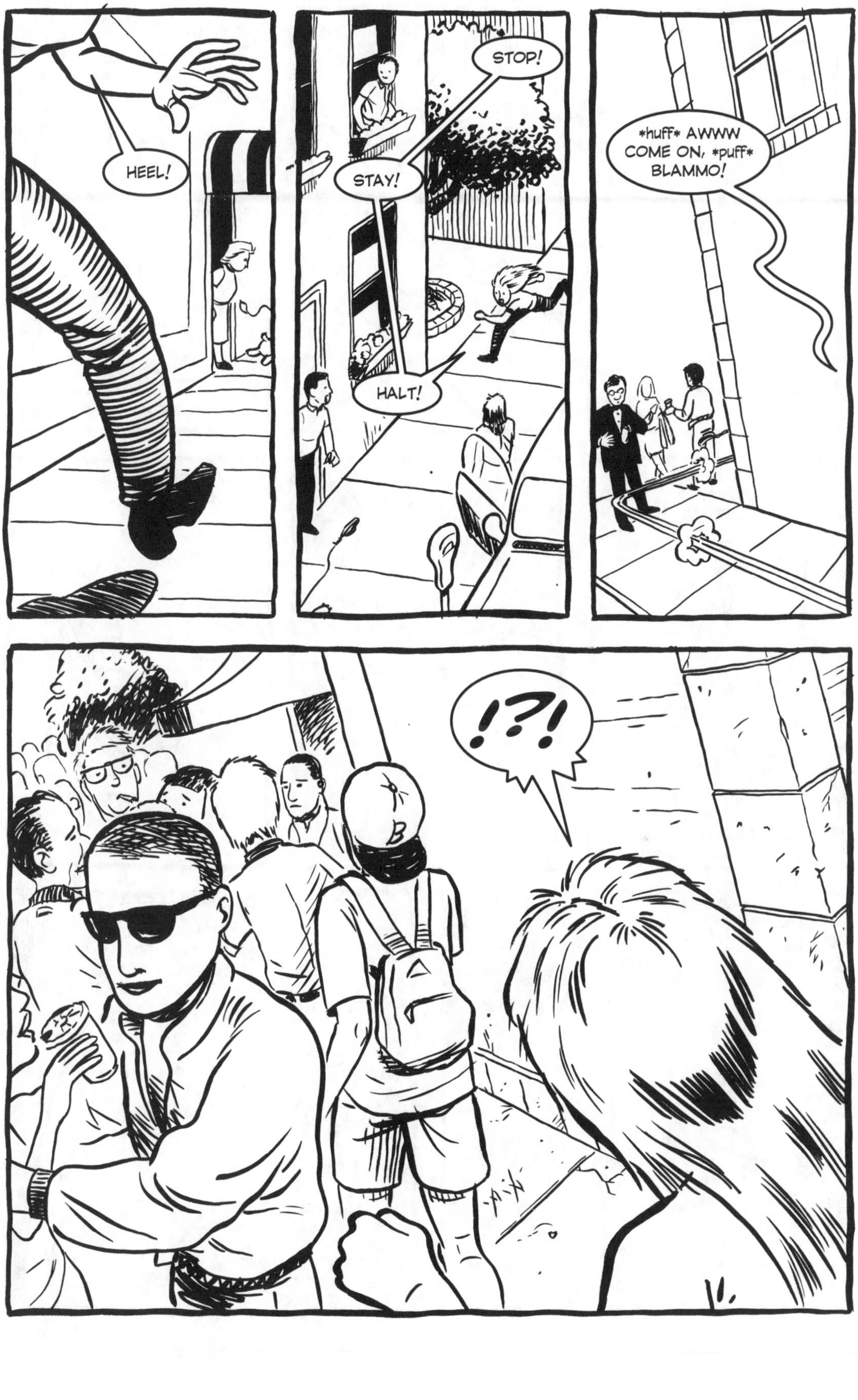
HEEL!
STOP!
STAY!
HALT!
huff AWWW COME ON, *puff* BLAMMO!
!?!

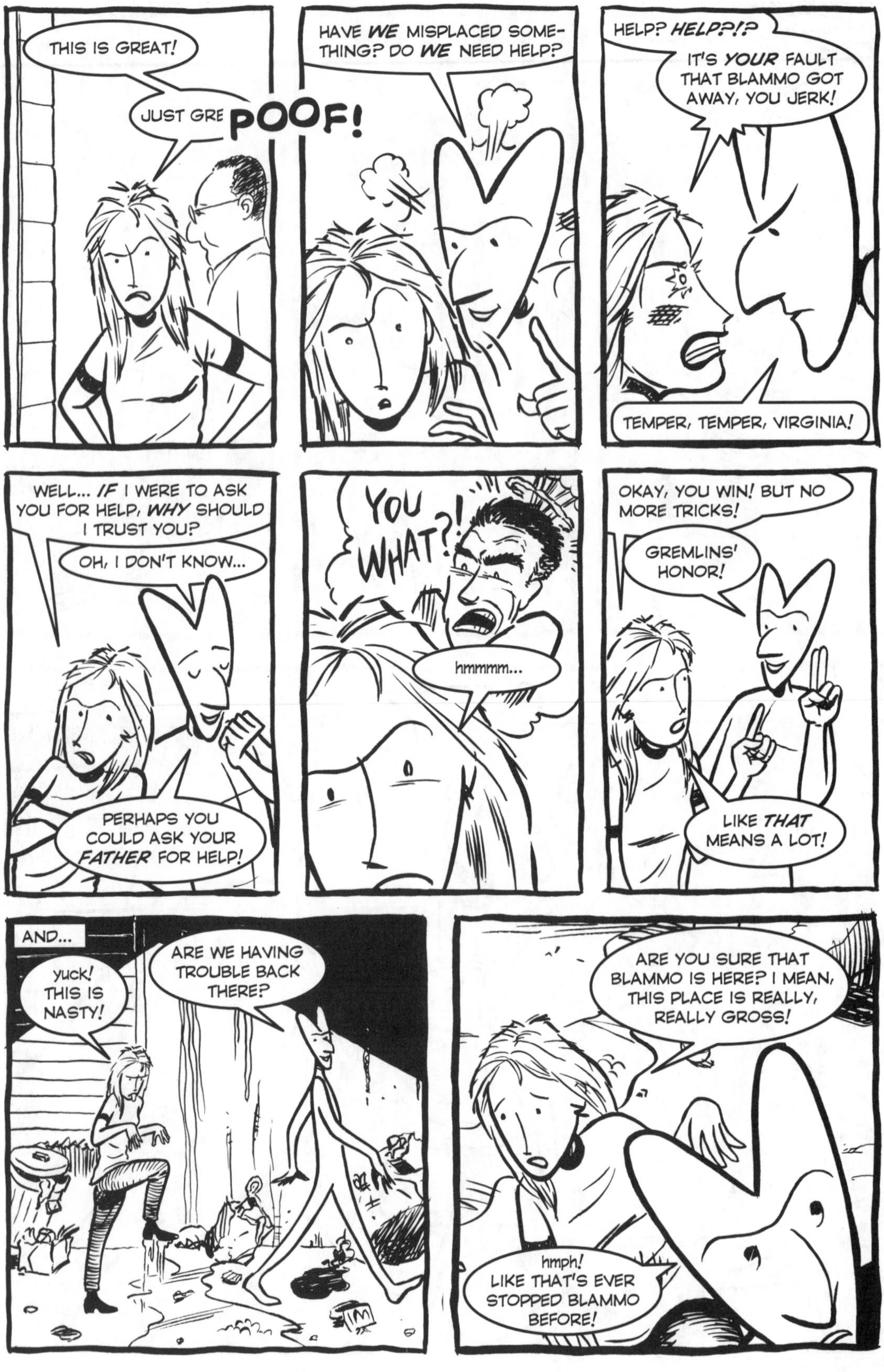
THIS IS GREAT!
JUST GRE
POOF!
HAVE WE MISPLACED SOMETHING? DO WE NEED HELP?
HELP? HELP?!?
IT'S YOUR FAULT THAT BLAMMO GOT AWAY, YOU JERK!
TEMPER, TEMPER, VIRGINIA!
WELL... IF I WERE TO ASK YOU FOR HELP, WHY SHOULD I TRUST YOU?
OH, I DON'T KNOW...
PERHAPS YOU COULD ASK YOUR FATHER FOR HELP!
YOU WHAT?!
hmmmm...
OKAY, YOU WIN! BUT NO MORE TRICKS!
GREMLINS' HONOR!
LIKE THAT MEANS A LOT!
AND...
yuck! THIS IS NASTY!
ARE WE HAVING TROUBLE BACK THERE?
ARE YOU SURE THAT BLAMMO IS HERE? I MEAN, THIS PLACE IS REALLY, REALLY GROSS!
hmph! LIKE THAT'S EVER STOPPED BLAMMO BEFORE!

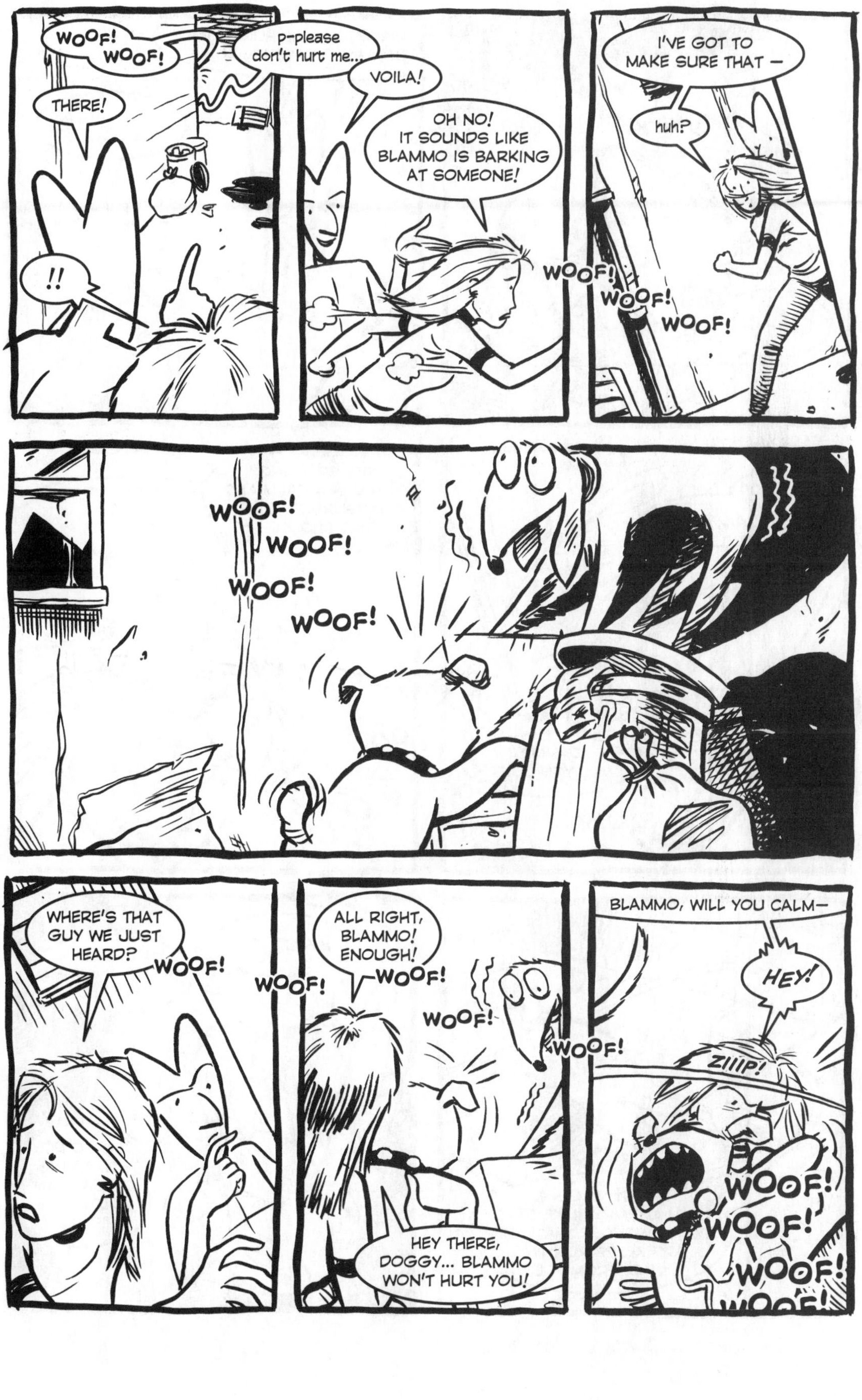

WOOF! WOOF!
p-please don't hurt me...
THERE!
!!
VOILA!
OH NO! IT SOUNDS LIKE BLAMMO IS BARKING AT SOMEONE!
I'VE GOT TO MAKE SURE THAT —
huh?
WOOF! WOOF! WOOF!
WOOF! WOOF! WOOF! WOOF!
WHERE'S THAT GUY WE JUST HEARD?
WOOF!
WOOF!
ALL RIGHT, BLAMMO! ENOUGH!
WOOF!
WOOF!
WOOF!
HEY THERE, DOGGY... BLAMMO WON'T HURT YOU!
BLAMMO, WILL YOU CALM—
HEY!
ZIIIP!
WOOF! WOOF! WOOF!

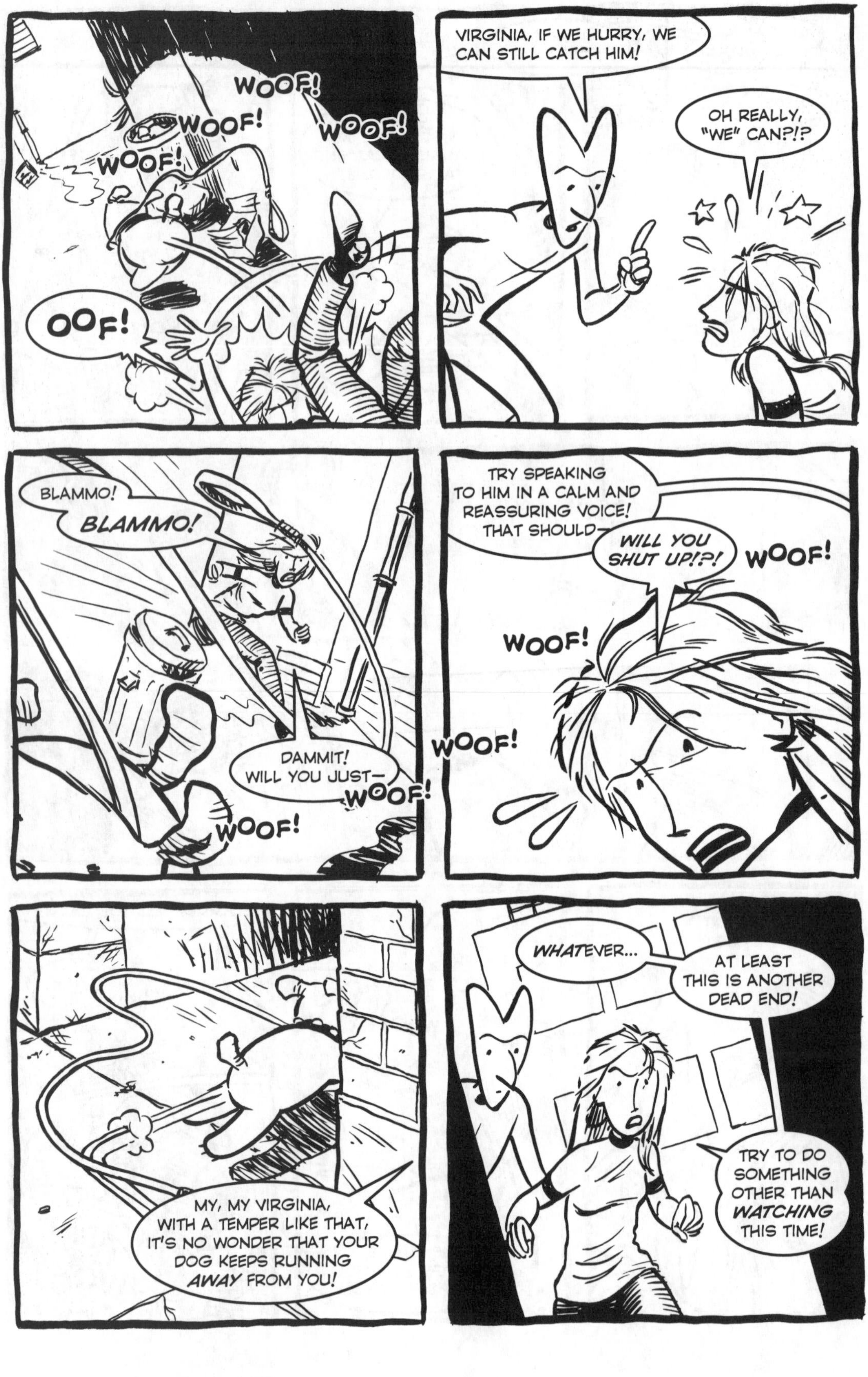
WOOF!
WOOF!
WOOF!
WOOF!
OOF!
VIRGINIA, IF WE HURRY, WE CAN STILL CATCH HIM!
OH REALLY, "WE" CAN?!?
BLAMMO! BLAMMO!
DAMMIT! WILL YOU JUST—
WOOF!
WOOF!
WOOF!
TRY SPEAKING TO HIM IN A CALM AND REASSURING VOICE! THAT SHOULD—
WILL YOU SHUT UP!?!
WOOF!
WOOF!
MY, MY VIRGINIA, WITH A TEMPER LIKE THAT, IT'S NO WONDER THAT YOUR DOG KEEPS RUNNING AWAY FROM YOU!
WHATEVER...
AT LEAST THIS IS ANOTHER DEAD END!
TRY TO DO SOMETHING OTHER THAN WATCHING THIS TIME!

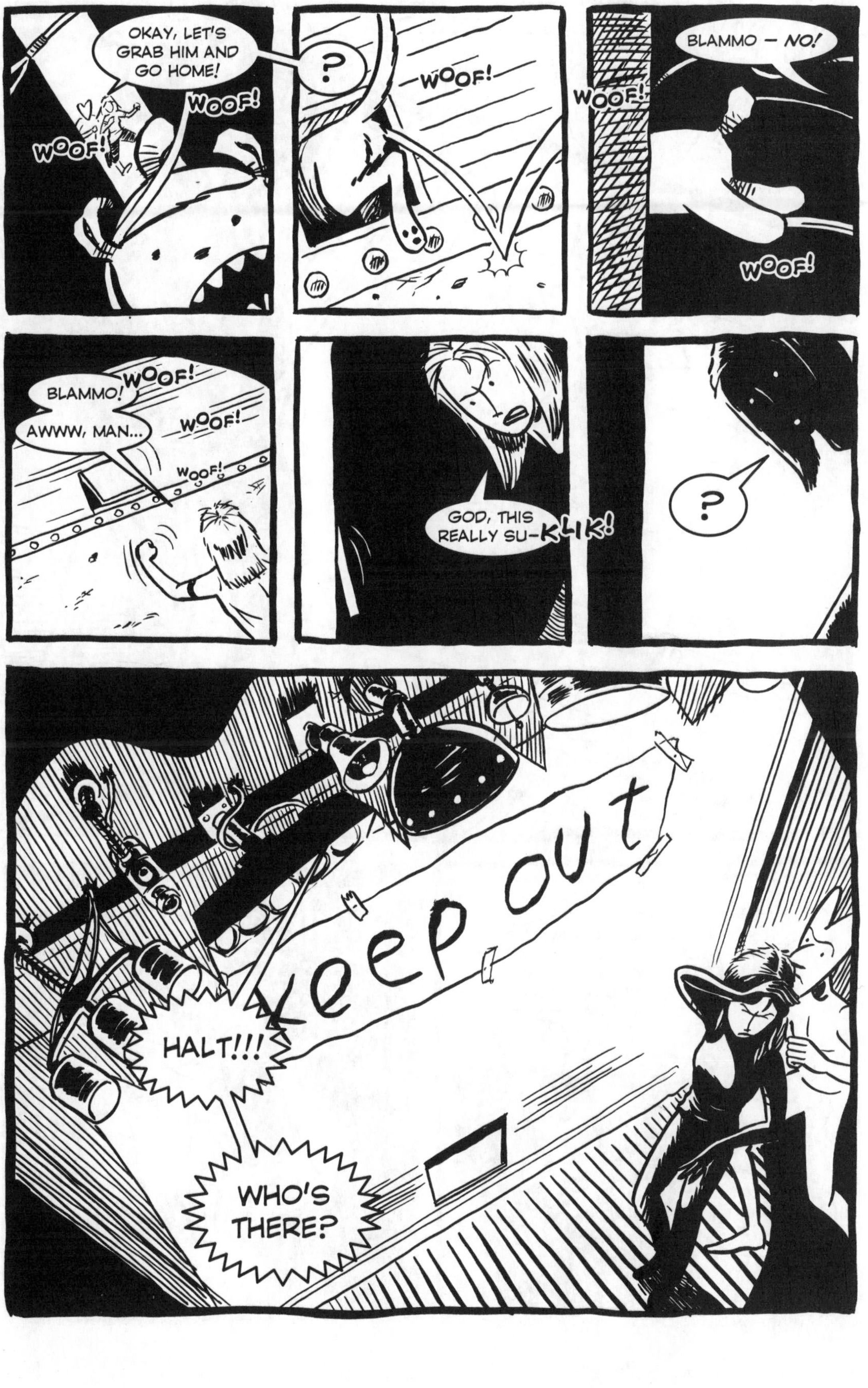
OKAY, LET'S GRAB HIM AND GO HOME!
WOOF!
WOOF!
?
WOOF!
WOOF!
BLAMMO – NO!
WOOF!
BLAMMO!
WOOF!
AWWW, MAN...
WOOF!
WOOF!
GOD, THIS REALLY SU-KLIK!
?
KEEP OUT
HALT!!!
WHO'S THERE?

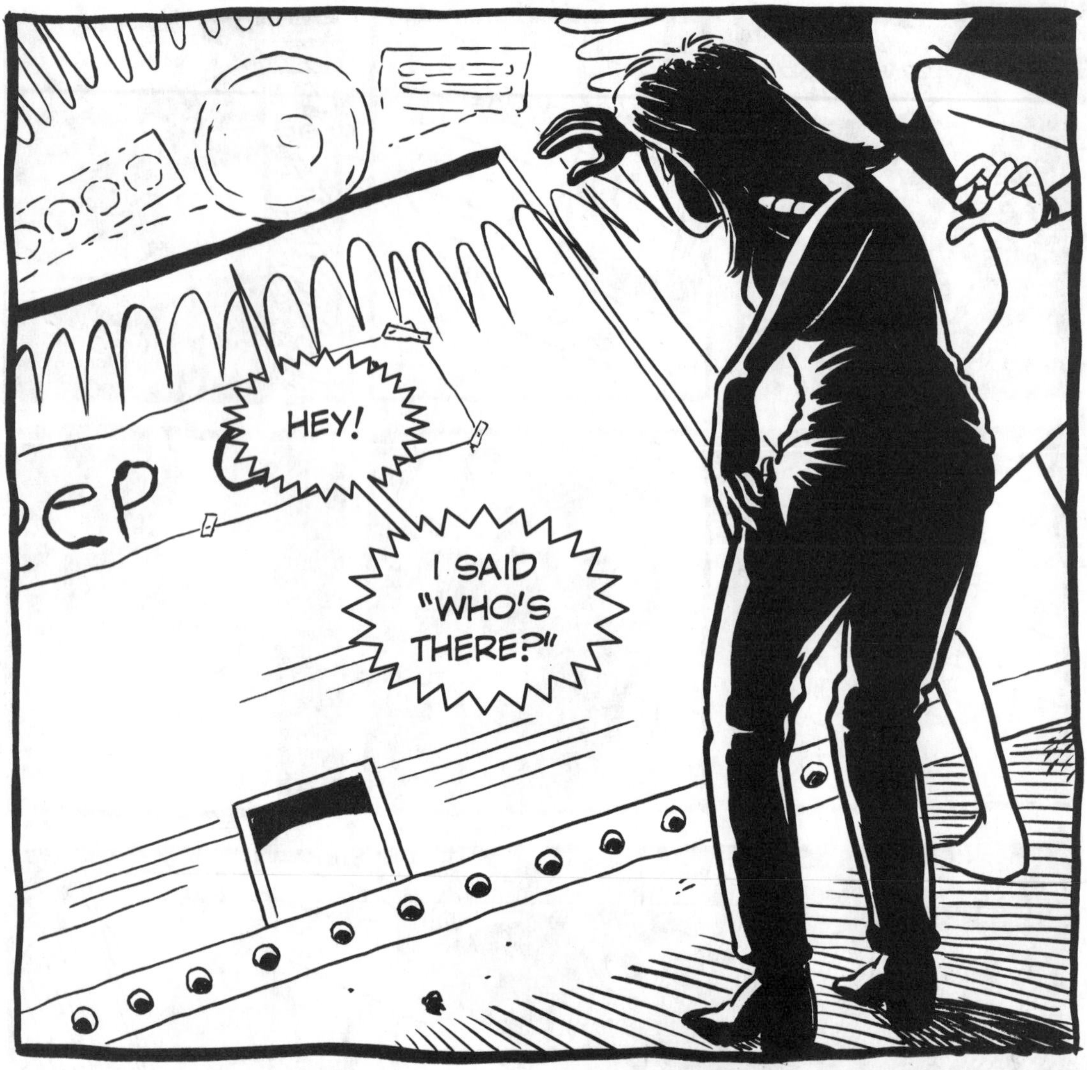
HEY!
I SAID "WHO'S THERE?"

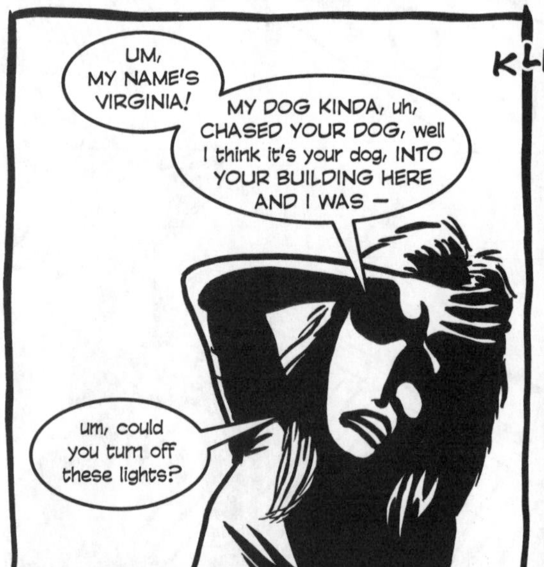
UM, MY NAME'S VIRGINIA!
MY DOG KINDA, uh, CHASED YOUR DOG, well I think it's your dog, INTO YOUR BUILDING HERE AND I WAS –
um, could you turn off these lights?

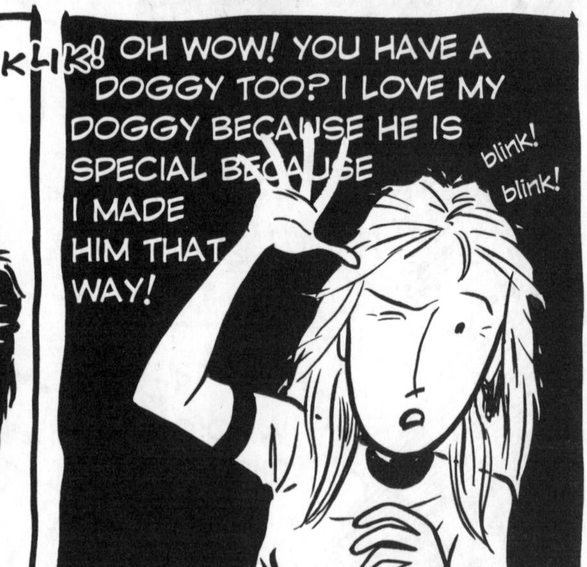
KLIK!
OH WOW! YOU HAVE A DOGGY TOO? I LOVE MY DOGGY BECAUSE HE IS SPECIAL BECAUSE I MADE HIM THAT WAY!
blink!
blink!

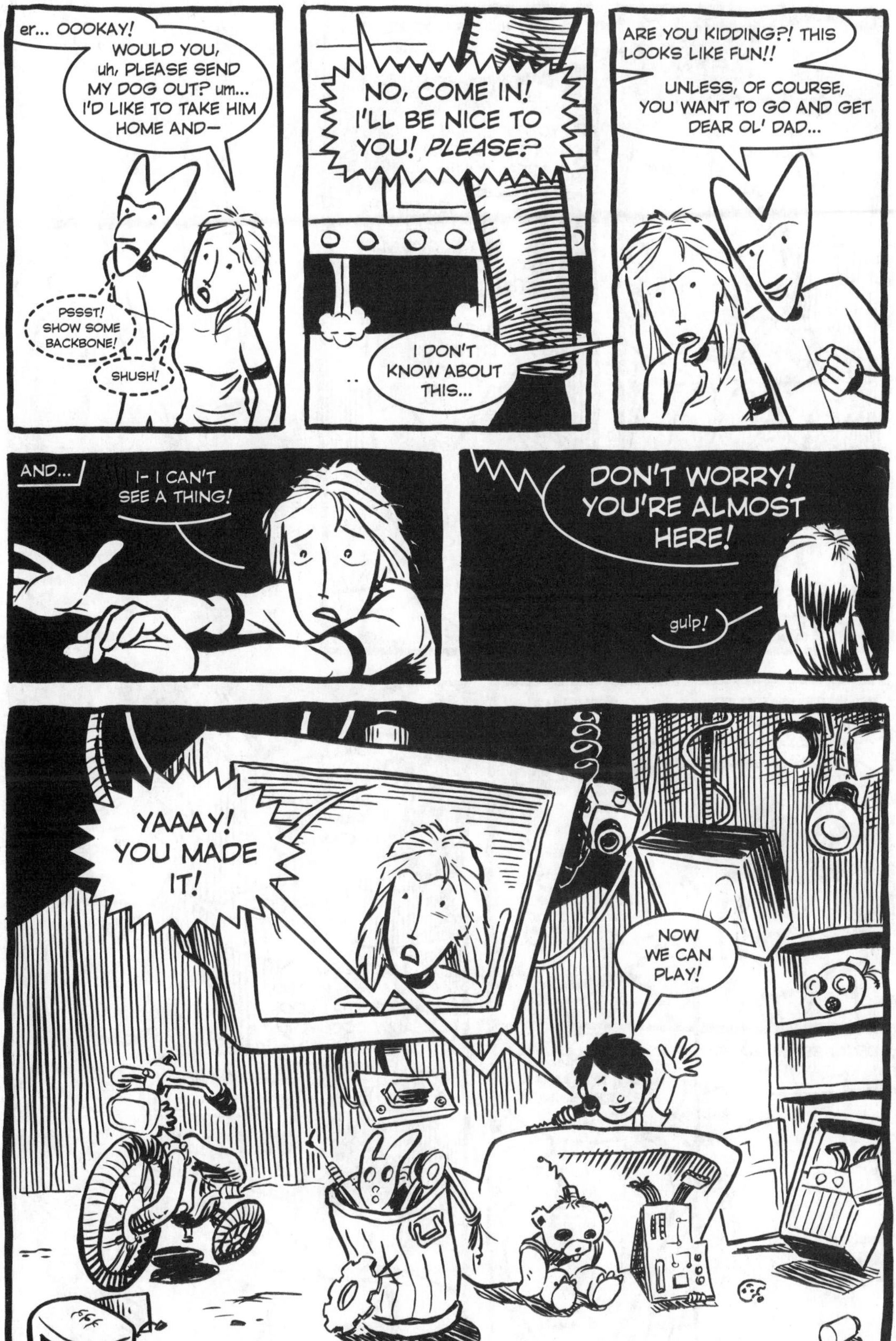

er... OOOKAY!
WOULD YOU, uh, PLEASE SEND MY DOG OUT? um... I'D LIKE TO TAKE HIM HOME AND—
PSSST! SHOW SOME BACKBONE!
SHUSH!
NO, COME IN! I'LL BE NICE TO YOU! PLEASE?
I DON'T KNOW ABOUT THIS...
ARE YOU KIDDING?! THIS LOOKS LIKE FUN!!
UNLESS, OF COURSE, YOU WANT TO GO AND GET DEAR OL' DAD...
AND...
I- I CAN'T SEE A THING!
DON'T WORRY! YOU'RE ALMOST HERE!
gulp!
YAAAY! YOU MADE IT!
NOW WE CAN PLAY!

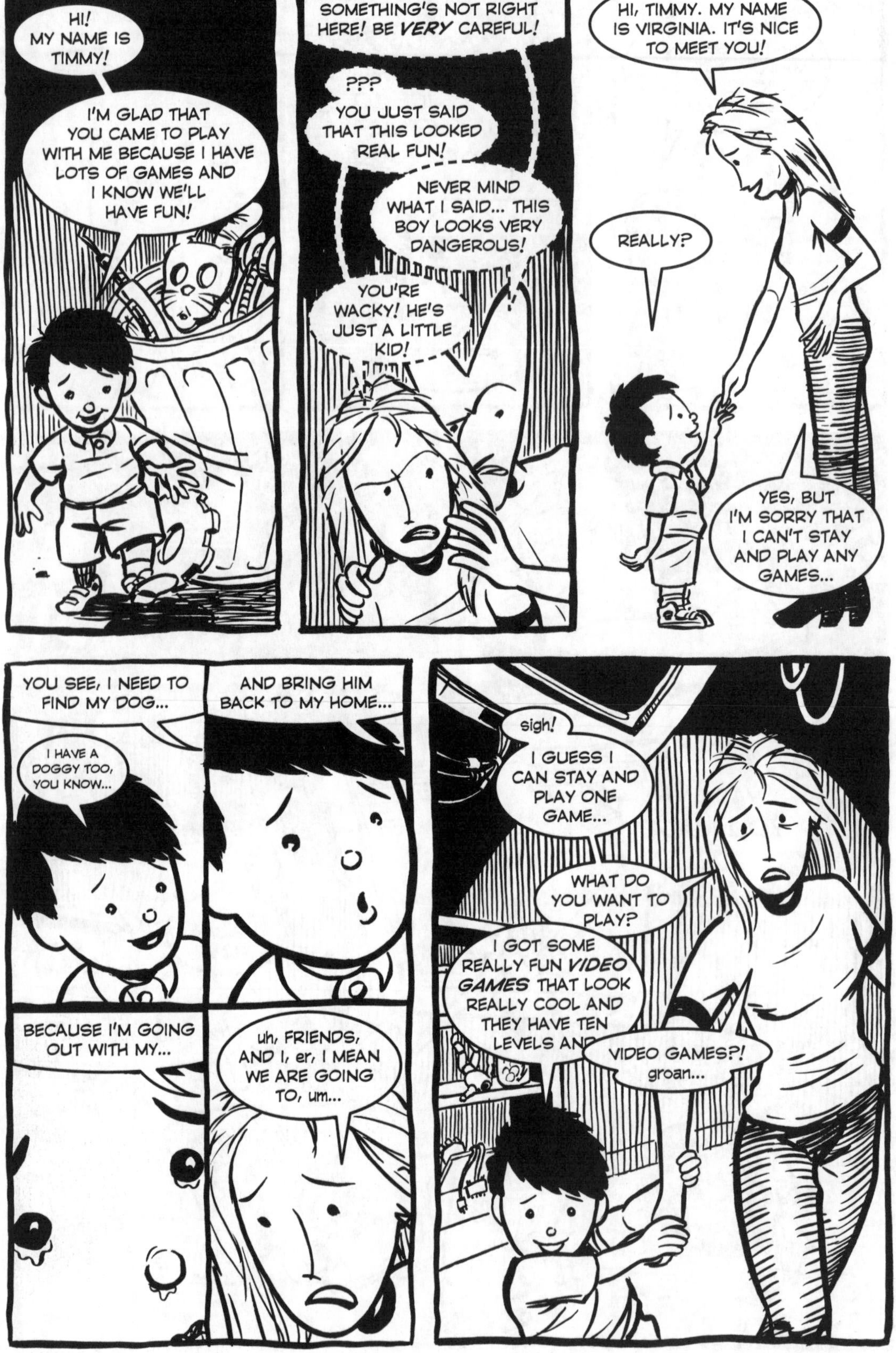
HI! MY NAME IS TIMMY!
I'M GLAD THAT YOU CAME TO PLAY WITH ME BECAUSE I HAVE LOTS OF GAMES AND I KNOW WE'LL HAVE FUN!
SOMETHING'S NOT RIGHT HERE! BE VERY CAREFUL!
???
YOU JUST SAID THAT THIS LOOKED REAL FUN!
NEVER MIND WHAT I SAID... THIS BOY LOOKS VERY DANGEROUS!
YOU'RE WACKY! HE'S JUST A LITTLE KID!
HI, TIMMY. MY NAME IS VIRGINIA. IT'S NICE TO MEET YOU!
REALLY?
YES, BUT I'M SORRY THAT I CAN'T STAY AND PLAY ANY GAMES...
YOU SEE, I NEED TO FIND MY DOG...
I HAVE A DOGGY TOO, YOU KNOW...
AND BRING HIM BACK TO MY HOME...
BECAUSE I'M GOING OUT WITH MY...
uh, FRIENDS, AND I, er, I MEAN WE ARE GOING TO, um...
sigh!
I GUESS I CAN STAY AND PLAY ONE GAME...
WHAT DO YOU WANT TO PLAY?
I GOT SOME REALLY FUN VIDEO GAMES THAT LOOK REALLY COOL AND THEY HAVE TEN LEVELS AND
VIDEO GAMES?! groan...

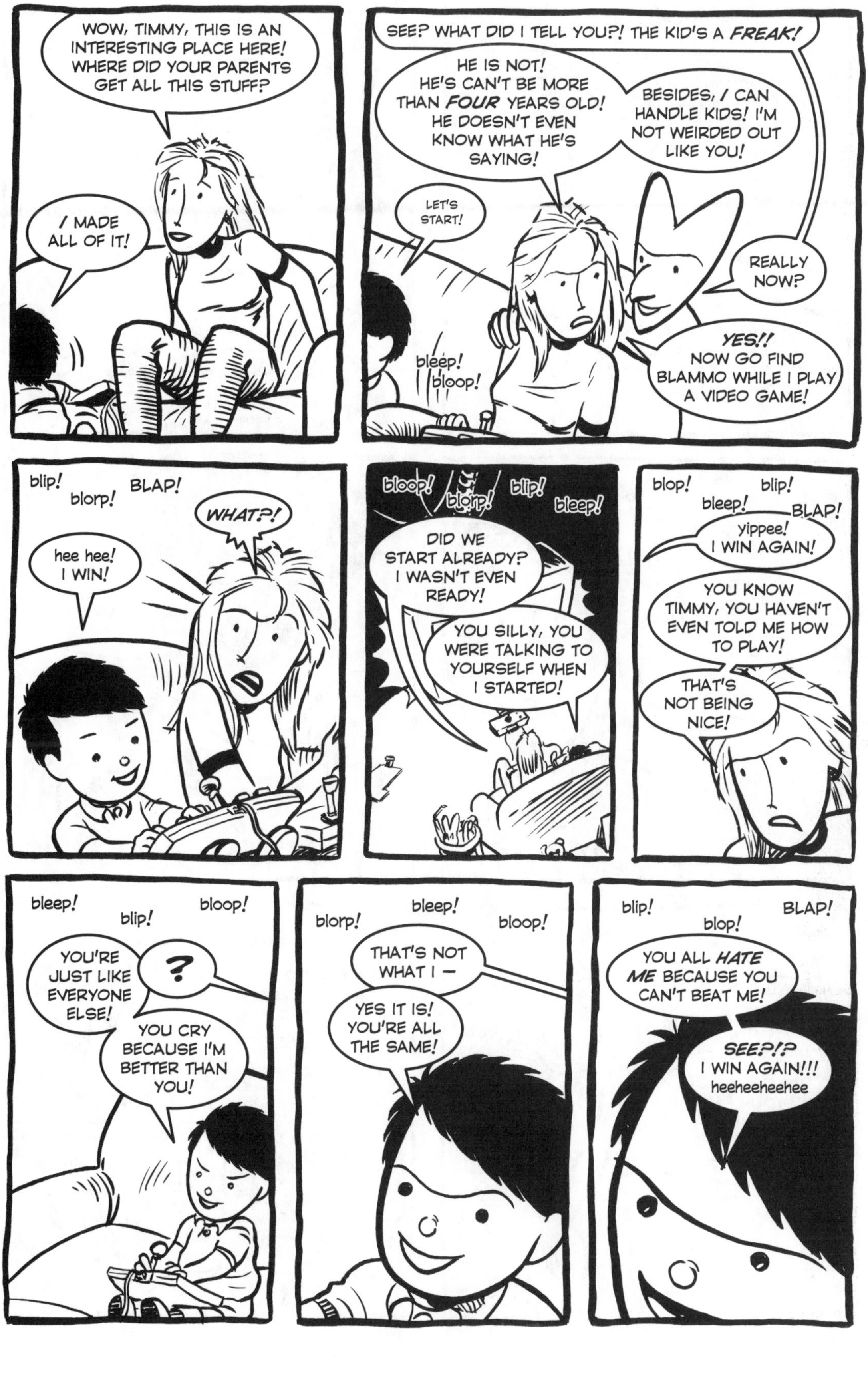
WOW, TIMMY, THIS IS AN INTERESTING PLACE HERE! WHERE DID YOUR PARENTS GET ALL THIS STUFF?
I MADE ALL OF IT!
SEE? WHAT DID I TELL YOU?! THE KID'S A FREAK!
HE IS NOT! HE'S CAN'T BE MORE THAN FOUR YEARS OLD! HE DOESN'T EVEN KNOW WHAT HE'S SAYING!
BESIDES, I CAN HANDLE KIDS! I'M NOT WEIRDED OUT LIKE YOU!
LET'S START!
REALLY NOW?
YES!! NOW GO FIND BLAMMO WHILE I PLAY A VIDEO GAME!
bleep! bloop!
blip! blorp! BLAP!
hee hee! I WIN!
WHAT?!
bloop! blorp! blip! bleep!
DID WE START ALREADY? I WASN'T EVEN READY!
YOU SILLY, YOU WERE TALKING TO YOURSELF WHEN I STARTED!
blop! bleep! blip! BLAP!
yippee! I WIN AGAIN!
YOU KNOW TIMMY, YOU HAVEN'T EVEN TOLD ME HOW TO PLAY!
THAT'S NOT BEING NICE!
bleep! blip! bloop!
YOU'RE JUST LIKE EVERYONE ELSE!
?
YOU CRY BECAUSE I'M BETTER THAN YOU!
blorp! bleep! bloop!
THAT'S NOT WHAT I —
YES IT IS! YOU'RE ALL THE SAME!
blip! blop! BLAP!
YOU ALL HATE ME BECAUSE YOU CAN'T BEAT ME!
SEE?!? I WIN AGAIN!!! heeheeheehee

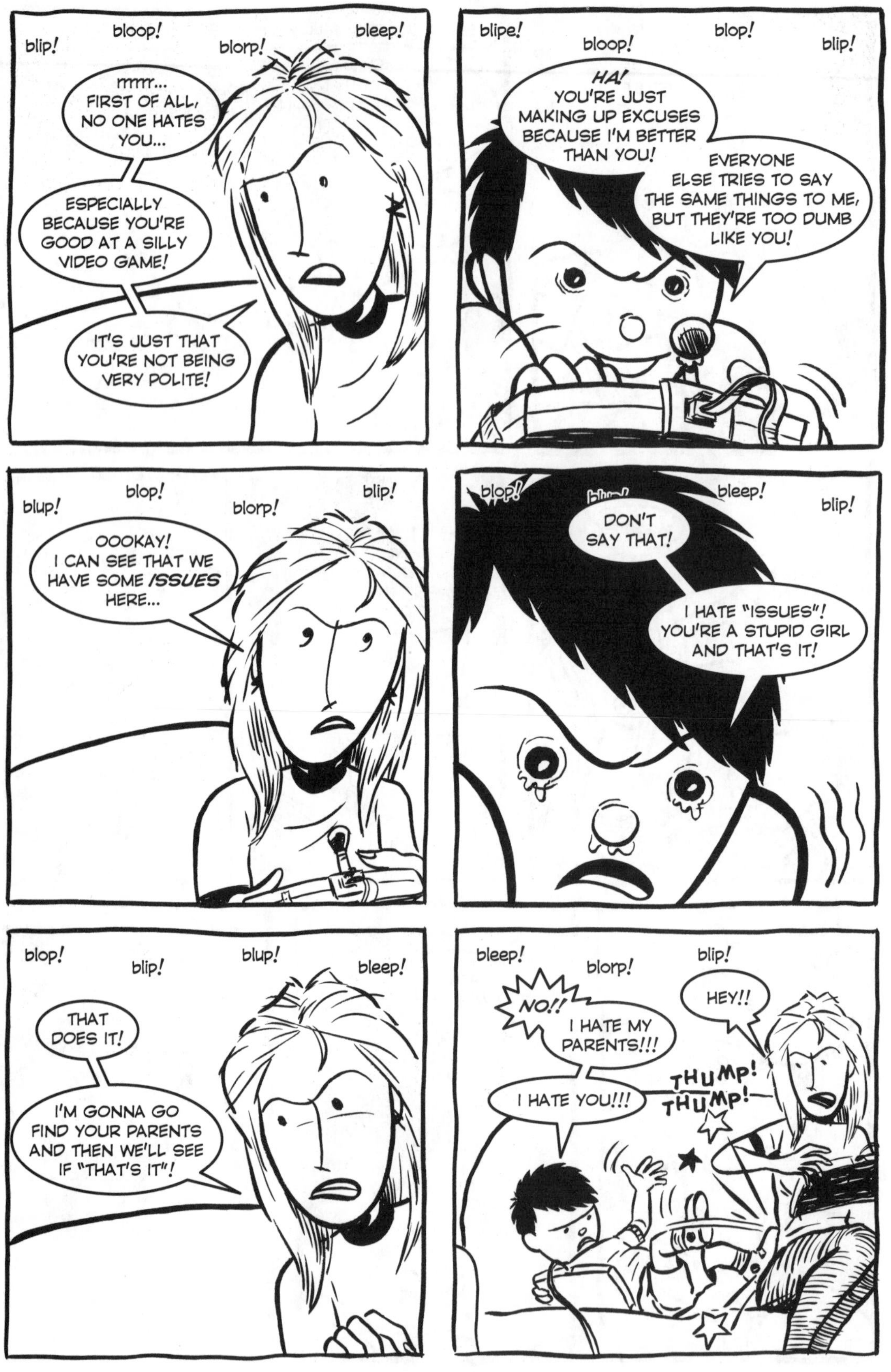
blip!
bloop!
blorp!
bleep!
rrrrr... FIRST OF ALL, NO ONE HATES YOU...
ESPECIALLY BECAUSE YOU'RE GOOD AT A SILLY VIDEO GAME!
IT'S JUST THAT YOU'RE NOT BEING VERY POLITE!
blipe!
bloop!
blop!
blip!
HA! YOU'RE JUST MAKING UP EXCUSES BECAUSE I'M BETTER THAN YOU!
EVERYONE ELSE TRIES TO SAY THE SAME THINGS TO ME, BUT THEY'RE TOO DUMB LIKE YOU!
blup!
blop!
blorp!
blip!
OOOKAY! I CAN SEE THAT WE HAVE SOME ISSUES HERE...
blop!
bleep!
blip!
DON'T SAY THAT!
I HATE "ISSUES"! YOU'RE A STUPID GIRL AND THAT'S IT!
blop!
blip!
blup!
bleep!
THAT DOES IT!
I'M GONNA GO FIND YOUR PARENTS AND THEN WE'LL SEE IF "THAT'S IT"!
bleep!
blorp!
blip!
NO!! I HATE MY PARENTS!!!
HEY!!
I HATE YOU!!!
THUMP! THUMP!

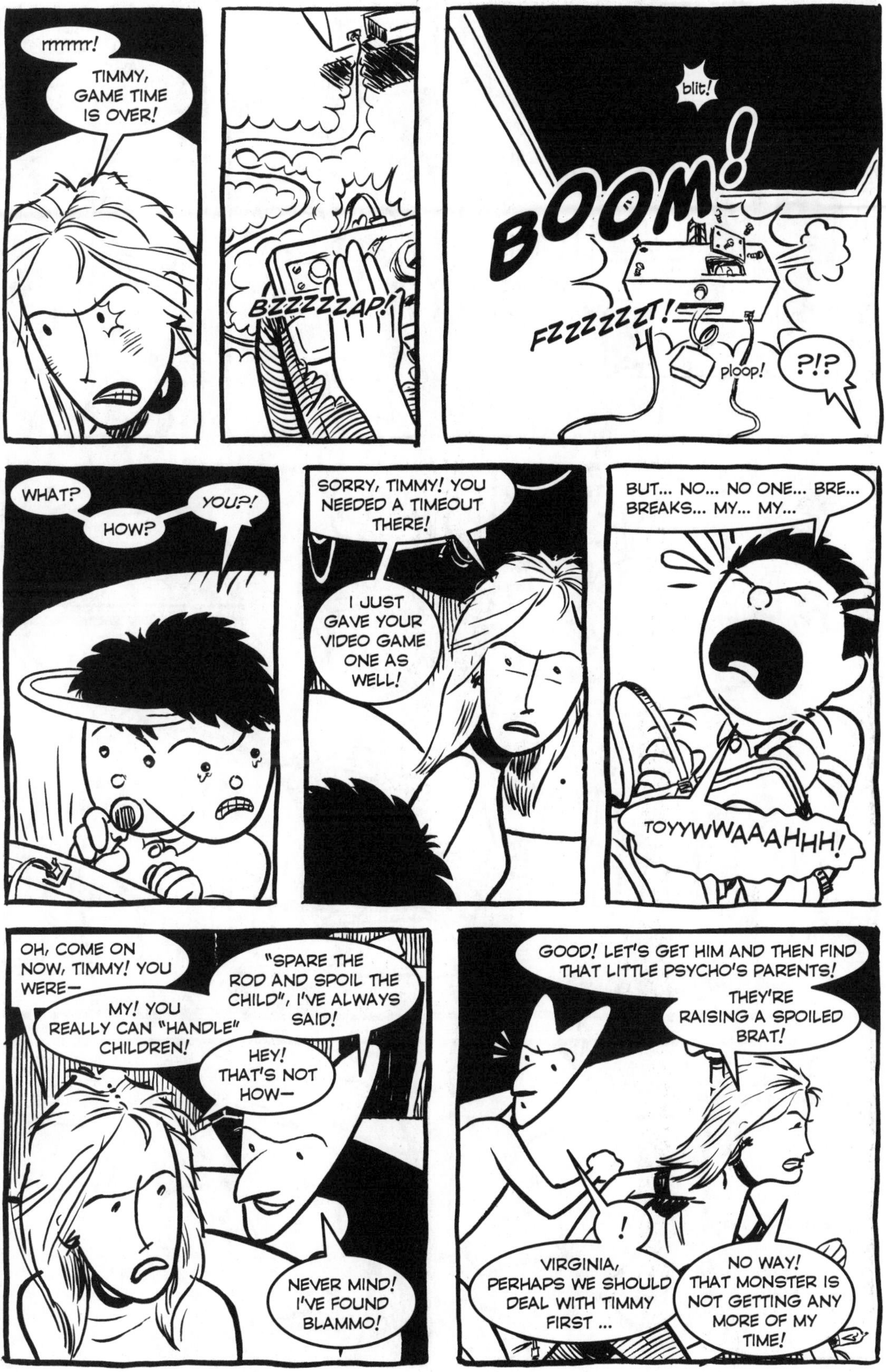
rrrrrrr!
TIMMY, GAME TIME IS OVER!
BZZZZZZAP!
blit!
BOOM!
FZZZZZZT!
ploop!
?!?
WHAT?
HOW?
YOU?!
SORRY, TIMMY! YOU NEEDED A TIMEOUT THERE!
I JUST GAVE YOUR VIDEO GAME ONE AS WELL!
BUT... NO... NO ONE... BRE... BREAKS... MY... MY...
TOYYWWAAAHHH!
OH, COME ON NOW, TIMMY! YOU WERE—
MY! YOU REALLY CAN "HANDLE" CHILDREN!
"SPARE THE ROD AND SPOIL THE CHILD", I'VE ALWAYS SAID!
HEY! THAT'S NOT HOW—
NEVER MIND! I'VE FOUND BLAMMO!
GOOD! LET'S GET HIM AND THEN FIND THAT LITTLE PSYCHO'S PARENTS!
THEY'RE RAISING A SPOILED BRAT!
!
VIRGINIA, PERHAPS WE SHOULD DEAL WITH TIMMY FIRST ...
NO WAY! THAT MONSTER IS NOT GETTING ANY MORE OF MY TIME!

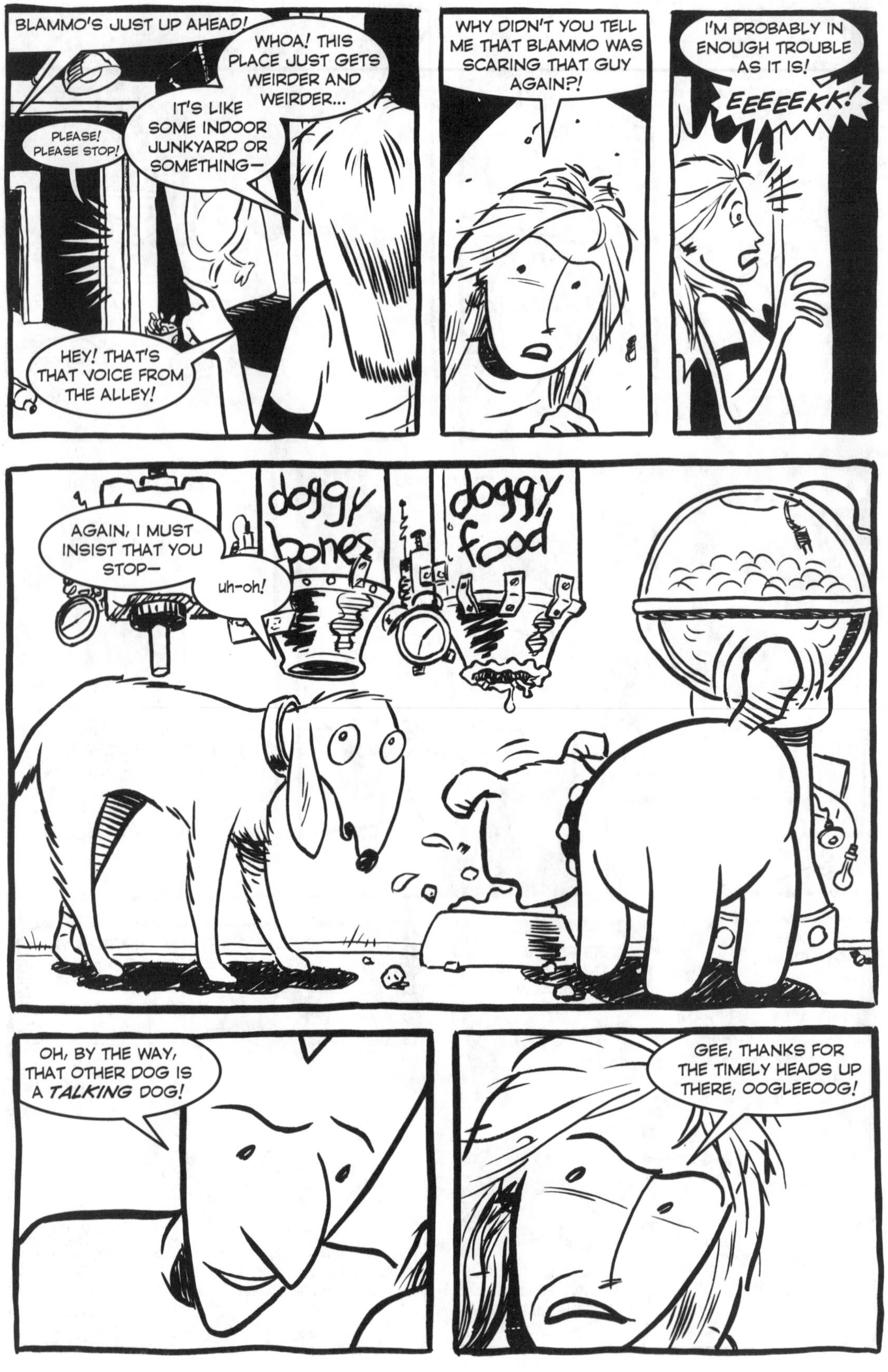

BLAMMO'S JUST UP AHEAD!
WHOA! THIS PLACE JUST GETS WEIRDER AND WEIRDER...
IT'S LIKE SOME INDOOR JUNKYARD OR SOMETHING—
PLEASE! PLEASE STOP!
HEY! THAT'S THAT VOICE FROM THE ALLEY!
WHY DIDN'T YOU TELL ME THAT BLAMMO WAS SCARING THAT GUY AGAIN?!
I'M PROBABLY IN ENOUGH TROUBLE AS IT IS!
EEEEEKK!
doggy bones
doggy food
AGAIN, I MUST INSIST THAT YOU STOP—
uh-oh!
OH, BY THE WAY, THAT OTHER DOG IS A *TALKING* DOG!
GEE, THANKS FOR THE TIMELY HEADS UP THERE, OOGLEEOOG!

WELL, SINCE YOU'VE PROBABLY MET MY MASTER TIMMY, YOU MAY HAVE NOTICED SEVERAL PECULIARITIES HERE. I AM ONE OF THEM.

?

ALLOW ME TO INTRODUCE MYSELF. MY NAME IS *SPARKY*. I AM MASTER TIMMY'S COMPANION!

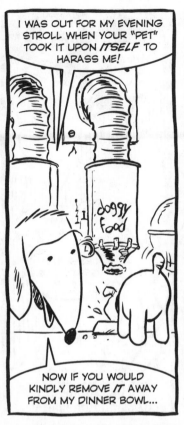

I WAS OUT FOR MY EVENING STROLL WHEN YOUR "PET" TOOK IT UPON *ITSELF* TO HARASS ME!

doggy food

NOW IF YOU WOULD KINDLY REMOVE *IT* AWAY FROM MY DINNER BOWL...

UH, SORRY ABOUT THAT! BLAMMO HADN'T HAD HIS DINNER YET!

BUT HE REALLY IS A VERY FRIENDLY DOG!

SEE, HE WON'T HURT YOU!

I- I'LL TAKE YOUR W-W-W-WORD ON I-I-IT!

SAY, IS THAT A *GREMLIN* THAT YOU HAVE WITH YOU?

?

uh-oh...

LISTEN HERE! YOU'RE A DOG, SO *I* KNOW THAT *YOU* KNOW THE RULES!

JUST BECAUSE YOU CAN SPEAK TO HUMANS DOESN'T CHANGE A THING!

UNDERSTAND?

Y-YES, SIR! C-C-C-COMPLETELY!

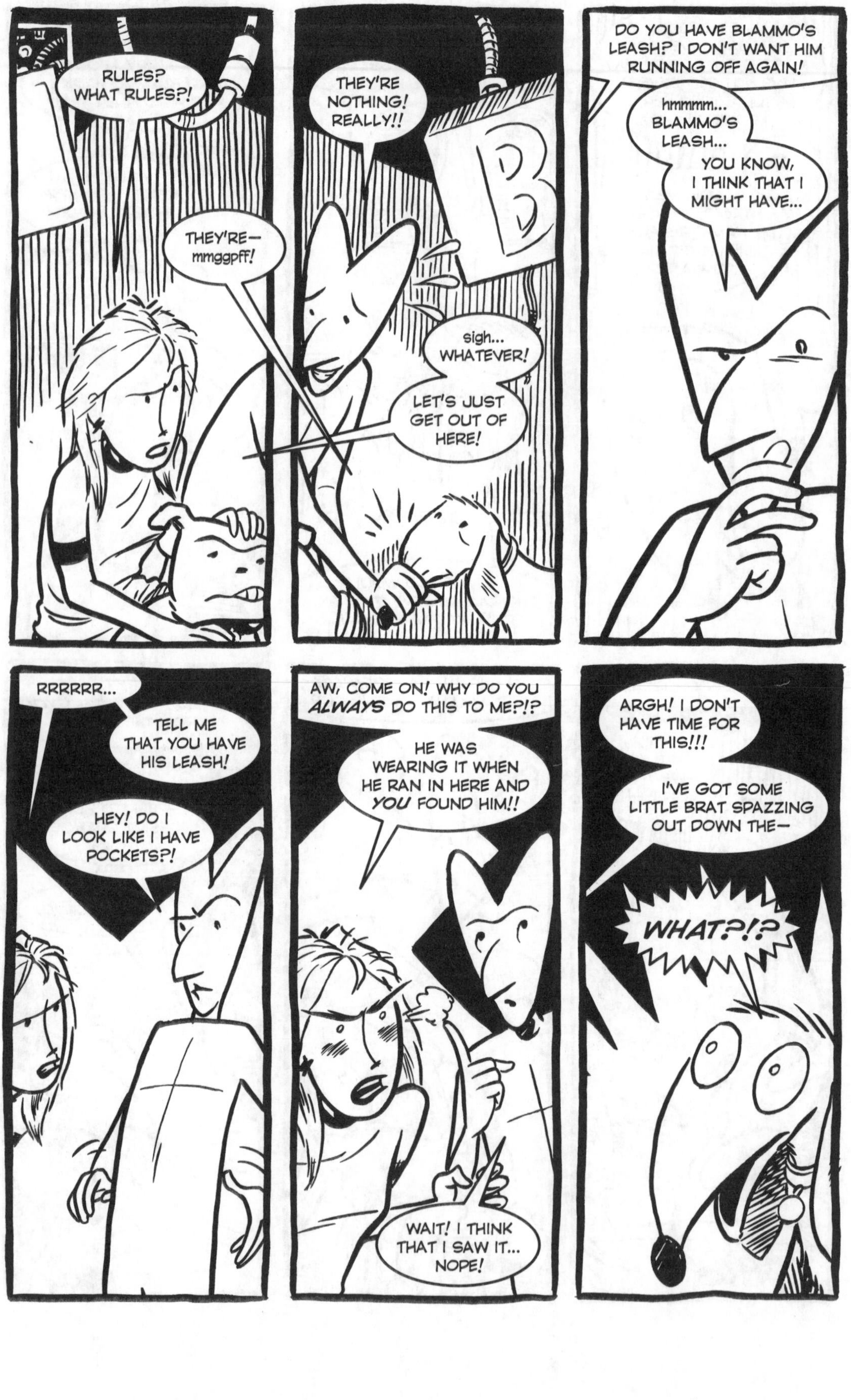
RULES? WHAT RULES?!
THEY'RE— mmggpff!
THEY'RE NOTHING! REALLY!!
sigh... WHATEVER!
LET'S JUST GET OUT OF HERE!
DO YOU HAVE BLAMMO'S LEASH? I DON'T WANT HIM RUNNING OFF AGAIN!
hmmmm... BLAMMO'S LEASH...
YOU KNOW, I THINK THAT I MIGHT HAVE...
RRRRRR...
TELL ME THAT YOU HAVE HIS LEASH!
HEY! DO I LOOK LIKE I HAVE POCKETS?!
AW, COME ON! WHY DO YOU ALWAYS DO THIS TO ME?!?
HE WAS WEARING IT WHEN HE RAN IN HERE AND YOU FOUND HIM!!
WAIT! I THINK THAT I SAW IT... NOPE!
ARGH! I DON'T HAVE TIME FOR THIS!!!
I'VE GOT SOME LITTLE BRAT SPAZZING OUT DOWN THE—
WHAT?!?

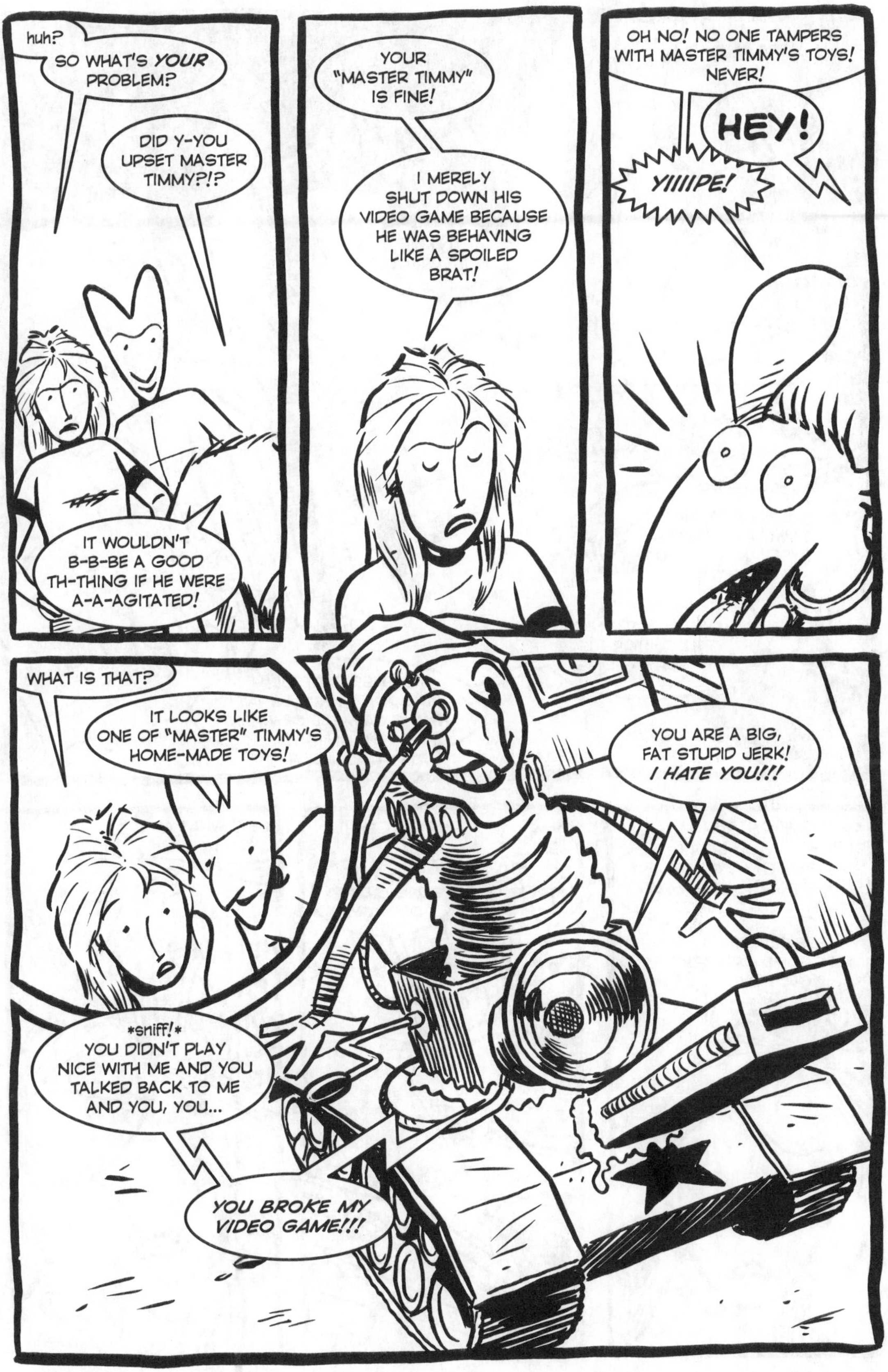
huh?
SO WHAT'S *YOUR* PROBLEM?
DID Y-YOU UPSET MASTER TIMMY?!?
IT WOULDN'T B-B-BE A GOOD TH-THING IF HE WERE A-A-AGITATED!
YOUR "MASTER TIMMY" IS FINE!
I MERELY SHUT DOWN HIS VIDEO GAME BECAUSE HE WAS BEHAVING LIKE A SPOILED BRAT!
OH NO! NO ONE TAMPERS WITH MASTER TIMMY'S TOYS! NEVER!
HEY!
YIIIIPE!
WHAT IS THAT?
IT LOOKS LIKE ONE OF "MASTER" TIMMY'S HOME-MADE TOYS!
YOU ARE A BIG, FAT STUPID JERK! *I HATE YOU!!!*
sniff! YOU DIDN'T PLAY NICE WITH ME AND YOU TALKED BACK TO ME AND YOU, YOU...
YOU BROKE MY VIDEO GAME!!!

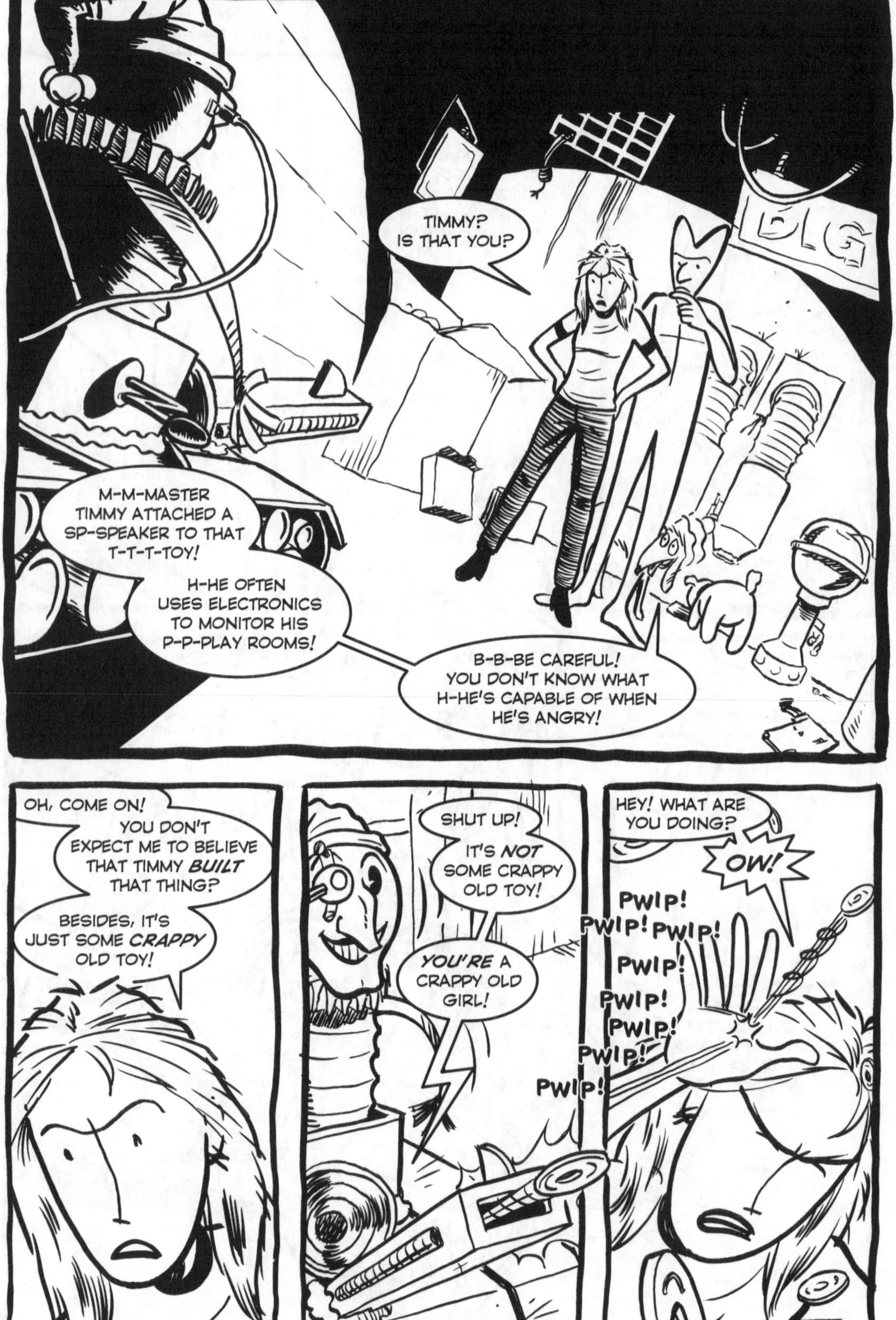
TIMMY? IS THAT YOU?
M-M-MASTER TIMMY ATTACHED A SP-SPEAKER TO THAT T-T-T-TOY!
H-HE OFTEN USES ELECTRONICS TO MONITOR HIS P-P-PLAY ROOMS!
B-B-BE CAREFUL! YOU DON'T KNOW WHAT H-HE'S CAPABLE OF WHEN HE'S ANGRY!
DLG
OH, COME ON!
YOU DON'T EXPECT ME TO BELIEVE THAT TIMMY *BUILT* THAT THING?
BESIDES, IT'S JUST SOME *CRAPPY* OLD TOY!
SHUT UP!
IT'S *NOT* SOME CRAPPY OLD TOY!
YOU'RE A CRAPPY OLD GIRL!
HEY! WHAT ARE YOU DOING?
OW!
PWIP! PWIP! PWIP! PWIP! PWIP! PWIP! PWIP! PWIP!

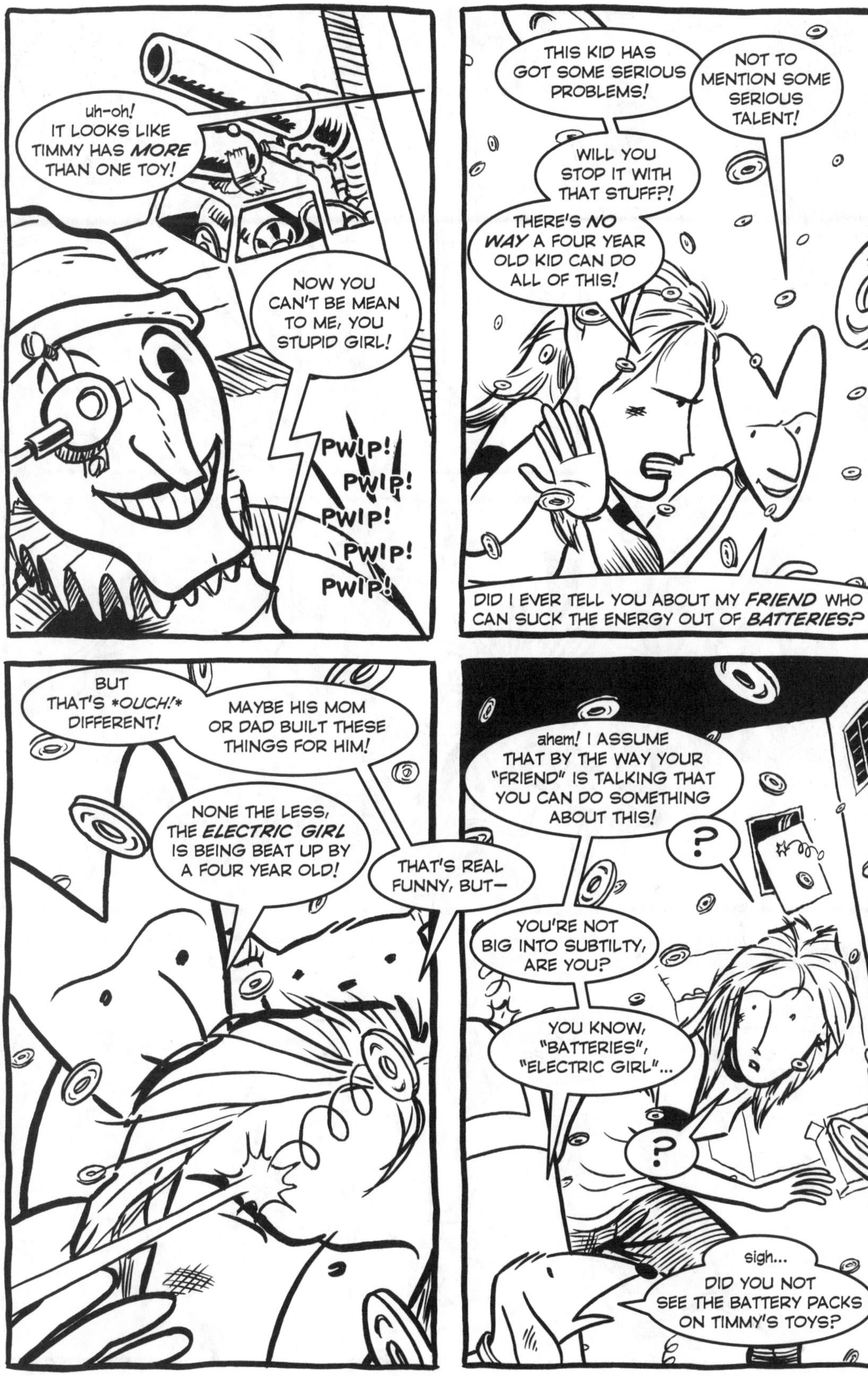
uh-oh! IT LOOKS LIKE TIMMY HAS MORE THAN ONE TOY!
NOW YOU CAN'T BE MEAN TO ME, YOU STUPID GIRL!
PWIP! PWIP! PWIP! PWIP! PWIP!
THIS KID HAS GOT SOME SERIOUS PROBLEMS!
NOT TO MENTION SOME SERIOUS TALENT!
WILL YOU STOP IT WITH THAT STUFF?!
THERE'S NO WAY A FOUR YEAR OLD KID CAN DO ALL OF THIS!
DID I EVER TELL YOU ABOUT MY FRIEND WHO CAN SUCK THE ENERGY OUT OF BATTERIES?
BUT THAT'S *OUCH!* DIFFERENT!
MAYBE HIS MOM OR DAD BUILT THESE THINGS FOR HIM!
NONE THE LESS, THE ELECTRIC GIRL IS BEING BEAT UP BY A FOUR YEAR OLD!
THAT'S REAL FUNNY, BUT—
ahem! I ASSUME THAT BY THE WAY YOUR "FRIEND" IS TALKING THAT YOU CAN DO SOMETHING ABOUT THIS!
?
YOU'RE NOT BIG INTO SUBTILTY, ARE YOU?
YOU KNOW, "BATTERIES", "ELECTRIC GIRL"...
?
sigh... DID YOU NOT SEE THE BATTERY PACKS ON TIMMY'S TOYS?

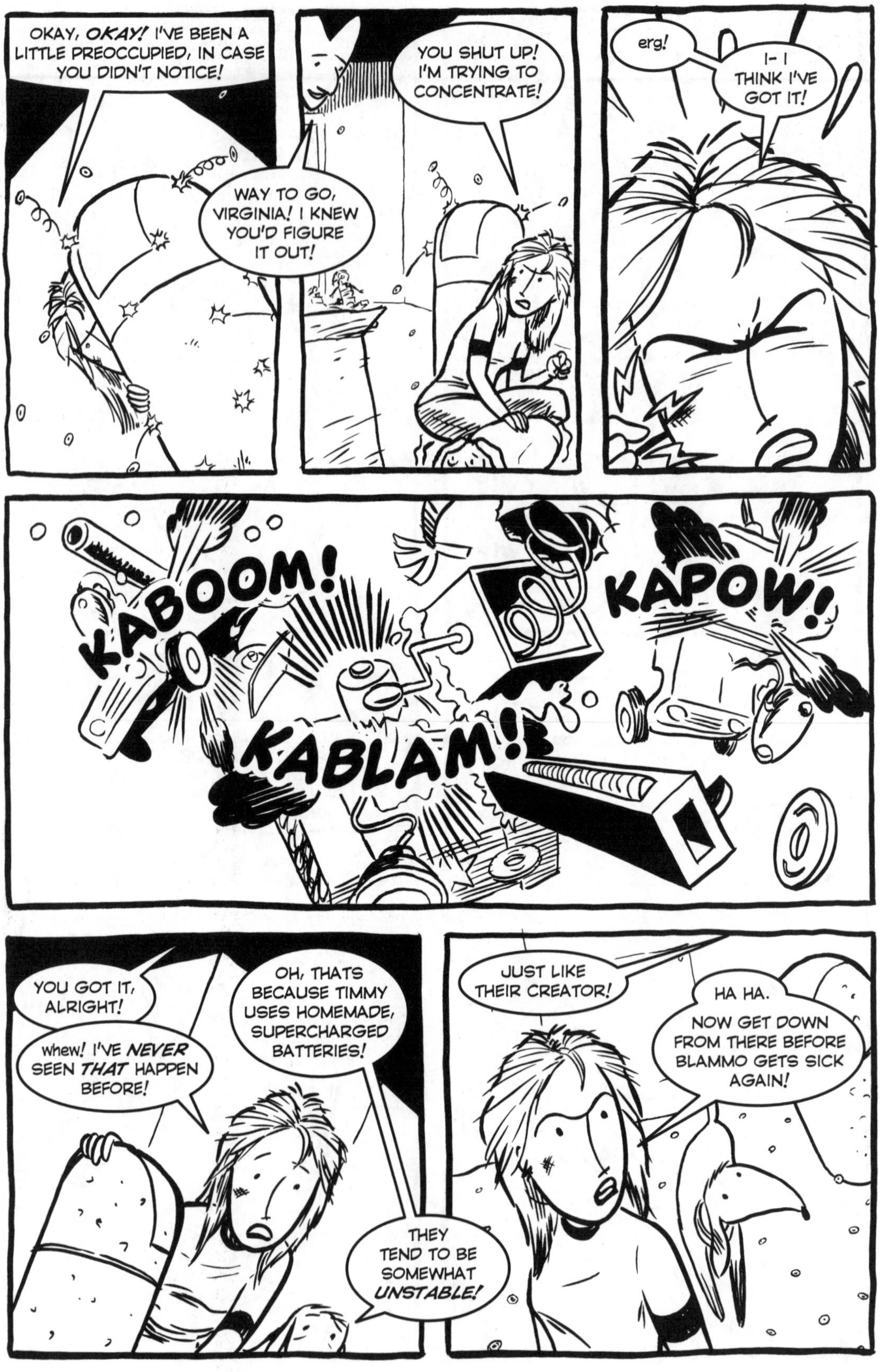

OKAY, OKAY! I'VE BEEN A LITTLE PREOCCUPIED, IN CASE YOU DIDN'T NOTICE!
WAY TO GO, VIRGINIA! I KNEW YOU'D FIGURE IT OUT!
YOU SHUT UP! I'M TRYING TO CONCENTRATE!
erg!
I- I THINK I'VE GOT IT!
KABOOM!
KAPOW!
KABLAM!
YOU GOT IT, ALRIGHT!
whew! I'VE NEVER SEEN THAT HAPPEN BEFORE!
OH, THATS BECAUSE TIMMY USES HOMEMADE, SUPERCHARGED BATTERIES!
THEY TEND TO BE SOMEWHAT UNSTABLE!
JUST LIKE THEIR CREATOR!
HA HA.
NOW GET DOWN FROM THERE BEFORE BLAMMO GETS SICK AGAIN!

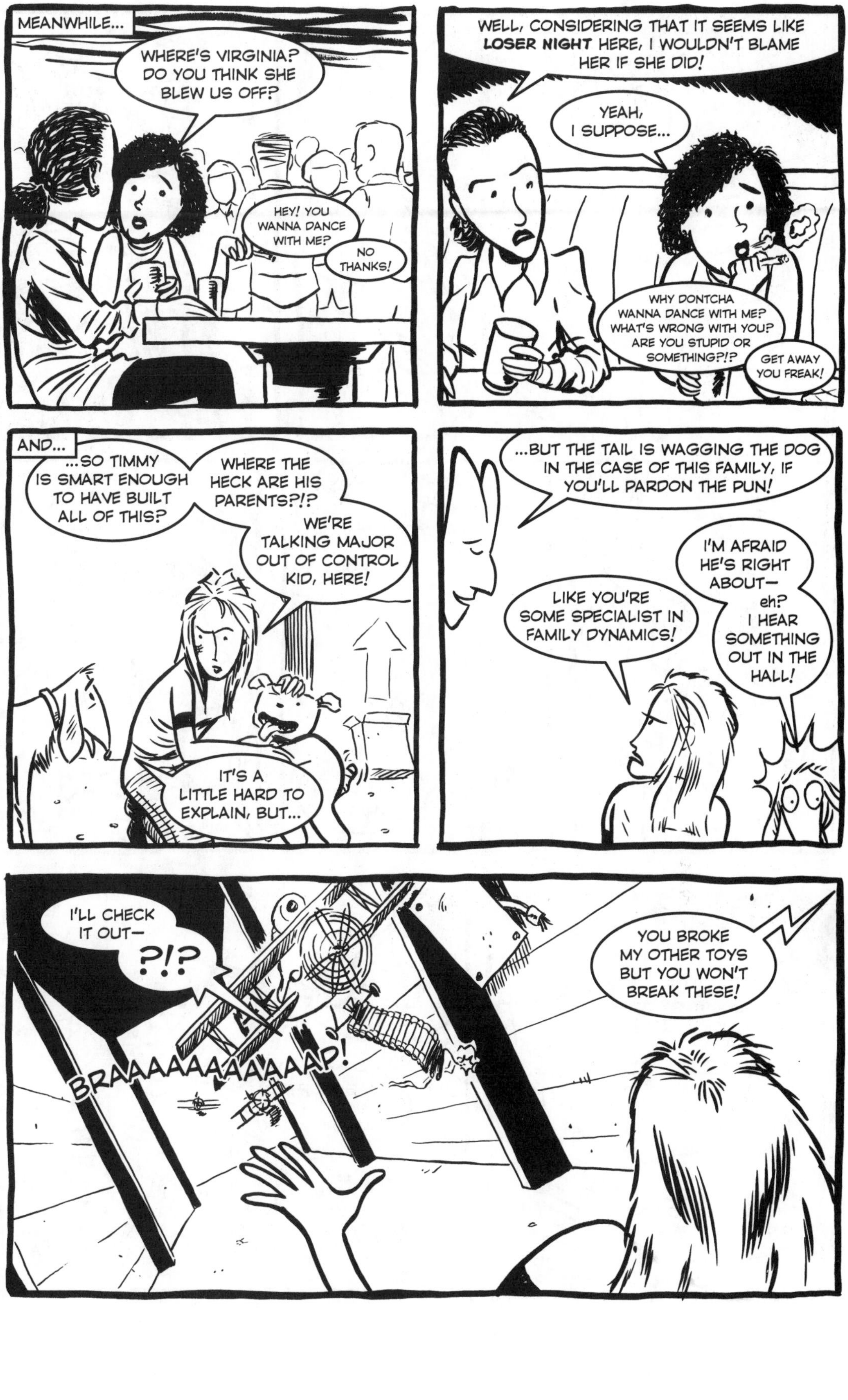
MEANWHILE...
WHERE'S VIRGINIA? DO YOU THINK SHE BLEW US OFF?
HEY! YOU WANNA DANCE WITH ME?
NO THANKS!
WELL, CONSIDERING THAT IT SEEMS LIKE **LOSER NIGHT** HERE, I WOULDN'T BLAME HER IF SHE DID!
YEAH, I SUPPOSE...
WHY DONTCHA WANNA DANCE WITH ME? WHAT'S WRONG WITH YOU? ARE YOU STUPID OR SOMETHING?!?
GET AWAY YOU FREAK!
AND...
...SO TIMMY IS SMART ENOUGH TO HAVE BUILT ALL OF THIS?
WHERE THE HECK ARE HIS PARENTS?!?
WE'RE TALKING MAJOR OUT OF CONTROL KID, HERE!
IT'S A LITTLE HARD TO EXPLAIN, BUT...
...BUT THE TAIL IS WAGGING THE DOG IN THE CASE OF THIS FAMILY, IF YOU'LL PARDON THE PUN!
LIKE YOU'RE SOME SPECIALIST IN FAMILY DYNAMICS!
I'M AFRAID HE'S RIGHT ABOUT— eh? I HEAR SOMETHING OUT IN THE HALL!
I'LL CHECK IT OUT—
?!?
BRAAAAAAAAAAP!
YOU BROKE MY OTHER TOYS BUT YOU WON'T BREAK THESE!

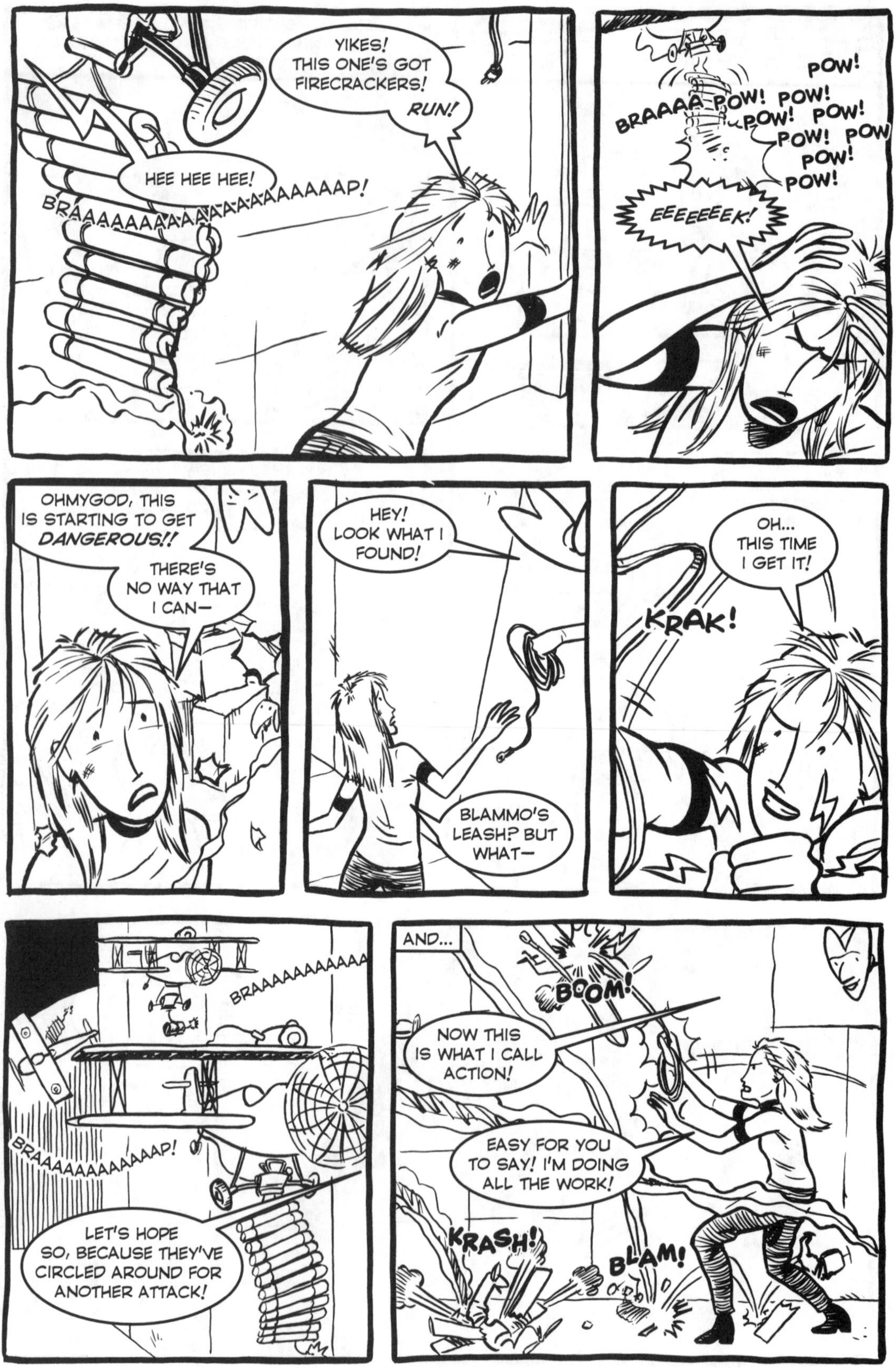
YIKES! THIS ONE'S GOT FIRECRACKERS!
RUN!
HEE HEE HEE!
BRAAAAAAAAAAAAAAAAAAAAAP!
POW!
BRAAAA POW! POW!
POW! POW!
POW! POW
POW!
POW!
EEEEEEEK!
OHMYGOD, THIS IS STARTING TO GET DANGEROUS!!
THERE'S NO WAY THAT I CAN—
HEY! LOOK WHAT I FOUND!
BLAMMO'S LEASH? BUT WHAT—
OH... THIS TIME I GET IT!
KRAK!
BRAAAAAAAAAAAA
BRAAAAAAAAAAAAP!
LET'S HOPE SO, BECAUSE THEY'VE CIRCLED AROUND FOR ANOTHER ATTACK!
AND...
BOOM!
NOW THIS IS WHAT I CALL ACTION!
EASY FOR YOU TO SAY! I'M DOING ALL THE WORK!
KRASH!
BLAM!

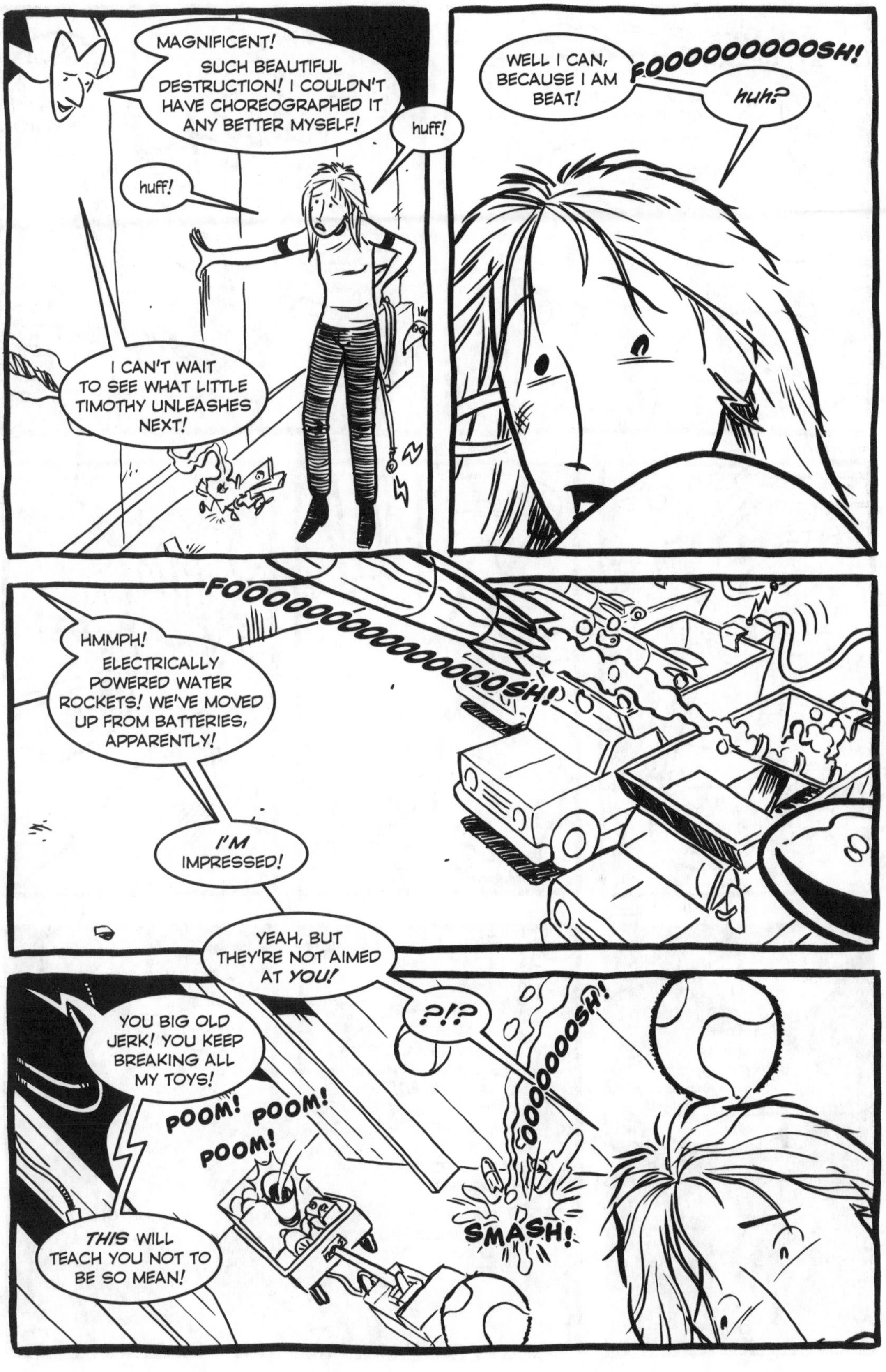

MAGNIFICENT!
SUCH BEAUTIFUL DESTRUCTION! I COULDN'T HAVE CHOREOGRAPHED IT ANY BETTER MYSELF!
huff!
huff!
I CAN'T WAIT TO SEE WHAT LITTLE TIMOTHY UNLEASHES NEXT!
WELL I CAN, BECAUSE I AM BEAT!
FOOOOOOOOOSH!
huh?
FOOOOOOOOOOOOOOOOOOOOSH!
HMMPH!
ELECTRICALLY POWERED WATER ROCKETS! WE'VE MOVED UP FROM BATTERIES, APPARENTLY!
I'M IMPRESSED!
YEAH, BUT THEY'RE NOT AIMED AT YOU!
?!?
YOU BIG OLD JERK! YOU KEEP BREAKING ALL MY TOYS!
OOOOOOOOSH!
POOM! POOM!
POOM!
SMASH!
THIS WILL TEACH YOU NOT TO BE SO MEAN!

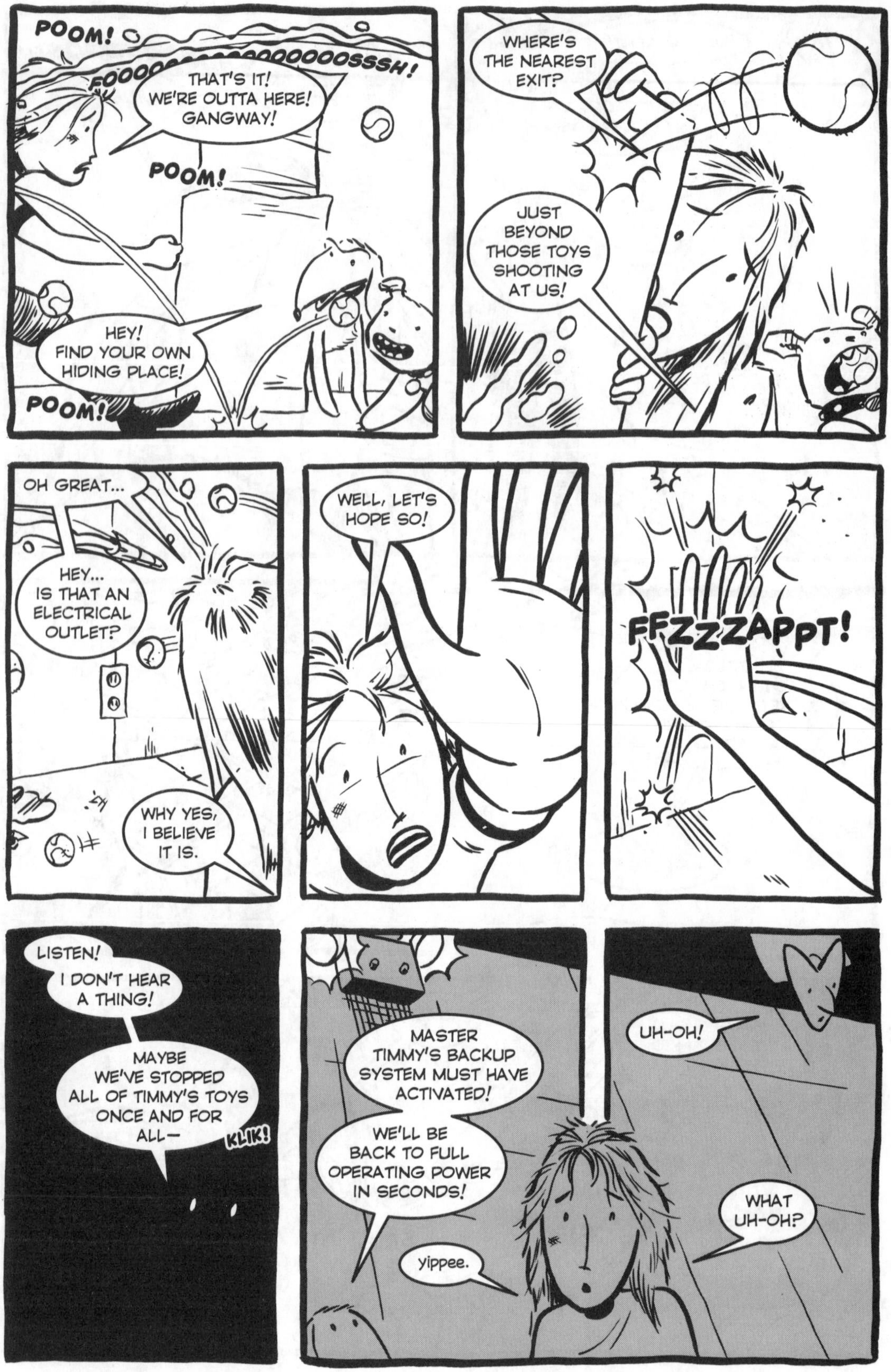
POOM!
FOOOOOOOOOOOOOOOOOOOSSSSH!
THAT'S IT! WE'RE OUTTA HERE! GANGWAY!
POOM!
HEY! FIND YOUR OWN HIDING PLACE!
POOM!
WHERE'S THE NEAREST EXIT?
JUST BEYOND THOSE TOYS SHOOTING AT US!
OH GREAT...
HEY... IS THAT AN ELECTRICAL OUTLET?
WHY YES, I BELIEVE IT IS.
WELL, LET'S HOPE SO!
FFZZZZAPPT!
LISTEN!
I DON'T HEAR A THING!
MAYBE WE'VE STOPPED ALL OF TIMMY'S TOYS ONCE AND FOR ALL—
KLIK!
MASTER TIMMY'S BACKUP SYSTEM MUST HAVE ACTIVATED!
WE'LL BE BACK TO FULL OPERATING POWER IN SECONDS!
yippee.
UH-OH!
WHAT UH-OH?

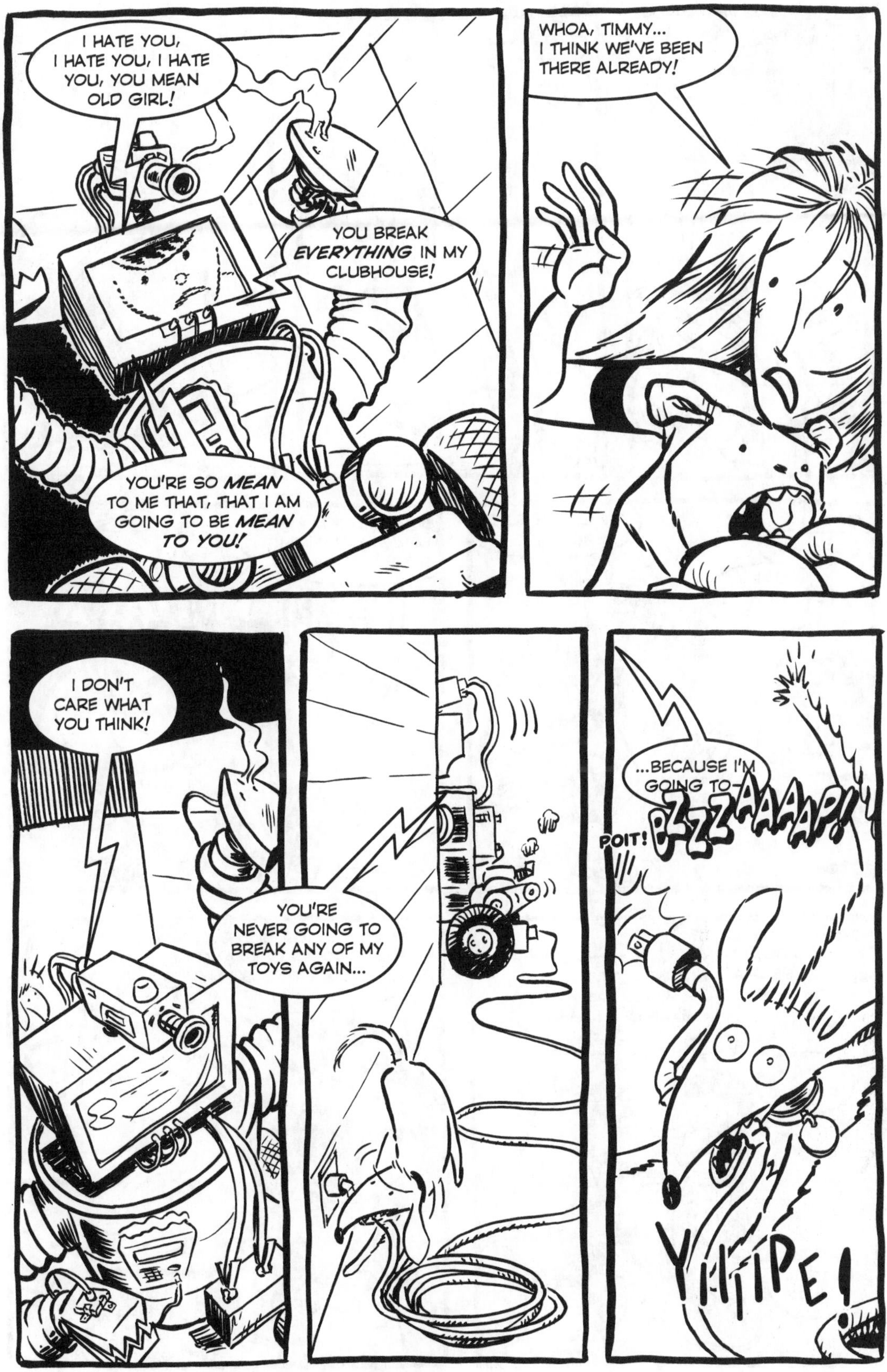
I HATE YOU, I HATE YOU, I HATE YOU, YOU MEAN OLD GIRL!
YOU BREAK EVERYTHING IN MY CLUBHOUSE!
YOU'RE SO MEAN TO ME THAT, THAT I AM GOING TO BE MEAN TO YOU!
WHOA, TIMMY... I THINK WE'VE BEEN THERE ALREADY!
I DON'T CARE WHAT YOU THINK!
YOU'RE NEVER GOING TO BREAK ANY OF MY TOYS AGAIN...
...BECAUSE I'M GOING TO–
BZZZAAAAP!
POIT!
YIIIIPE!

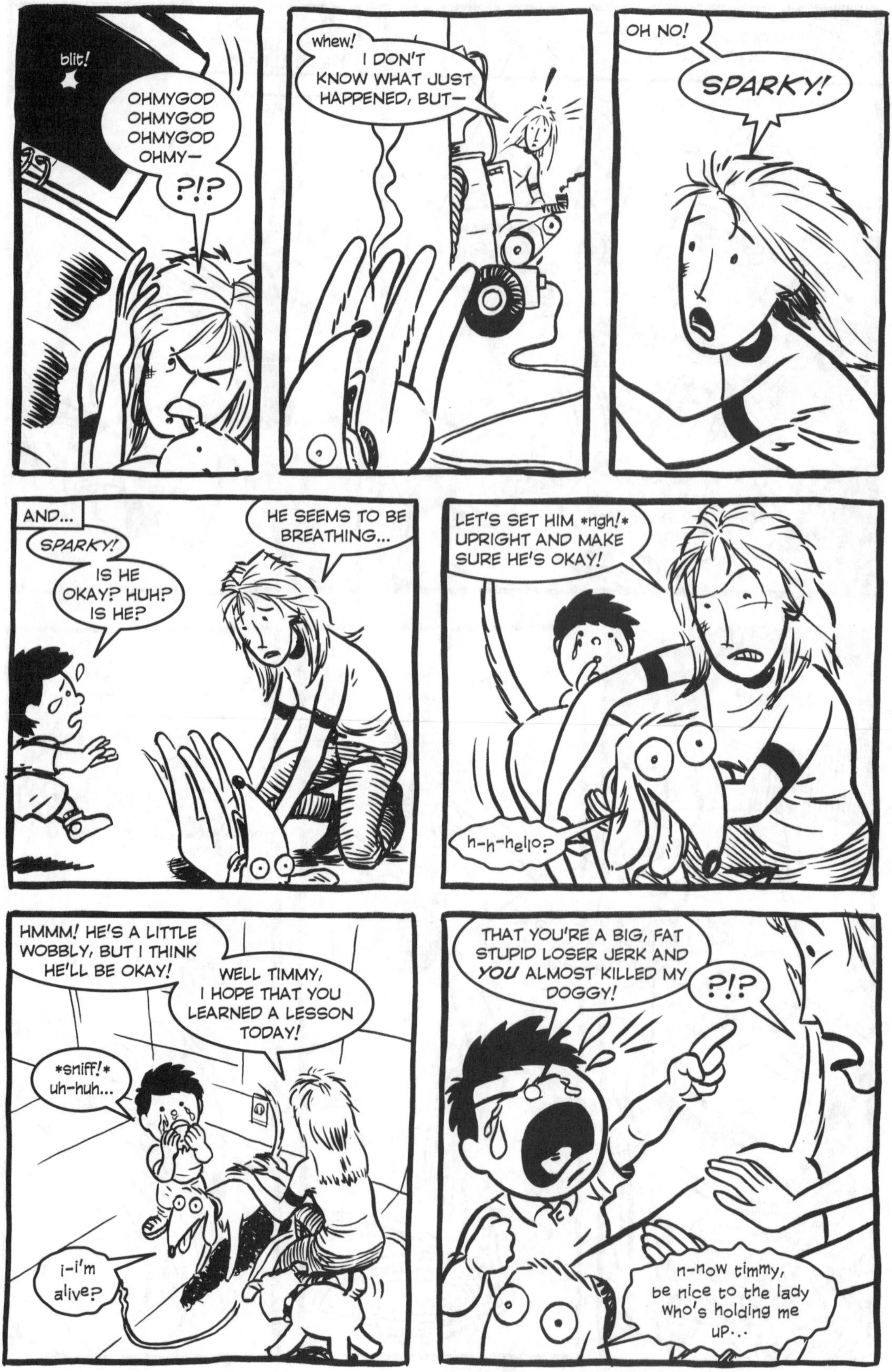
blit!
OHMYGOD OHMYGOD OHMYGOD OHMY—
?!?
whew! I DON'T KNOW WHAT JUST HAPPENED, BUT—
!
OH NO!
SPARKY!
AND...
SPARKY!
IS HE OKAY? HUH? IS HE?
HE SEEMS TO BE BREATHING...
LET'S SET HIM *ngh!* UPRIGHT AND MAKE SURE HE'S OKAY!
h-h-hello?
HMMM! HE'S A LITTLE WOBBLY, BUT I THINK HE'LL BE OKAY!
WELL TIMMY, I HOPE THAT YOU LEARNED A LESSON TODAY!
sniff! uh-huh...
i-i'm alive?
THAT YOU'RE A BIG, FAT STUPID LOSER JERK AND YOU ALMOST KILLED MY DOGGY!
?!?
n-now timmy, be nice to the lady who's holding me up...

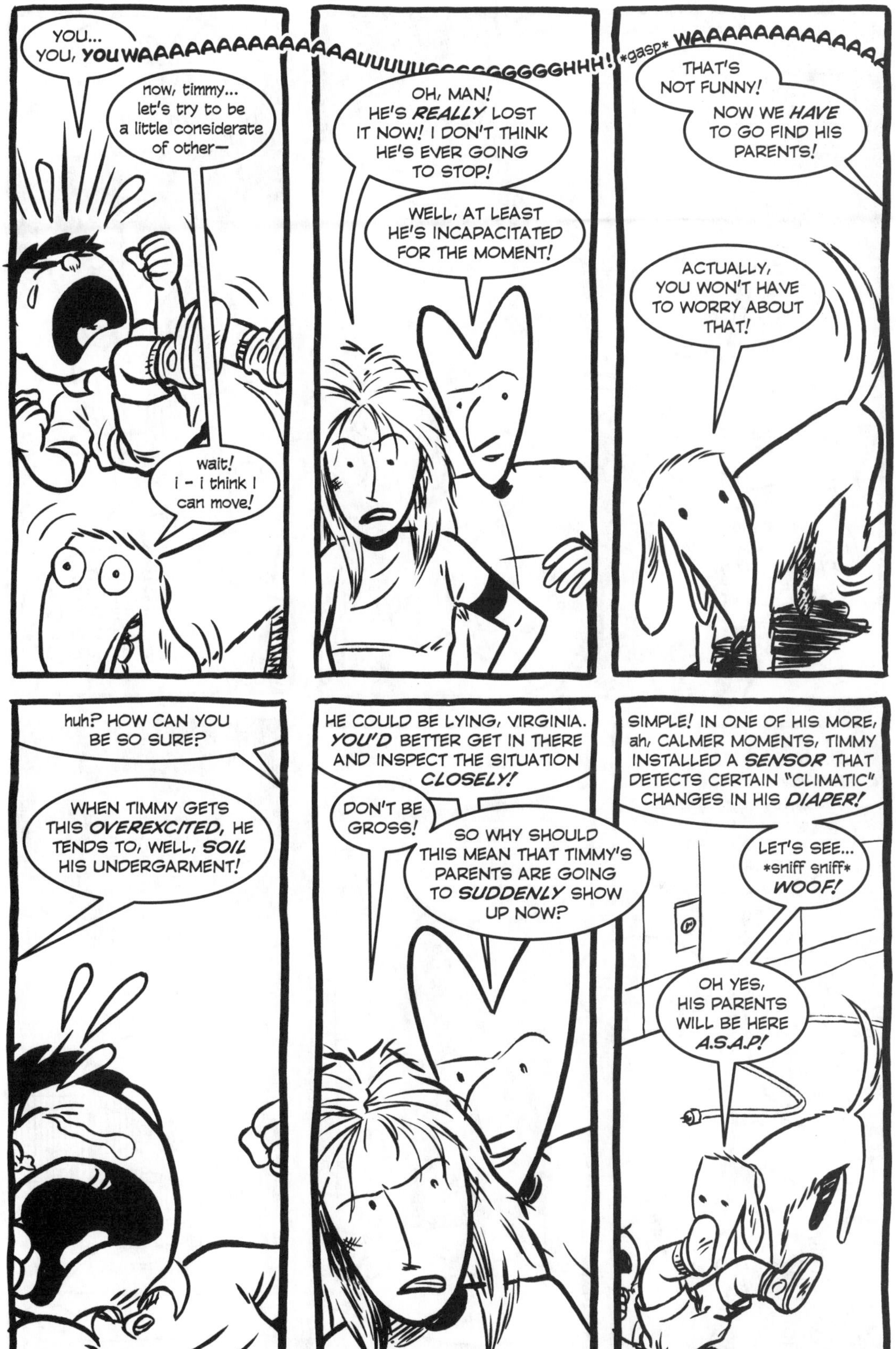
YOU... YOU, YOU WAAAAAAAAAAAAAAAAUUUUUGGGGGGGGGHHH! *gasp* WAAAAAAAAAAAAA
now, timmy... let's try to be a little considerate of other—
wait! i - i think I can move!
OH, MAN! HE'S REALLY LOST IT NOW! I DON'T THINK HE'S EVER GOING TO STOP!
WELL, AT LEAST HE'S INCAPACITATED FOR THE MOMENT!
THAT'S NOT FUNNY!
NOW WE HAVE TO GO FIND HIS PARENTS!
ACTUALLY, YOU WON'T HAVE TO WORRY ABOUT THAT!
huh? HOW CAN YOU BE SO SURE?
WHEN TIMMY GETS THIS OVEREXCITED, HE TENDS TO, WELL, SOIL HIS UNDERGARMENT!
HE COULD BE LYING, VIRGINIA. YOU'D BETTER GET IN THERE AND INSPECT THE SITUATION CLOSELY!
DON'T BE GROSS!
SO WHY SHOULD THIS MEAN THAT TIMMY'S PARENTS ARE GOING TO SUDDENLY SHOW UP NOW?
SIMPLE! IN ONE OF HIS MORE, ah, CALMER MOMENTS, TIMMY INSTALLED A SENSOR THAT DETECTS CERTAIN "CLIMATIC" CHANGES IN HIS DIAPER!
LET'S SEE... *sniff sniff* WOOF!
OH YES, HIS PARENTS WILL BE HERE A.S.A.P!

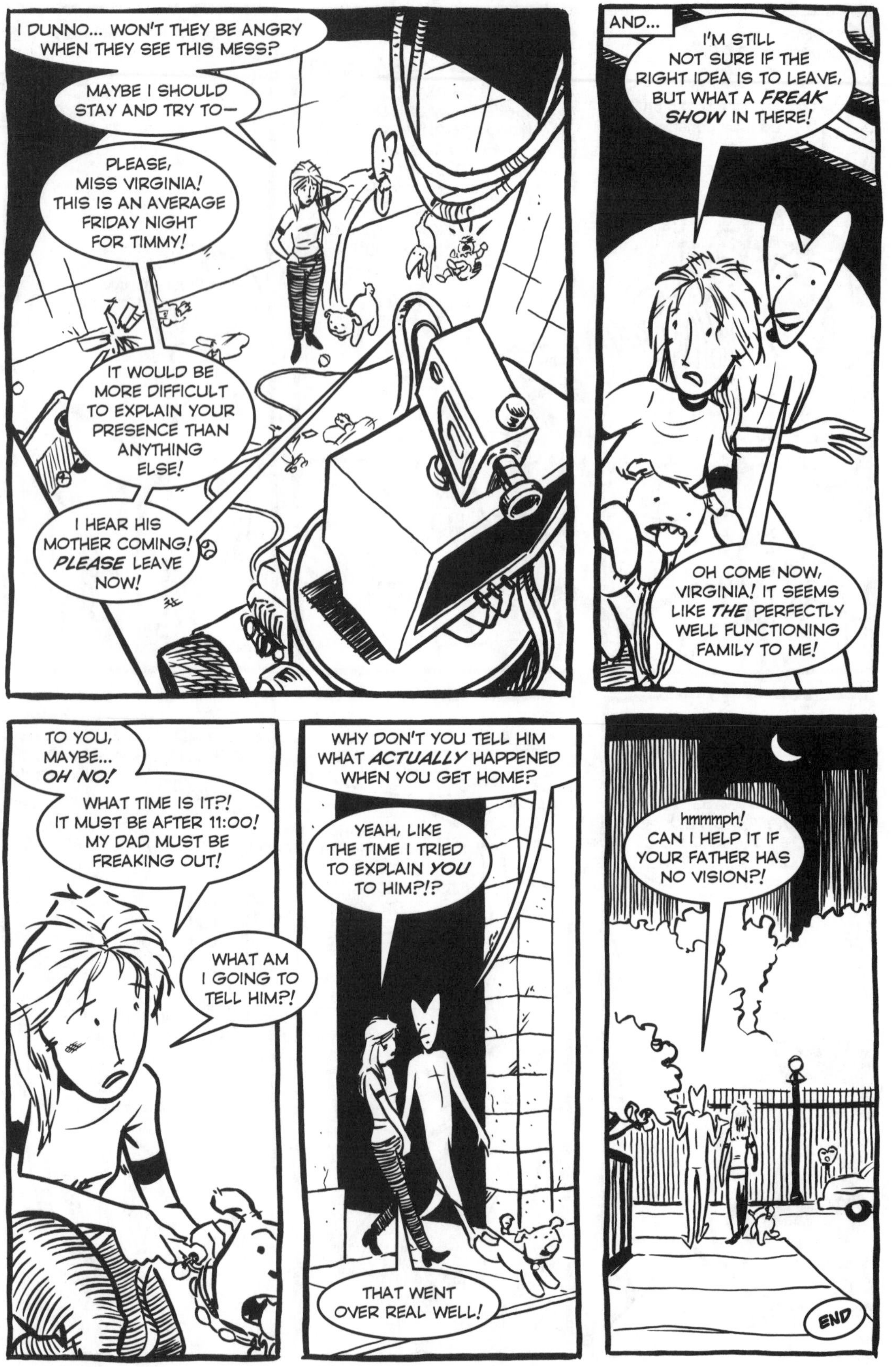

I DUNNO... WON'T THEY BE ANGRY WHEN THEY SEE THIS MESS?
MAYBE I SHOULD STAY AND TRY TO—
PLEASE, MISS VIRGINIA! THIS IS AN AVERAGE FRIDAY NIGHT FOR TIMMY!
IT WOULD BE MORE DIFFICULT TO EXPLAIN YOUR PRESENCE THAN ANYTHING ELSE!
I HEAR HIS MOTHER COMING! PLEASE LEAVE NOW!
AND...
I'M STILL NOT SURE IF THE RIGHT IDEA IS TO LEAVE, BUT WHAT A FREAK SHOW IN THERE!
OH COME NOW, VIRGINIA! IT SEEMS LIKE THE PERFECTLY WELL FUNCTIONING FAMILY TO ME!
TO YOU, MAYBE... OH NO!
WHAT TIME IS IT?! IT MUST BE AFTER 11:00! MY DAD MUST BE FREAKING OUT!
WHAT AM I GOING TO TELL HIM?!
WHY DON'T YOU TELL HIM WHAT ACTUALLY HAPPENED WHEN YOU GET HOME?
YEAH, LIKE THE TIME I TRIED TO EXPLAIN YOU TO HIM?!?
THAT WENT OVER REAL WELL!
hmmmph! CAN I HELP IT IF YOUR FATHER HAS NO VISION?!
END

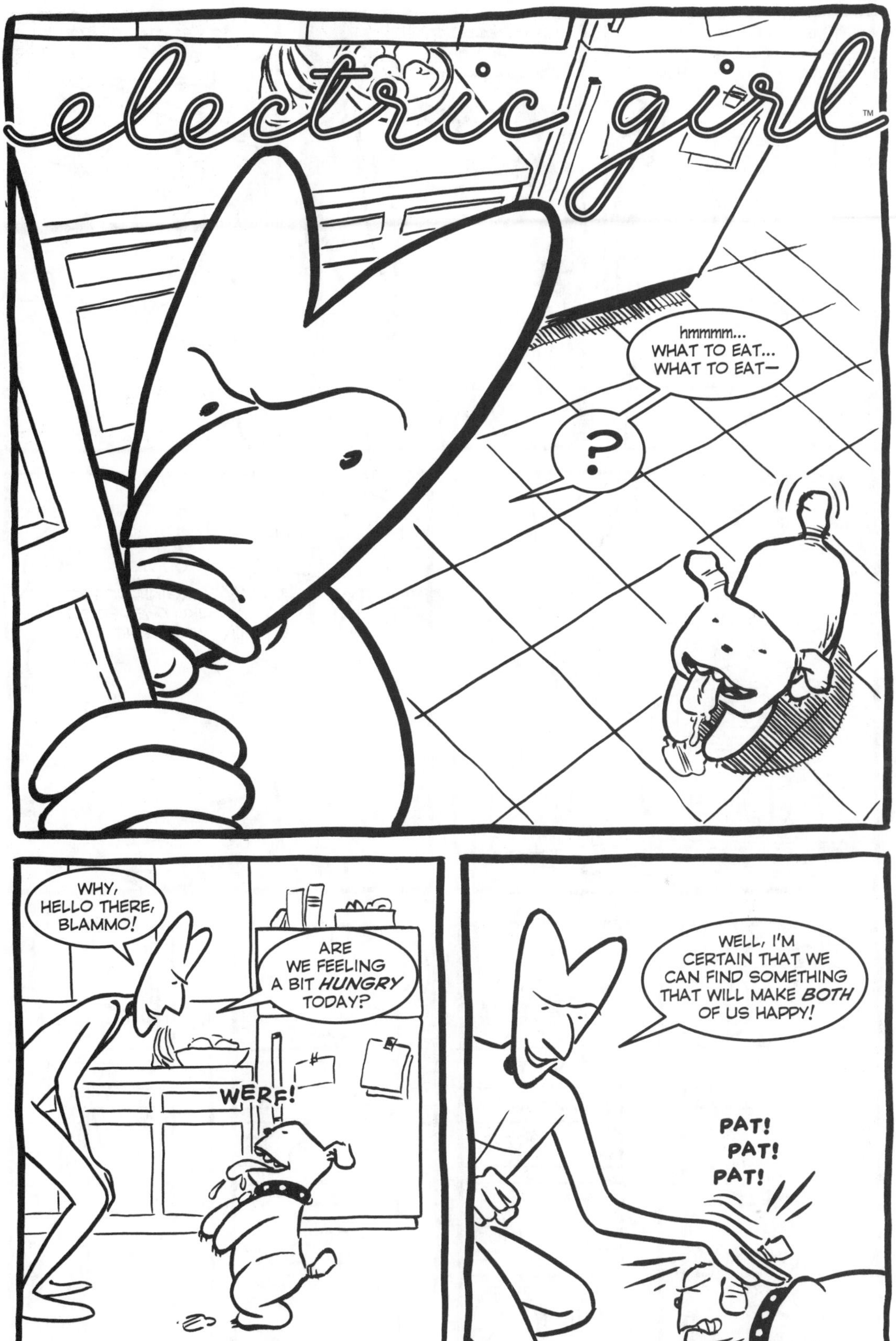
electric girl™
hmmmm...
WHAT TO EAT...
WHAT TO EAT—
?
WHY, HELLO THERE, BLAMMO!
ARE WE FEELING A BIT *HUNGRY* TODAY?
WERF!
WELL, I'M CERTAIN THAT WE CAN FIND SOMETHING THAT WILL MAKE *BOTH* OF US HAPPY!
PAT! PAT! PAT!

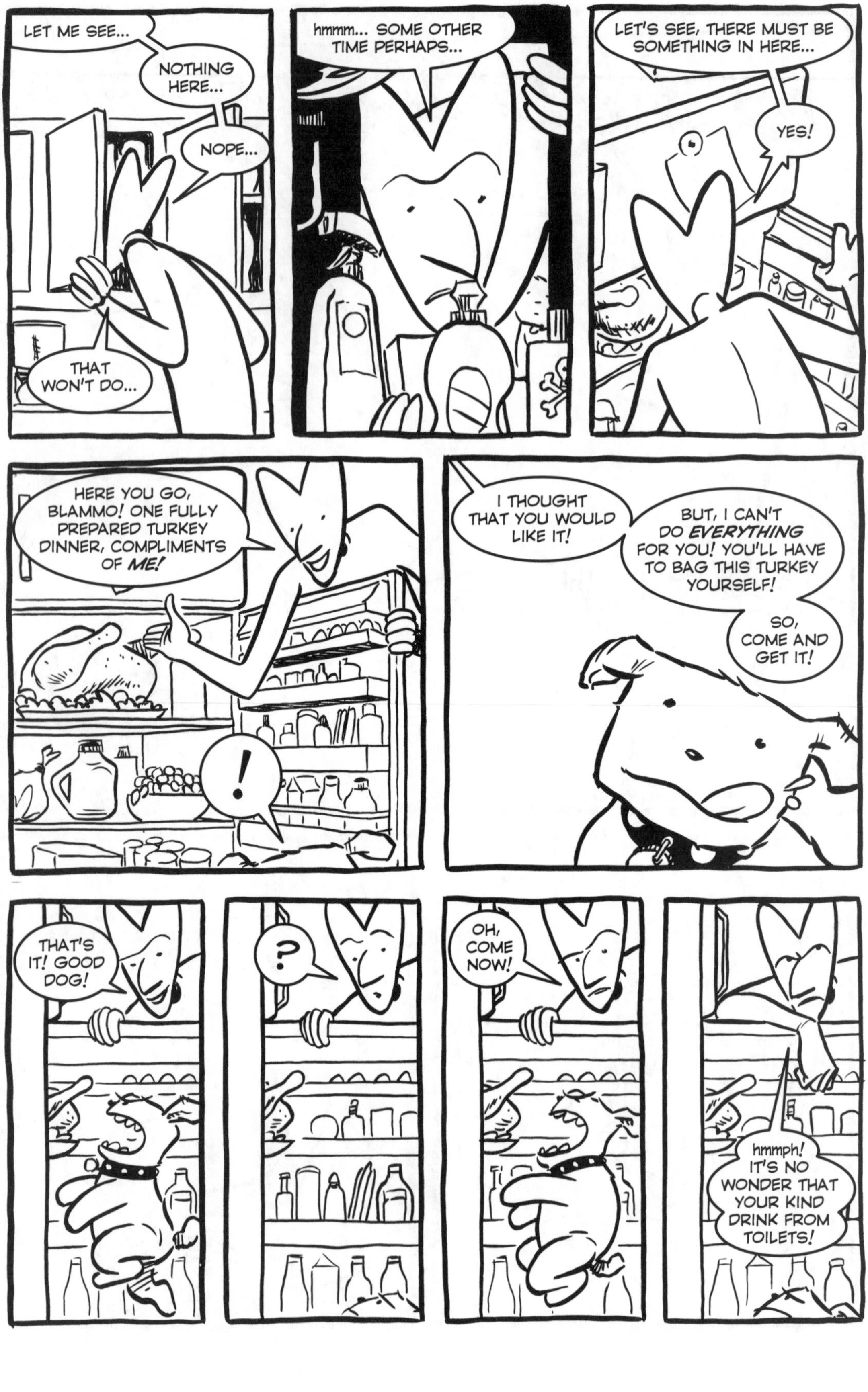
LET ME SEE...
NOTHING HERE...
NOPE...
THAT WON'T DO...
hmmm... SOME OTHER TIME PERHAPS...
LET'S SEE, THERE MUST BE SOMETHING IN HERE...
YES!
HERE YOU GO, BLAMMO! ONE FULLY PREPARED TURKEY DINNER, COMPLIMENTS OF *ME!*
!
I THOUGHT THAT YOU WOULD LIKE IT!
BUT, I CAN'T DO ***EVERYTHING*** FOR YOU! YOU'LL HAVE TO BAG THIS TURKEY YOURSELF!
SO, COME AND GET IT!
THAT'S IT! GOOD DOG!
?
OH, COME NOW!
hmmph! IT'S NO WONDER THAT YOUR KIND DRINK FROM TOILETS!

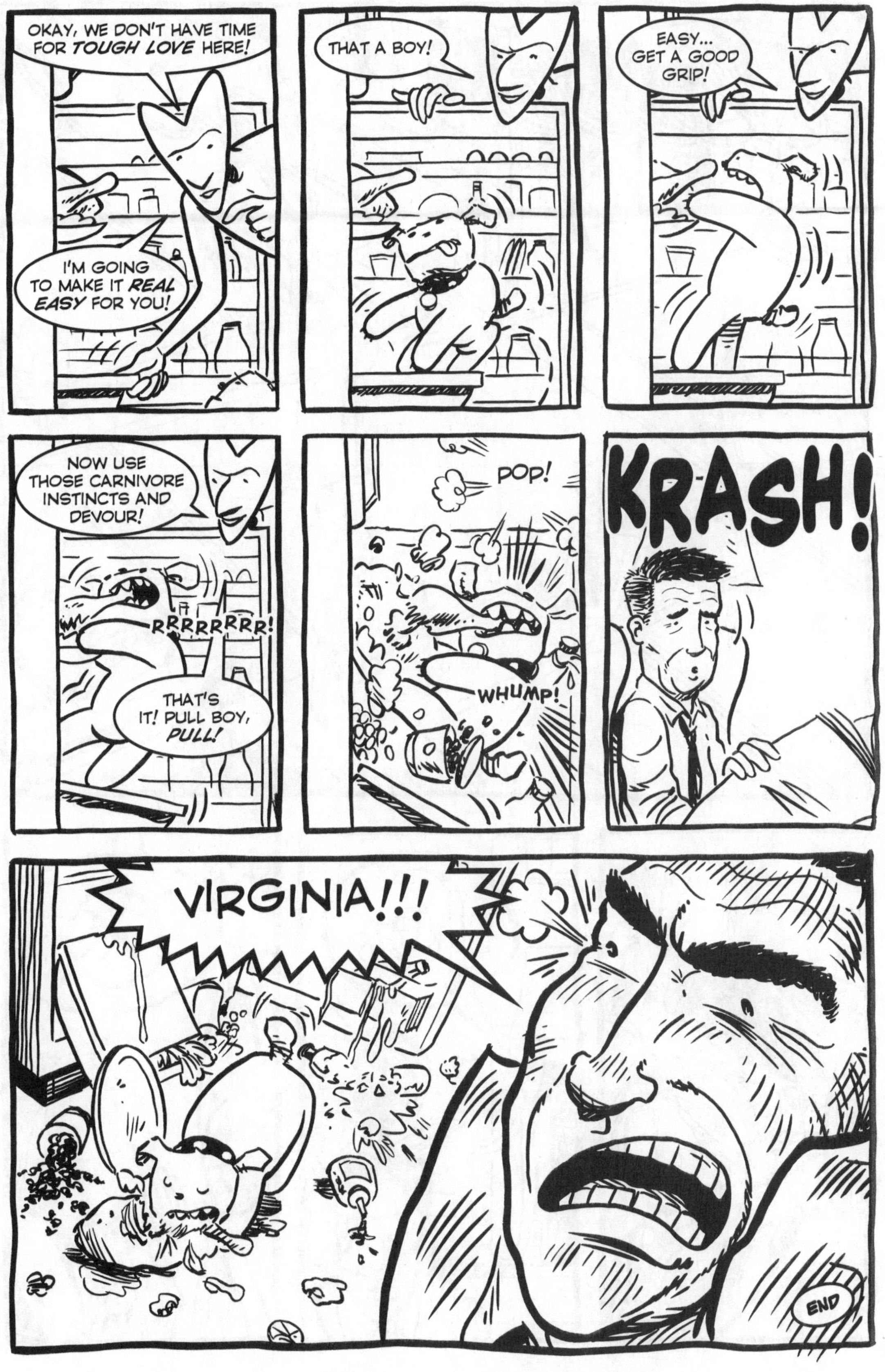
OKAY, WE DON'T HAVE TIME FOR TOUGH LOVE HERE!
I'M GOING TO MAKE IT REAL EASY FOR YOU!
THAT A BOY!
EASY... GET A GOOD GRIP!
NOW USE THOSE CARNIVORE INSTINCTS AND DEVOUR!
RRRRRRRR!
THAT'S IT! PULL BOY, PULL!
POP!
WHUMP!
KRASH!
VIRGINIA!!!
END

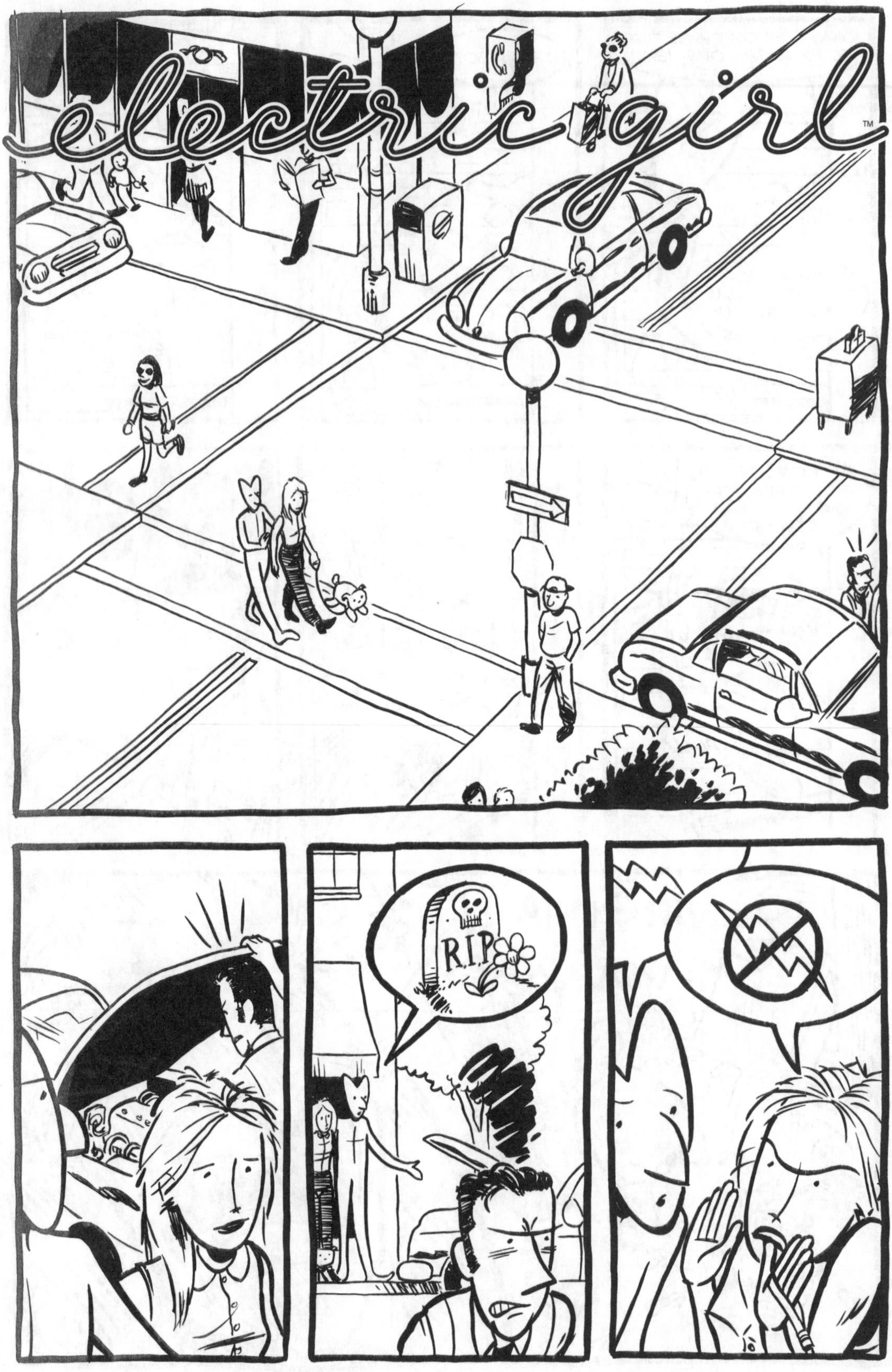
electric girl™
R.I.P.

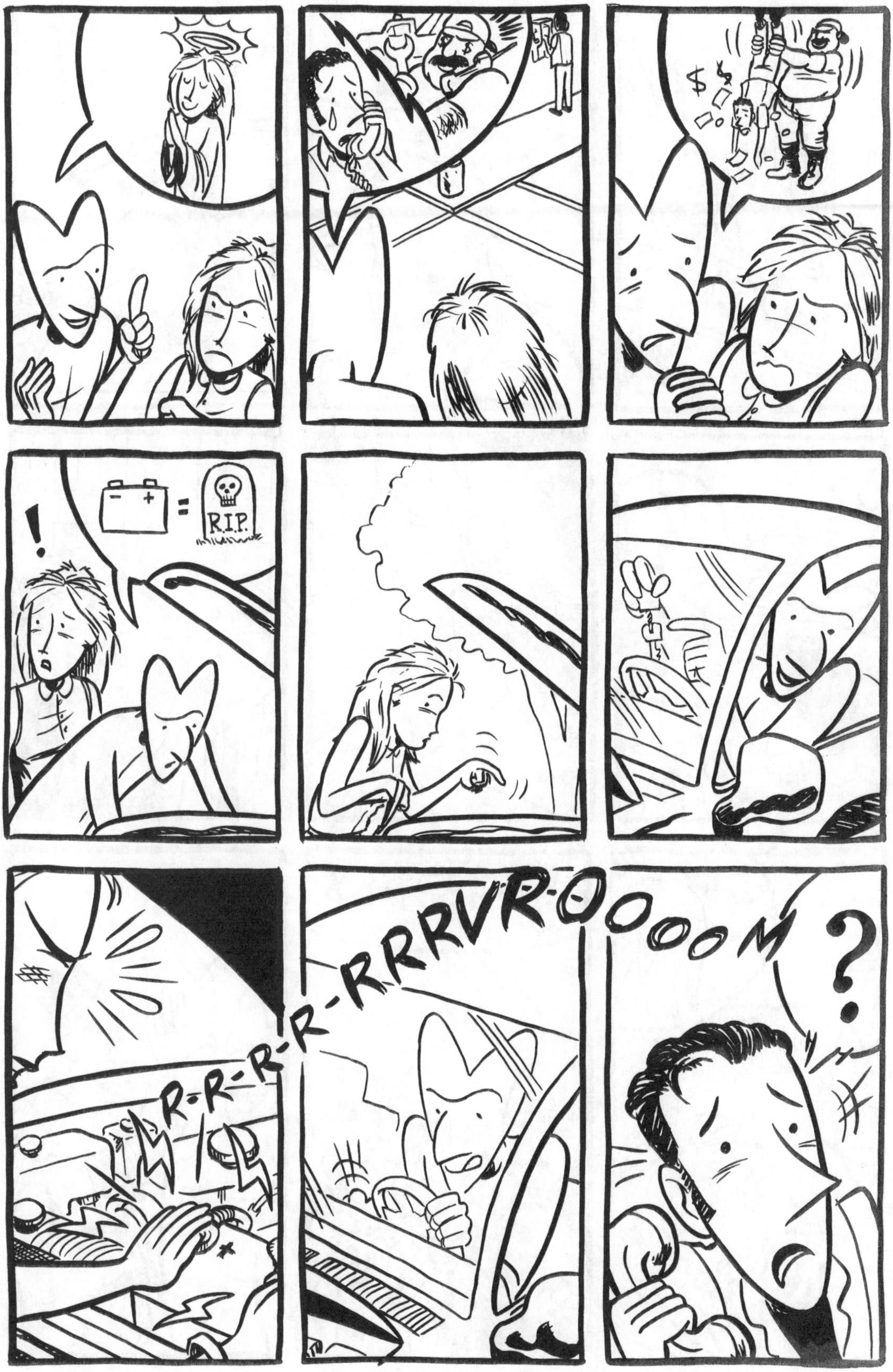

R.I.P.
!
R-R-R-R-R-RRRVR-OOOOOM
?

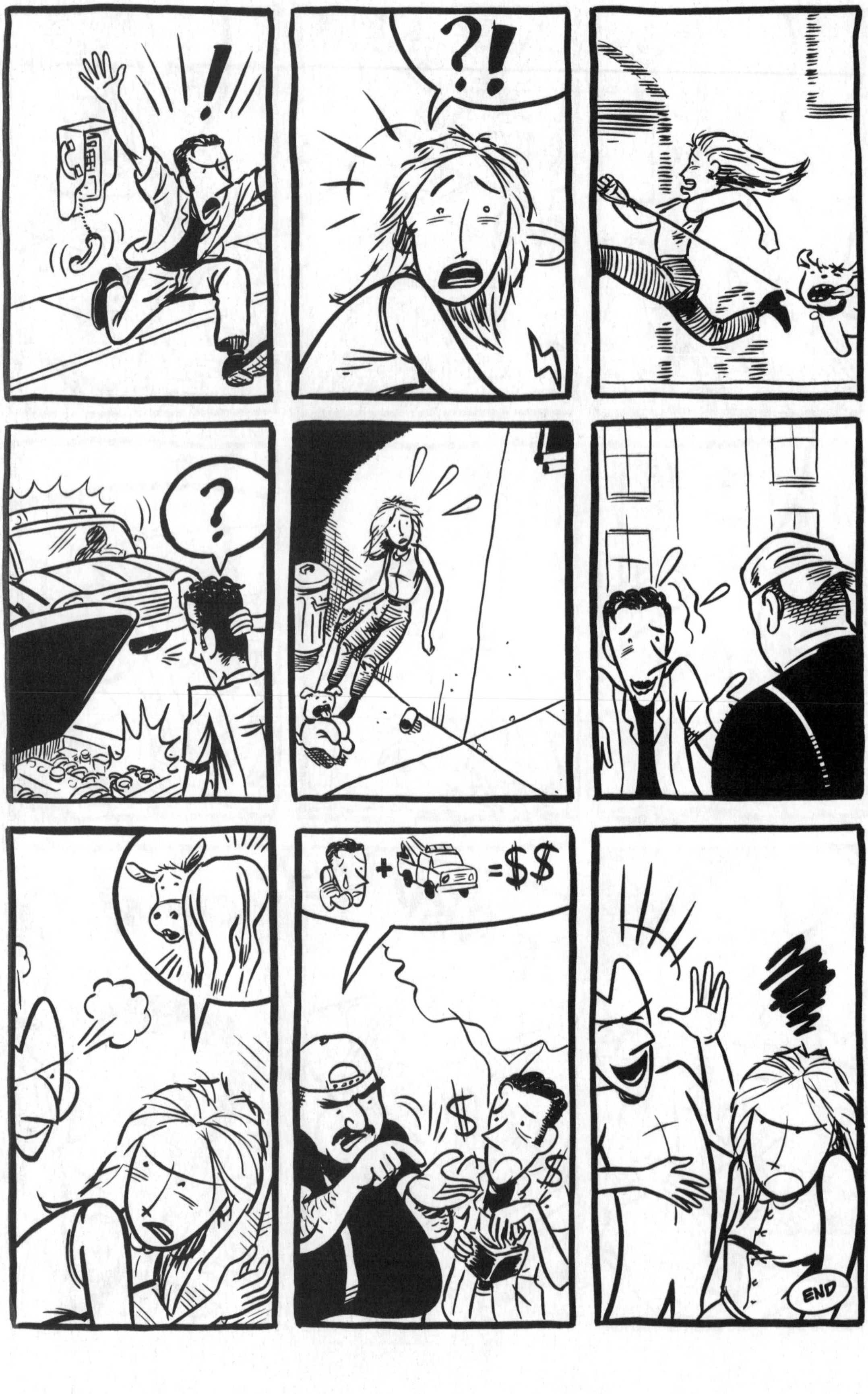
!
?!
?
=$$
$
$
END

electric girl issue ②

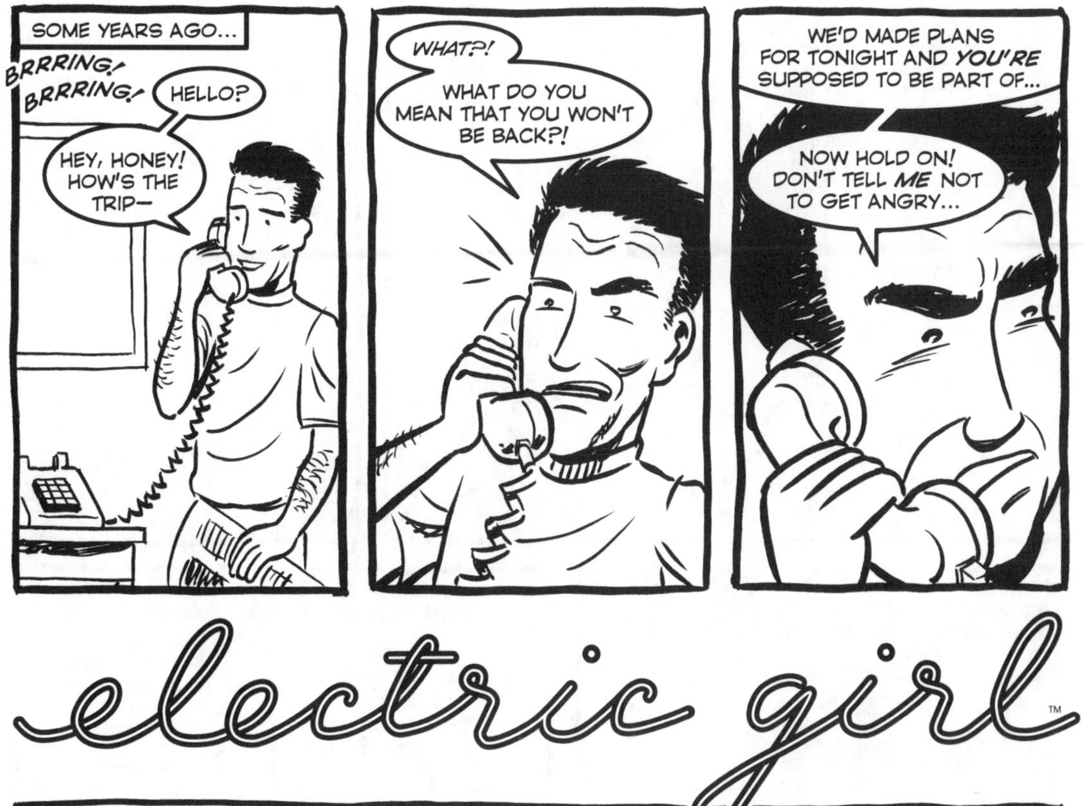
SOME YEARS AGO...
BRRRING! BRRRING!
HELLO?
HEY, HONEY! HOW'S THE TRIP—
WHAT?!
WHAT DO YOU MEAN THAT YOU WON'T BE BACK?!
WE'D MADE PLANS FOR TONIGHT AND YOU'RE SUPPOSED TO BE PART OF...
NOW HOLD ON! DON'T TELL ME NOT TO GET ANGRY...

electric girl™

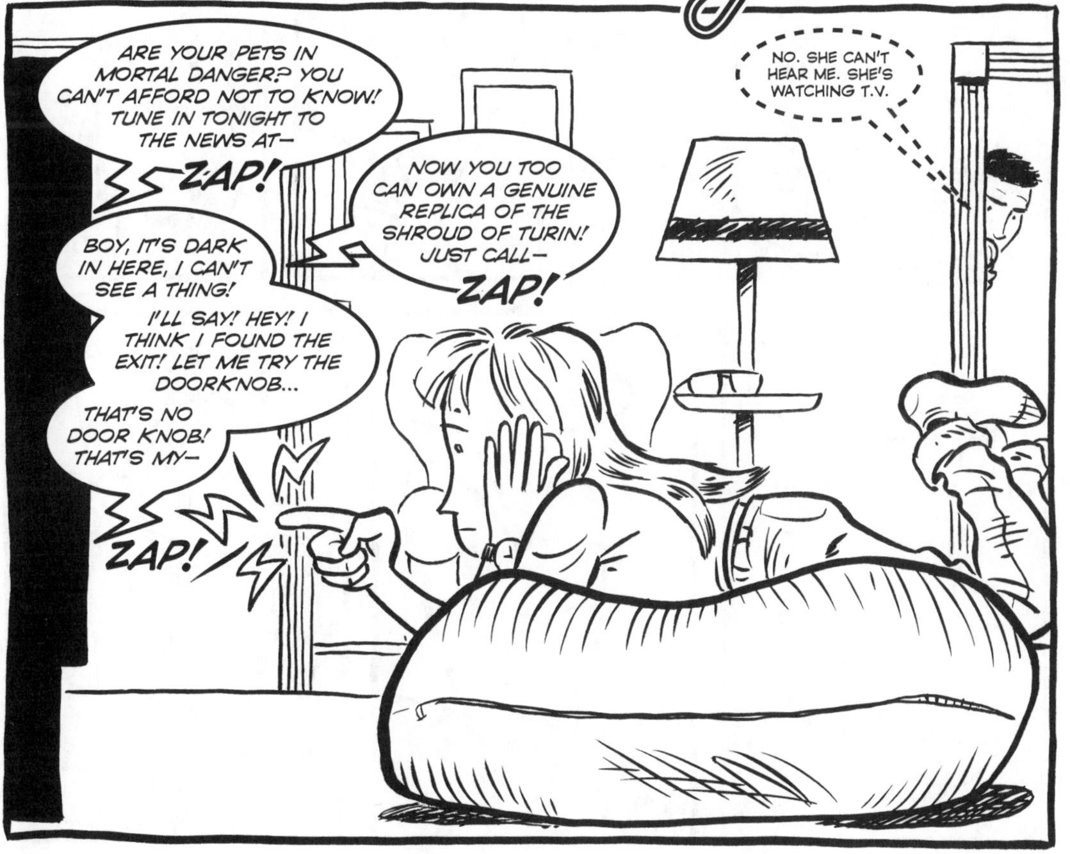
ARE YOUR PETS IN MORTAL DANGER? YOU CAN'T AFFORD NOT TO KNOW! TUNE IN TONIGHT TO THE NEWS AT—
ZAP!
NOW YOU TOO CAN OWN A GENUINE REPLICA OF THE SHROUD OF TURIN! JUST CALL—
ZAP!
BOY, IT'S DARK IN HERE, I CAN'T SEE A THING!
I'LL SAY! HEY! I THINK I FOUND THE EXIT! LET ME TRY THE DOORKNOB...
THAT'S NO DOOR KNOB! THAT'S MY—
ZAP!
NO. SHE CAN'T HEAR ME. SHE'S WATCHING T.V.

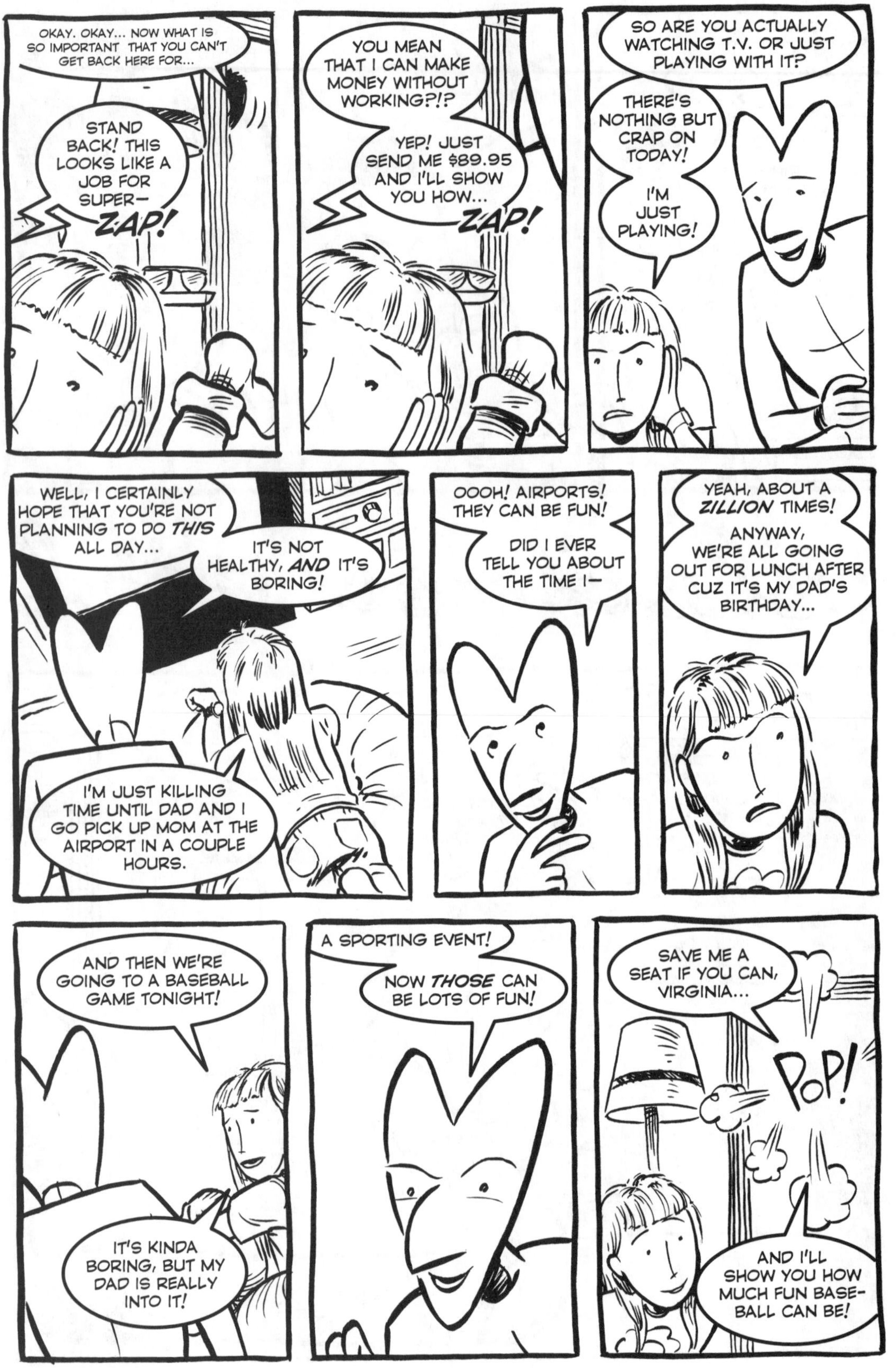

OKAY. OKAY... NOW WHAT IS SO IMPORTANT THAT YOU CAN'T GET BACK HERE FOR...
STAND BACK! THIS LOOKS LIKE A JOB FOR SUPER—
ZAP!
YOU MEAN THAT I CAN MAKE MONEY WITHOUT WORKING?!?
YEP! JUST SEND ME $89.95 AND I'LL SHOW YOU HOW...
ZAP!
SO ARE YOU ACTUALLY WATCHING T.V. OR JUST PLAYING WITH IT?
THERE'S NOTHING BUT CRAP ON TODAY!
I'M JUST PLAYING!
WELL, I CERTAINLY HOPE THAT YOU'RE NOT PLANNING TO DO *THIS* ALL DAY...
IT'S NOT HEALTHY, *AND* IT'S BORING!
I'M JUST KILLING TIME UNTIL DAD AND I GO PICK UP MOM AT THE AIRPORT IN A COUPLE HOURS.
OOOH! AIRPORTS! THEY CAN BE FUN!
DID I EVER TELL YOU ABOUT THE TIME I—
YEAH, ABOUT A *ZILLION* TIMES!
ANYWAY, WE'RE ALL GOING OUT FOR LUNCH AFTER CUZ IT'S MY DAD'S BIRTHDAY...
AND THEN WE'RE GOING TO A BASEBALL GAME TONIGHT!
IT'S KINDA BORING, BUT MY DAD IS REALLY INTO IT!
A SPORTING EVENT!
NOW *THOSE* CAN BE LOTS OF FUN!
SAVE ME A SEAT IF YOU CAN, VIRGINIA...
POP!
AND I'LL SHOW YOU HOW MUCH FUN BASE-BALL CAN BE!

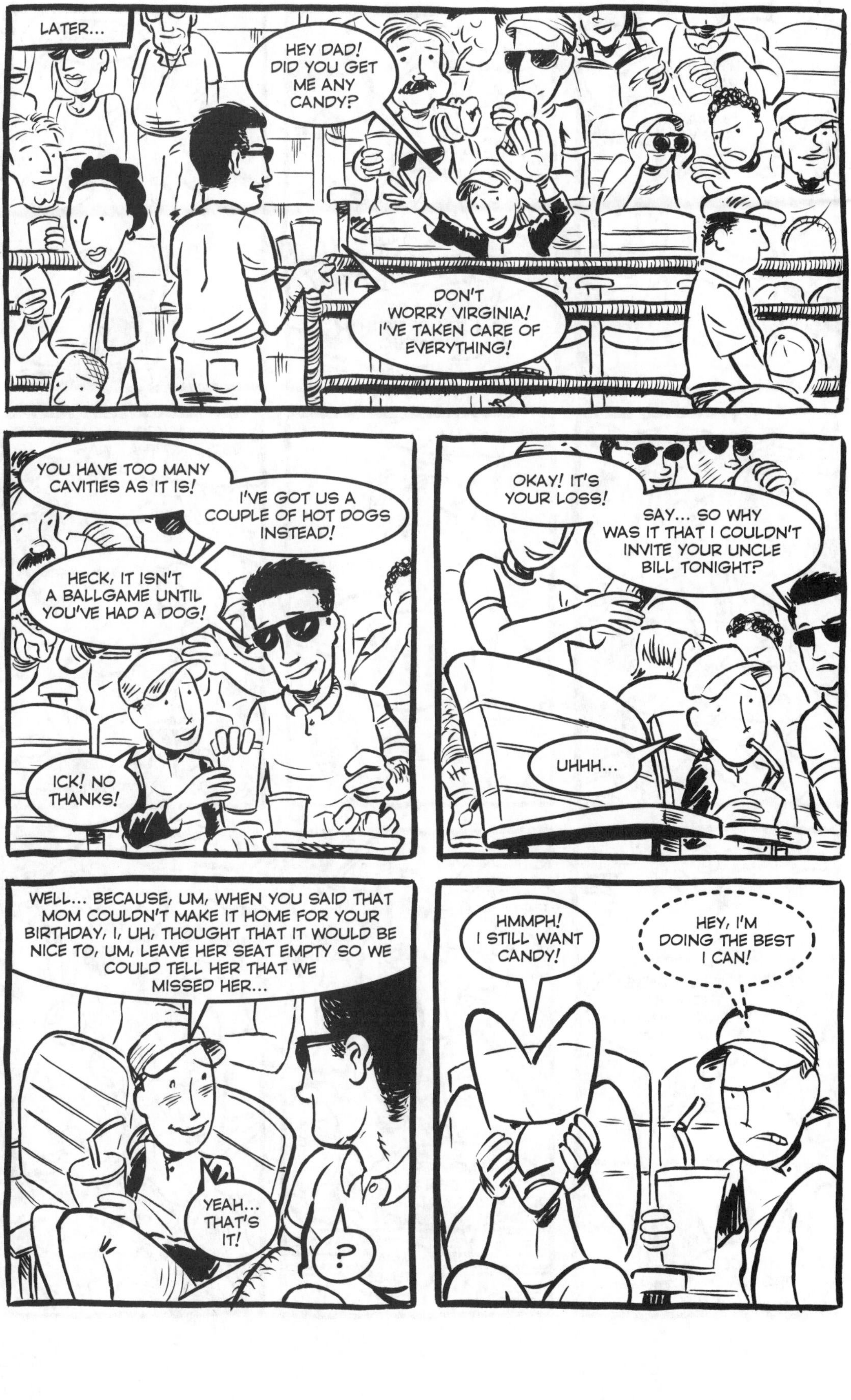
LATER...
HEY DAD! DID YOU GET ME ANY CANDY?
DON'T WORRY VIRGINIA! I'VE TAKEN CARE OF EVERYTHING!
YOU HAVE TOO MANY CAVITIES AS IT IS!
I'VE GOT US A COUPLE OF HOT DOGS INSTEAD!
HECK, IT ISN'T A BALLGAME UNTIL YOU'VE HAD A DOG!
ICK! NO THANKS!
OKAY! IT'S YOUR LOSS!
SAY... SO WHY WAS IT THAT I COULDN'T INVITE YOUR UNCLE BILL TONIGHT?
UHHH...
WELL... BECAUSE, UM, WHEN YOU SAID THAT MOM COULDN'T MAKE IT HOME FOR YOUR BIRTHDAY, I, UH, THOUGHT THAT IT WOULD BE NICE TO, UM, LEAVE HER SEAT EMPTY SO WE COULD TELL HER THAT WE MISSED HER...
YEAH... THAT'S IT!
?
HMMPH! I STILL WANT CANDY!
HEY, I'M DOING THE BEST I CAN!

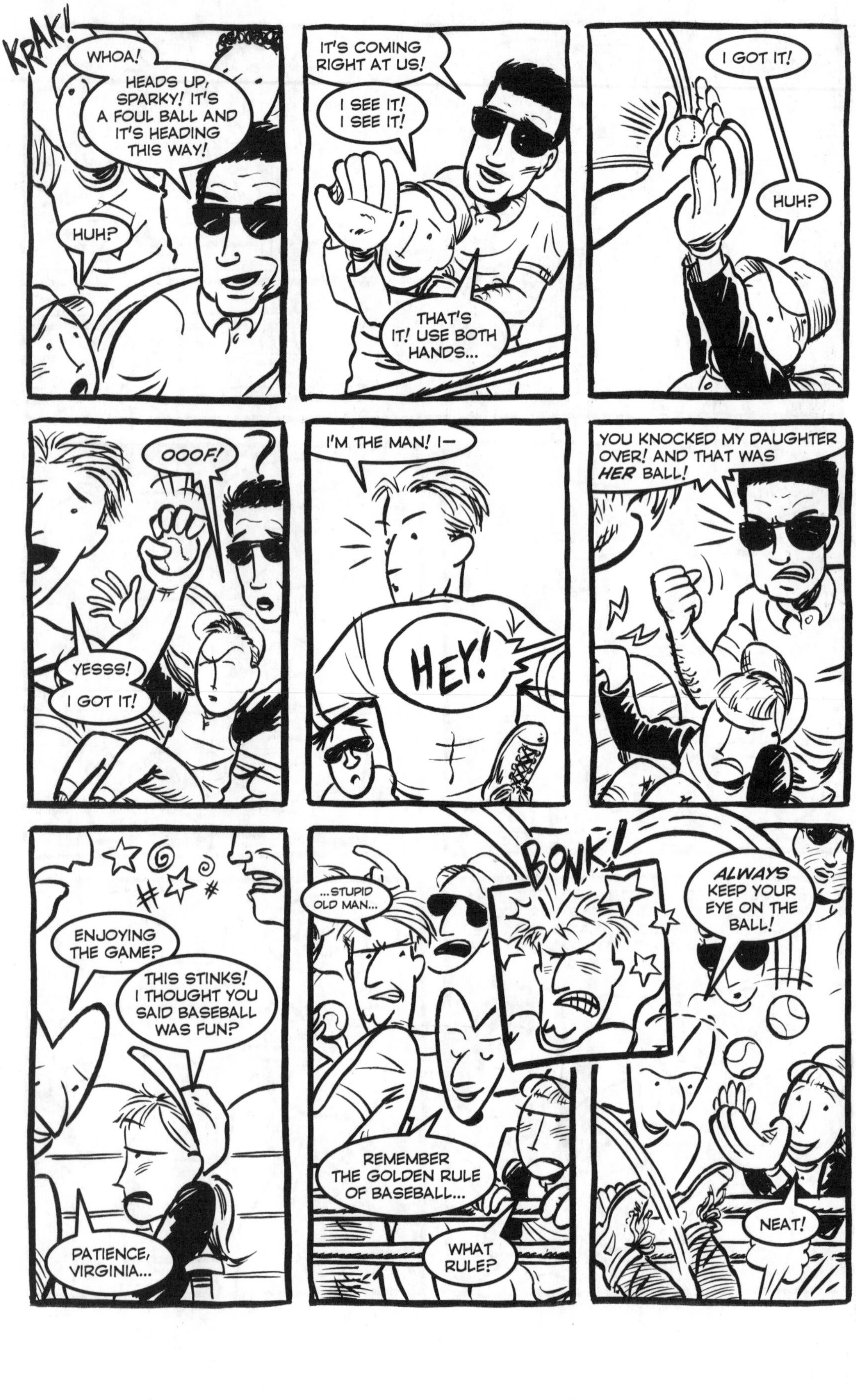
KRAK!
WHOA!
HEADS UP, SPARKY! IT'S A FOUL BALL AND IT'S HEADING THIS WAY!
HUH?
IT'S COMING RIGHT AT US!
I SEE IT! I SEE IT!
THAT'S IT! USE BOTH HANDS...
I GOT IT!
HUH?
OOOF!
YESSS! I GOT IT!
I'M THE MAN! I–
HEY!
YOU KNOCKED MY DAUGHTER OVER! AND THAT WAS HER BALL!
ENJOYING THE GAME?
THIS STINKS! I THOUGHT YOU SAID BASEBALL WAS FUN?
PATIENCE, VIRGINIA...
...STUPID OLD MAN...
REMEMBER THE GOLDEN RULE OF BASEBALL...
WHAT RULE?
BONK!
ALWAYS KEEP YOUR EYE ON THE BALL!
NEAT!

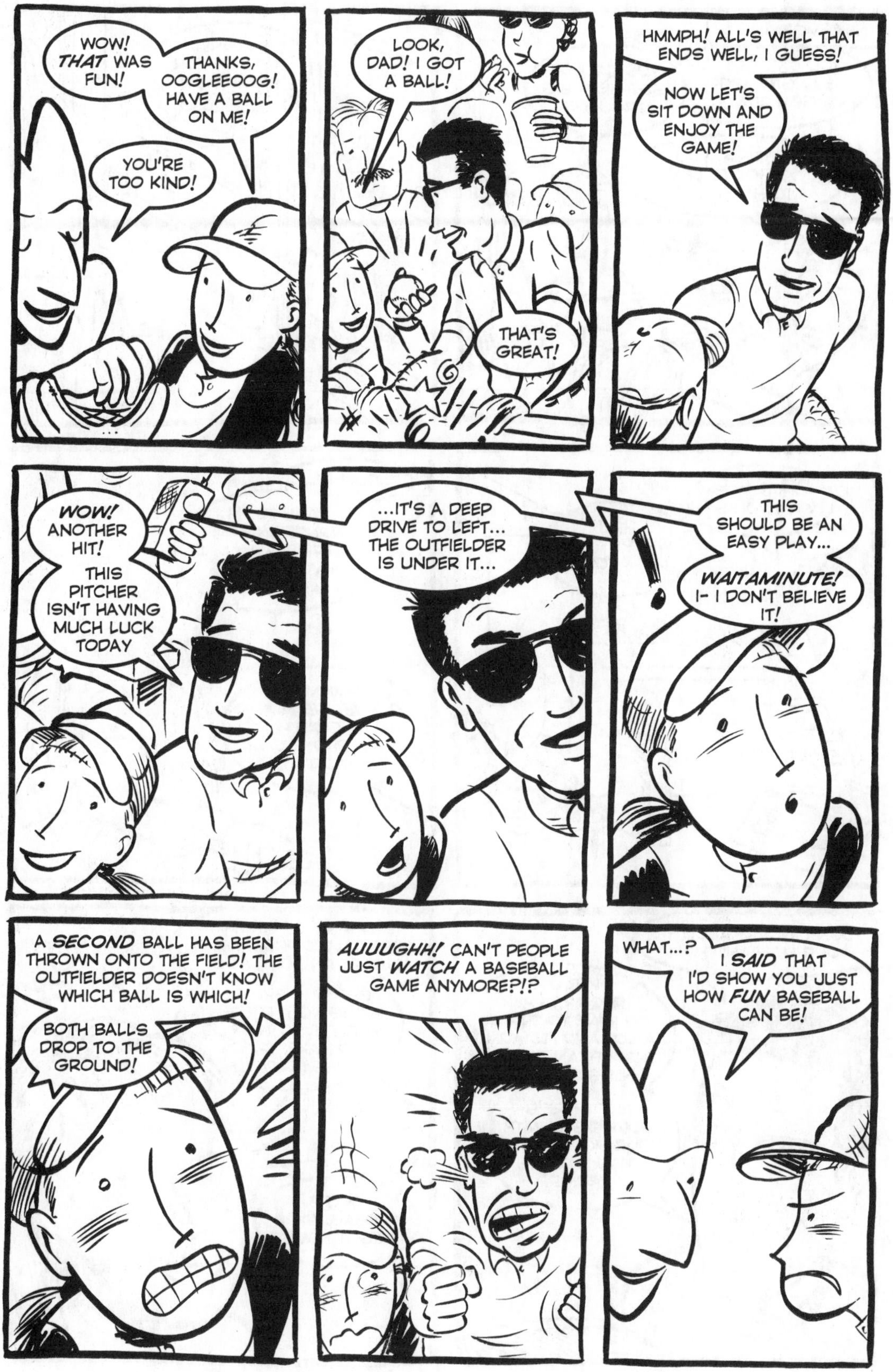

WOW! THAT WAS FUN!
THANKS, OOGLEEOOG! HAVE A BALL ON ME!
YOU'RE TOO KIND!
LOOK, DAD! I GOT A BALL!
THAT'S GREAT!
HMMPH! ALL'S WELL THAT ENDS WELL, I GUESS!
NOW LET'S SIT DOWN AND ENJOY THE GAME!
WOW! ANOTHER HIT!
THIS PITCHER ISN'T HAVING MUCH LUCK TODAY
...IT'S A DEEP DRIVE TO LEFT... THE OUTFIELDER IS UNDER IT...
THIS SHOULD BE AN EASY PLAY...
WAITAMINUTE! I- I DON'T BELIEVE IT!
A SECOND BALL HAS BEEN THROWN ONTO THE FIELD! THE OUTFIELDER DOESN'T KNOW WHICH BALL IS WHICH!
BOTH BALLS DROP TO THE GROUND!
AUUUGHH! CAN'T PEOPLE JUST WATCH A BASEBALL GAME ANYMORE?!?
WHAT...?
I SAID THAT I'D SHOW YOU JUST HOW FUN BASEBALL CAN BE!

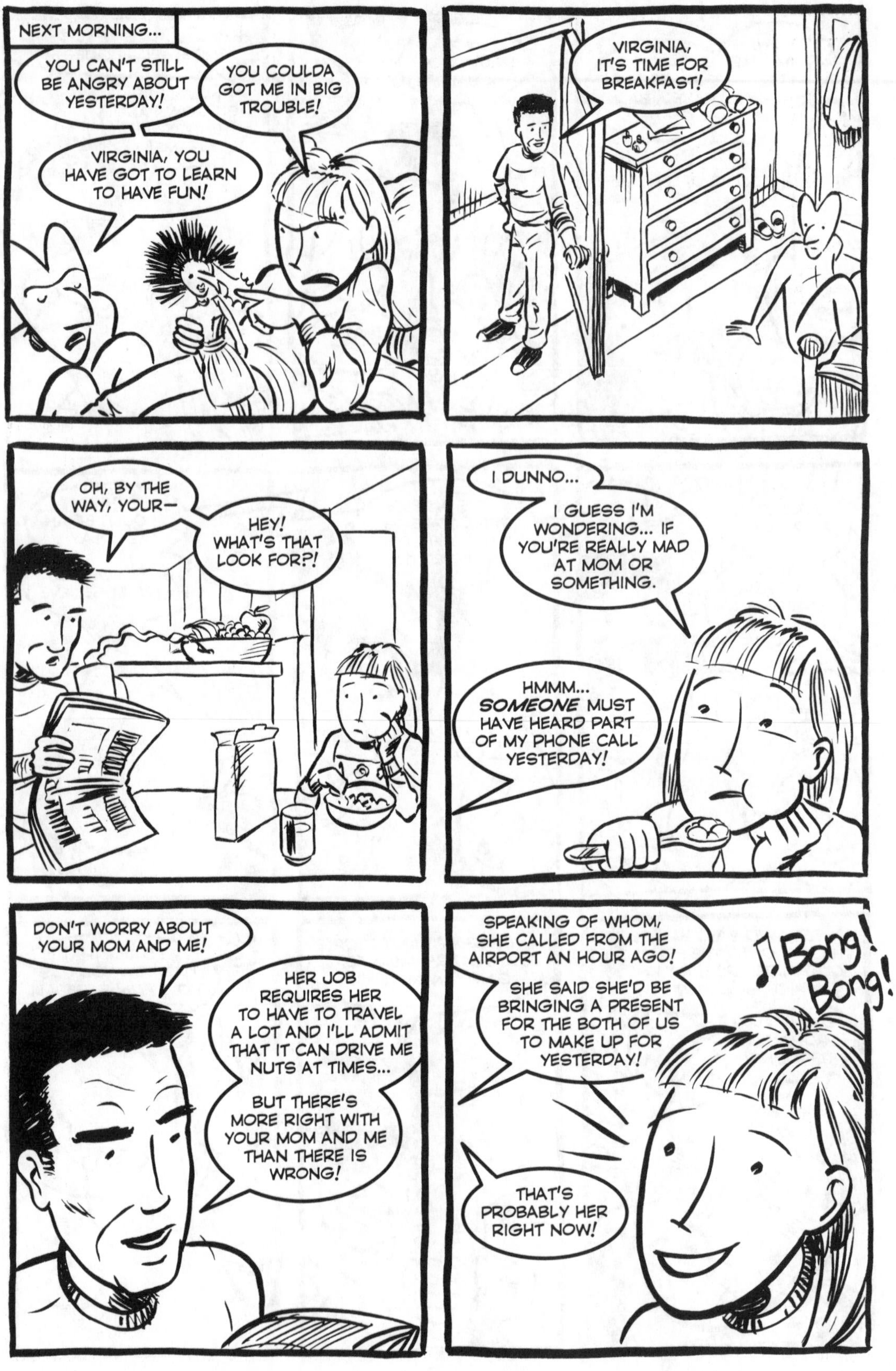
NEXT MORNING...
YOU CAN'T STILL BE ANGRY ABOUT YESTERDAY!
YOU COULDA GOT ME IN BIG TROUBLE!
VIRGINIA, YOU HAVE GOT TO LEARN TO HAVE FUN!
VIRGINIA, IT'S TIME FOR BREAKFAST!
OH, BY THE WAY, YOUR—
HEY! WHAT'S THAT LOOK FOR?!
I DUNNO...
I GUESS I'M WONDERING... IF YOU'RE REALLY MAD AT MOM OR SOMETHING.
HMMM... SOMEONE MUST HAVE HEARD PART OF MY PHONE CALL YESTERDAY!
DON'T WORRY ABOUT YOUR MOM AND ME!
HER JOB REQUIRES HER TO HAVE TO TRAVEL A LOT AND I'LL ADMIT THAT IT CAN DRIVE ME NUTS AT TIMES...
BUT THERE'S MORE RIGHT WITH YOUR MOM AND ME THAN THERE IS WRONG!
SPEAKING OF WHOM, SHE CALLED FROM THE AIRPORT AN HOUR AGO!
SHE SAID SHE'D BE BRINGING A PRESENT FOR THE BOTH OF US TO MAKE UP FOR YESTERDAY!
Bong! Bong!
THAT'S PROBABLY HER RIGHT NOW!

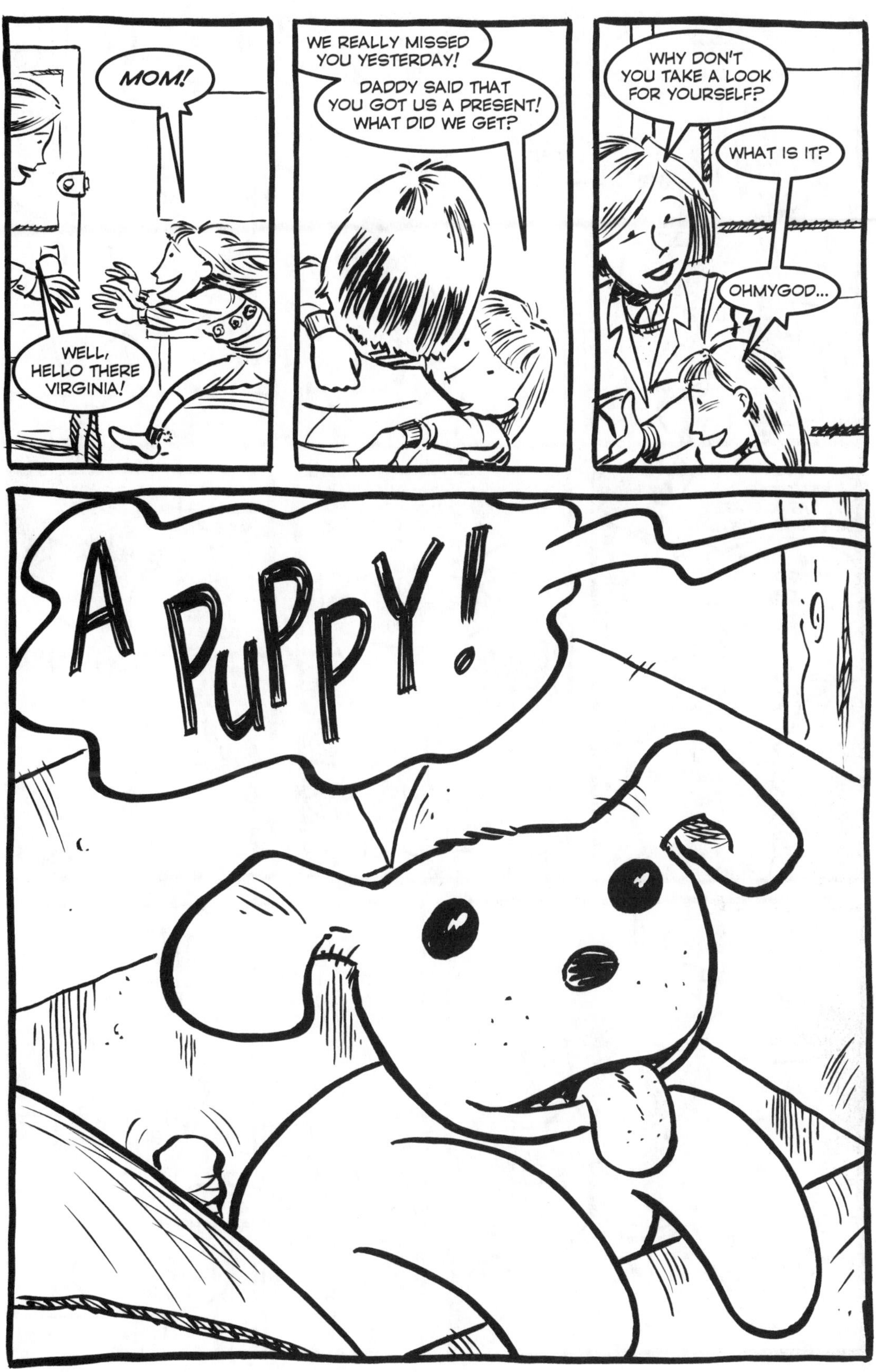
MOM!
WELL, HELLO THERE VIRGINIA!
WE REALLY MISSED YOU YESTERDAY!
DADDY SAID THAT YOU GOT US A PRESENT! WHAT DID WE GET?
WHY DON'T YOU TAKE A LOOK FOR YOURSELF?
WHAT IS IT?
OHMYGOD...
A PUPPY!

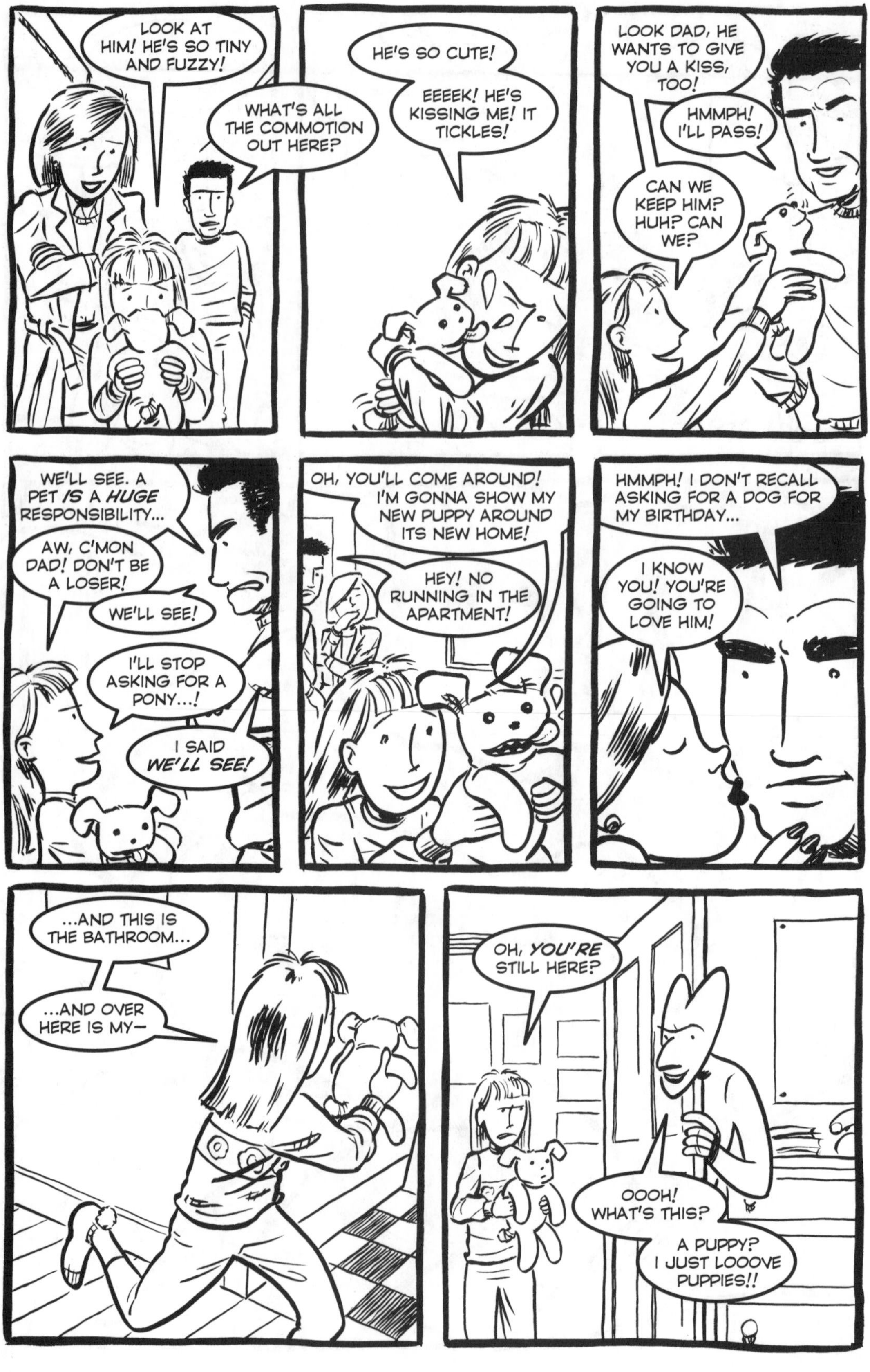
LOOK AT HIM! HE'S SO TINY AND FUZZY!
WHAT'S ALL THE COMMOTION OUT HERE?
HE'S SO CUTE!
EEEEK! HE'S KISSING ME! IT TICKLES!
LOOK DAD, HE WANTS TO GIVE YOU A KISS, TOO!
HMMPH! I'LL PASS!
CAN WE KEEP HIM? HUH? CAN WE?
WE'LL SEE. A PET IS A HUGE RESPONSIBILITY...
AW, C'MON DAD! DON'T BE A LOSER!
WE'LL SEE!
I'LL STOP ASKING FOR A PONY...!
I SAID WE'LL SEE!
OH, YOU'LL COME AROUND!
I'M GONNA SHOW MY NEW PUPPY AROUND ITS NEW HOME!
HEY! NO RUNNING IN THE APARTMENT!
HMMPH! I DON'T RECALL ASKING FOR A DOG FOR MY BIRTHDAY...
I KNOW YOU! YOU'RE GOING TO LOVE HIM!
...AND THIS IS THE BATHROOM...
...AND OVER HERE IS MY—
OH, YOU'RE STILL HERE?
OOOH! WHAT'S THIS?
A PUPPY? I JUST LOOOVE PUPPIES!!

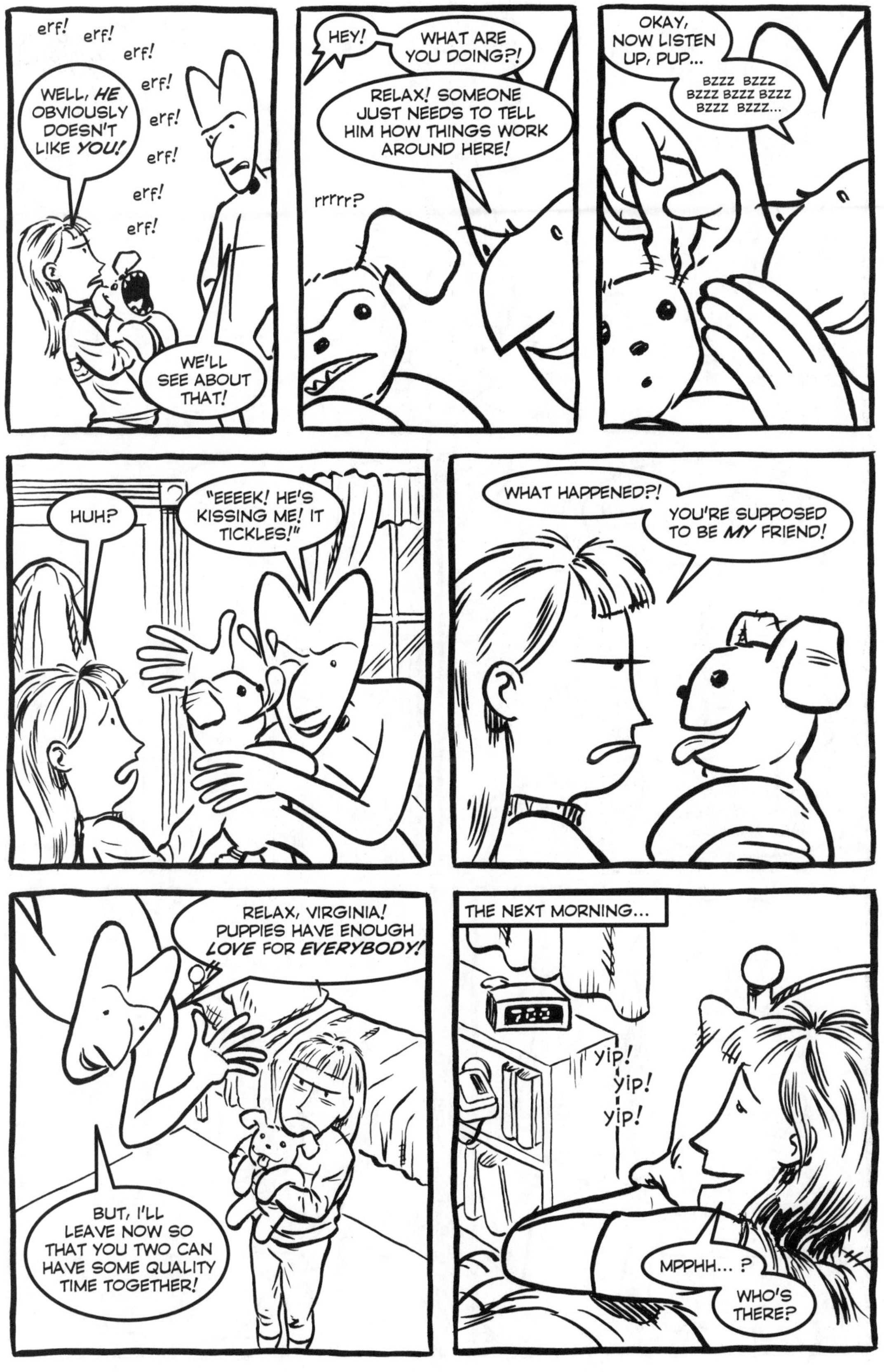
erf! erf! erf! erf! erf! erf! erf! erf!
WELL, *HE* OBVIOUSLY DOESN'T LIKE *YOU!*
WE'LL SEE ABOUT THAT!
HEY!
WHAT ARE YOU DOING?!
RELAX! SOMEONE JUST NEEDS TO TELL HIM HOW THINGS WORK AROUND HERE!
rrrrr?
OKAY, NOW LISTEN UP, PUP...
BZZZ BZZZ BZZZ BZZZ BZZZ BZZZ BZZZ...
HUH?
"EEEEK! HE'S KISSING ME! IT TICKLES!"
WHAT HAPPENED?!
YOU'RE SUPPOSED TO BE *MY* FRIEND!
RELAX, VIRGINIA! PUPPIES HAVE ENOUGH *LOVE* FOR *EVERYBODY!*
BUT, I'LL LEAVE NOW SO THAT YOU TWO CAN HAVE SOME QUALITY TIME TOGETHER!
THE NEXT MORNING...
yip! yip! yip!
MPPHH... ?
WHO'S THERE?

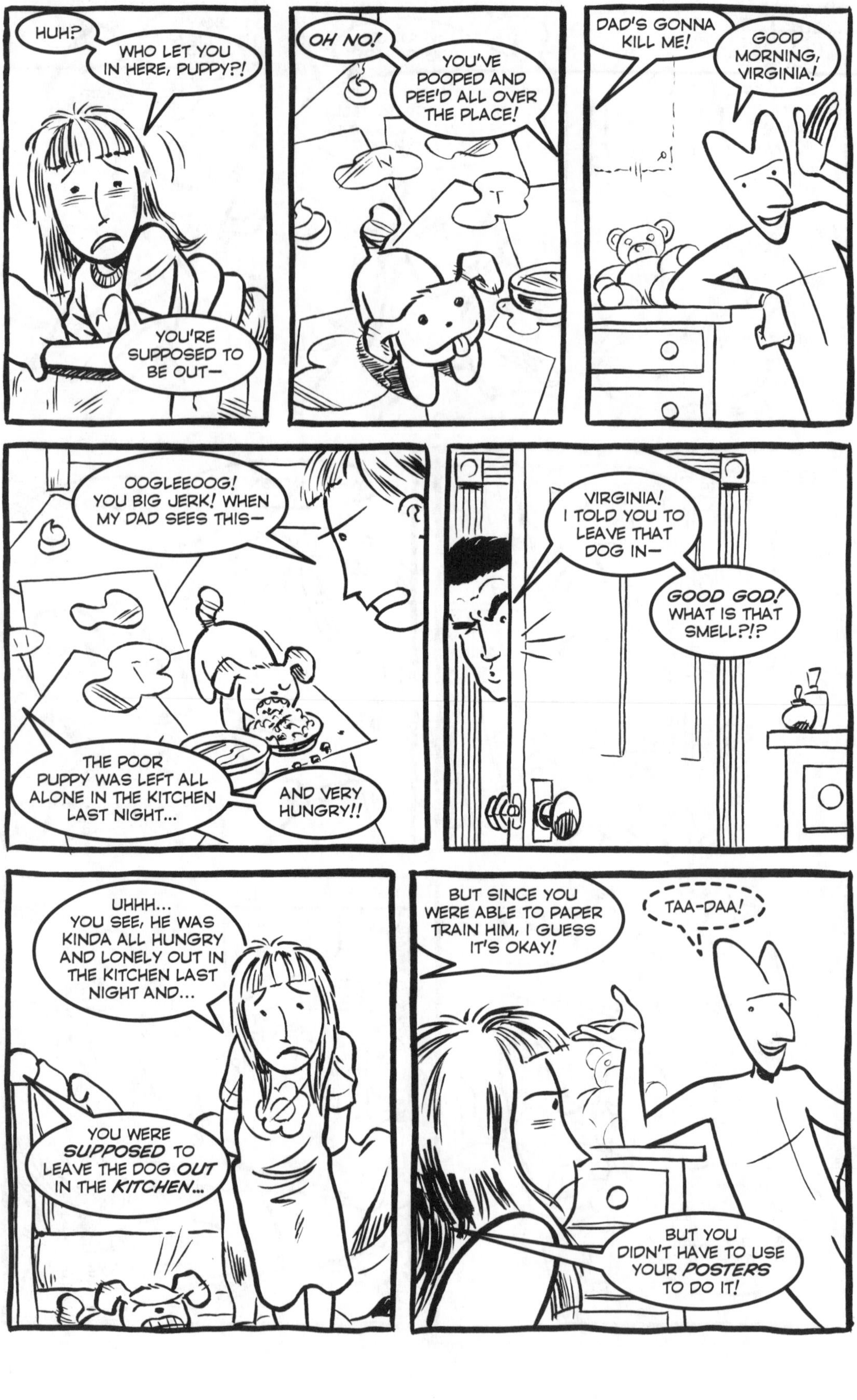
HUH?
WHO LET YOU IN HERE, PUPPY?!
YOU'RE SUPPOSED TO BE OUT—
OH NO!
YOU'VE POOPED AND PEE'D ALL OVER THE PLACE!
DAD'S GONNA KILL ME!
GOOD MORNING, VIRGINIA!
OOGLEEOOG! YOU BIG JERK! WHEN MY DAD SEES THIS—
THE POOR PUPPY WAS LEFT ALL ALONE IN THE KITCHEN LAST NIGHT...
AND VERY HUNGRY!!
VIRGINIA! I TOLD YOU TO LEAVE THAT DOG IN—
GOOD GOD! WHAT IS THAT SMELL?!?
UHHH... YOU SEE, HE WAS KINDA ALL HUNGRY AND LONELY OUT IN THE KITCHEN LAST NIGHT AND...
YOU WERE SUPPOSED TO LEAVE THE DOG OUT IN THE KITCHEN...
BUT SINCE YOU WERE ABLE TO PAPER TRAIN HIM, I GUESS IT'S OKAY!
TAA-DAA!
BUT YOU DIDN'T HAVE TO USE YOUR POSTERS TO DO IT!

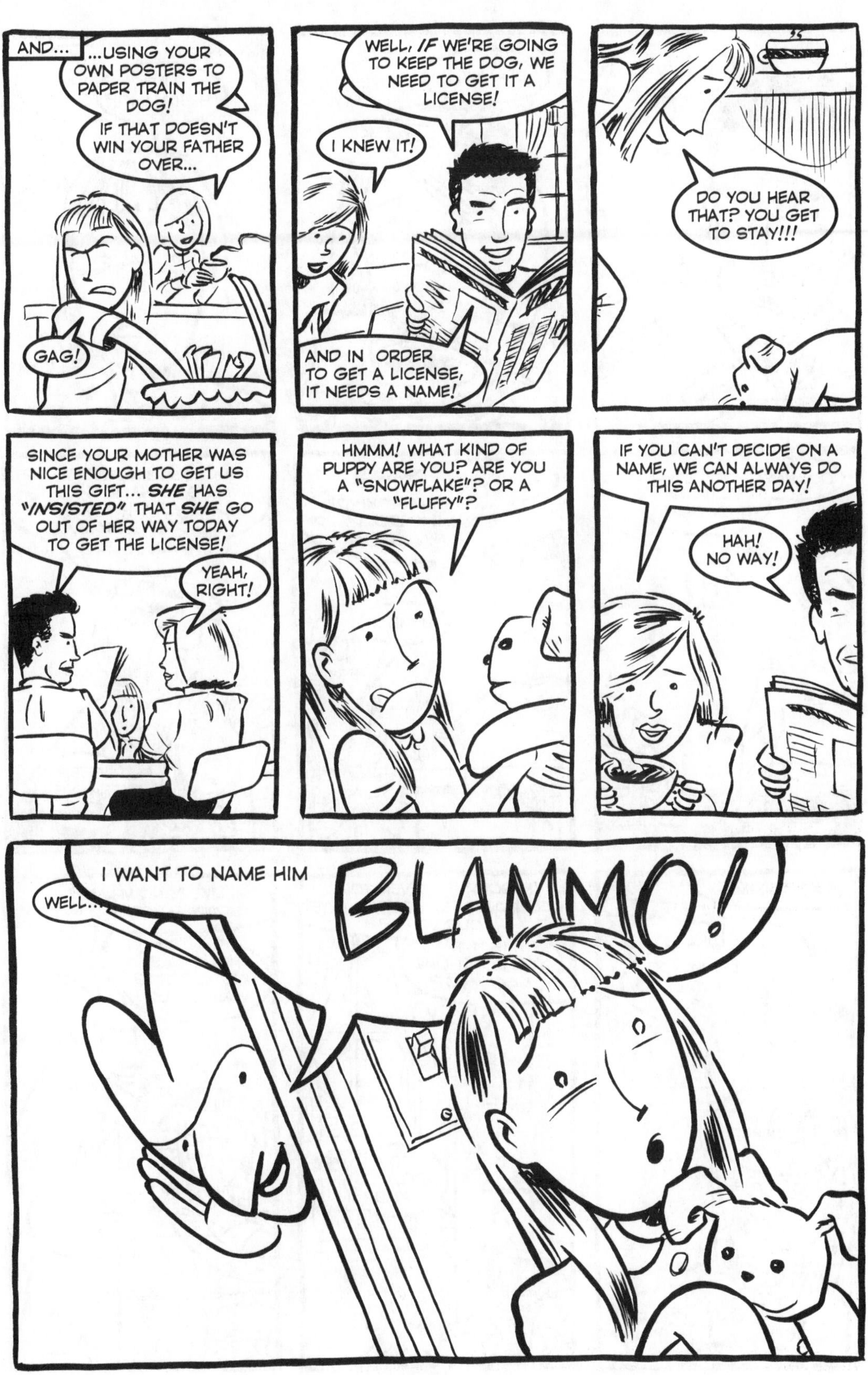
AND...
...USING YOUR OWN POSTERS TO PAPER TRAIN THE DOG!
IF THAT DOESN'T WIN YOUR FATHER OVER...
GAG!
WELL, *IF* WE'RE GOING TO KEEP THE DOG, WE NEED TO GET IT A LICENSE!
I KNEW IT!
AND IN ORDER TO GET A LICENSE, IT NEEDS A NAME!
DO YOU HEAR THAT? YOU GET TO STAY!!!
SINCE YOUR MOTHER WAS NICE ENOUGH TO GET US THIS GIFT... *SHE* HAS *"INSISTED"* THAT *SHE* GO OUT OF HER WAY TODAY TO GET THE LICENSE!
YEAH, RIGHT!
HMMM! WHAT KIND OF PUPPY ARE YOU? ARE YOU A "SNOWFLAKE"? OR A "FLUFFY"?
IF YOU CAN'T DECIDE ON A NAME, WE CAN ALWAYS DO THIS ANOTHER DAY!
HAH! NO WAY!
WELL...
I WANT TO NAME HIM
BLAMMO!

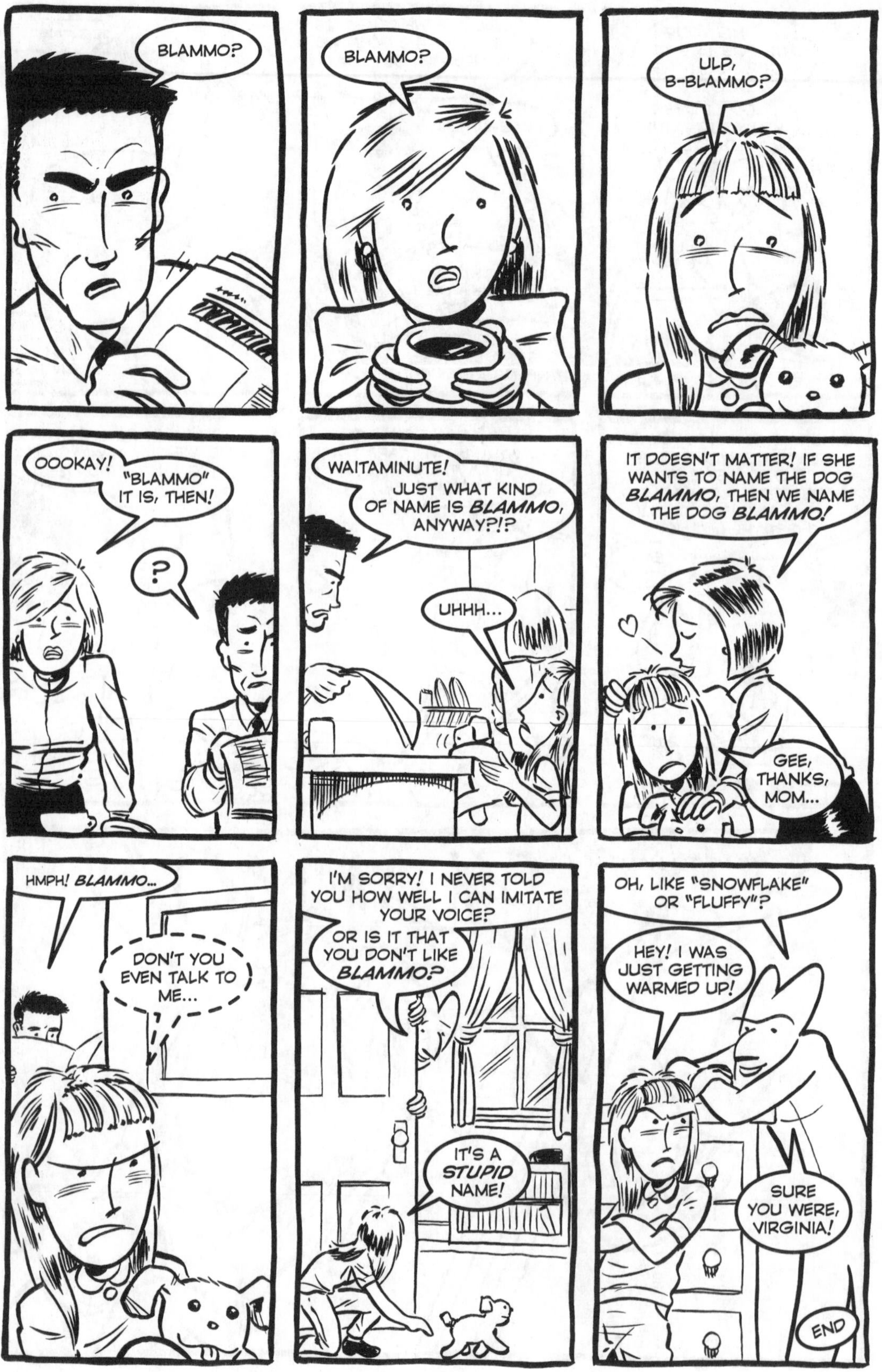

BLAMMO?
BLAMMO?
ULP, B-BLAMMO?
OOOKAY!
"BLAMMO" IT IS, THEN!
?
WAITAMINUTE!
JUST WHAT KIND OF NAME IS *BLAMMO*, ANYWAY?!?
UHHH...
IT DOESN'T MATTER! IF SHE WANTS TO NAME THE DOG *BLAMMO*, THEN WE NAME THE DOG *BLAMMO!*
GEE, THANKS, MOM...
HMPH! *BLAMMO*...
DON'T YOU EVEN TALK TO ME...
I'M SORRY! I NEVER TOLD YOU HOW WELL I CAN IMITATE YOUR VOICE?
OR IS IT THAT YOU DON'T LIKE *BLAMMO?*
IT'S A *STUPID* NAME!
OH, LIKE "SNOWFLAKE" OR "FLUFFY"?
HEY! I WAS JUST GETTING WARMED UP!
SURE YOU WERE, VIRGINIA!
END

electric girl™

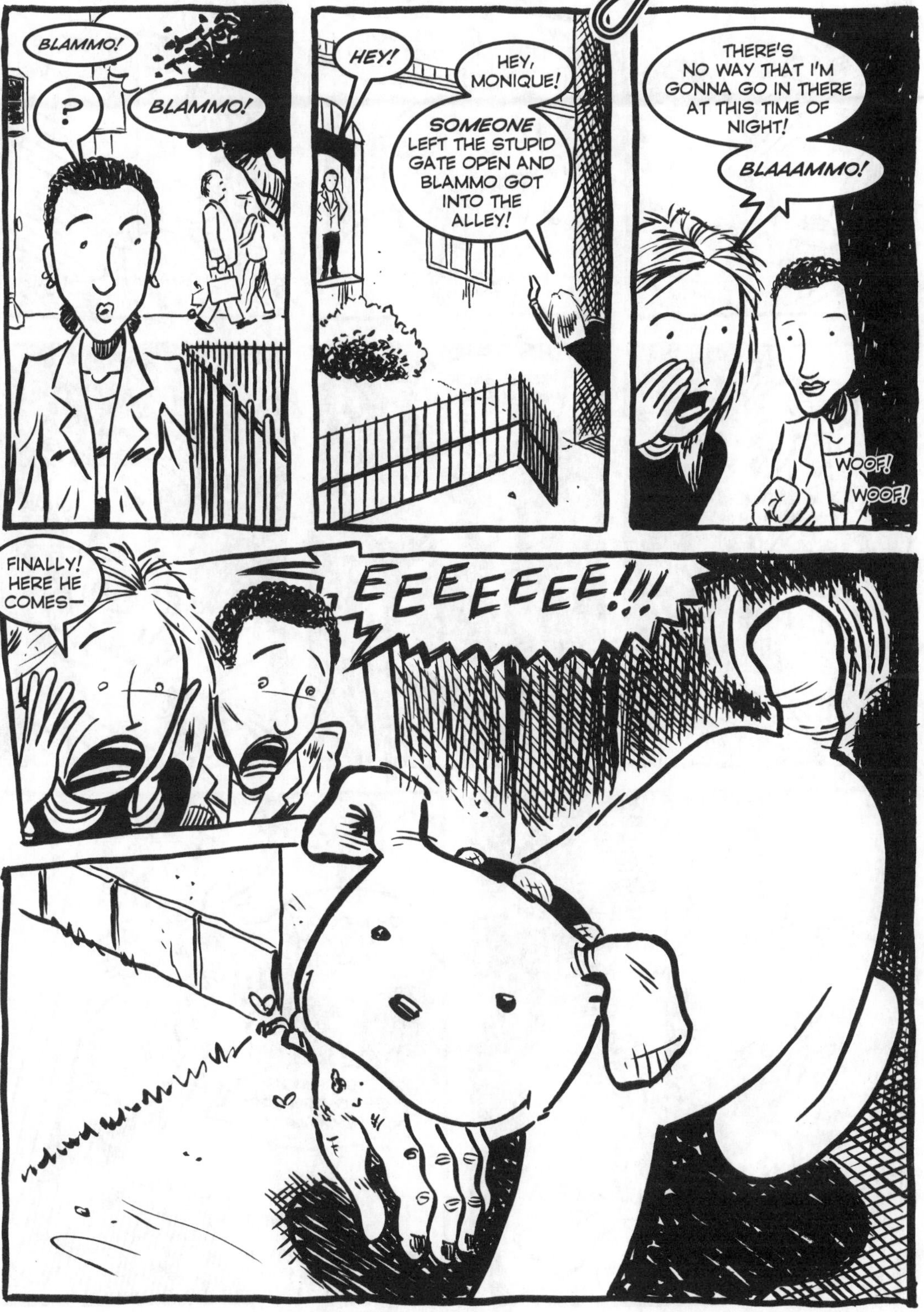

BLAMMO!
?
BLAMMO!
HEY!
HEY, MONIQUE!
SOMEONE LEFT THE STUPID GATE OPEN AND BLAMMO GOT INTO THE ALLEY!
THERE'S NO WAY THAT I'M GONNA GO IN THERE AT THIS TIME OF NIGHT!
BLAAAMMO!
WOOF!
WOOF!
FINALLY! HERE HE COMES—
EEEEEEEE!!!

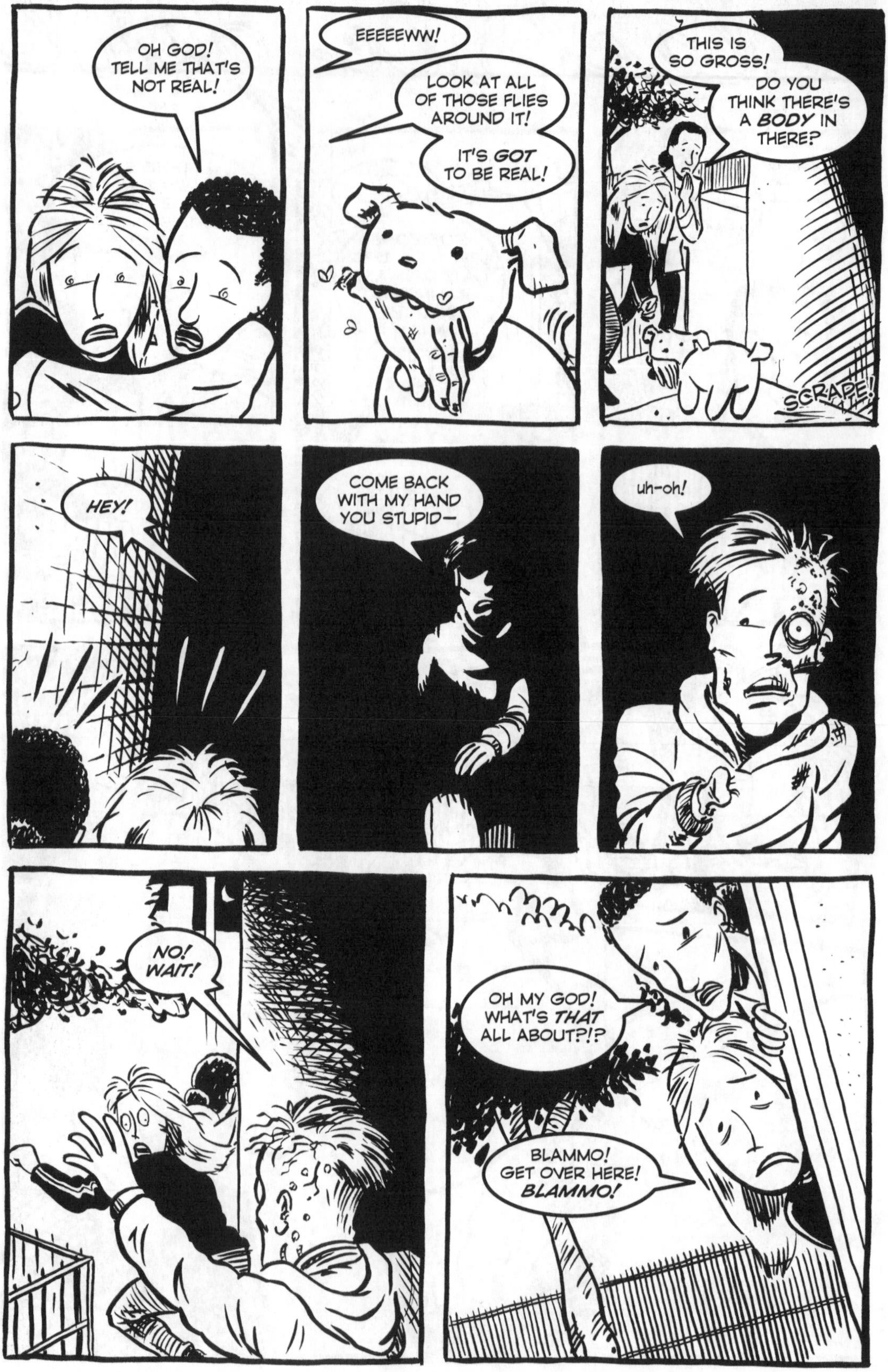

OH GOD! TELL ME THAT'S NOT REAL!
EEEEEWW!
LOOK AT ALL OF THOSE FLIES AROUND IT!
IT'S GOT TO BE REAL!
THIS IS SO GROSS!
DO YOU THINK THERE'S A BODY IN THERE?
SCRAPE!
HEY!
COME BACK WITH MY HAND YOU STUPID—
uh-oh!
NO! WAIT!
OH MY GOD! WHAT'S THAT ALL ABOUT?!?
BLAMMO! GET OVER HERE! BLAMMO!

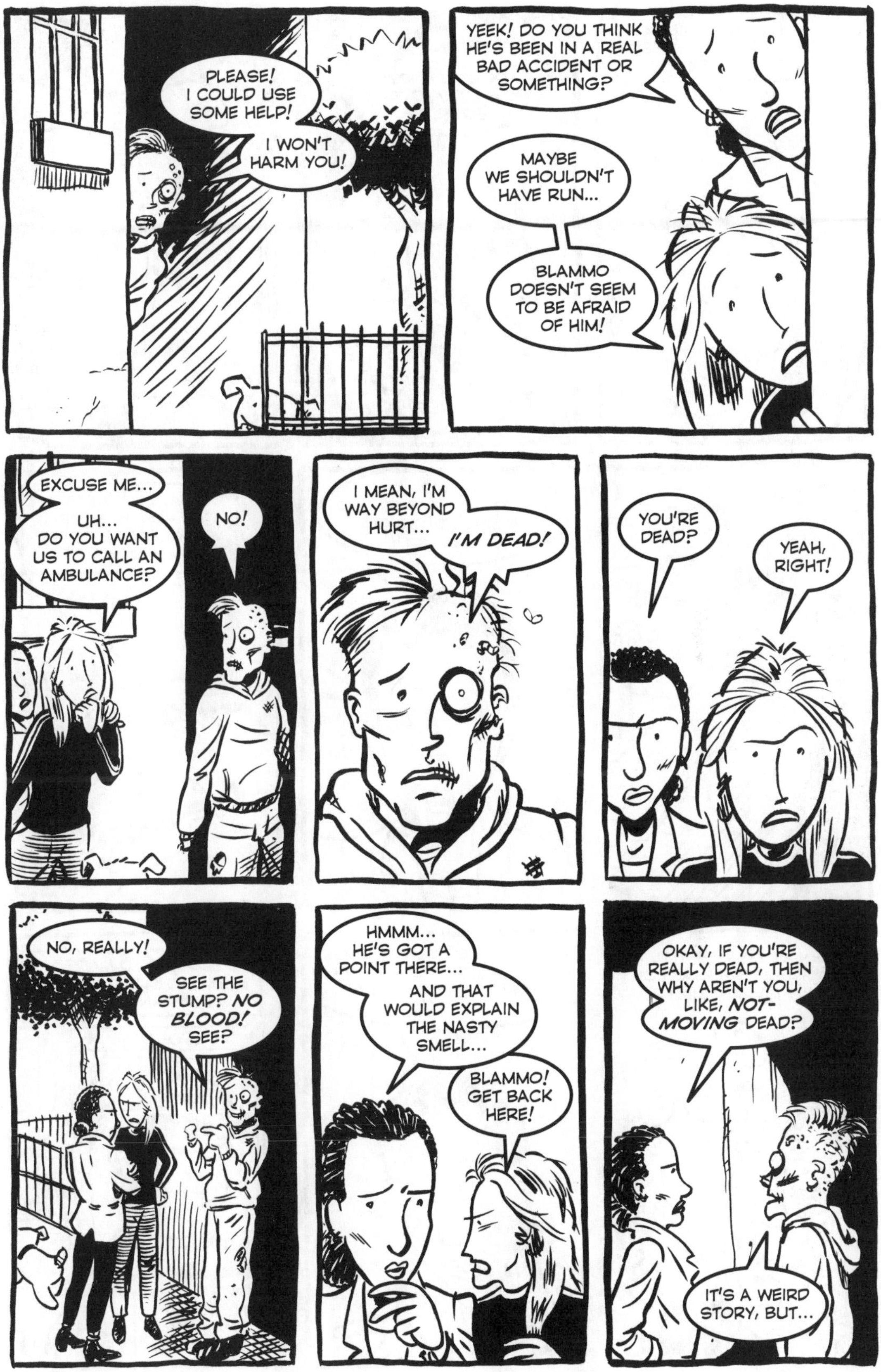
PLEASE! I COULD USE SOME HELP!
I WON'T HARM YOU!
YEEK! DO YOU THINK HE'S BEEN IN A REAL BAD ACCIDENT OR SOMETHING?
MAYBE WE SHOULDN'T HAVE RUN...
BLAMMO DOESN'T SEEM TO BE AFRAID OF HIM!
EXCUSE ME...
UH... DO YOU WANT US TO CALL AN AMBULANCE?
NO!
I MEAN, I'M WAY BEYOND HURT...
I'M DEAD!
YOU'RE DEAD?
YEAH, RIGHT!
NO, REALLY!
SEE THE STUMP? NO BLOOD! SEE?
HMMM... HE'S GOT A POINT THERE...
AND THAT WOULD EXPLAIN THE NASTY SMELL...
BLAMMO! GET BACK HERE!
OKAY, IF YOU'RE REALLY DEAD, THEN WHY AREN'T YOU, LIKE, NOT-MOVING DEAD?
IT'S A WEIRD STORY, BUT...

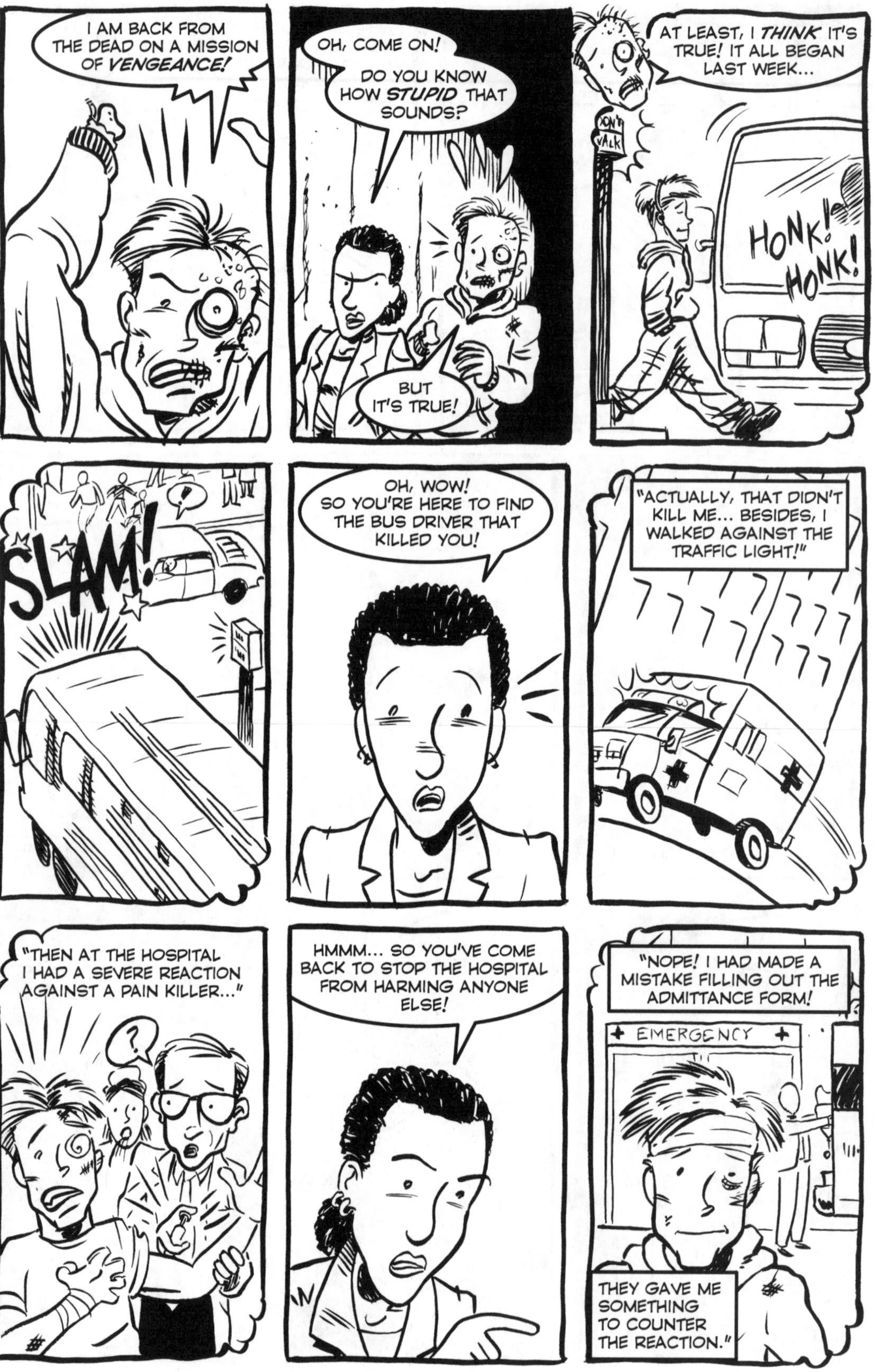

I AM BACK FROM THE DEAD ON A MISSION OF *VENGEANCE!*
OH, COME ON!
DO YOU KNOW HOW *STUPID* THAT SOUNDS?
BUT IT'S TRUE!
AT LEAST, I *THINK* IT'S TRUE! IT ALL BEGAN LAST WEEK...
HONK! HONK!
SLAM!
OH, WOW! SO YOU'RE HERE TO FIND THE BUS DRIVER THAT KILLED YOU!
"ACTUALLY, THAT DIDN'T KILL ME... BESIDES, I WALKED AGAINST THE TRAFFIC LIGHT!"
"THEN AT THE HOSPITAL I HAD A SEVERE REACTION AGAINST A PAIN KILLER..."
HMMM... SO YOU'VE COME BACK TO STOP THE HOSPITAL FROM HARMING ANYONE ELSE!
"NOPE! I HAD MADE A MISTAKE FILLING OUT THE ADMITTANCE FORM!
EMERGENCY
THEY GAVE ME SOMETHING TO COUNTER THE REACTION."

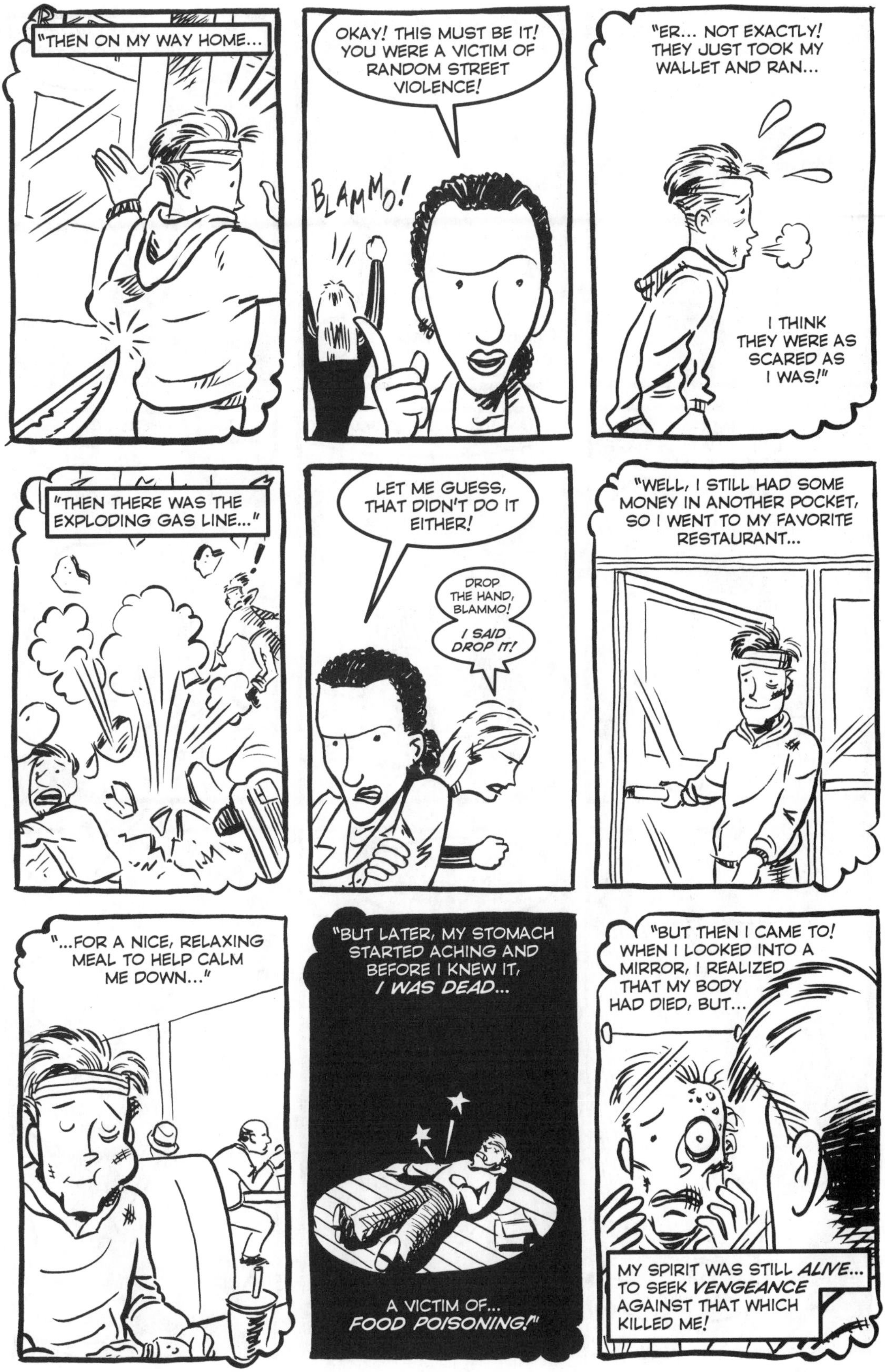
"THEN ON MY WAY HOME...
OKAY! THIS MUST BE IT! YOU WERE A VICTIM OF RANDOM STREET VIOLENCE!
BLAMMO!
"ER... NOT EXACTLY! THEY JUST TOOK MY WALLET AND RAN...
I THINK THEY WERE AS SCARED AS I WAS!"
"THEN THERE WAS THE EXPLODING GAS LINE..."
LET ME GUESS, THAT DIDN'T DO IT EITHER!
DROP THE HAND, BLAMMO!
I SAID DROP IT!
"WELL, I STILL HAD SOME MONEY IN ANOTHER POCKET, SO I WENT TO MY FAVORITE RESTAURANT...
"...FOR A NICE, RELAXING MEAL TO HELP CALM ME DOWN..."
"BUT LATER, MY STOMACH STARTED ACHING AND BEFORE I KNEW IT, I WAS DEAD...
A VICTIM OF... FOOD POISONING!"
"BUT THEN I CAME TO! WHEN I LOOKED INTO A MIRROR, I REALIZED THAT MY BODY HAD DIED, BUT...
MY SPIRIT WAS STILL ALIVE... TO SEEK VENGEANCE AGAINST THAT WHICH KILLED ME!

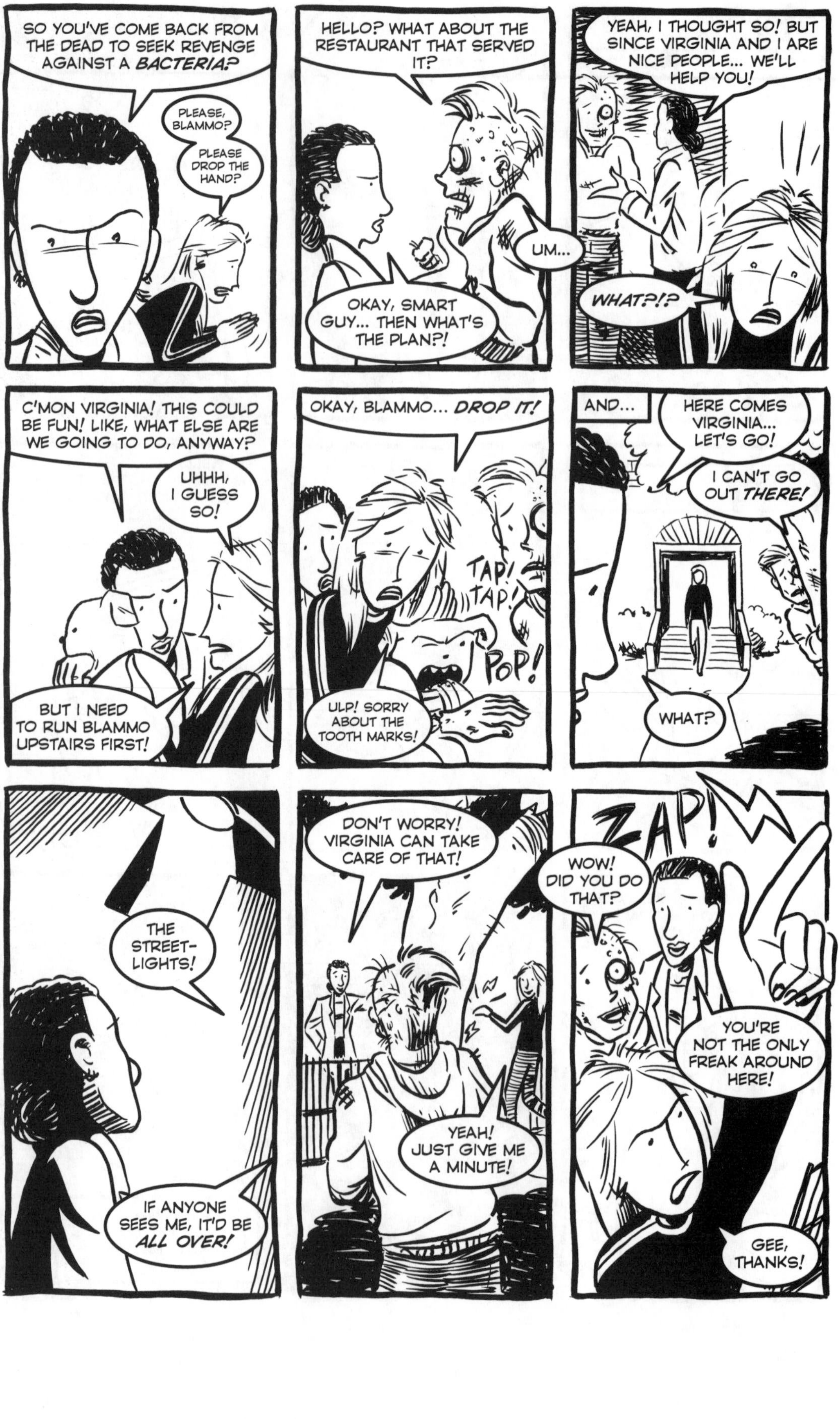
SO YOU'VE COME BACK FROM THE DEAD TO SEEK REVENGE AGAINST A BACTERIA?
PLEASE, BLAMMO?
PLEASE DROP THE HAND?
HELLO? WHAT ABOUT THE RESTAURANT THAT SERVED IT?
OKAY, SMART GUY... THEN WHAT'S THE PLAN?!
UM...
YEAH, I THOUGHT SO! BUT SINCE VIRGINIA AND I ARE NICE PEOPLE... WE'LL HELP YOU!
WHAT?!?
C'MON VIRGINIA! THIS COULD BE FUN! LIKE, WHAT ELSE ARE WE GOING TO DO, ANYWAY?
UHHH, I GUESS SO!
BUT I NEED TO RUN BLAMMO UPSTAIRS FIRST!
OKAY, BLAMMO... DROP IT!
TAP! TAP!
POP!
ULP! SORRY ABOUT THE TOOTH MARKS!
AND...
HERE COMES VIRGINIA... LET'S GO!
I CAN'T GO OUT THERE!
WHAT?
THE STREET-LIGHTS!
IF ANYONE SEES ME, IT'D BE ALL OVER!
DON'T WORRY! VIRGINIA CAN TAKE CARE OF THAT!
YEAH! JUST GIVE ME A MINUTE!
ZAP!
WOW! DID YOU DO THAT?
YOU'RE NOT THE ONLY FREAK AROUND HERE!
GEE, THANKS!

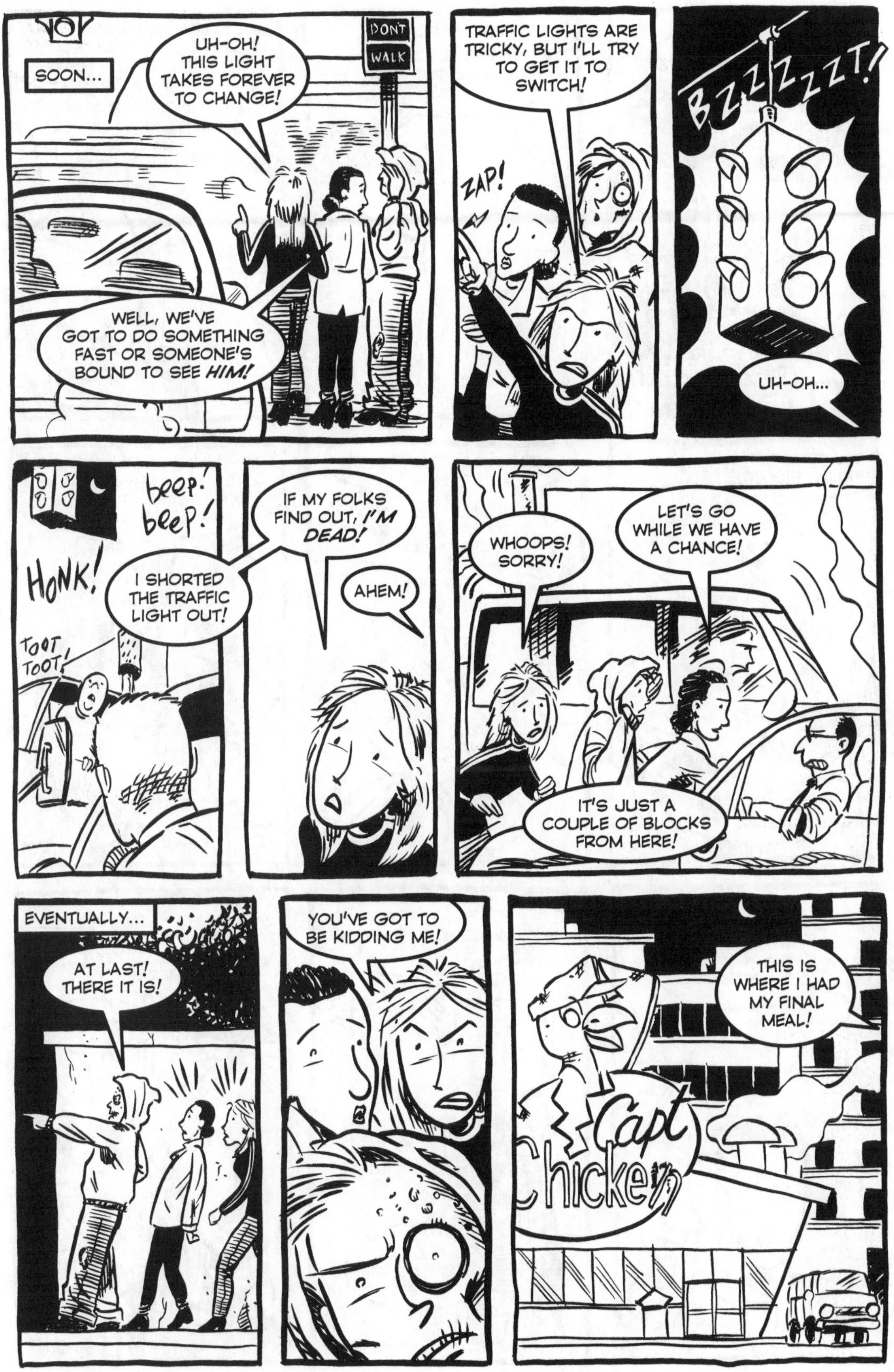
SOON...
UH-OH! THIS LIGHT TAKES FOREVER TO CHANGE!
DON'T WALK
WELL, WE'VE GOT TO DO SOMETHING FAST OR SOMEONE'S BOUND TO SEE *HIM!*
TRAFFIC LIGHTS ARE TRICKY, BUT I'LL TRY TO GET IT TO SWITCH!
ZAP!
BZZZZZZT!
UH-OH...
beep! beep!
HONK!
TOOT TOOT!
I SHORTED THE TRAFFIC LIGHT OUT!
IF MY FOLKS FIND OUT, *I'M DEAD!*
AHEM!
WHOOPS! SORRY!
LET'S GO WHILE WE HAVE A CHANCE!
IT'S JUST A COUPLE OF BLOCKS FROM HERE!
EVENTUALLY...
AT LAST! THERE IT IS!
YOU'VE GOT TO BE KIDDING ME!
THIS IS WHERE I HAD MY FINAL MEAL!
Capt Chicken

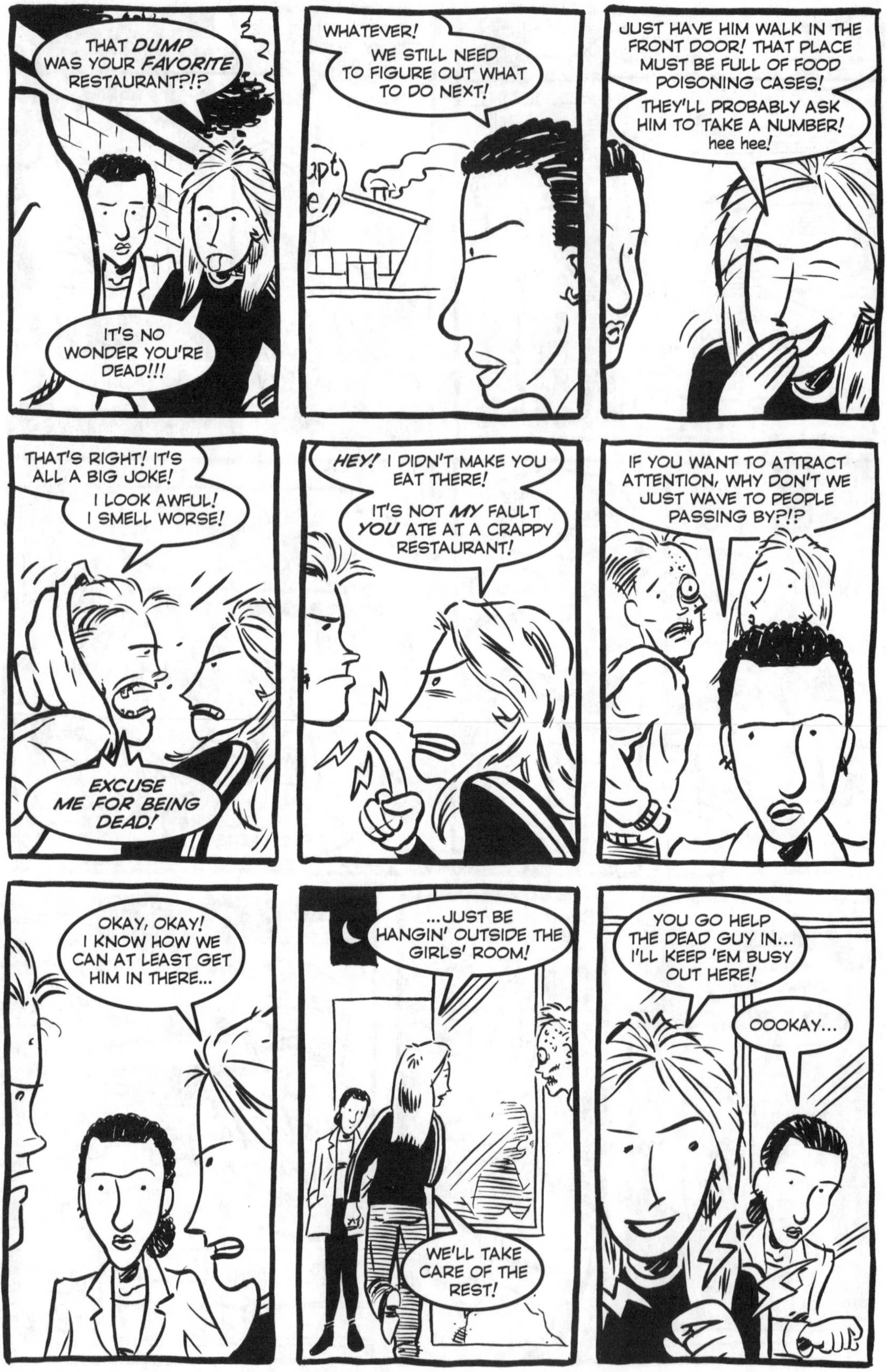
THAT DUMP WAS YOUR FAVORITE RESTAURANT?!?
IT'S NO WONDER YOU'RE DEAD!!!
WHATEVER!
WE STILL NEED TO FIGURE OUT WHAT TO DO NEXT!
JUST HAVE HIM WALK IN THE FRONT DOOR! THAT PLACE MUST BE FULL OF FOOD POISONING CASES!
THEY'LL PROBABLY ASK HIM TO TAKE A NUMBER! hee hee!
THAT'S RIGHT! IT'S ALL A BIG JOKE!
I LOOK AWFUL! I SMELL WORSE!
EXCUSE ME FOR BEING DEAD!
HEY! I DIDN'T MAKE YOU EAT THERE!
IT'S NOT MY FAULT YOU ATE AT A CRAPPY RESTAURANT!
IF YOU WANT TO ATTRACT ATTENTION, WHY DON'T WE JUST WAVE TO PEOPLE PASSING BY?!?
OKAY, OKAY! I KNOW HOW WE CAN AT LEAST GET HIM IN THERE...
...JUST BE HANGIN' OUTSIDE THE GIRLS' ROOM!
WE'LL TAKE CARE OF THE REST!
YOU GO HELP THE DEAD GUY IN... I'LL KEEP 'EM BUSY OUT HERE!
OOOKAY...

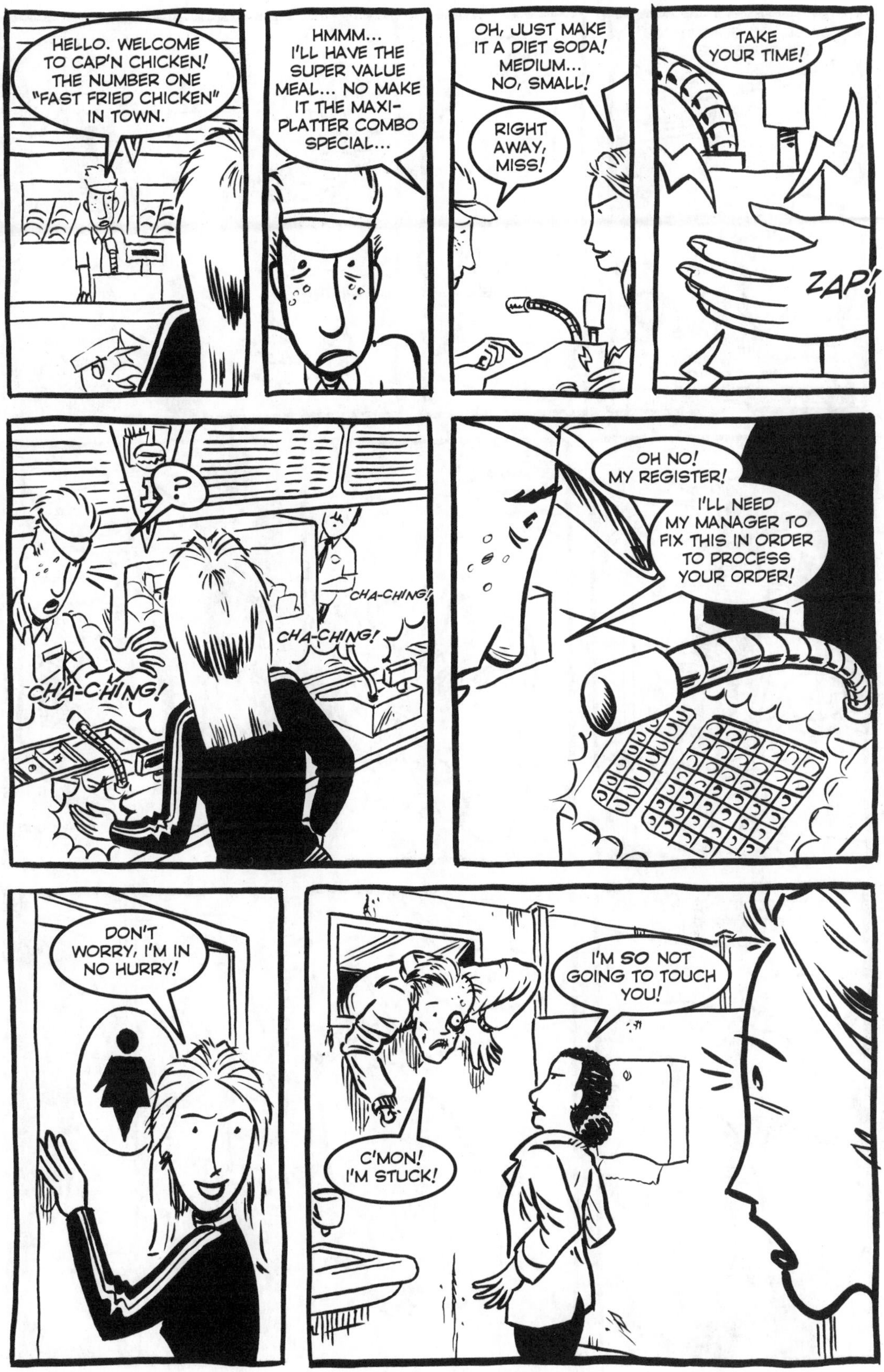
HELLO. WELCOME TO CAP'N CHICKEN! THE NUMBER ONE "FAST FRIED CHICKEN" IN TOWN.
HMMM... I'LL HAVE THE SUPER VALUE MEAL... NO MAKE IT THE MAXI-PLATTER COMBO SPECIAL...
OH, JUST MAKE IT A DIET SODA! MEDIUM... NO, SMALL!
RIGHT AWAY, MISS!
TAKE YOUR TIME!
ZAP!
?
CHA-CHING!
CHA-CHING!
CHA-CHING!
OH NO! MY REGISTER!
I'LL NEED MY MANAGER TO FIX THIS IN ORDER TO PROCESS YOUR ORDER!
DON'T WORRY, I'M IN NO HURRY!
I'M SO NOT GOING TO TOUCH YOU!
C'MON! I'M STUCK!

WELL, DO SOMETHING! SOMEONE'S GONNA SEE ME!
HMMM...
OKAY! ON THREE— PULL!
POP!
ULP!
THUD!
boink!
YEEEK!
GROSS!
WOULD SOMEONE PLEASE GET THAT FOR ME?
ERR, I'LL PASS!
ME TOO!
I'VE GOT IT!
GASP!
OH NO...

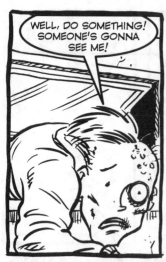

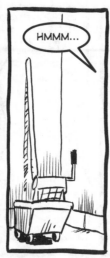

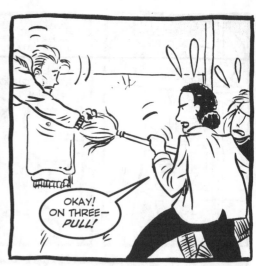

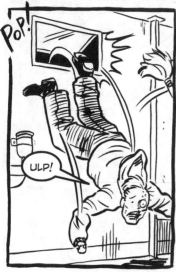

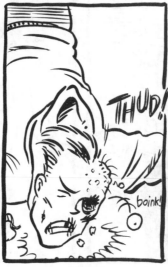

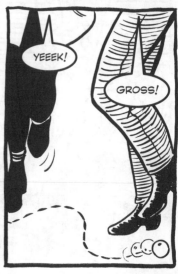

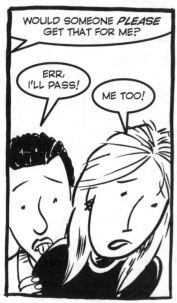

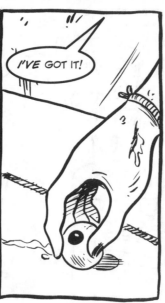

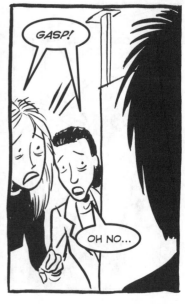

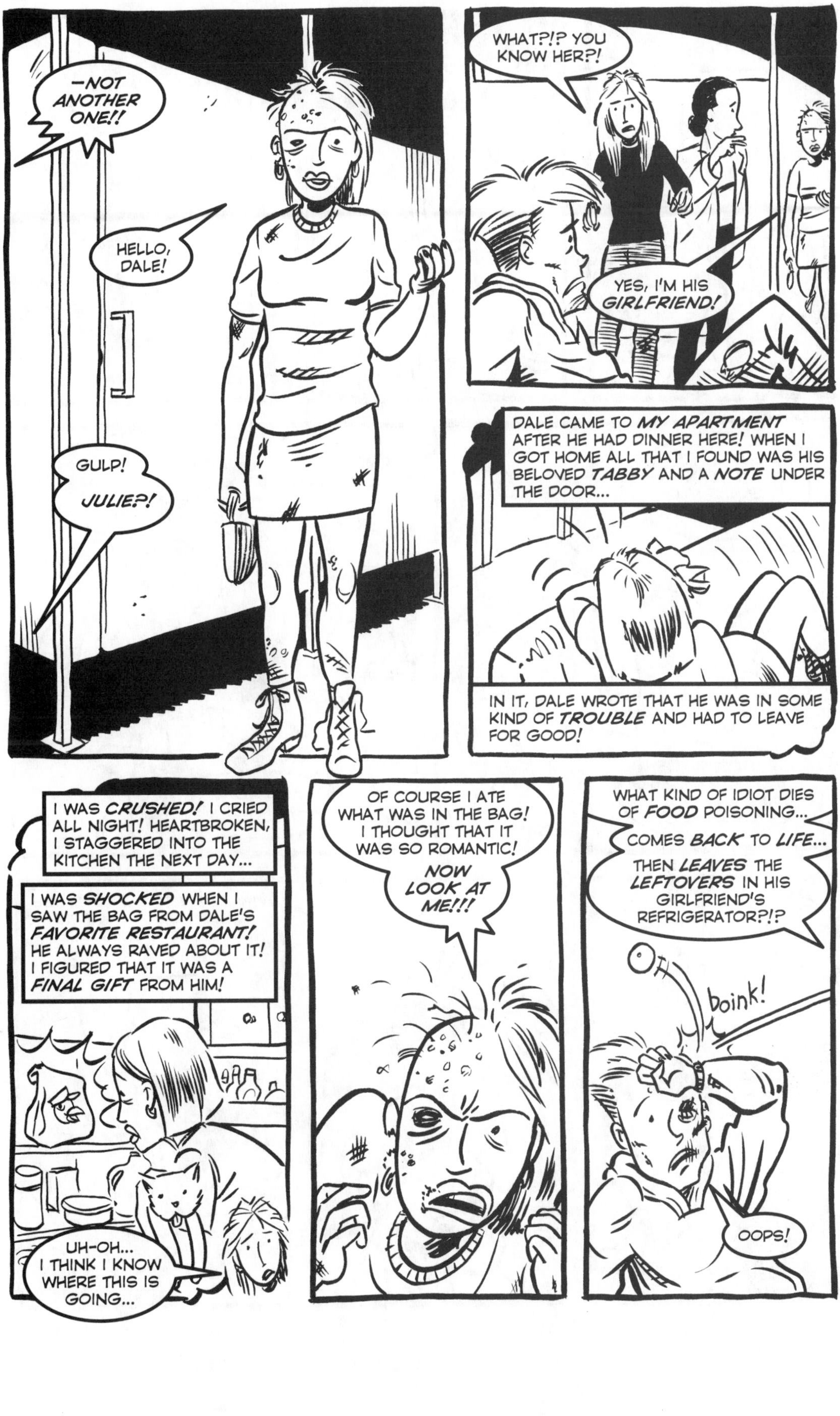

—NOT ANOTHER ONE!!
HELLO, DALE!
GULP!
JULIE?!
WHAT?!? YOU KNOW HER?!
YES, I'M HIS GIRLFRIEND!
DALE CAME TO MY APARTMENT AFTER HE HAD DINNER HERE! WHEN I GOT HOME ALL THAT I FOUND WAS HIS BELOVED TABBY AND A NOTE UNDER THE DOOR...
IN IT, DALE WROTE THAT HE WAS IN SOME KIND OF TROUBLE AND HAD TO LEAVE FOR GOOD!
I WAS CRUSHED! I CRIED ALL NIGHT! HEARTBROKEN, I STAGGERED INTO THE KITCHEN THE NEXT DAY...
I WAS SHOCKED WHEN I SAW THE BAG FROM DALE'S FAVORITE RESTAURANT! HE ALWAYS RAVED ABOUT IT! I FIGURED THAT IT WAS A FINAL GIFT FROM HIM!
UH-OH... I THINK I KNOW WHERE THIS IS GOING...
OF COURSE I ATE WHAT WAS IN THE BAG! I THOUGHT THAT IT WAS SO ROMANTIC!
NOW LOOK AT ME!!!
WHAT KIND OF IDIOT DIES OF FOOD POISONING...
COMES BACK TO LIFE...
THEN LEAVES THE LEFTOVERS IN HIS GIRLFRIEND'S REFRIGERATOR?!?
boink!
OOPS!

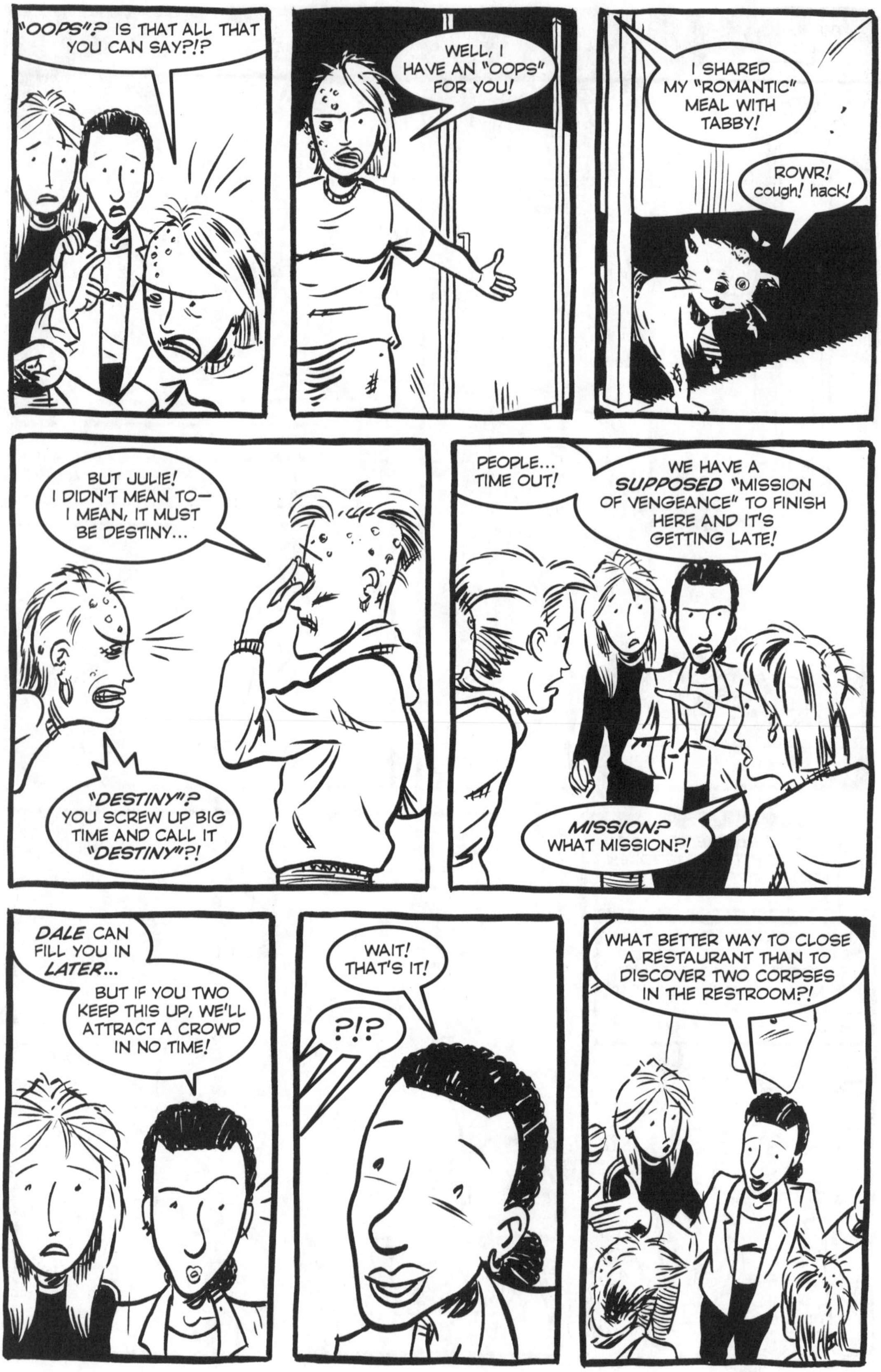
"OOPS"? IS THAT ALL THAT YOU CAN SAY?!?
WELL, I HAVE AN "OOPS" FOR YOU!
I SHARED MY "ROMANTIC" MEAL WITH TABBY!
ROWR! cough! hack!
BUT JULIE! I DIDN'T MEAN TO— I MEAN, IT MUST BE DESTINY...
"DESTINY"? YOU SCREW UP BIG TIME AND CALL IT "DESTINY"?!
PEOPLE... TIME OUT!
WE HAVE A SUPPOSED "MISSION OF VENGEANCE" TO FINISH HERE AND IT'S GETTING LATE!
MISSION? WHAT MISSION?!
DALE CAN FILL YOU IN LATER...
BUT IF YOU TWO KEEP THIS UP, WE'LL ATTRACT A CROWD IN NO TIME!
WAIT! THAT'S IT!
?!?
WHAT BETTER WAY TO CLOSE A RESTAURANT THAN TO DISCOVER TWO CORPSES IN THE RESTROOM?!

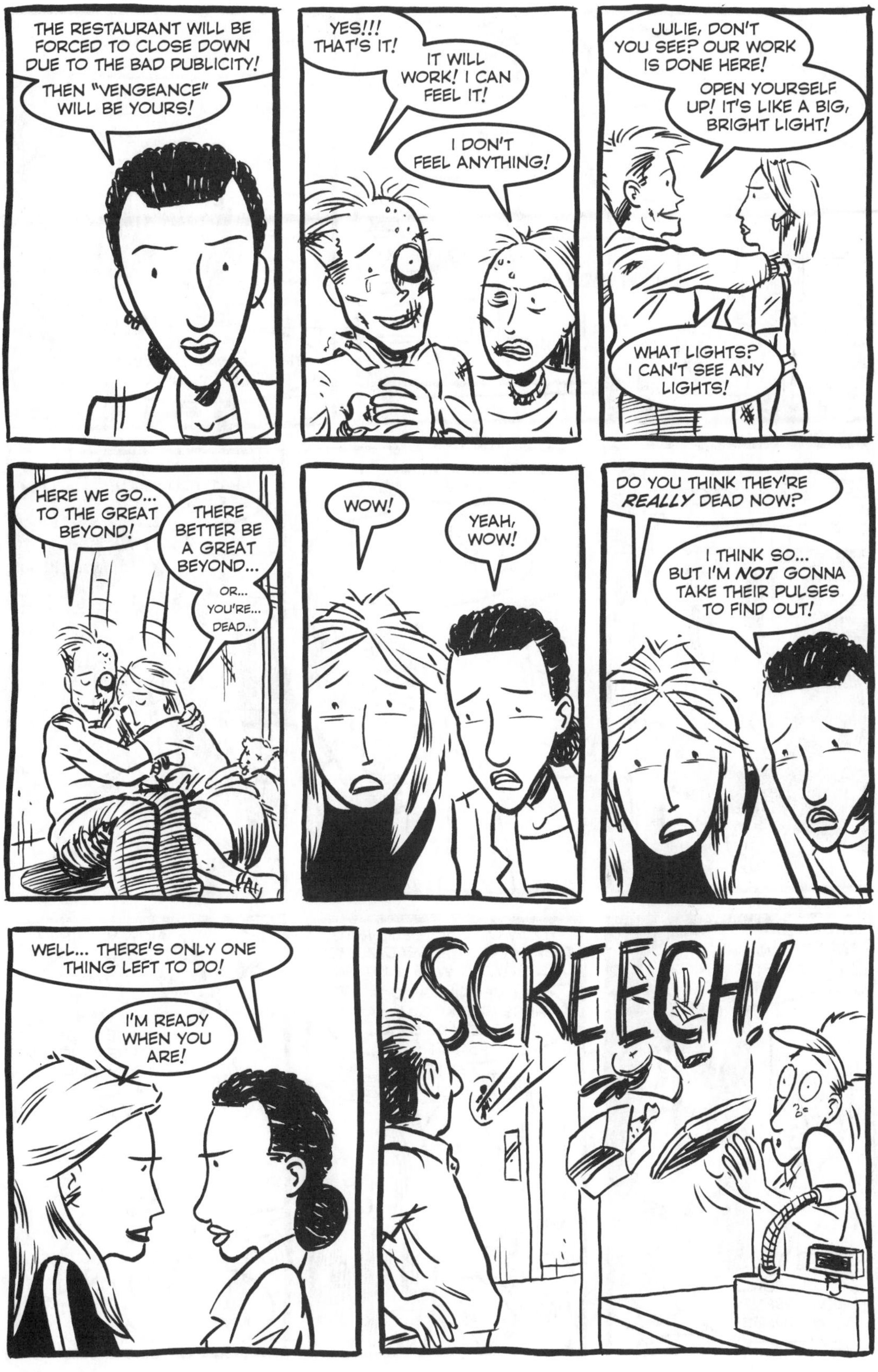
THE RESTAURANT WILL BE FORCED TO CLOSE DOWN DUE TO THE BAD PUBLICITY!
THEN "VENGEANCE" WILL BE YOURS!
YES!!! THAT'S IT!
IT WILL WORK! I CAN FEEL IT!
I DON'T FEEL ANYTHING!
JULIE, DON'T YOU SEE? OUR WORK IS DONE HERE!
OPEN YOURSELF UP! IT'S LIKE A BIG, BRIGHT LIGHT!
WHAT LIGHTS? I CAN'T SEE ANY LIGHTS!
HERE WE GO... TO THE GREAT BEYOND!
THERE BETTER BE A GREAT BEYOND...
OR... YOU'RE... DEAD...
WOW!
YEAH, WOW!
DO YOU THINK THEY'RE *REALLY* DEAD NOW?
I THINK SO... BUT I'M ***NOT*** GONNA TAKE THEIR PULSES TO FIND OUT!
WELL... THERE'S ONLY ONE THING LEFT TO DO!
I'M READY WHEN YOU ARE!
SCREECH!

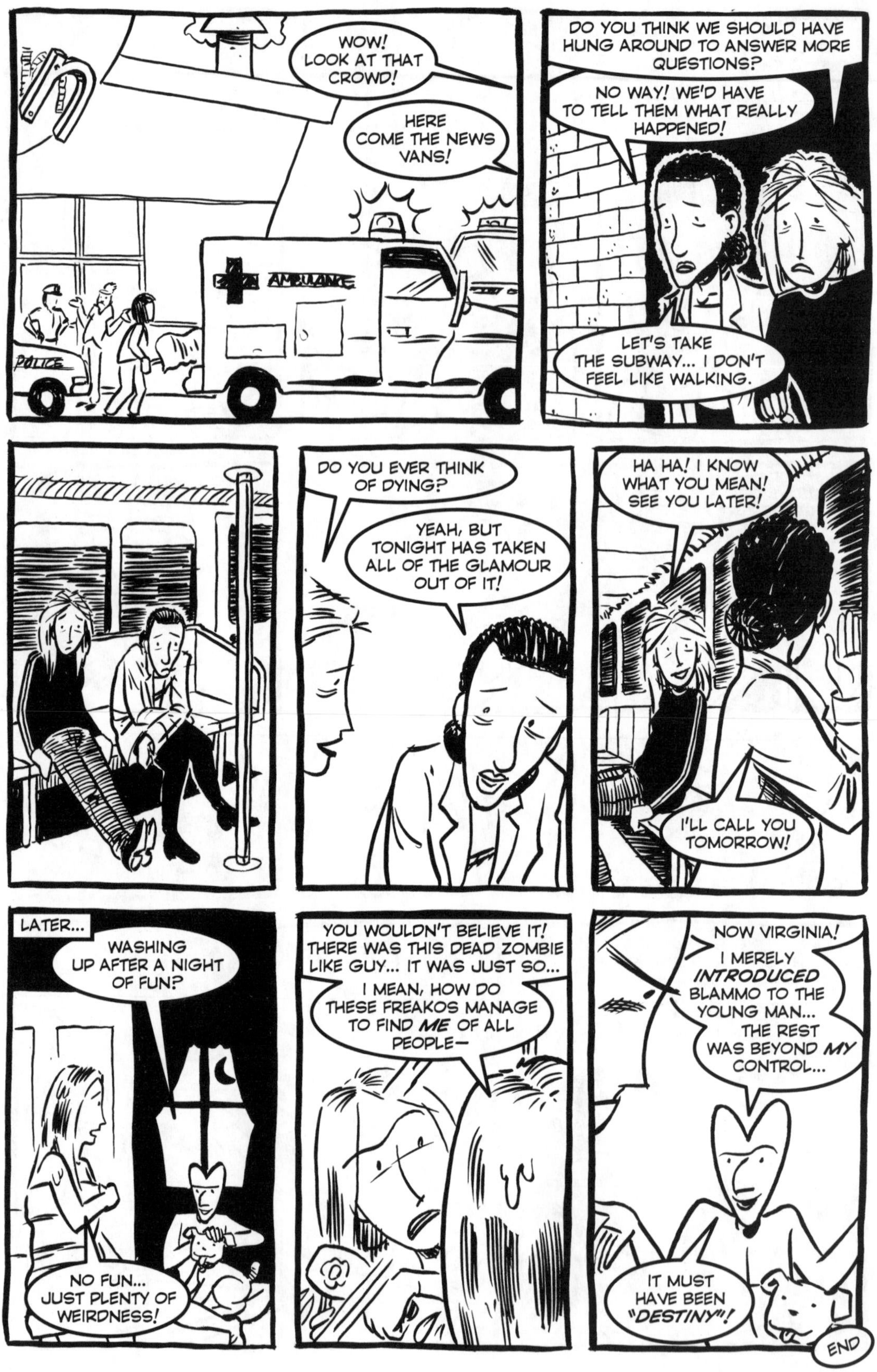

WOW! LOOK AT THAT CROWD!
HERE COME THE NEWS VANS!
AMBULANCE
POLICE
DO YOU THINK WE SHOULD HAVE HUNG AROUND TO ANSWER MORE QUESTIONS?
NO WAY! WE'D HAVE TO TELL THEM WHAT REALLY HAPPENED!
LET'S TAKE THE SUBWAY... I DON'T FEEL LIKE WALKING.
DO YOU EVER THINK OF DYING?
YEAH, BUT TONIGHT HAS TAKEN ALL OF THE GLAMOUR OUT OF IT!
HA HA! I KNOW WHAT YOU MEAN! SEE YOU LATER!
I'LL CALL YOU TOMORROW!
LATER...
WASHING UP AFTER A NIGHT OF FUN?
NO FUN... JUST PLENTY OF WEIRDNESS!
YOU WOULDN'T BELIEVE IT! THERE WAS THIS DEAD ZOMBIE LIKE GUY... IT WAS JUST SO...
I MEAN, HOW DO THESE FREAKOS MANAGE TO FIND ME OF ALL PEOPLE—
NOW VIRGINIA!
I MERELY INTRODUCED BLAMMO TO THE YOUNG MAN... THE REST WAS BEYOND MY CONTROL...
IT MUST HAVE BEEN "DESTINY"!
END

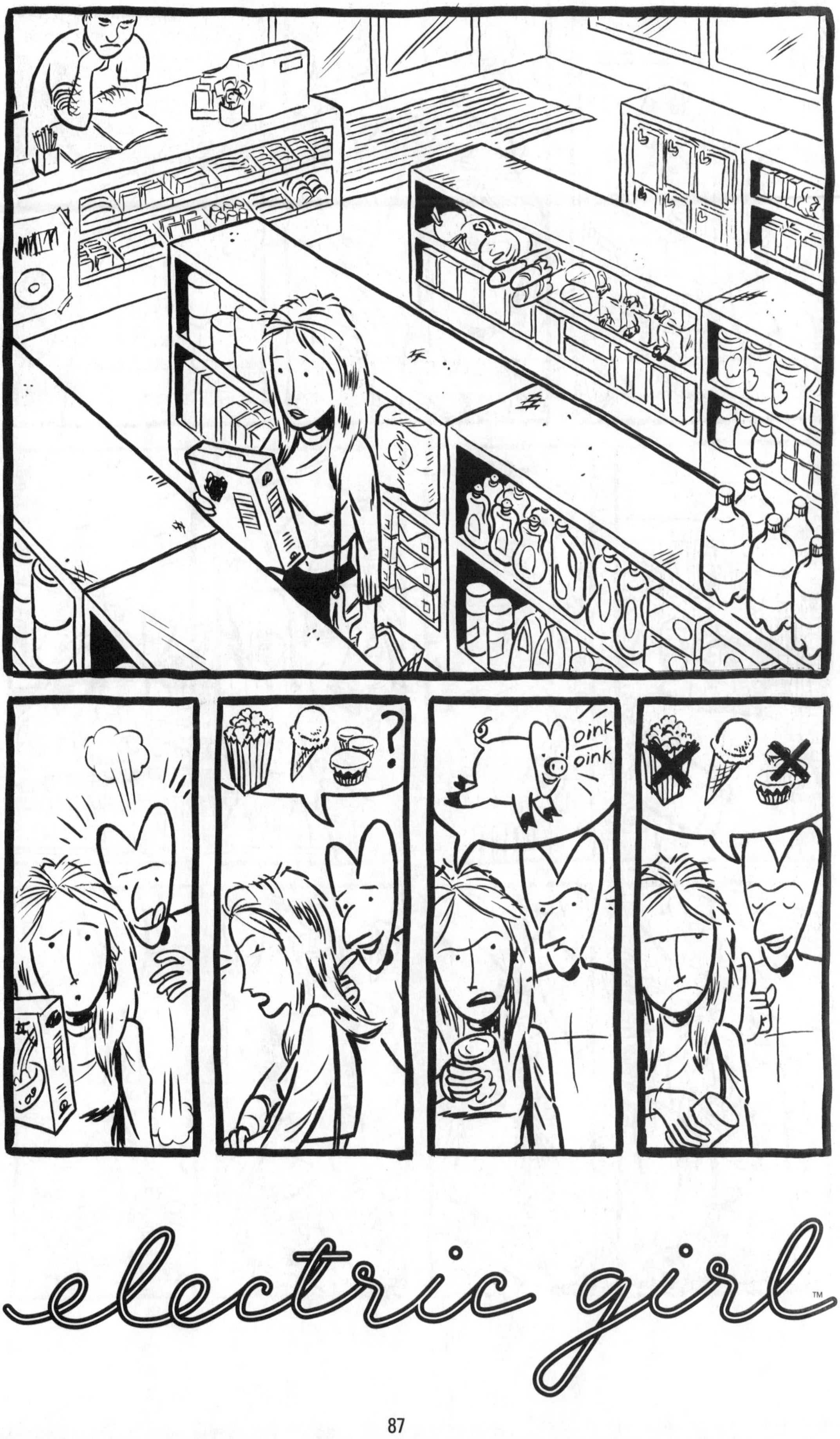
?
oink
oink

electric girl™

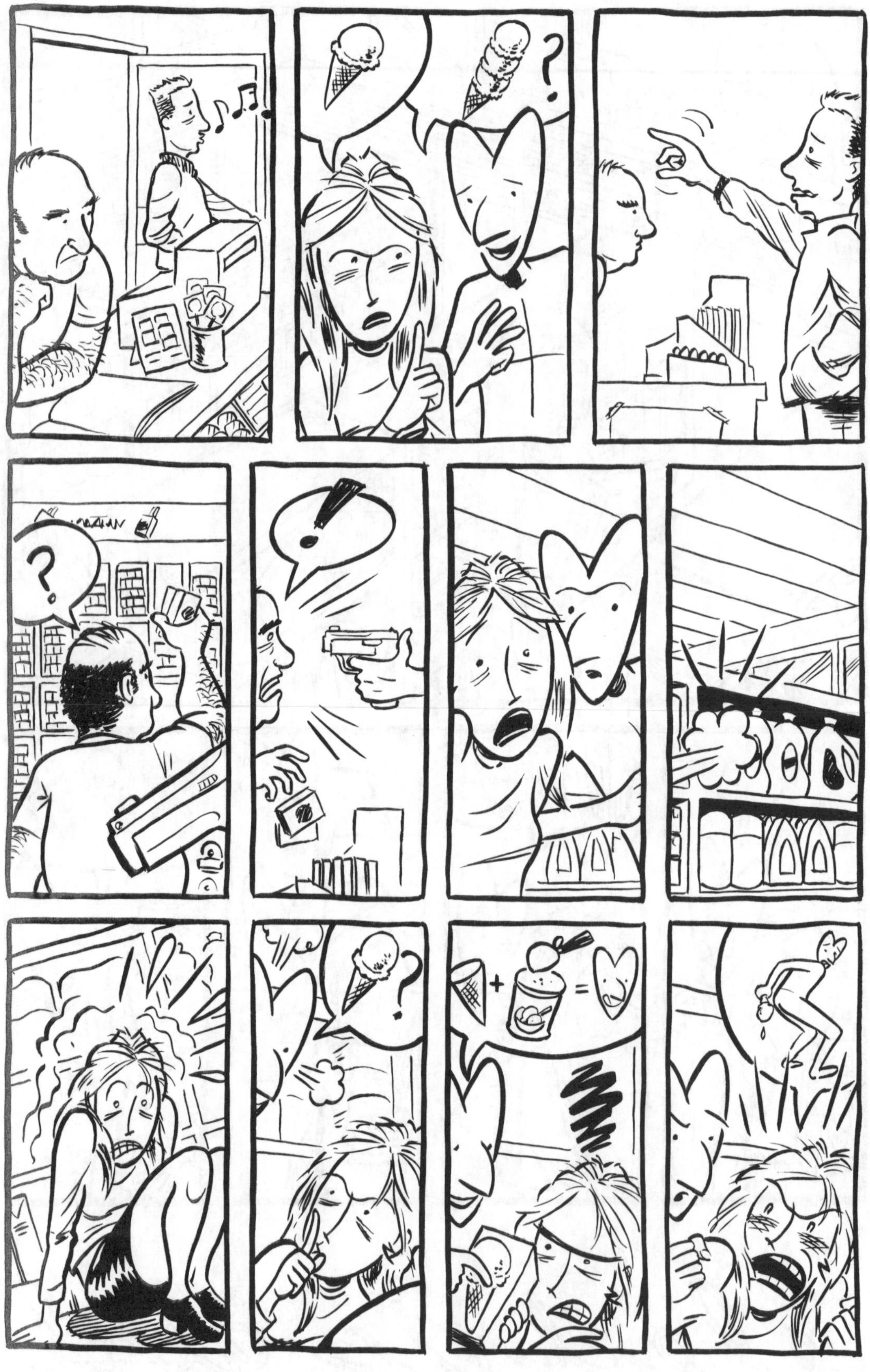

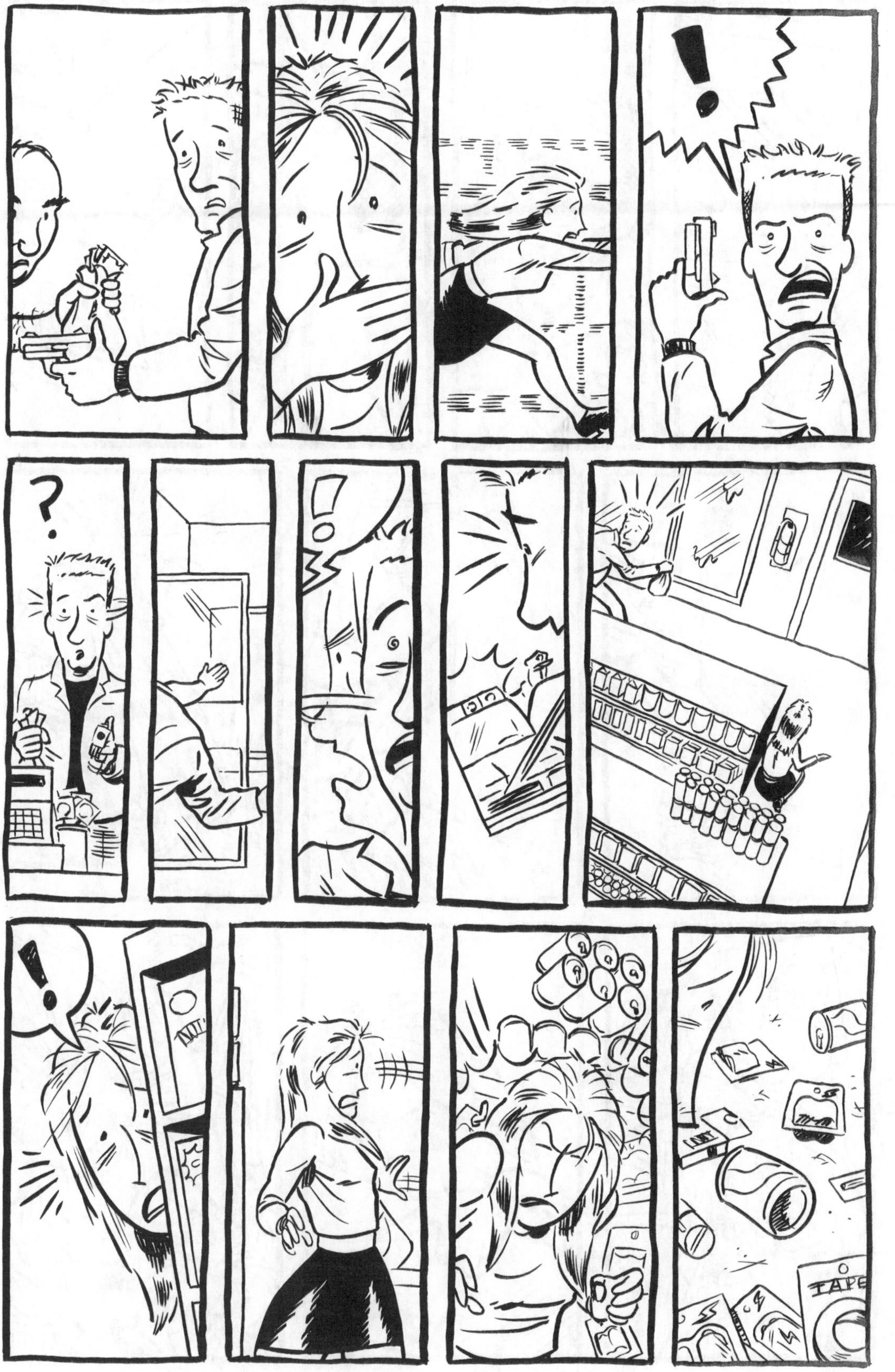
!
?
!
!
TAPE

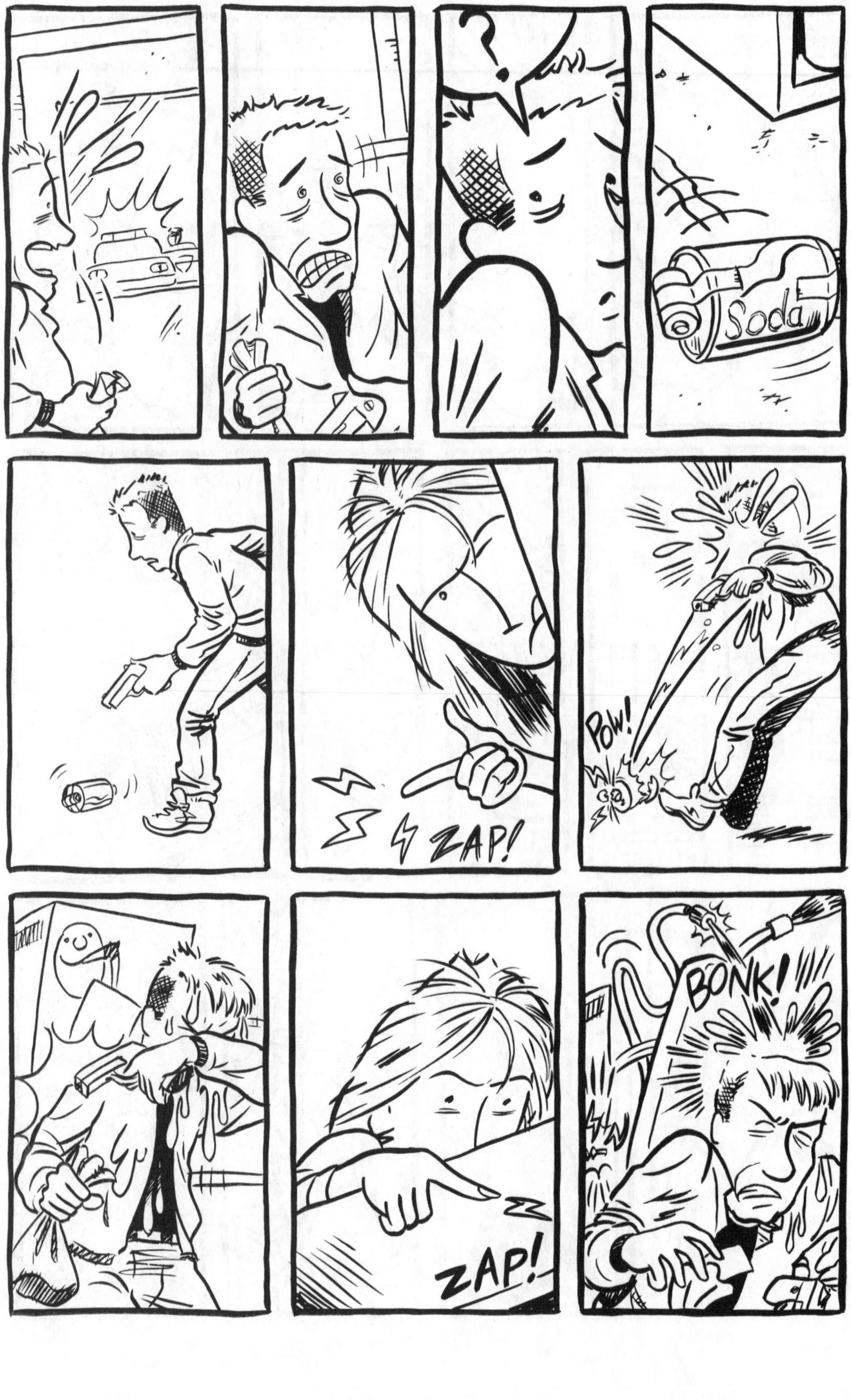
?
!
Soda
ZAP!
POW!
ZAP!
BONK!

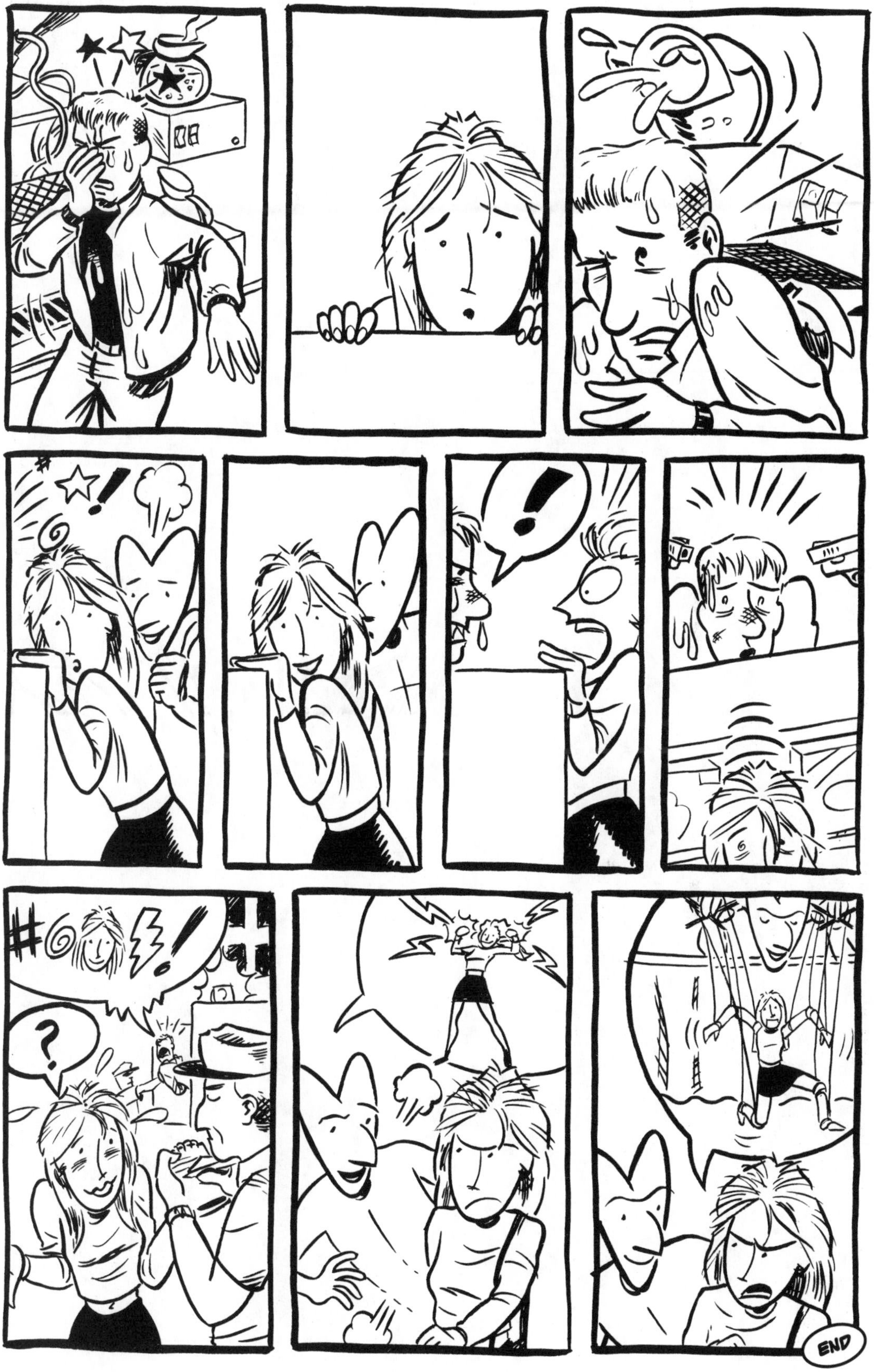

!
?
END

electric girl issue ③

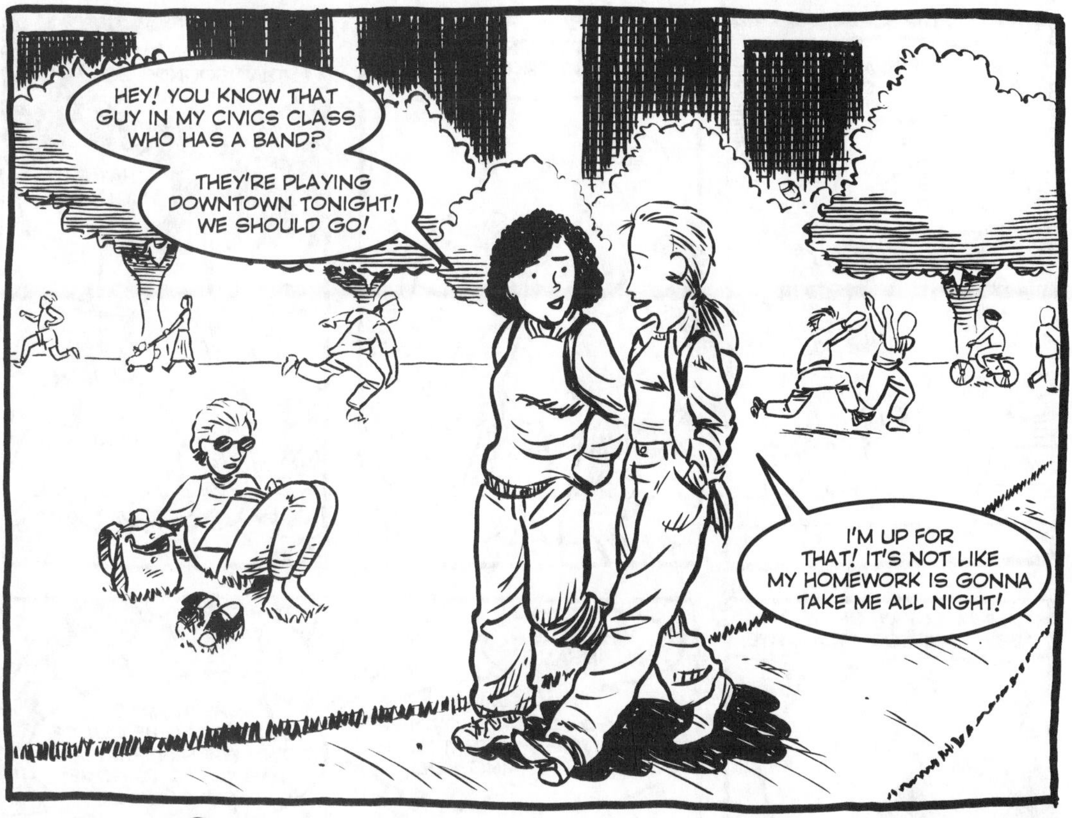
HEY! YOU KNOW THAT GUY IN MY CIVICS CLASS WHO HAS A BAND?
THEY'RE PLAYING DOWNTOWN TONIGHT! WE SHOULD GO!
I'M UP FOR THAT! IT'S NOT LIKE MY HOMEWORK IS GONNA TAKE ME ALL NIGHT!

electric girl™

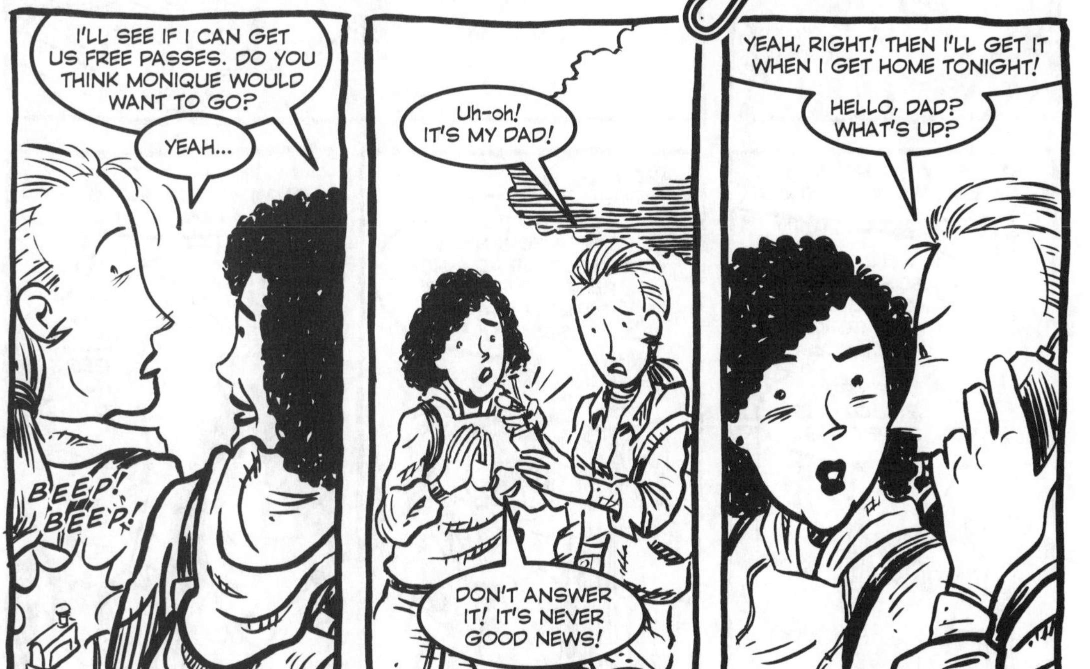
I'LL SEE IF I CAN GET US FREE PASSES. DO YOU THINK MONIQUE WOULD WANT TO GO?
YEAH...
BEEP! BEEP!
Uh-oh! IT'S MY DAD!
DON'T ANSWER IT! IT'S NEVER GOOD NEWS!
YEAH, RIGHT! THEN I'LL GET IT WHEN I GET HOME TONIGHT!
HELLO, DAD? WHAT'S UP?

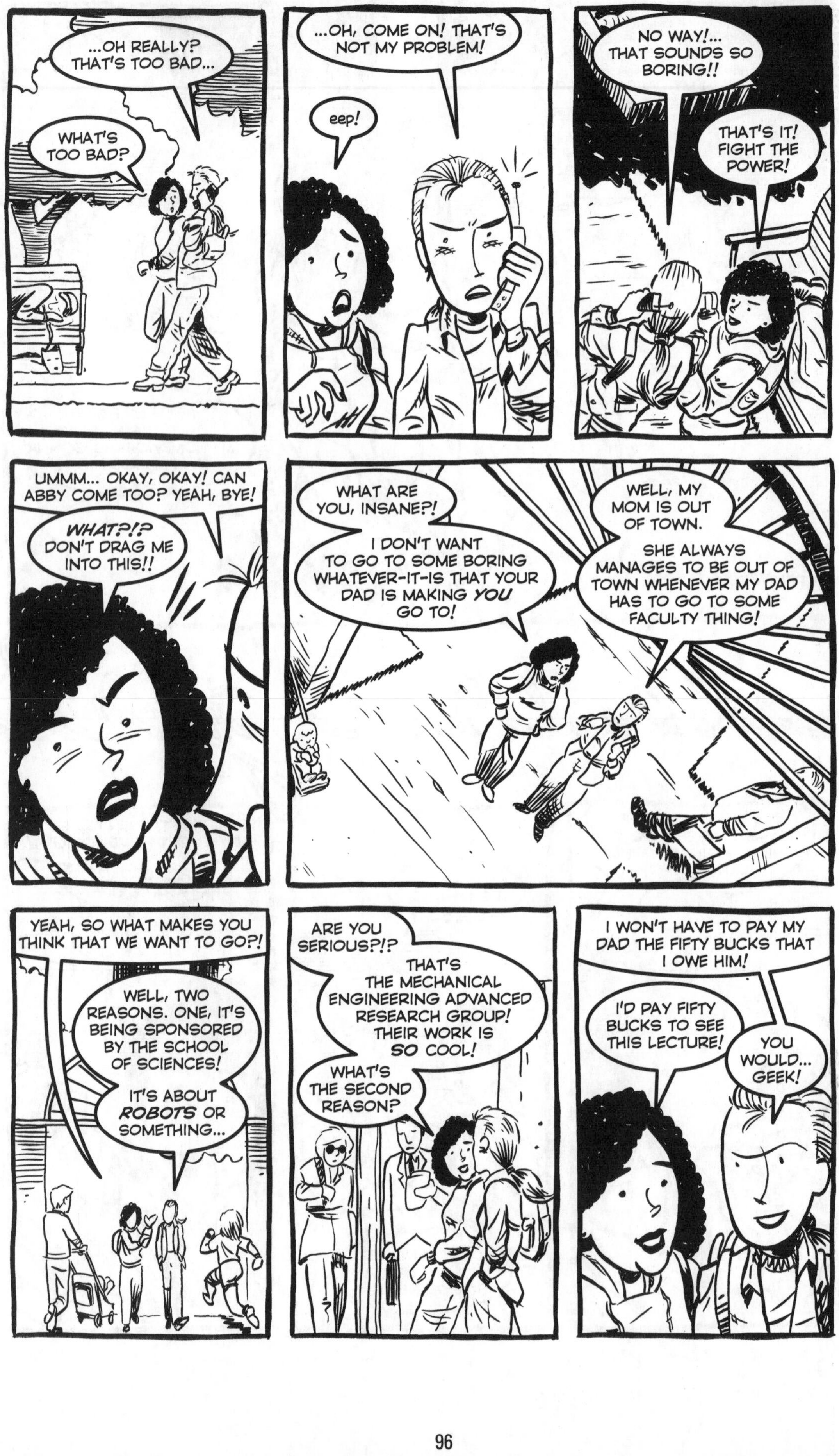

...OH REALLY? THAT'S TOO BAD...
WHAT'S TOO BAD?
...OH, COME ON! THAT'S NOT MY PROBLEM!
eep!
NO WAY!... THAT SOUNDS SO BORING!!
THAT'S IT! FIGHT THE POWER!
UMMM... OKAY, OKAY! CAN ABBY COME TOO? YEAH, BYE!
WHAT?!? DON'T DRAG ME INTO THIS!!
WHAT ARE YOU, INSANE?!
I DON'T WANT TO GO TO SOME BORING WHATEVER-IT-IS THAT YOUR DAD IS MAKING YOU GO TO!
WELL, MY MOM IS OUT OF TOWN.
SHE ALWAYS MANAGES TO BE OUT OF TOWN WHENEVER MY DAD HAS TO GO TO SOME FACULTY THING!
YEAH, SO WHAT MAKES YOU THINK THAT WE WANT TO GO?!
WELL, TWO REASONS. ONE, IT'S BEING SPONSORED BY THE SCHOOL OF SCIENCES!
IT'S ABOUT ROBOTS OR SOMETHING...
ARE YOU SERIOUS?!?
THAT'S THE MECHANICAL ENGINEERING ADVANCED RESEARCH GROUP! THEIR WORK IS SO COOL!
WHAT'S THE SECOND REASON?
I WON'T HAVE TO PAY MY DAD THE FIFTY BUCKS THAT I OWE HIM!
I'D PAY FIFTY BUCKS TO SEE THIS LECTURE!
YOU WOULD... GEEK!

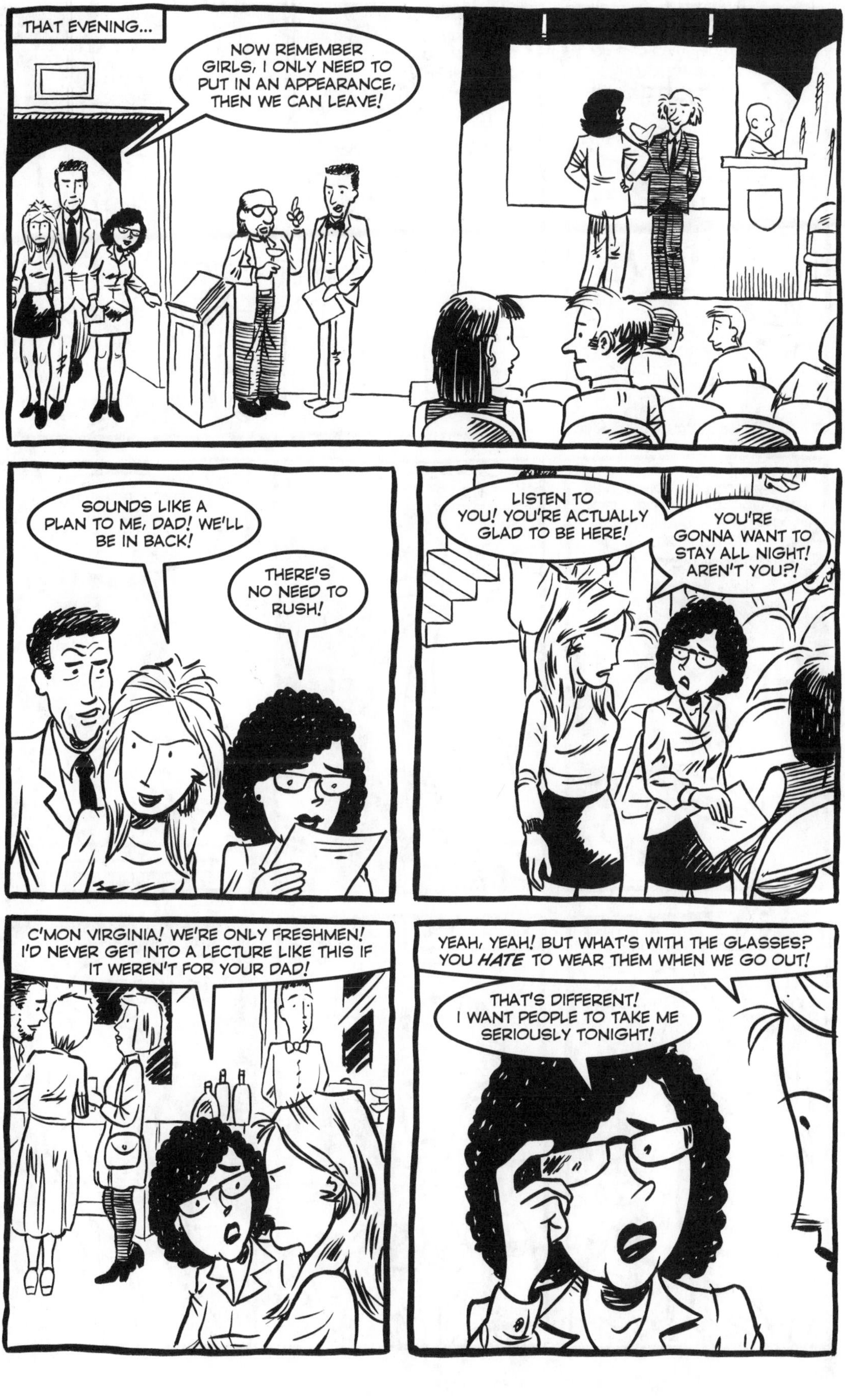
THAT EVENING...
NOW REMEMBER GIRLS, I ONLY NEED TO PUT IN AN APPEARANCE, THEN WE CAN LEAVE!
SOUNDS LIKE A PLAN TO ME, DAD! WE'LL BE IN BACK!
THERE'S NO NEED TO RUSH!
LISTEN TO YOU! YOU'RE ACTUALLY GLAD TO BE HERE!
YOU'RE GONNA WANT TO STAY ALL NIGHT! AREN'T YOU?!
C'MON VIRGINIA! WE'RE ONLY FRESHMEN! I'D NEVER GET INTO A LECTURE LIKE THIS IF IT WEREN'T FOR YOUR DAD!
YEAH, YEAH! BUT WHAT'S WITH THE GLASSES? YOU HATE TO WEAR THEM WHEN WE GO OUT!
THAT'S DIFFERENT! I WANT PEOPLE TO TAKE ME SERIOUSLY TONIGHT!

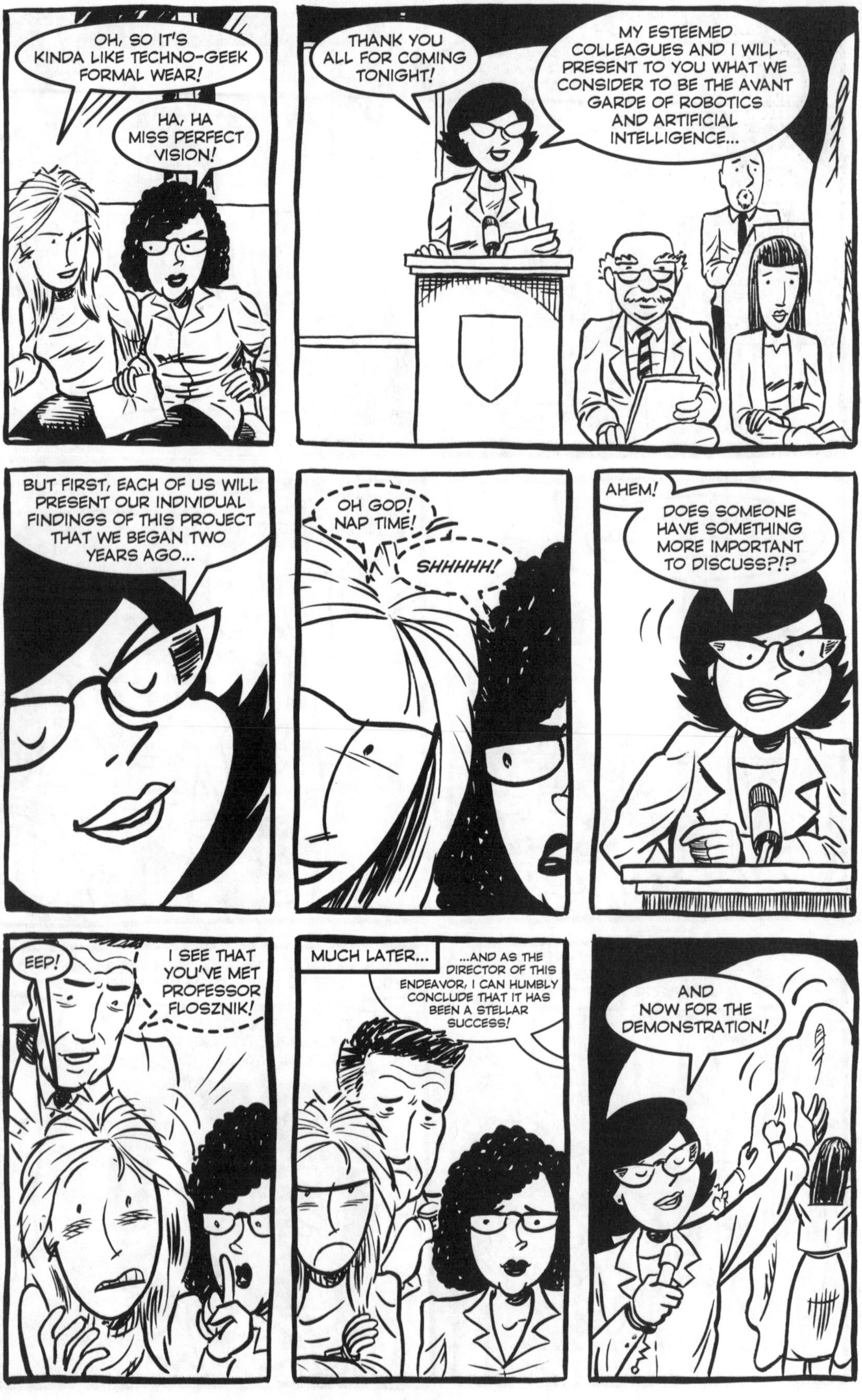

OH, SO IT'S KINDA LIKE TECHNO-GEEK FORMAL WEAR!
HA, HA MISS PERFECT VISION!
THANK YOU ALL FOR COMING TONIGHT!
MY ESTEEMED COLLEAGUES AND I WILL PRESENT TO YOU WHAT WE CONSIDER TO BE THE AVANT GARDE OF ROBOTICS AND ARTIFICIAL INTELLIGENCE...
BUT FIRST, EACH OF US WILL PRESENT OUR INDIVIDUAL FINDINGS OF THIS PROJECT THAT WE BEGAN TWO YEARS AGO...
OH GOD! NAP TIME!
SHHHHH!
AHEM!
DOES SOMEONE HAVE SOMETHING MORE IMPORTANT TO DISCUSS?!?
EEP!
I SEE THAT YOU'VE MET PROFESSOR FLOSZNIK!
MUCH LATER...
...AND AS THE DIRECTOR OF THIS ENDEAVOR, I CAN HUMBLY CONCLUDE THAT IT HAS BEEN A STELLAR SUCCESS!
AND NOW FOR THE DEMONSTRATION!

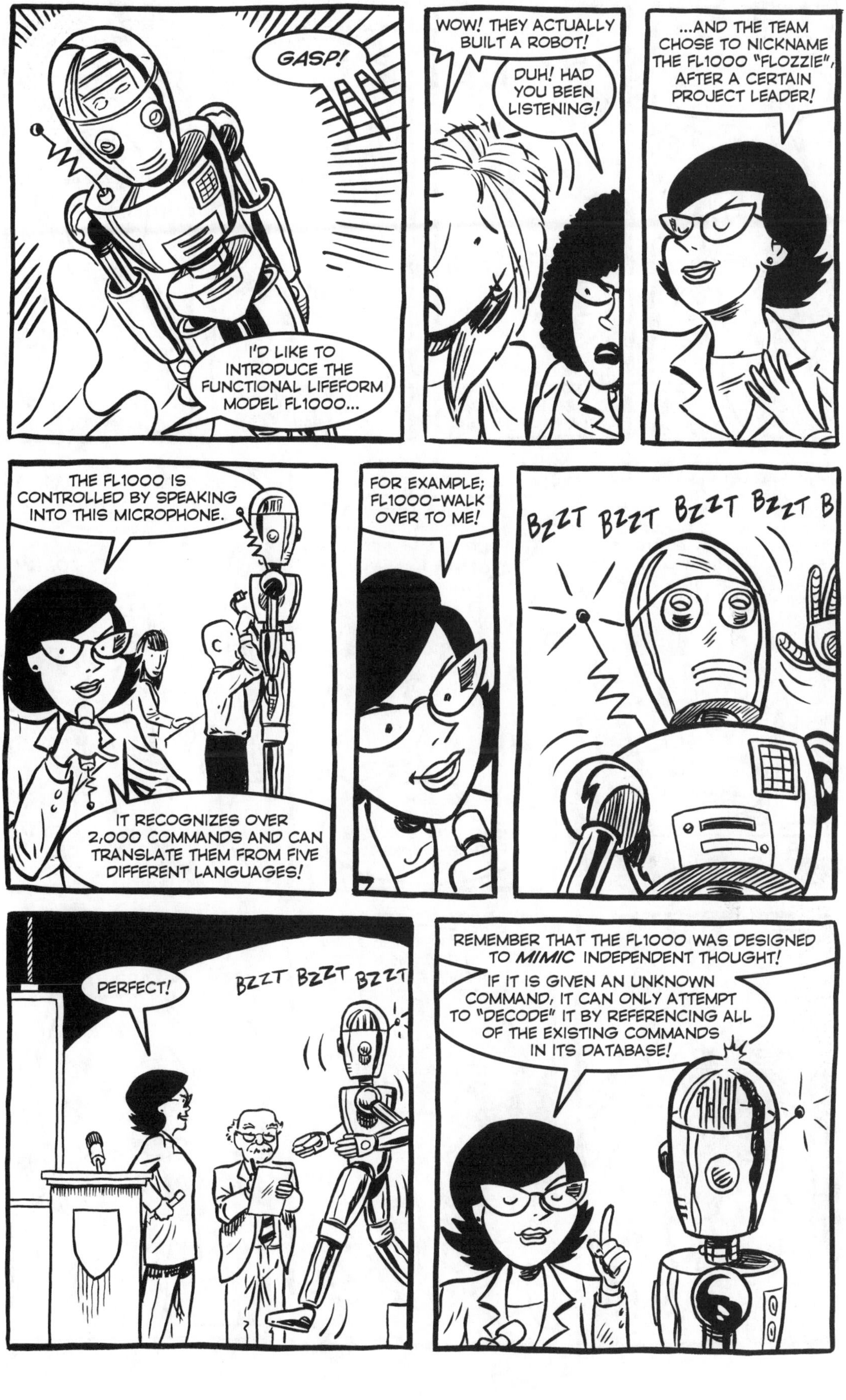
GASP!
I'D LIKE TO INTRODUCE THE FUNCTIONAL LIFEFORM MODEL FL1000...
WOW! THEY ACTUALLY BUILT A ROBOT!
DUH! HAD YOU BEEN LISTENING!
...AND THE TEAM CHOSE TO NICKNAME THE FL1000 "FLOZZIE", AFTER A CERTAIN PROJECT LEADER!
THE FL1000 IS CONTROLLED BY SPEAKING INTO THIS MICROPHONE.
IT RECOGNIZES OVER 2,000 COMMANDS AND CAN TRANSLATE THEM FROM FIVE DIFFERENT LANGUAGES!
FOR EXAMPLE; FL1000-WALK OVER TO ME!
BZZT BZZT BZZT BZZT B
PERFECT!
BZZT BZZT BZZT
REMEMBER THAT THE FL1000 WAS DESIGNED TO *MIMIC* INDEPENDENT THOUGHT!
IF IT IS GIVEN AN UNKNOWN COMMAND, IT CAN ONLY ATTEMPT TO "DECODE" IT BY REFERENCING ALL OF THE EXISTING COMMANDS IN ITS DATABASE!

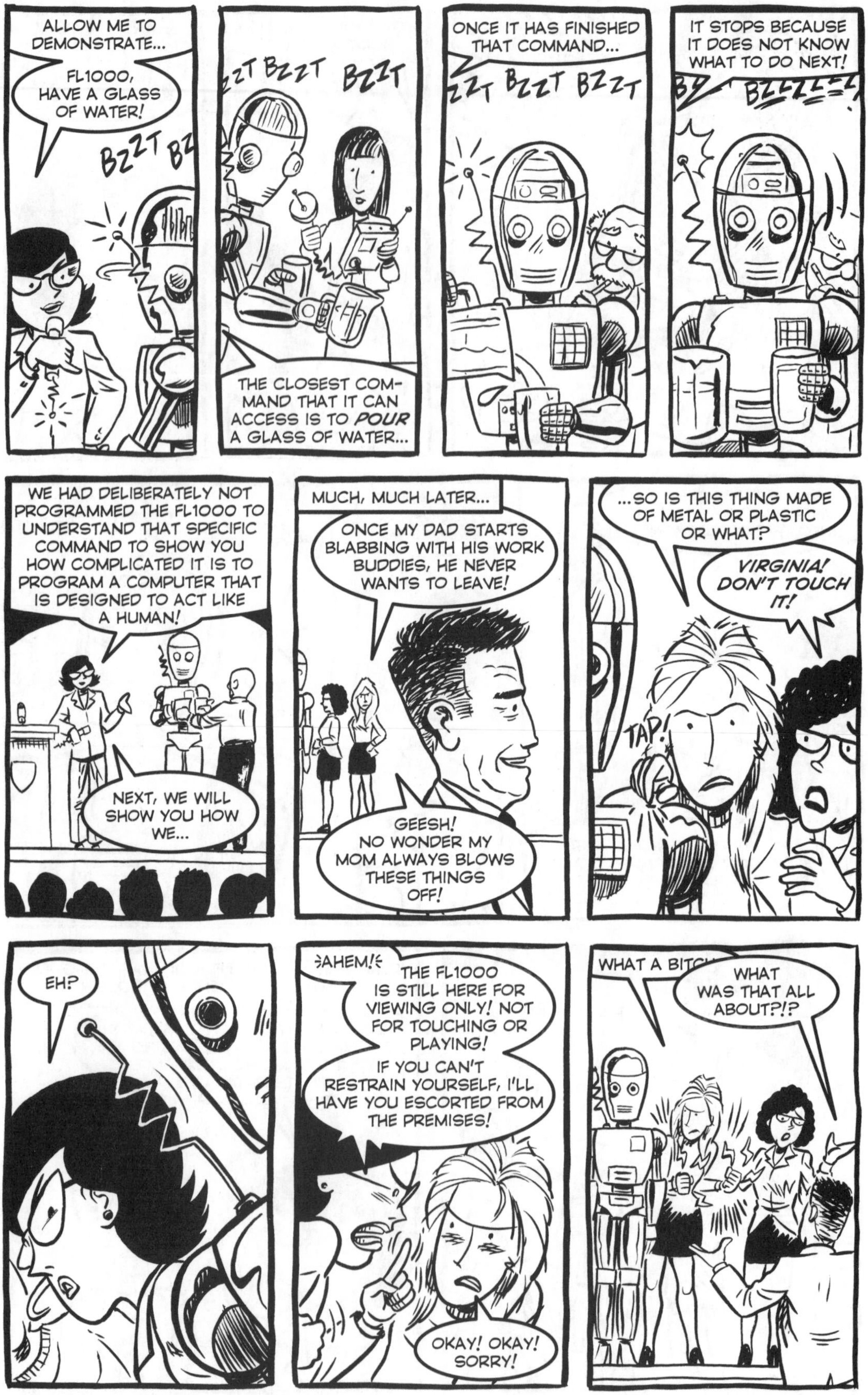
ALLOW ME TO DEMONSTRATE...
FL1000, HAVE A GLASS OF WATER!
BZZT BZ
ZZT BZZT BZZT
THE CLOSEST COMMAND THAT IT CAN ACCESS IS TO POUR A GLASS OF WATER...
ONCE IT HAS FINISHED THAT COMMAND...
ZZT BZZT BZZT
IT STOPS BECAUSE IT DOES NOT KNOW WHAT TO DO NEXT!
BZZZZZZ
WE HAD DELIBERATELY NOT PROGRAMMED THE FL1000 TO UNDERSTAND THAT SPECIFIC COMMAND TO SHOW YOU HOW COMPLICATED IT IS TO PROGRAM A COMPUTER THAT IS DESIGNED TO ACT LIKE A HUMAN!
NEXT, WE WILL SHOW YOU HOW WE...
MUCH, MUCH LATER...
ONCE MY DAD STARTS BLABBING WITH HIS WORK BUDDIES, HE NEVER WANTS TO LEAVE!
GEESH! NO WONDER MY MOM ALWAYS BLOWS THESE THINGS OFF!
...SO IS THIS THING MADE OF METAL OR PLASTIC OR WHAT?
VIRGINIA! DON'T TOUCH IT!
TAP!
EH?
AHEM!
THE FL1000 IS STILL HERE FOR VIEWING ONLY! NOT FOR TOUCHING OR PLAYING!
IF YOU CAN'T RESTRAIN YOURSELF, I'LL HAVE YOU ESCORTED FROM THE PREMISES!
OKAY! OKAY! SORRY!
WHAT A BITC
WHAT WAS THAT ALL ABOUT?!?

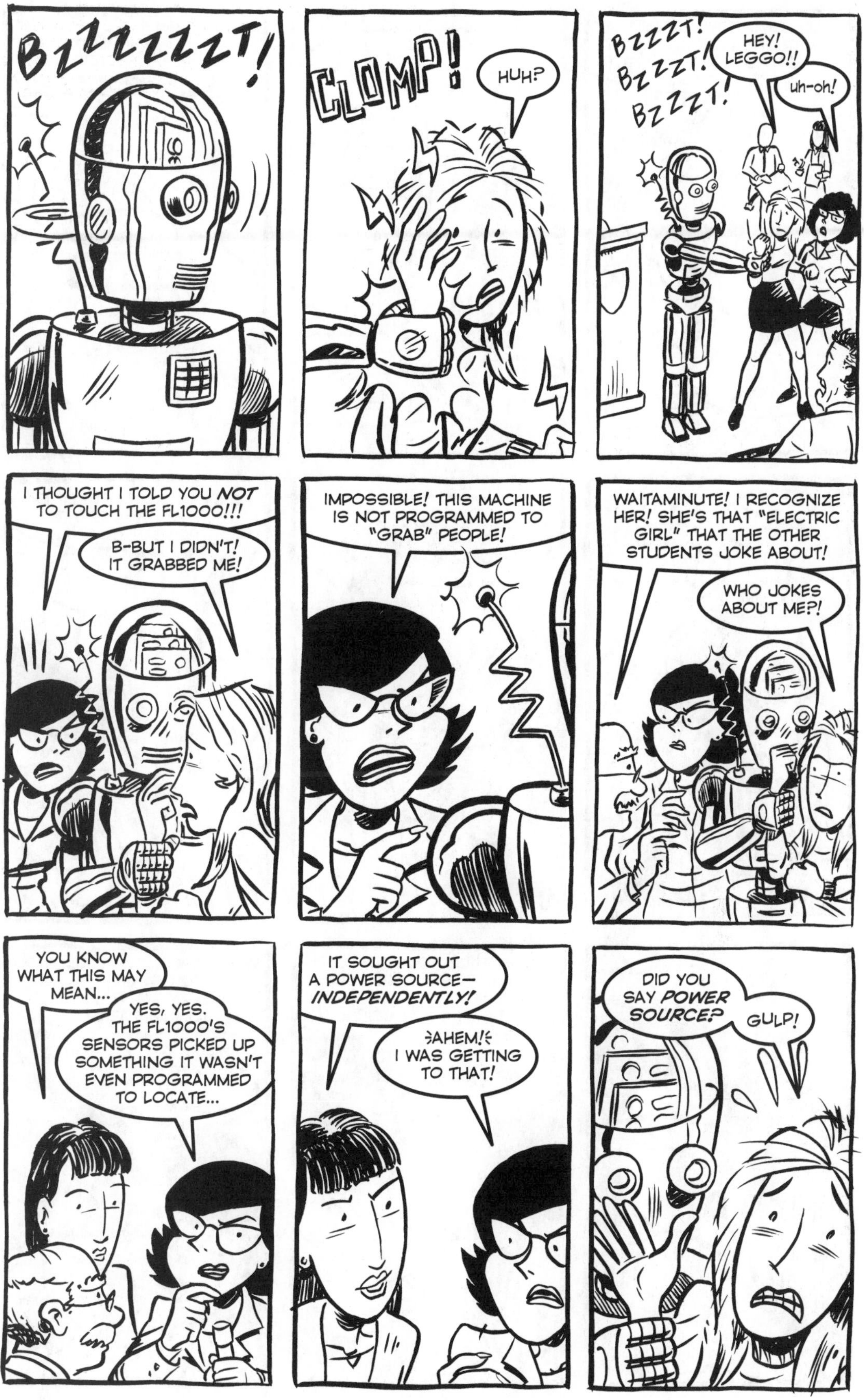
BZZZZZZZT!
CLOMP!
HUH?
BZZZT! BZZZT! BZZZT!
HEY! LEGGO!!
uh-oh!
I THOUGHT I TOLD YOU *NOT* TO TOUCH THE FL1000!!!
B-BUT I DIDN'T! IT GRABBED ME!
IMPOSSIBLE! THIS MACHINE IS NOT PROGRAMMED TO "GRAB" PEOPLE!
WAITAMINUTE! I RECOGNIZE HER! SHE'S THAT "ELECTRIC GIRL" THAT THE OTHER STUDENTS JOKE ABOUT!
WHO JOKES ABOUT ME?!
YOU KNOW WHAT THIS MAY MEAN...
YES, YES. THE FL1000'S SENSORS PICKED UP SOMETHING IT WASN'T EVEN PROGRAMMED TO LOCATE...
IT SOUGHT OUT A POWER SOURCE— *INDEPENDENTLY!*
AHEM! I WAS GETTING TO THAT!
DID YOU SAY *POWER SOURCE?*
GULP!

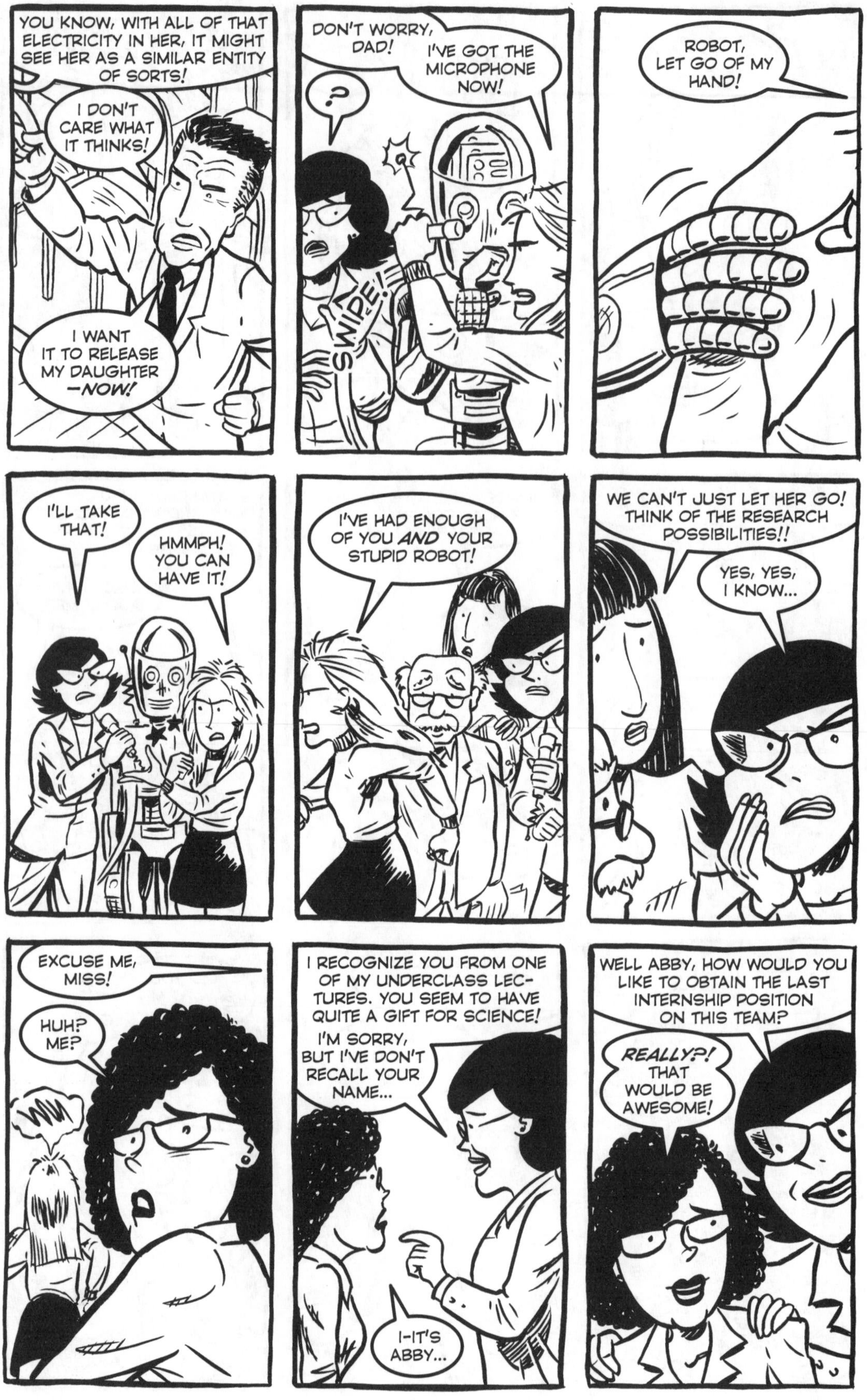
YOU KNOW, WITH ALL OF THAT ELECTRICITY IN HER, IT MIGHT SEE HER AS A SIMILAR ENTITY OF SORTS!
I DON'T CARE WHAT IT THINKS!
I WANT IT TO RELEASE MY DAUGHTER —NOW!
DON'T WORRY, DAD!
I'VE GOT THE MICROPHONE NOW!
?
SWIPE!
ROBOT, LET GO OF MY HAND!
I'LL TAKE THAT!
HMMPH! YOU CAN HAVE IT!
I'VE HAD ENOUGH OF YOU AND YOUR STUPID ROBOT!
WE CAN'T JUST LET HER GO! THINK OF THE RESEARCH POSSIBILITIES!!
YES, YES, I KNOW...
EXCUSE ME, MISS!
HUH? ME?
I RECOGNIZE YOU FROM ONE OF MY UNDERCLASS LECTURES. YOU SEEM TO HAVE QUITE A GIFT FOR SCIENCE!
I'M SORRY, BUT I'VE DON'T RECALL YOUR NAME...
I-IT'S ABBY...
WELL ABBY, HOW WOULD YOU LIKE TO OBTAIN THE LAST INTERNSHIP POSITION ON THIS TEAM?
REALLY?! THAT WOULD BE AWESOME!

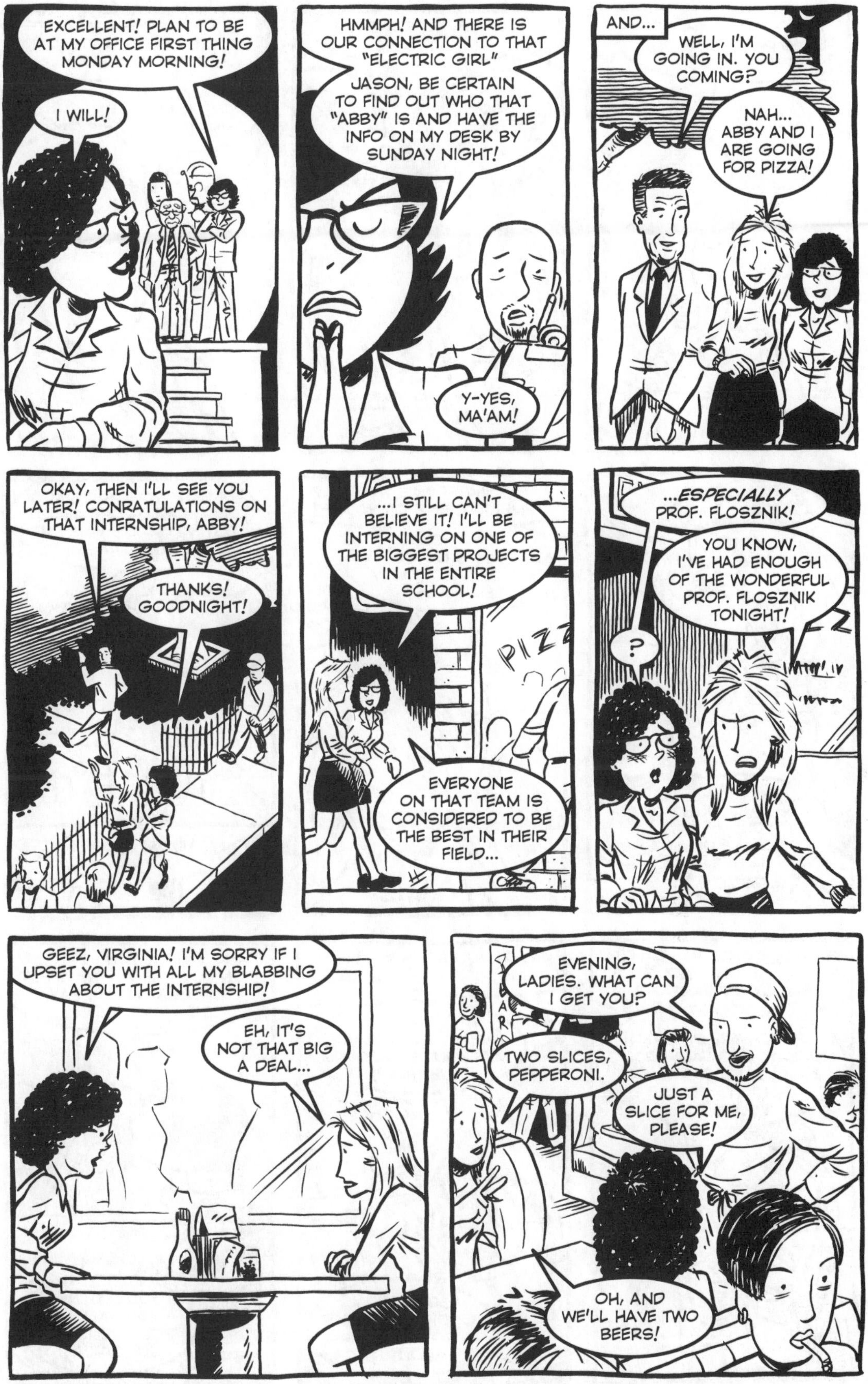
EXCELLENT! PLAN TO BE AT MY OFFICE FIRST THING MONDAY MORNING!
I WILL!
HMMPH! AND THERE IS OUR CONNECTION TO THAT "ELECTRIC GIRL"
JASON, BE CERTAIN TO FIND OUT WHO THAT "ABBY" IS AND HAVE THE INFO ON MY DESK BY SUNDAY NIGHT!
Y-YES, MA'AM!
AND...
WELL, I'M GOING IN. YOU COMING?
NAH... ABBY AND I ARE GOING FOR PIZZA!
OKAY, THEN I'LL SEE YOU LATER! CONRATULATIONS ON THAT INTERNSHIP, ABBY!
THANKS! GOODNIGHT!
...I STILL CAN'T BELIEVE IT! I'LL BE INTERNING ON ONE OF THE BIGGEST PROJECTS IN THE ENTIRE SCHOOL!
EVERYONE ON THAT TEAM IS CONSIDERED TO BE THE BEST IN THEIR FIELD...
...*ESPECIALLY* PROF. FLOSZNIK!
YOU KNOW, I'VE HAD ENOUGH OF THE WONDERFUL PROF. FLOSZNIK TONIGHT!
?
GEEZ, VIRGINIA! I'M SORRY IF I UPSET YOU WITH ALL MY BLABBING ABOUT THE INTERNSHIP!
EH, IT'S NOT THAT BIG A DEAL...
EVENING, LADIES. WHAT CAN I GET YOU?
TWO SLICES, PEPPERONI.
JUST A SLICE FOR ME, PLEASE!
OH, AND WE'LL HAVE TWO BEERS!

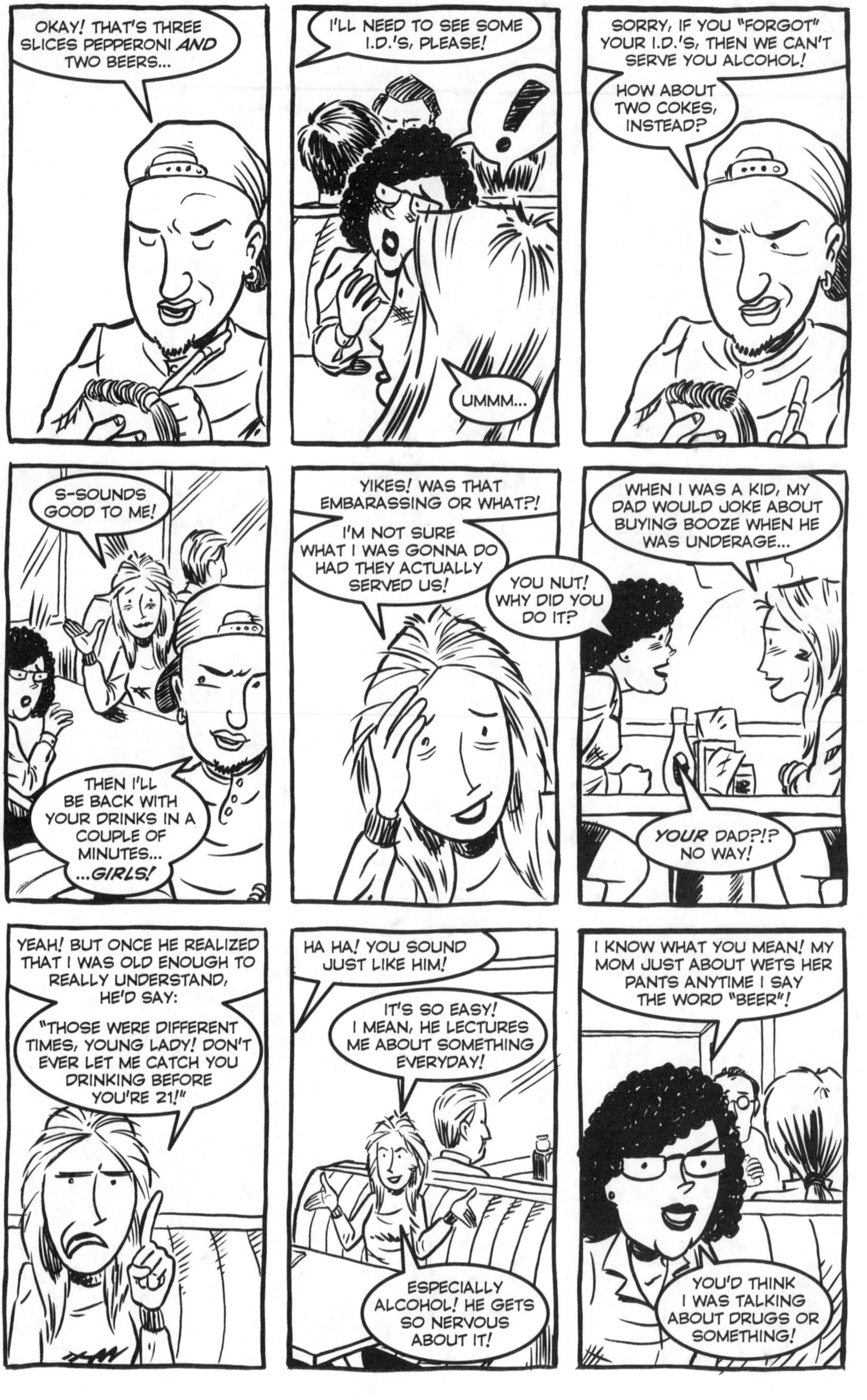
OKAY! THAT'S THREE SLICES PEPPERONI *AND* TWO BEERS...
I'LL NEED TO SEE SOME I.D.'S, PLEASE!
!
UMMM...
SORRY, IF YOU "FORGOT" YOUR I.D.'S, THEN WE CAN'T SERVE YOU ALCOHOL!
HOW ABOUT TWO COKES, INSTEAD?
S-SOUNDS GOOD TO ME!
THEN I'LL BE BACK WITH YOUR DRINKS IN A COUPLE OF MINUTES... ...*GIRLS!*
YIKES! WAS THAT EMBARASSING OR WHAT?!
I'M NOT SURE WHAT I WAS GONNA DO HAD THEY ACTUALLY SERVED US!
YOU NUT! WHY DID YOU DO IT?
WHEN I WAS A KID, MY DAD WOULD JOKE ABOUT BUYING BOOZE WHEN HE WAS UNDERAGE...
YOUR DAD?!? NO WAY!
YEAH! BUT ONCE HE REALIZED THAT I WAS OLD ENOUGH TO REALLY UNDERSTAND, HE'D SAY:
"THOSE WERE DIFFERENT TIMES, YOUNG LADY! DON'T EVER LET ME CATCH YOU DRINKING BEFORE YOU'RE 21!"
HA HA! YOU SOUND JUST LIKE HIM!
IT'S SO EASY! I MEAN, HE LECTURES ME ABOUT SOMETHING EVERYDAY!
ESPECIALLY ALCOHOL! HE GETS SO NERVOUS ABOUT IT!
I KNOW WHAT YOU MEAN! MY MOM JUST ABOUT WETS HER PANTS ANYTIME I SAY THE WORD "BEER"!
YOU'D THINK I WAS TALKING ABOUT DRUGS OR SOMETHING!

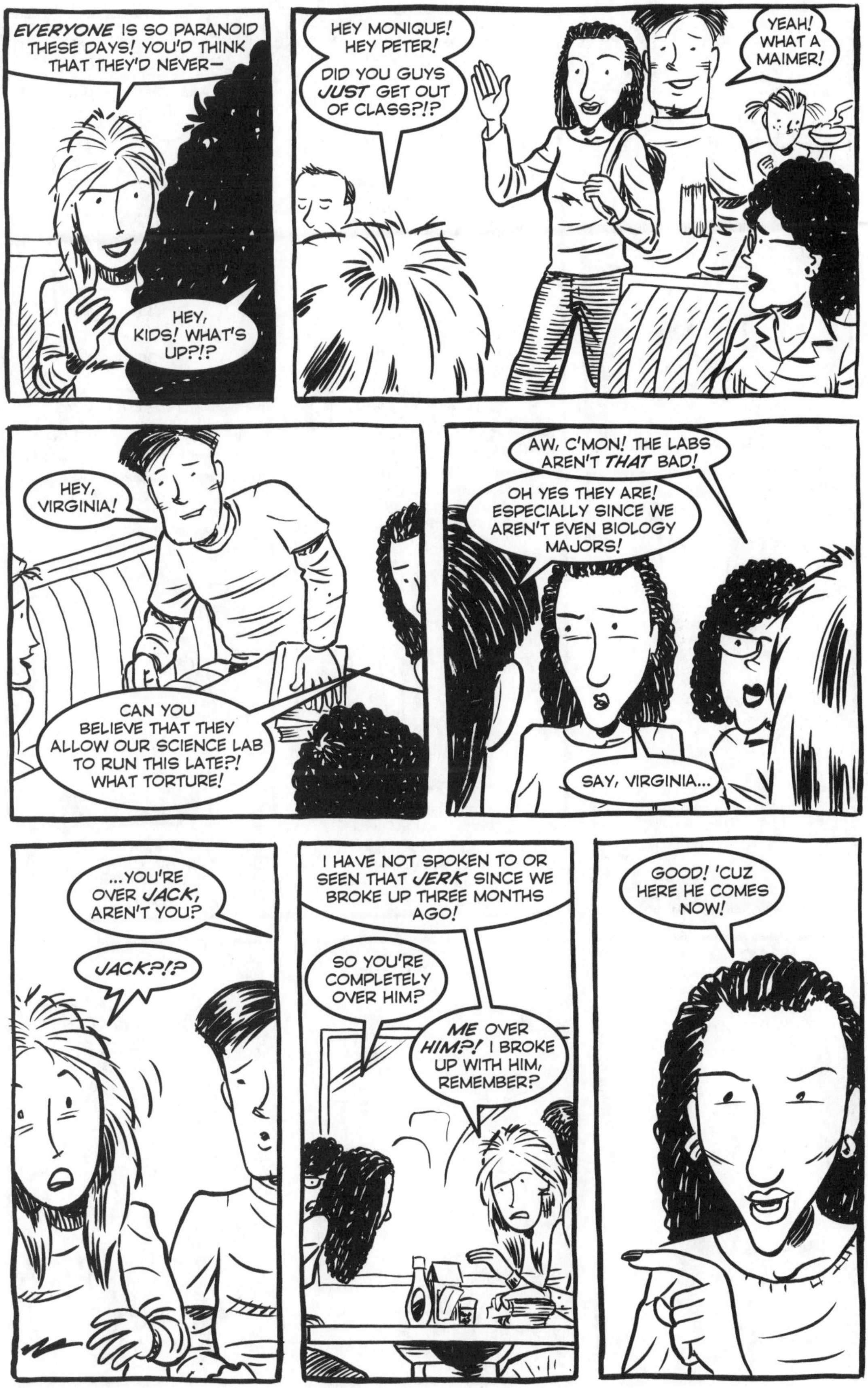

EVERYONE IS SO PARANOID THESE DAYS! YOU'D THINK THAT THEY'D NEVER—
HEY, KIDS! WHAT'S UP?!?
HEY MONIQUE! HEY PETER!
DID YOU GUYS JUST GET OUT OF CLASS?!?
YEAH! WHAT A MAIMER!
HEY, VIRGINIA!
CAN YOU BELIEVE THAT THEY ALLOW OUR SCIENCE LAB TO RUN THIS LATE?! WHAT TORTURE!
AW, C'MON! THE LABS AREN'T THAT BAD!
OH YES THEY ARE! ESPECIALLY SINCE WE AREN'T EVEN BIOLOGY MAJORS!
SAY, VIRGINIA...
...YOU'RE OVER JACK, AREN'T YOU?
JACK?!?
I HAVE NOT SPOKEN TO OR SEEN THAT JERK SINCE WE BROKE UP THREE MONTHS AGO!
SO YOU'RE COMPLETELY OVER HIM?
ME OVER HIM?! I BROKE UP WITH HIM, REMEMBER?
GOOD! 'CUZ HERE HE COMES NOW!

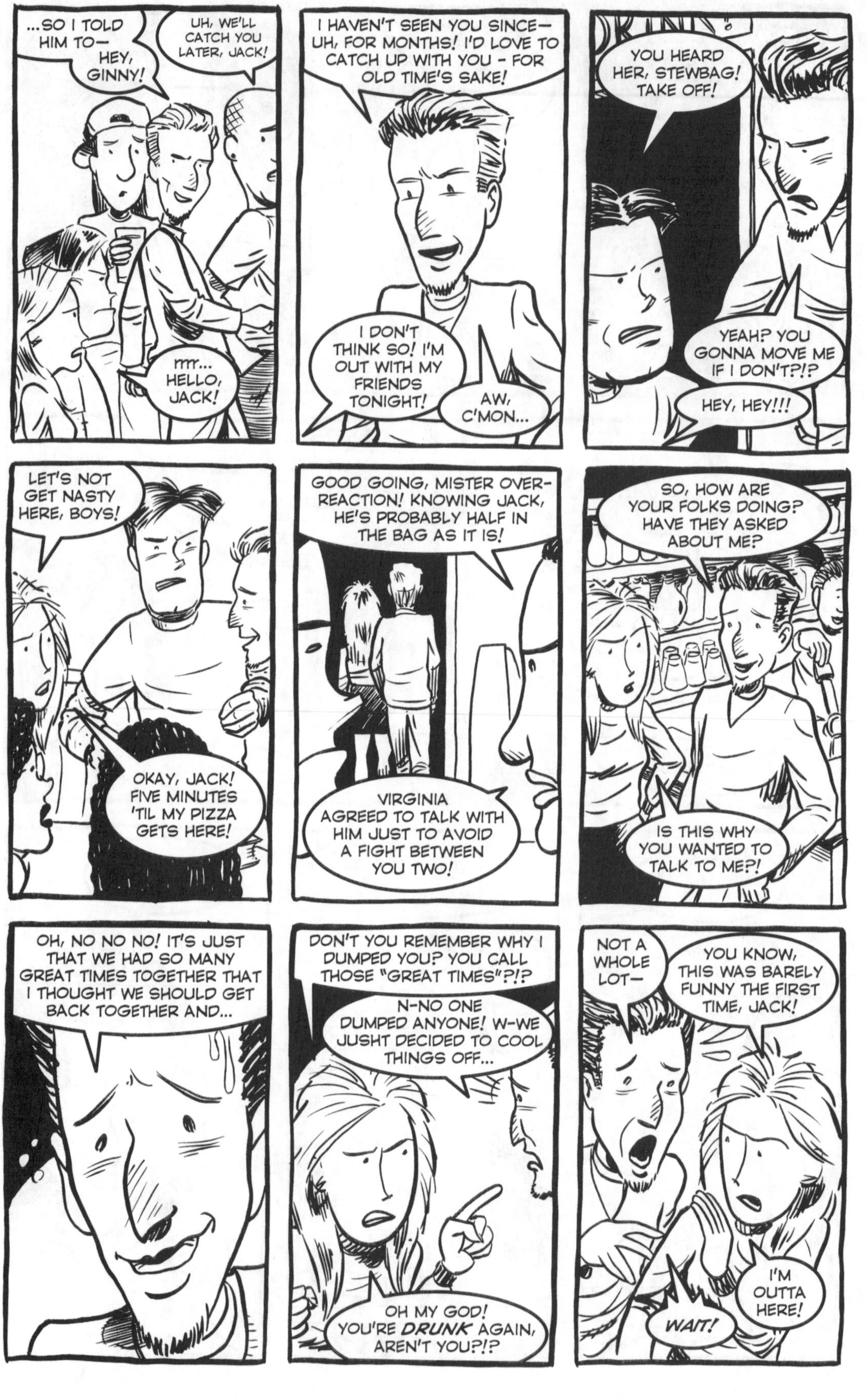
...SO I TOLD HIM TO—
HEY, GINNY!
UH, WE'LL CATCH YOU LATER, JACK!
mrr... HELLO, JACK!
I HAVEN'T SEEN YOU SINCE— UH, FOR MONTHS! I'D LOVE TO CATCH UP WITH YOU - FOR OLD TIME'S SAKE!
I DON'T THINK SO! I'M OUT WITH MY FRIENDS TONIGHT!
AW, C'MON...
YOU HEARD HER, STEWBAG! TAKE OFF!
YEAH? YOU GONNA MOVE ME IF I DON'T?!?
HEY, HEY!!!
LET'S NOT GET NASTY HERE, BOYS!
OKAY, JACK! FIVE MINUTES 'TIL MY PIZZA GETS HERE!
GOOD GOING, MISTER OVER-REACTION! KNOWING JACK, HE'S PROBABLY HALF IN THE BAG AS IT IS!
VIRGINIA AGREED TO TALK WITH HIM JUST TO AVOID A FIGHT BETWEEN YOU TWO!
SO, HOW ARE YOUR FOLKS DOING? HAVE THEY ASKED ABOUT ME?
IS THIS WHY YOU WANTED TO TALK TO ME?!
OH, NO NO NO! IT'S JUST THAT WE HAD SO MANY GREAT TIMES TOGETHER THAT I THOUGHT WE SHOULD GET BACK TOGETHER AND...
DON'T YOU REMEMBER WHY I DUMPED YOU? YOU CALL THOSE "GREAT TIMES"?!?
N-NO ONE DUMPED ANYONE! W-WE JUSHT DECIDED TO COOL THINGS OFF...
OH MY GOD! YOU'RE DRUNK AGAIN, AREN'T YOU?!?
NOT A WHOLE LOT—
YOU KNOW, THIS WAS BARELY FUNNY THE FIRST TIME, JACK!
I'M OUTTA HERE!
WAIT!

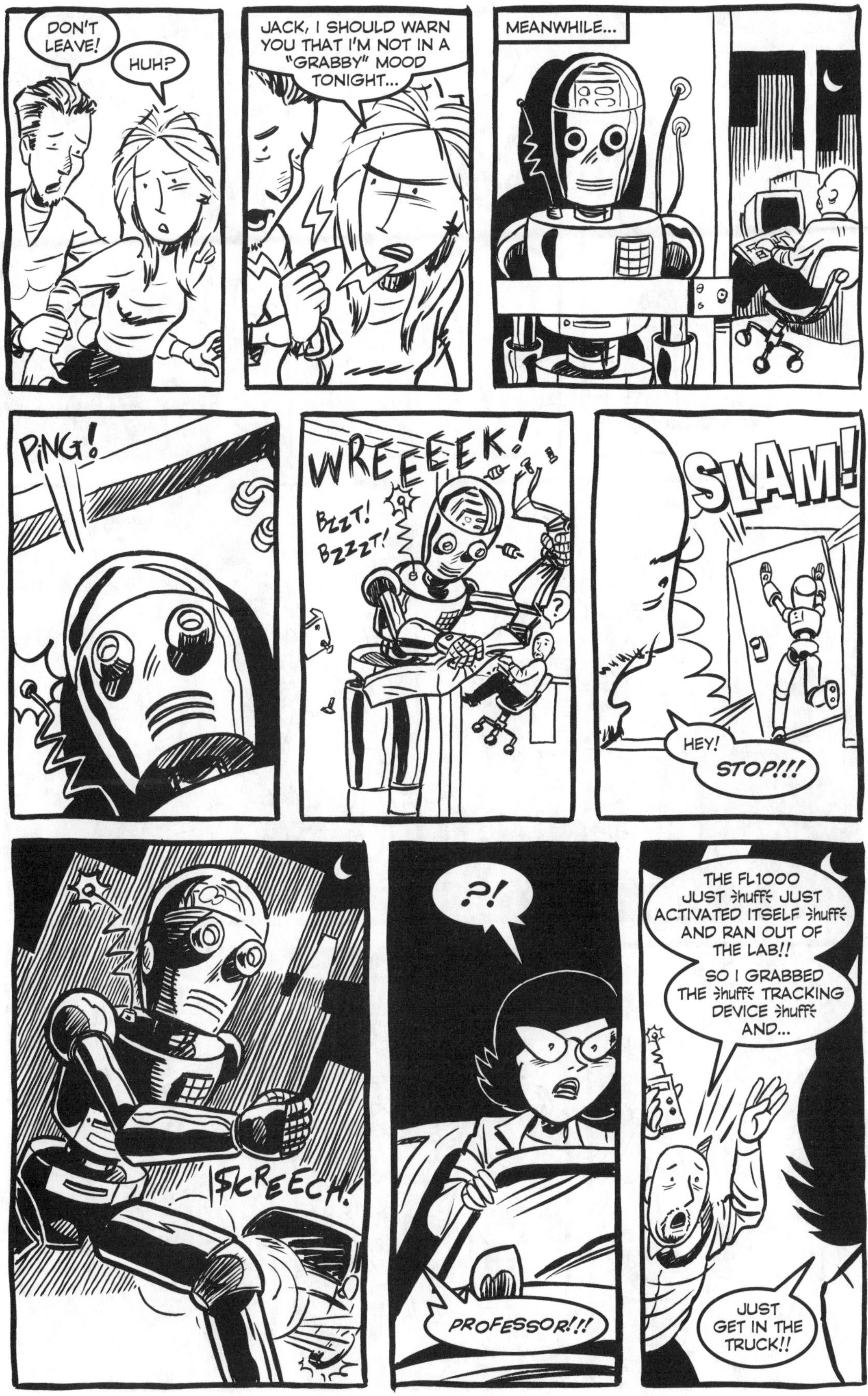

DON'T LEAVE!
HUH?
JACK, I SHOULD WARN YOU THAT I'M NOT IN A "GRABBY" MOOD TONIGHT...
MEANWHILE...
PING!
WREEEEK!
BZZT! BZZZT!
SLAM!
HEY! STOP!!!
SCREECH!
?!
PROFESSOR!!!
THE FL1000 JUST *huff* JUST ACTIVATED ITSELF *huff* AND RAN OUT OF THE LAB!!
SO I GRABBED THE *huff* TRACKING DEVICE *huff* AND...
JUST GET IN THE TRUCK!!

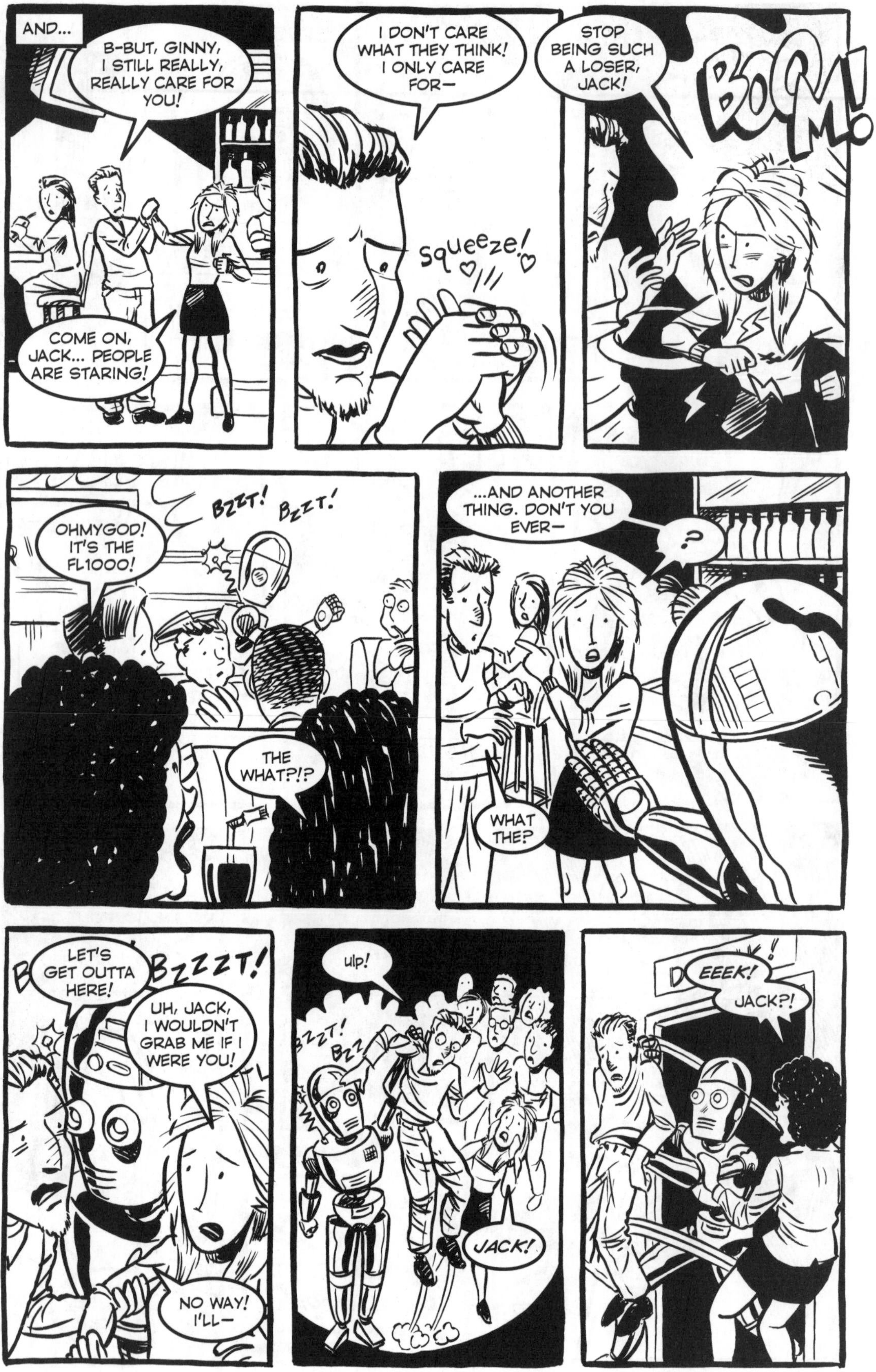

AND...
B-BUT, GINNY, I STILL REALLY, REALLY CARE FOR YOU!
COME ON, JACK... PEOPLE ARE STARING!
I DON'T CARE WHAT THEY THINK! I ONLY CARE FOR—
squeeze!
STOP BEING SUCH A LOSER, JACK!
BOOM!
BZZT! BZZT!
OHMYGOD! IT'S THE FL1000!
THE WHAT?!?
...AND ANOTHER THING. DON'T YOU EVER—
?
WHAT THE?
LET'S GET OUTTA HERE!
BZZZT!
UH, JACK, I WOULDN'T GRAB ME IF I WERE YOU!
NO WAY! I'LL—
ulp!
BZZT! BZZ
JACK!
EEEK! JACK?!

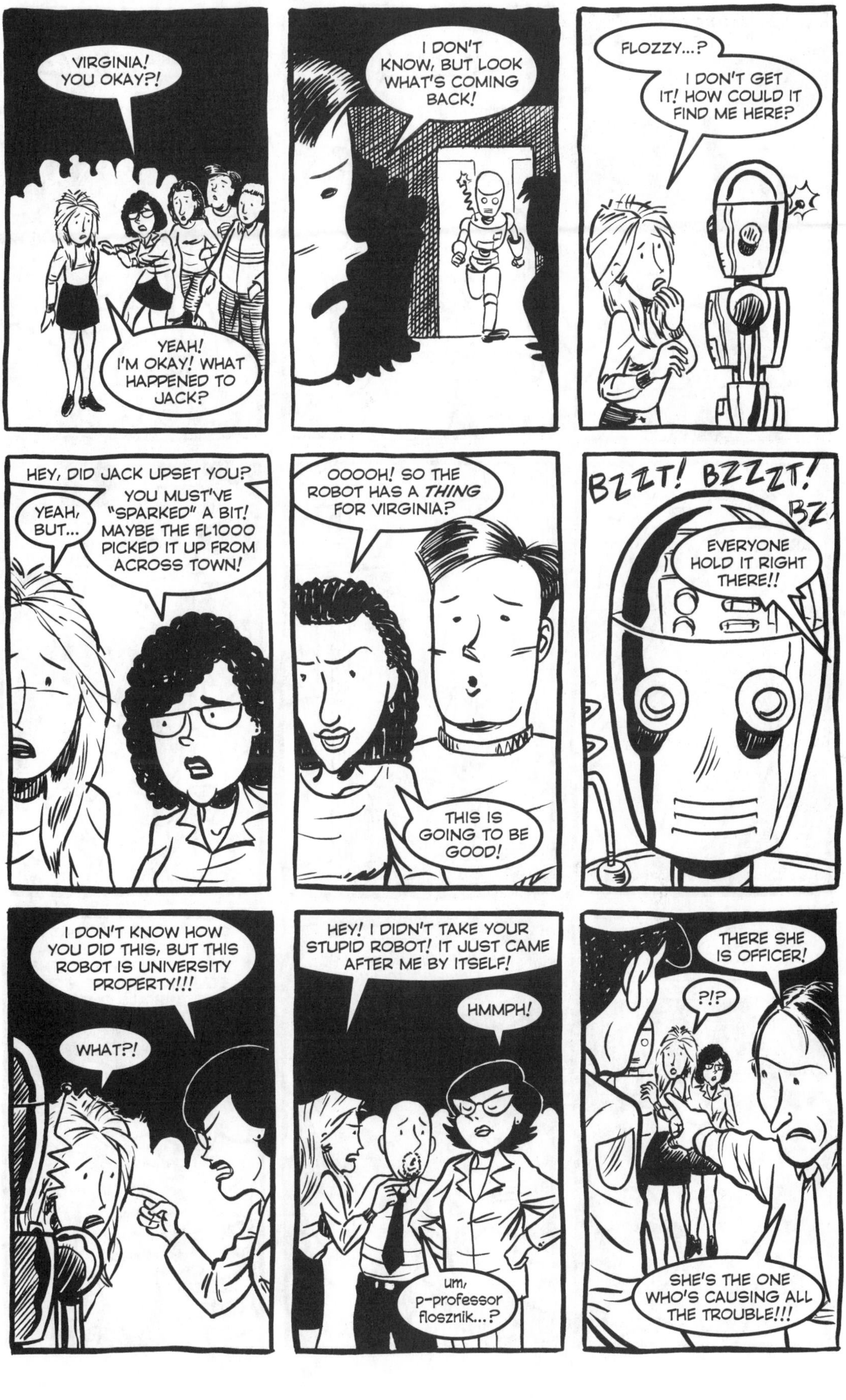
VIRGINIA! YOU OKAY?!
YEAH! I'M OKAY! WHAT HAPPENED TO JACK?
I DON'T KNOW, BUT LOOK WHAT'S COMING BACK!
FLOZZY...?
I DON'T GET IT! HOW COULD IT FIND ME HERE?
HEY, DID JACK UPSET YOU?
YEAH, BUT...
YOU MUST'VE "SPARKED" A BIT! MAYBE THE FL1000 PICKED IT UP FROM ACROSS TOWN!
OOOOH! SO THE ROBOT HAS A *THING* FOR VIRGINIA?
THIS IS GOING TO BE GOOD!
BZZT! BZZZT!
EVERYONE HOLD IT RIGHT THERE!!
I DON'T KNOW HOW YOU DID THIS, BUT THIS ROBOT IS UNIVERSITY PROPERTY!!!
WHAT?!
HEY! I DIDN'T TAKE YOUR STUPID ROBOT! IT JUST CAME AFTER ME BY ITSELF!
HMMPH!
um, p-professor flosznik...?
THERE SHE IS OFFICER!
?!?
SHE'S THE ONE WHO'S CAUSING ALL THE TROUBLE!!!

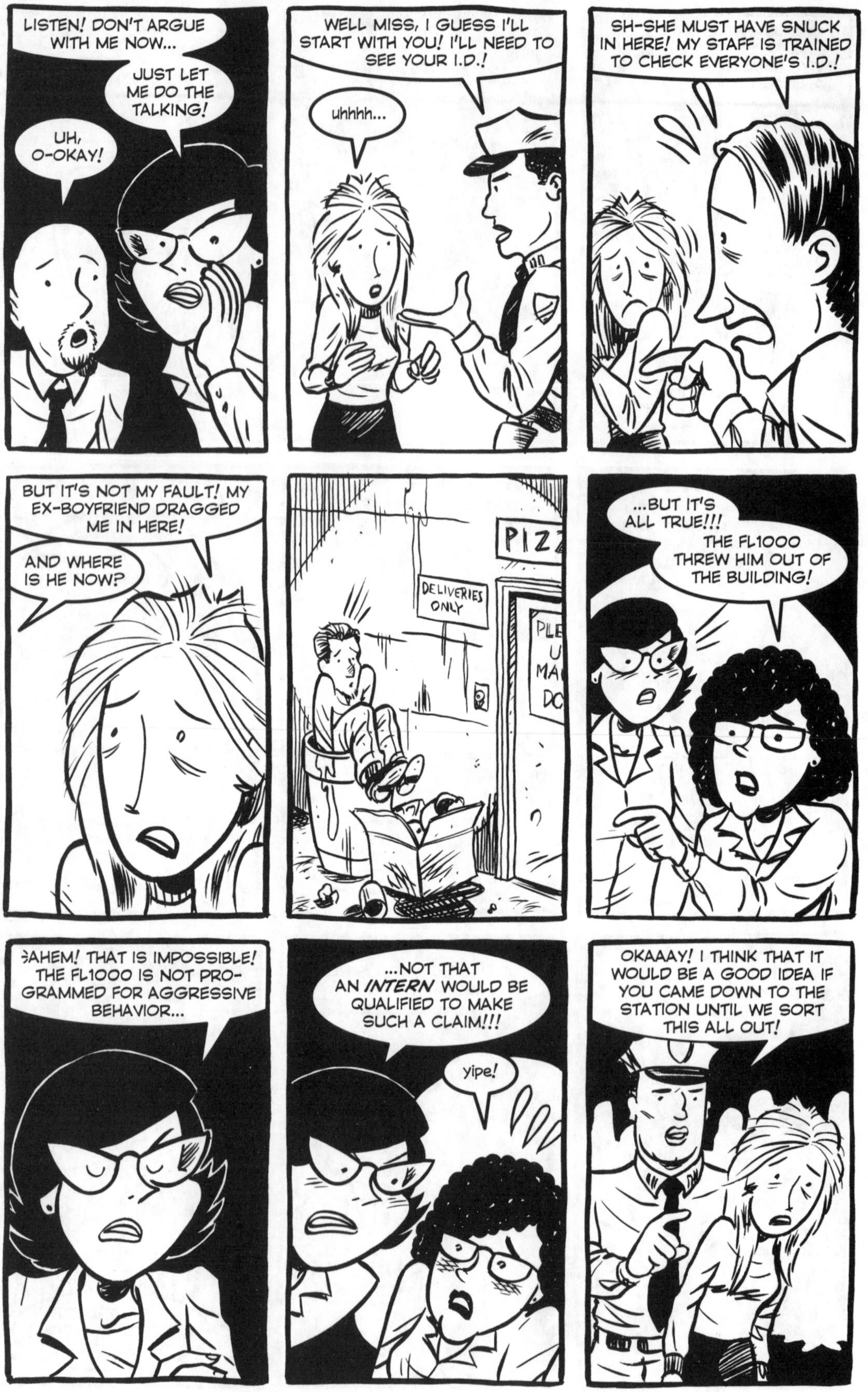
LISTEN! DON'T ARGUE WITH ME NOW...
JUST LET ME DO THE TALKING!
UH, O-OKAY!
WELL MISS, I GUESS I'LL START WITH YOU! I'LL NEED TO SEE YOUR I.D.!
uhhhh...
SH-SHE MUST HAVE SNUCK IN HERE! MY STAFF IS TRAINED TO CHECK EVERYONE'S I.D.!
BUT IT'S NOT MY FAULT! MY EX-BOYFRIEND DRAGGED ME IN HERE!
AND WHERE IS HE NOW?
DELIVERIES ONLY
...BUT IT'S ALL TRUE!!!
THE FL1000 THREW HIM OUT OF THE BUILDING!
AHEM! THAT IS IMPOSSIBLE! THE FL1000 IS NOT PRO-GRAMMED FOR AGGRESSIVE BEHAVIOR...
...NOT THAT AN INTERN WOULD BE QUALIFIED TO MAKE SUCH A CLAIM!!!
yipe!
OKAAAY! I THINK THAT IT WOULD BE A GOOD IDEA IF YOU CAME DOWN TO THE STATION UNTIL WE SORT THIS ALL OUT!

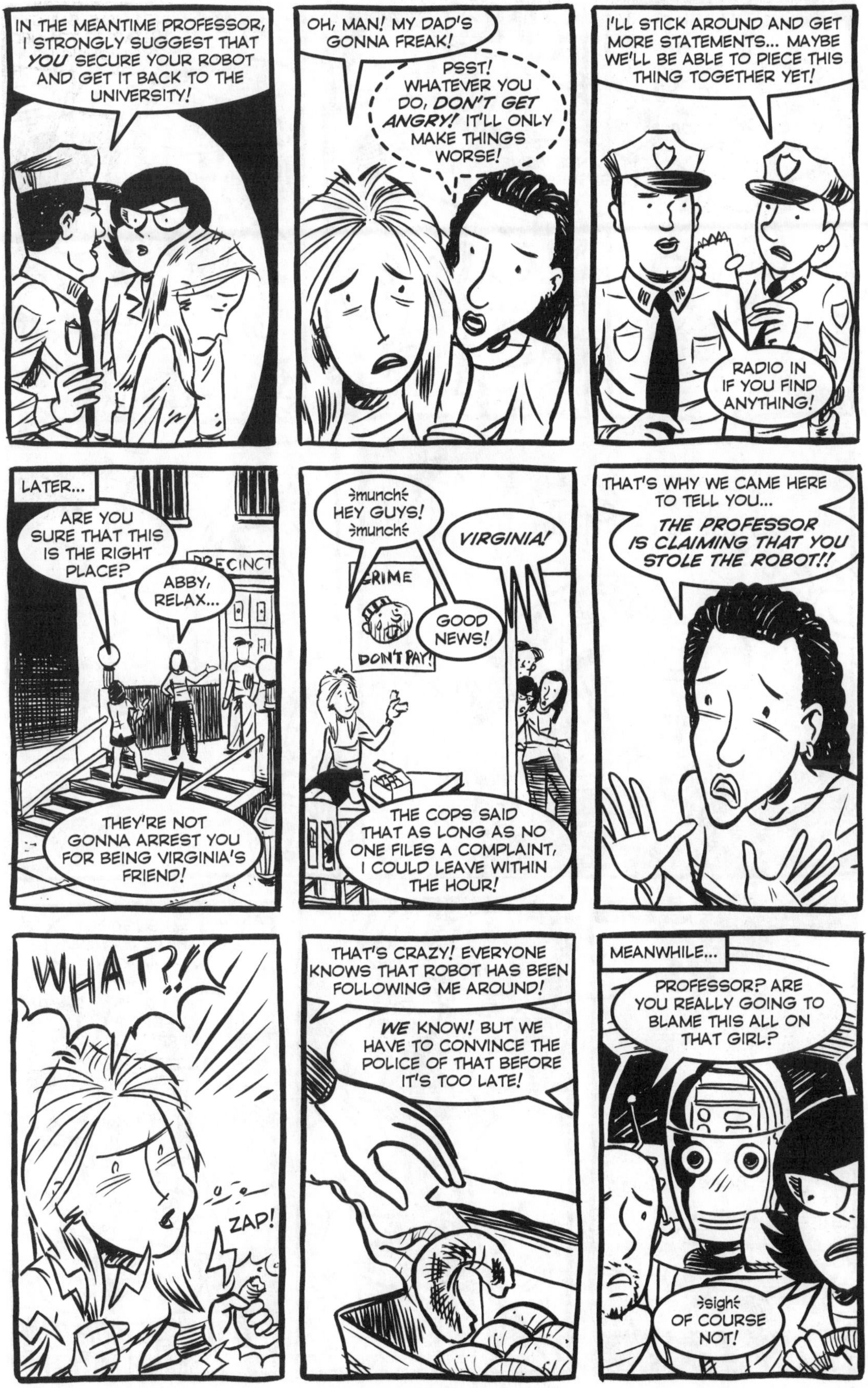
IN THE MEANTIME PROFESSOR, I STRONGLY SUGGEST THAT YOU SECURE YOUR ROBOT AND GET IT BACK TO THE UNIVERSITY!
OH, MAN! MY DAD'S GONNA FREAK!
PSST! WHATEVER YOU DO, DON'T GET ANGRY! IT'LL ONLY MAKE THINGS WORSE!
I'LL STICK AROUND AND GET MORE STATEMENTS... MAYBE WE'LL BE ABLE TO PIECE THIS THING TOGETHER YET!
RADIO IN IF YOU FIND ANYTHING!
LATER...
ARE YOU SURE THAT THIS IS THE RIGHT PLACE?
PRECINCT
ABBY, RELAX...
THEY'RE NOT GONNA ARREST YOU FOR BEING VIRGINIA'S FRIEND!
munch HEY GUYS! munch
VIRGINIA!
CRIME
DON'T PAY!
GOOD NEWS!
THE COPS SAID THAT AS LONG AS NO ONE FILES A COMPLAINT, I COULD LEAVE WITHIN THE HOUR!
THAT'S WHY WE CAME HERE TO TELL YOU... THE PROFESSOR IS CLAIMING THAT YOU STOLE THE ROBOT!!
WHAT?!
ZAP!
THAT'S CRAZY! EVERYONE KNOWS THAT ROBOT HAS BEEN FOLLOWING ME AROUND!
WE KNOW! BUT WE HAVE TO CONVINCE THE POLICE OF THAT BEFORE IT'S TOO LATE!
MEANWHILE...
PROFESSOR? ARE YOU REALLY GOING TO BLAME THIS ALL ON THAT GIRL?
sigh OF COURSE NOT!

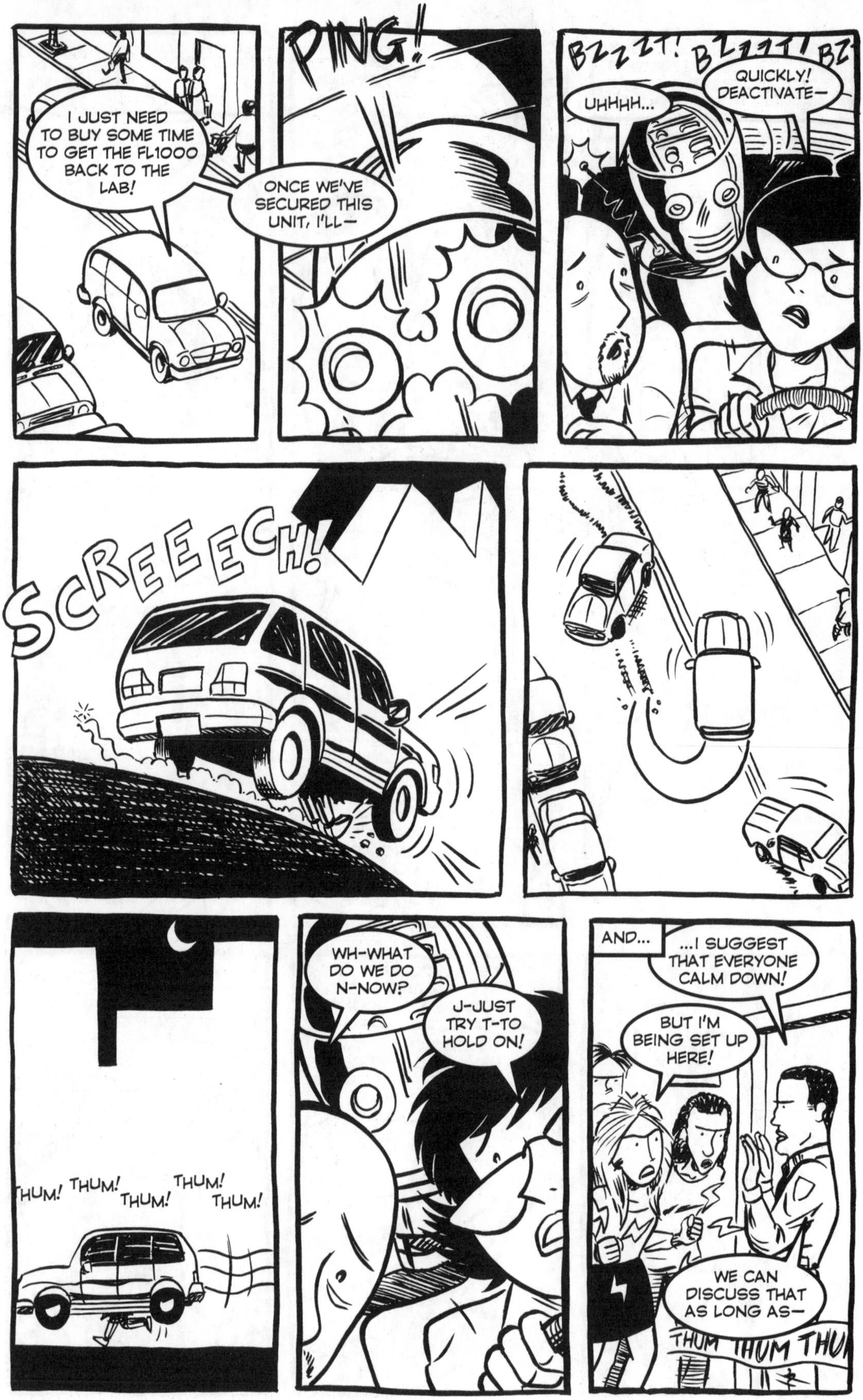
I JUST NEED TO BUY SOME TIME TO GET THE FL1000 BACK TO THE LAB!
PING!
ONCE WE'VE SECURED THIS UNIT, I'LL—
UHHHH...
QUICKLY! DEACTIVATE—
SCREEECH!
THUM! THUM! THUM! THUM! THUM!
WH-WHAT DO WE DO N-NOW?
J-JUST TRY T-TO HOLD ON!
AND...
...I SUGGEST THAT EVERYONE CALM DOWN!
BUT I'M BEING SET UP HERE!
WE CAN DISCUSS THAT AS LONG AS—
THUM THUM THUM

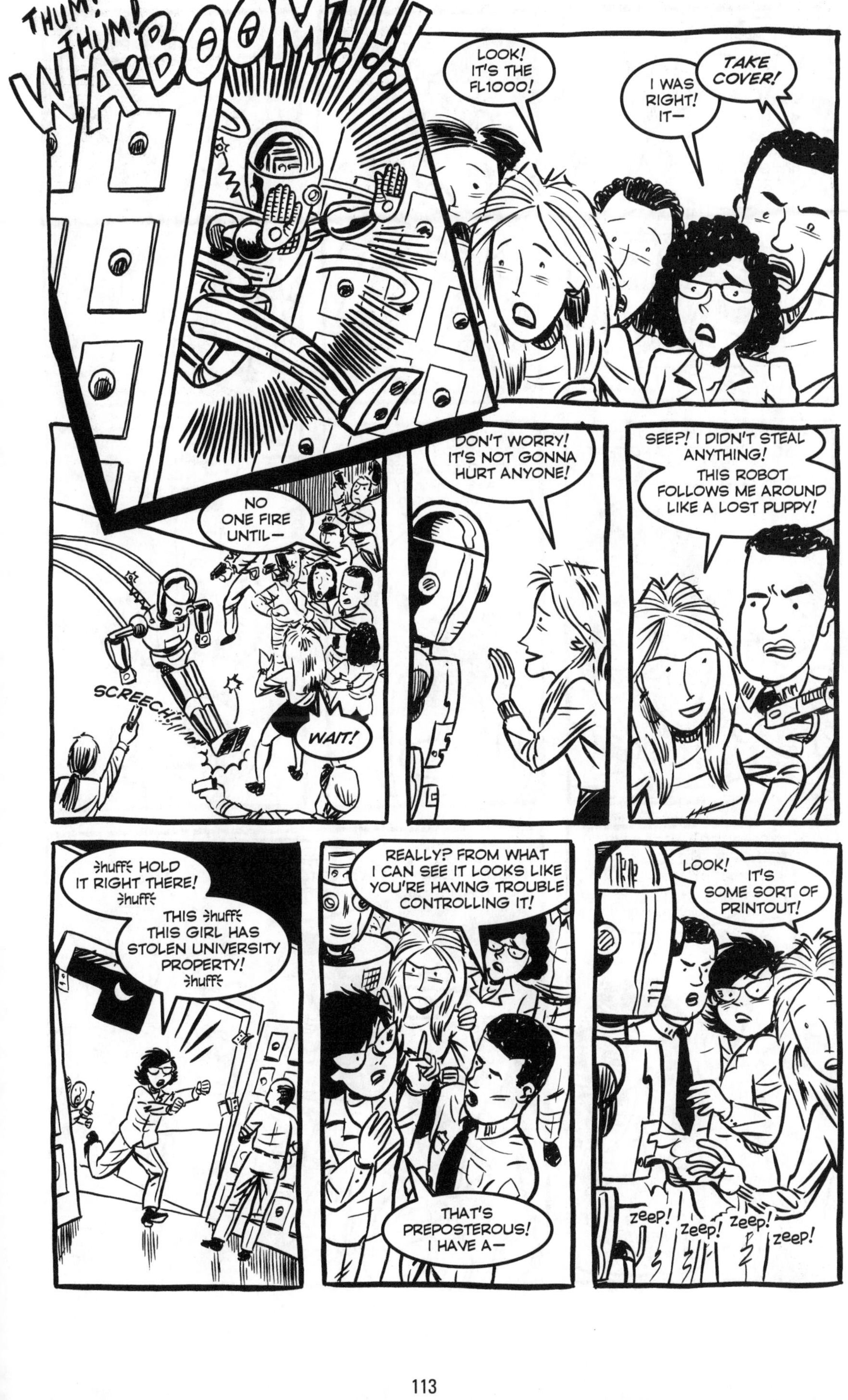
THUM! THUM!
WA-BOOM!!!!
LOOK! IT'S THE FL1000!
I WAS RIGHT! IT—
TAKE COVER!
NO ONE FIRE UNTIL—
SCREECH!
WAIT!
DON'T WORRY! IT'S NOT GONNA HURT ANYONE!
SEE?! I DIDN'T STEAL ANYTHING!
THIS ROBOT FOLLOWS ME AROUND LIKE A LOST PUPPY!
huff HOLD IT RIGHT THERE! *huff*
THIS *huff* THIS GIRL HAS STOLEN UNIVERSITY PROPERTY! *huff*
REALLY? FROM WHAT I CAN SEE IT LOOKS LIKE YOU'RE HAVING TROUBLE CONTROLLING IT!
THAT'S PREPOSTEROUS! I HAVE A—
LOOK!
IT'S SOME SORT OF PRINTOUT!
zeep! zeep! zeep! zeep!

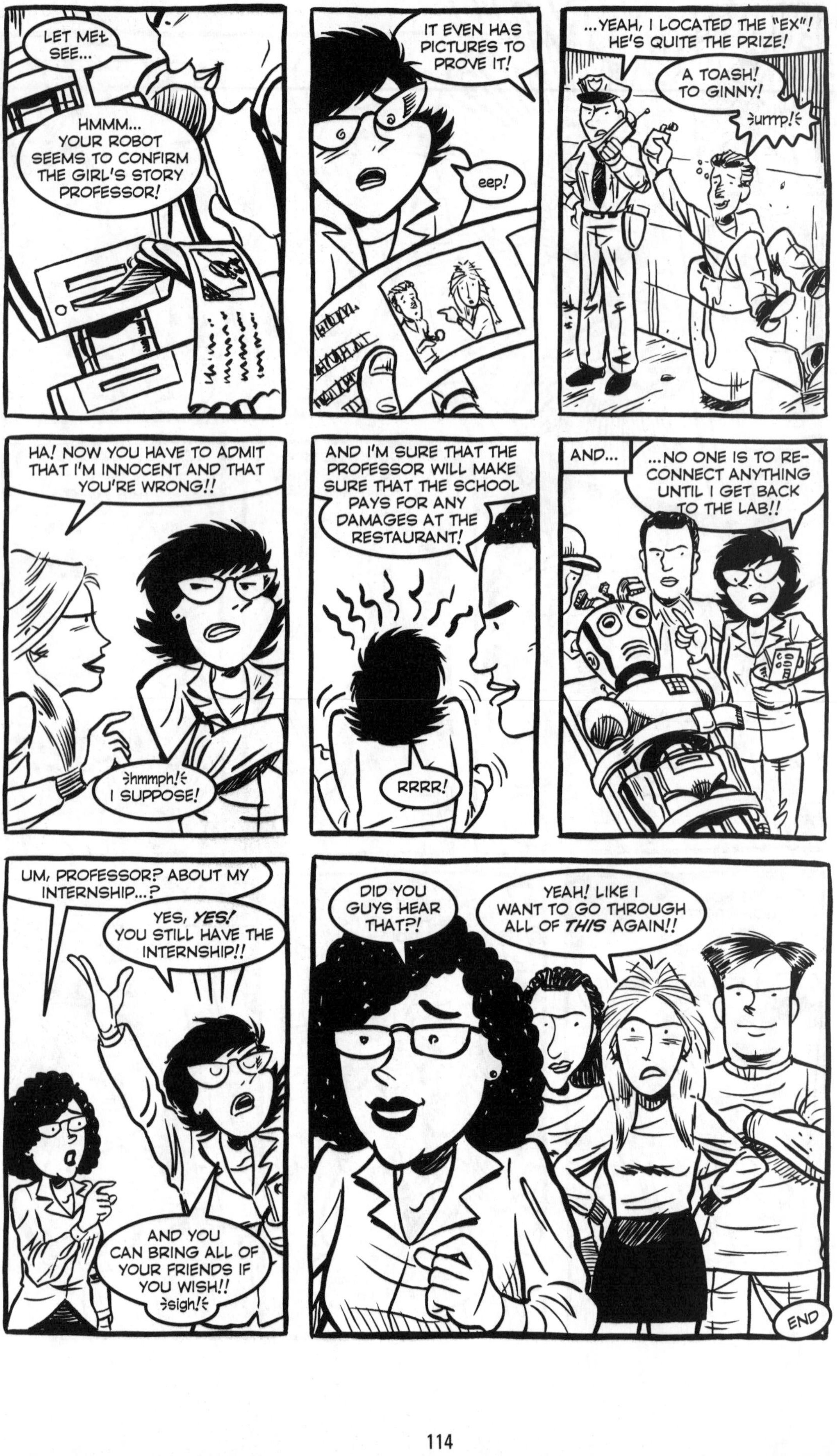
LET ME SEE...
HMMM... YOUR ROBOT SEEMS TO CONFIRM THE GIRL'S STORY PROFESSOR!
IT EVEN HAS PICTURES TO PROVE IT!
eep!
...YEAH, I LOCATED THE "EX"! HE'S QUITE THE PRIZE!
A TOASH! TO GINNY!
urrrp!
HA! NOW YOU HAVE TO ADMIT THAT I'M INNOCENT AND THAT YOU'RE WRONG!!
hmmph! I SUPPOSE!
AND I'M SURE THAT THE PROFESSOR WILL MAKE SURE THAT THE SCHOOL PAYS FOR ANY DAMAGES AT THE RESTAURANT!
RRRR!
AND...
...NO ONE IS TO RE-CONNECT ANYTHING UNTIL I GET BACK TO THE LAB!!
UM, PROFESSOR? ABOUT MY INTERNSHIP...?
YES, YES! YOU STILL HAVE THE INTERNSHIP!!
AND YOU CAN BRING ALL OF YOUR FRIENDS IF YOU WISH!! sigh!
DID YOU GUYS HEAR THAT?!
YEAH! LIKE I WANT TO GO THROUGH ALL OF THIS AGAIN!!
END

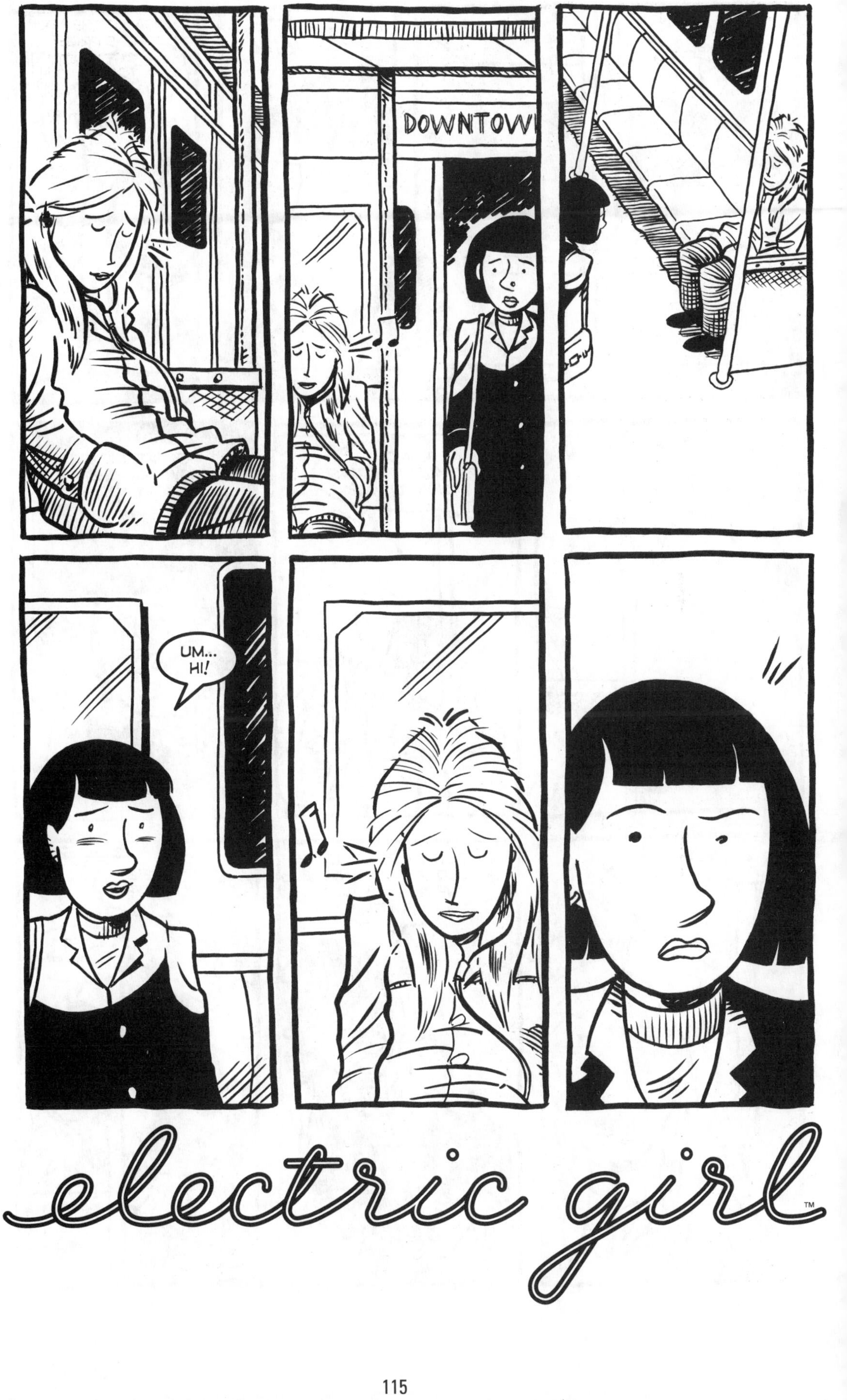
DOWNTOWN
UM... HI!

electric girl™

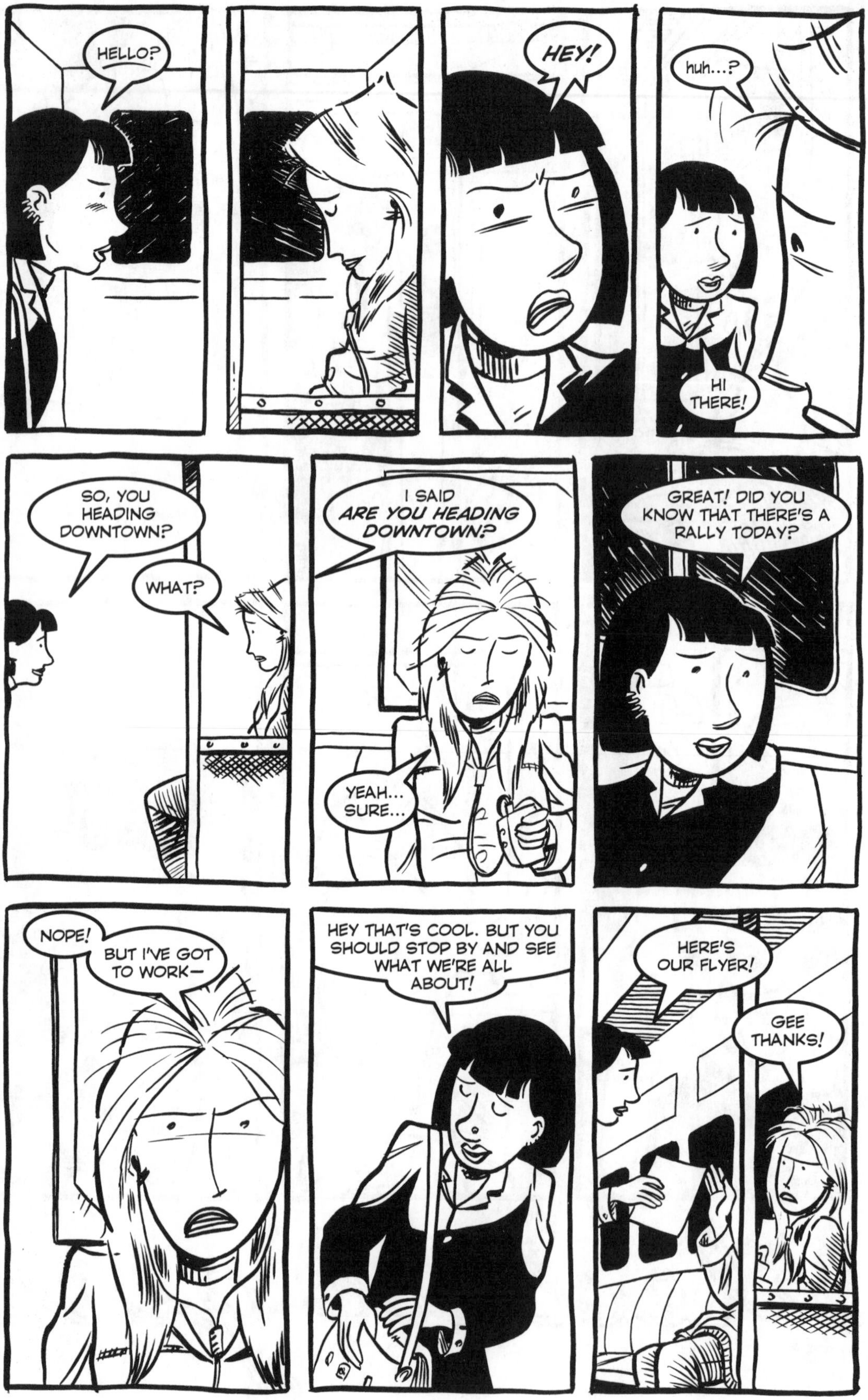
HELLO?
HEY!
huh...?
HI THERE!
SO, YOU HEADING DOWNTOWN?
WHAT?
I SAID *ARE YOU HEADING DOWNTOWN?*
YEAH... SURE...
GREAT! DID YOU KNOW THAT THERE'S A RALLY TODAY?
NOPE!
BUT I'VE GOT TO WORK—
HEY THAT'S COOL. BUT YOU SHOULD STOP BY AND SEE WHAT WE'RE ALL ABOUT!
HERE'S OUR FLYER!
GEE THANKS!

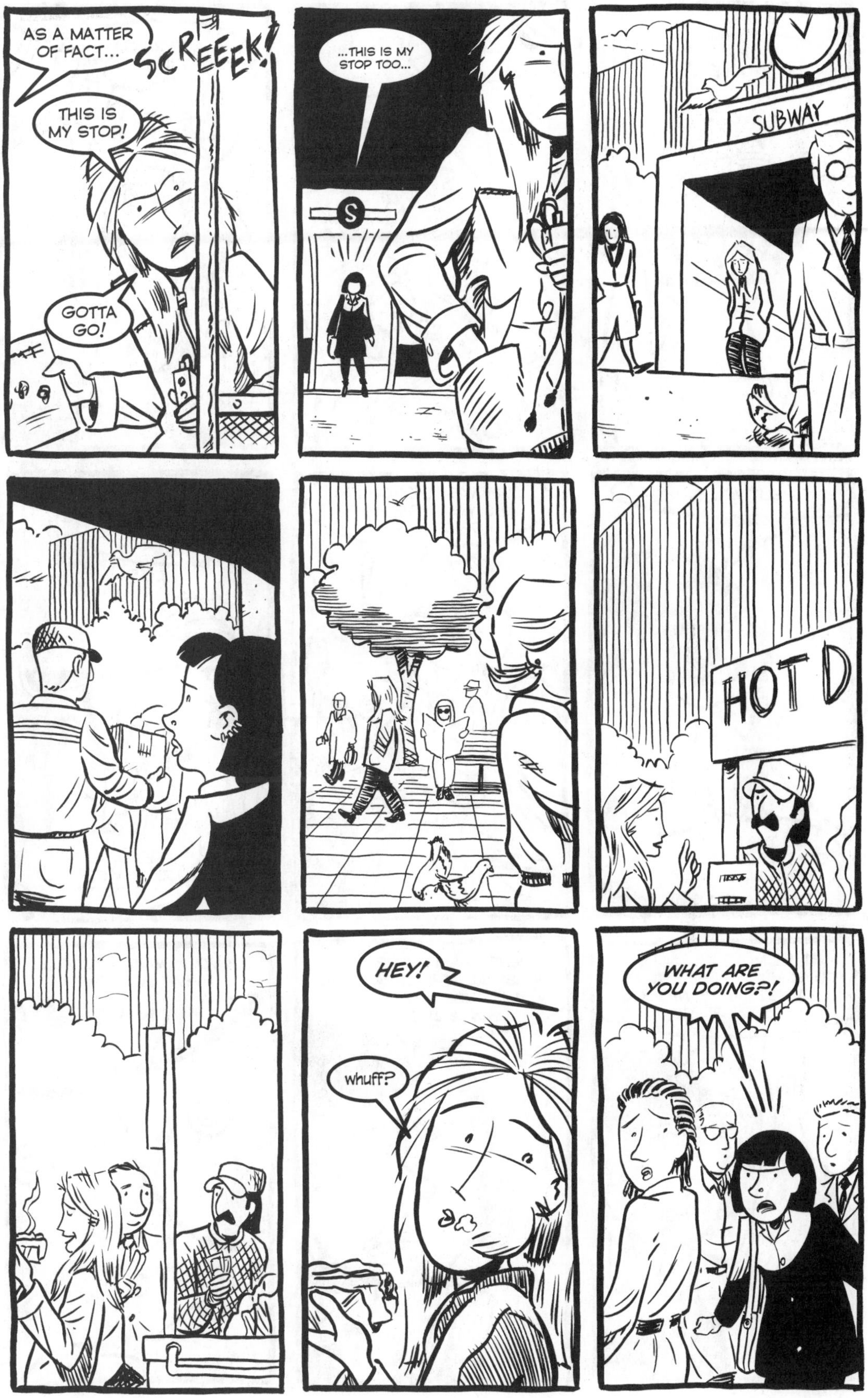
AS A MATTER OF FACT...
SCREEEK!
THIS IS MY STOP!
GOTTA GO!
...THIS IS MY STOP TOO...
S
SUBWAY
HOT D
HEY!
whuff?
WHAT ARE YOU DOING?!

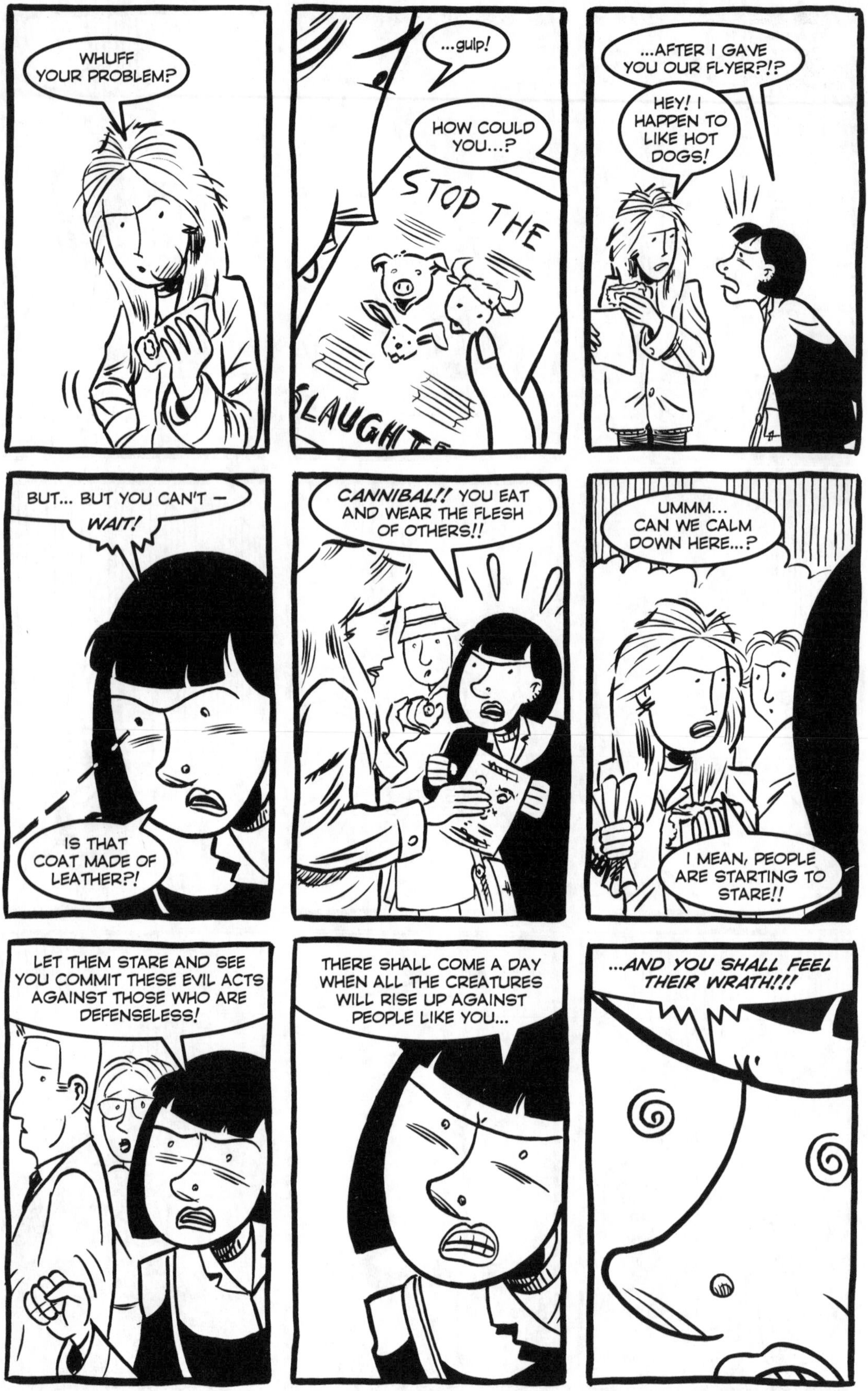
WHUFF YOUR PROBLEM?
...gulp!
HOW COULD YOU...?
STOP THE
SLAUGHT
...AFTER I GAVE YOU OUR FLYER?!?
HEY! I HAPPEN TO LIKE HOT DOGS!
BUT... BUT YOU CAN'T — WAIT!
IS THAT COAT MADE OF LEATHER?!
CANNIBAL!! YOU EAT AND WEAR THE FLESH OF OTHERS!!
UMMM... CAN WE CALM DOWN HERE...?
I MEAN, PEOPLE ARE STARTING TO STARE!!
LET THEM STARE AND SEE YOU COMMIT THESE EVIL ACTS AGAINST THOSE WHO ARE DEFENSELESS!
THERE SHALL COME A DAY WHEN ALL THE CREATURES WILL RISE UP AGAINST PEOPLE LIKE YOU...
...AND YOU SHALL FEEL THEIR WRATH!!!

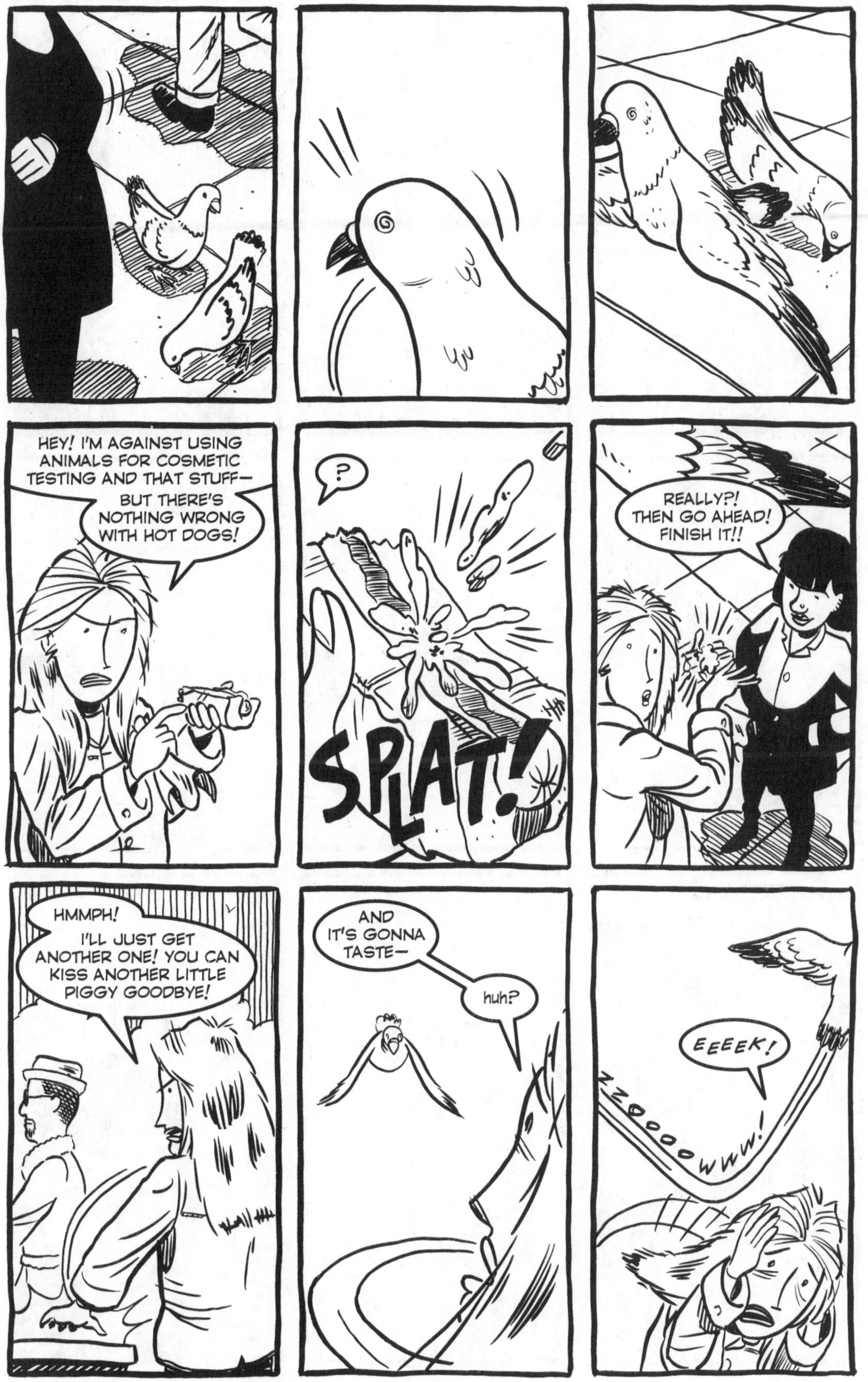
HEY! I'M AGAINST USING ANIMALS FOR COSMETIC TESTING AND THAT STUFF—
BUT THERE'S NOTHING WRONG WITH HOT DOGS!
?
SPLAT!
REALLY?! THEN GO AHEAD! FINISH IT!!
HMMPH!
I'LL JUST GET ANOTHER ONE! YOU CAN KISS ANOTHER LITTLE PIGGY GOODBYE!
AND IT'S GONNA TASTE—
huh?
EEEEK!
ZZOOOOOWWW!

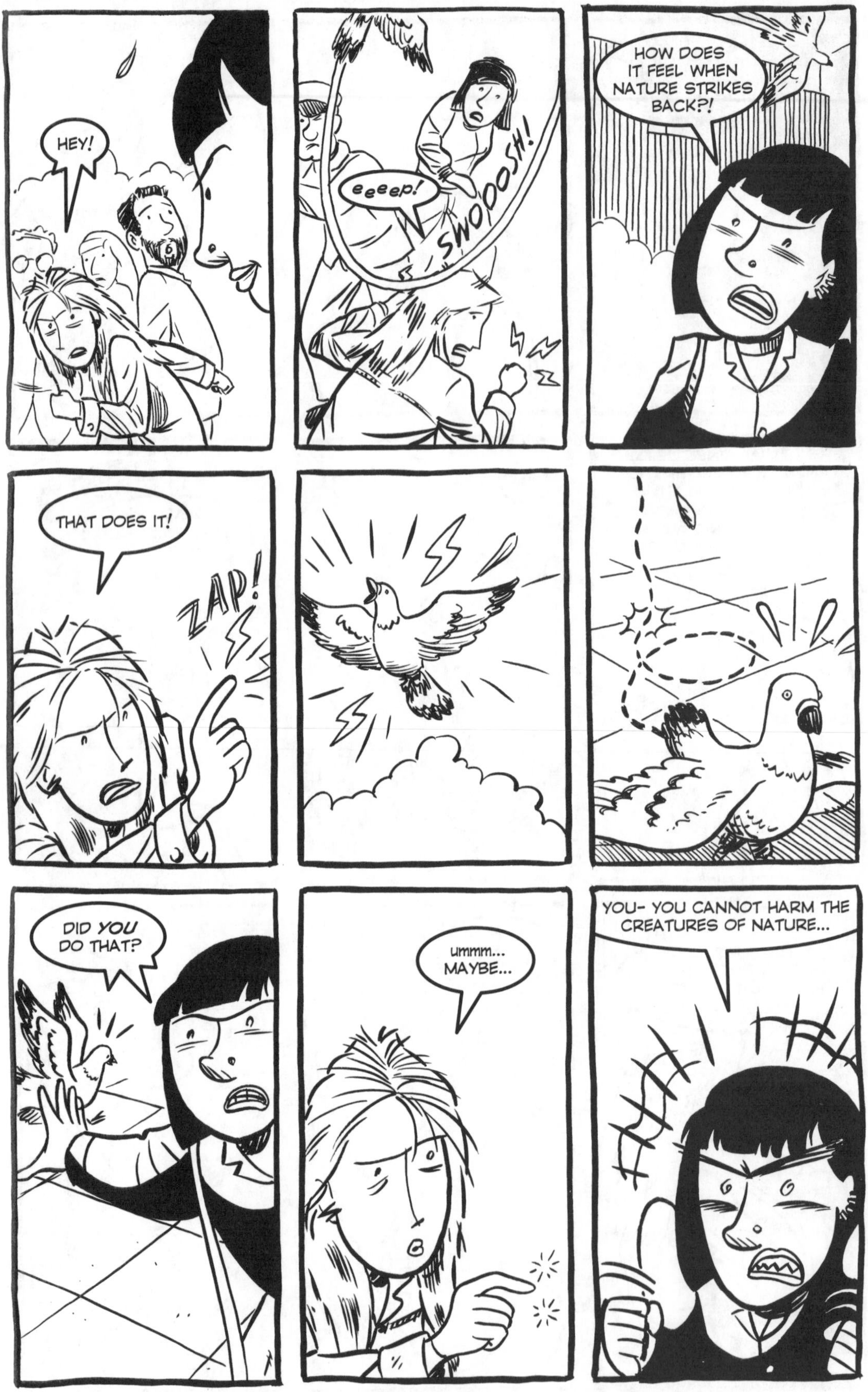

HEY!
eeeep!
SWOOOSH!
HOW DOES IT FEEL WHEN NATURE STRIKES BACK?!
THAT DOES IT!
ZAP!
DID YOU DO THAT?
ummm... MAYBE...
YOU- YOU CANNOT HARM THE CREATURES OF NATURE...

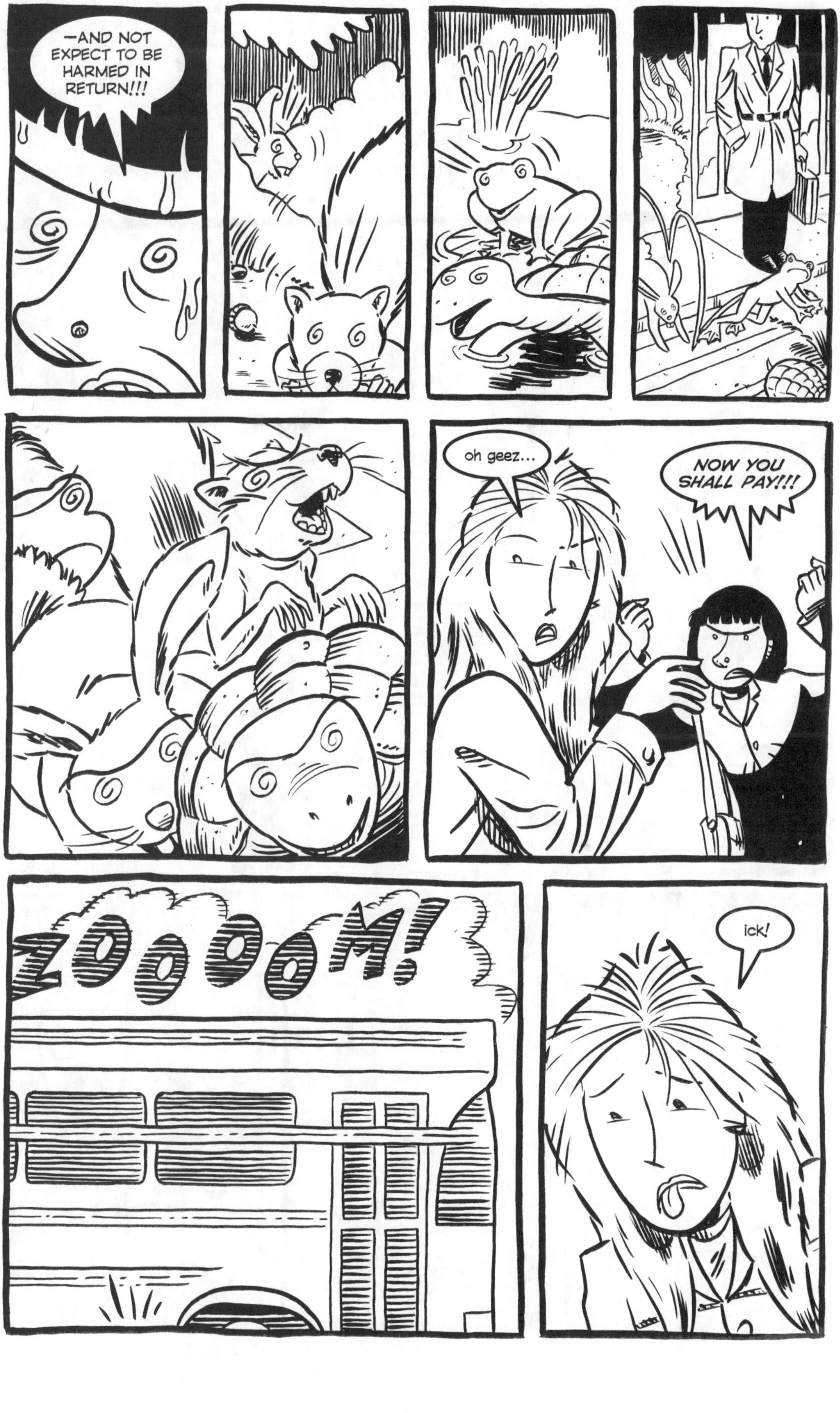
—AND NOT EXPECT TO BE HARMED IN RETURN!!!
oh geez...
NOW YOU SHALL PAY!!!
ZOOOOM!
ick!

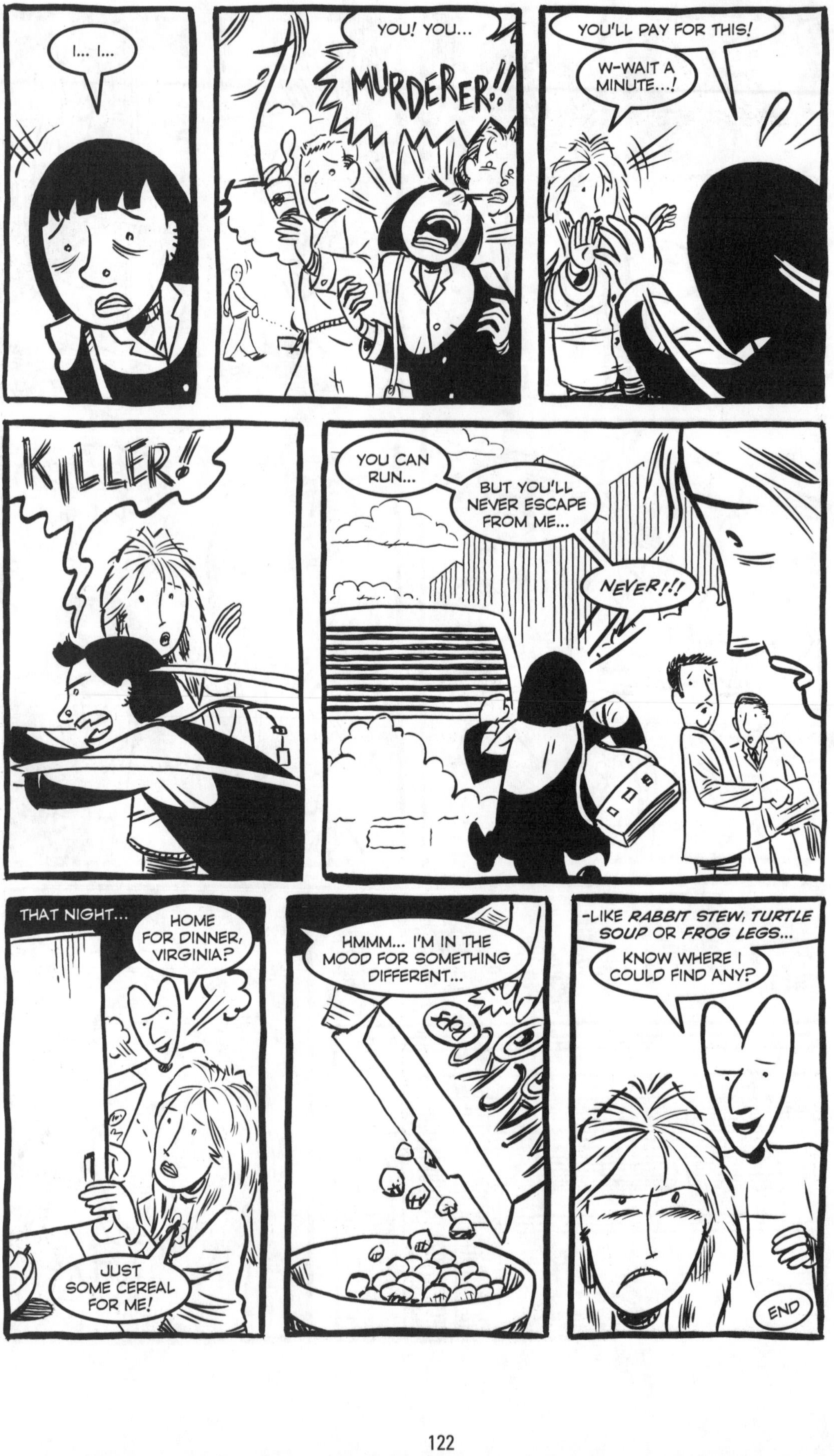

I... I...
YOU! YOU...
MURDERER!!
YOU'LL PAY FOR THIS!
W-WAIT A MINUTE...!
KILLER!
YOU CAN RUN...
BUT YOU'LL NEVER ESCAPE FROM ME...
NEVER!!!
THAT NIGHT...
HOME FOR DINNER, VIRGINIA?
JUST SOME CEREAL FOR ME!
HMMM... I'M IN THE MOOD FOR SOMETHING DIFFERENT...
-LIKE RABBIT STEW, TURTLE SOUP OR FROG LEGS...
KNOW WHERE I COULD FIND ANY?
END

electric girl™

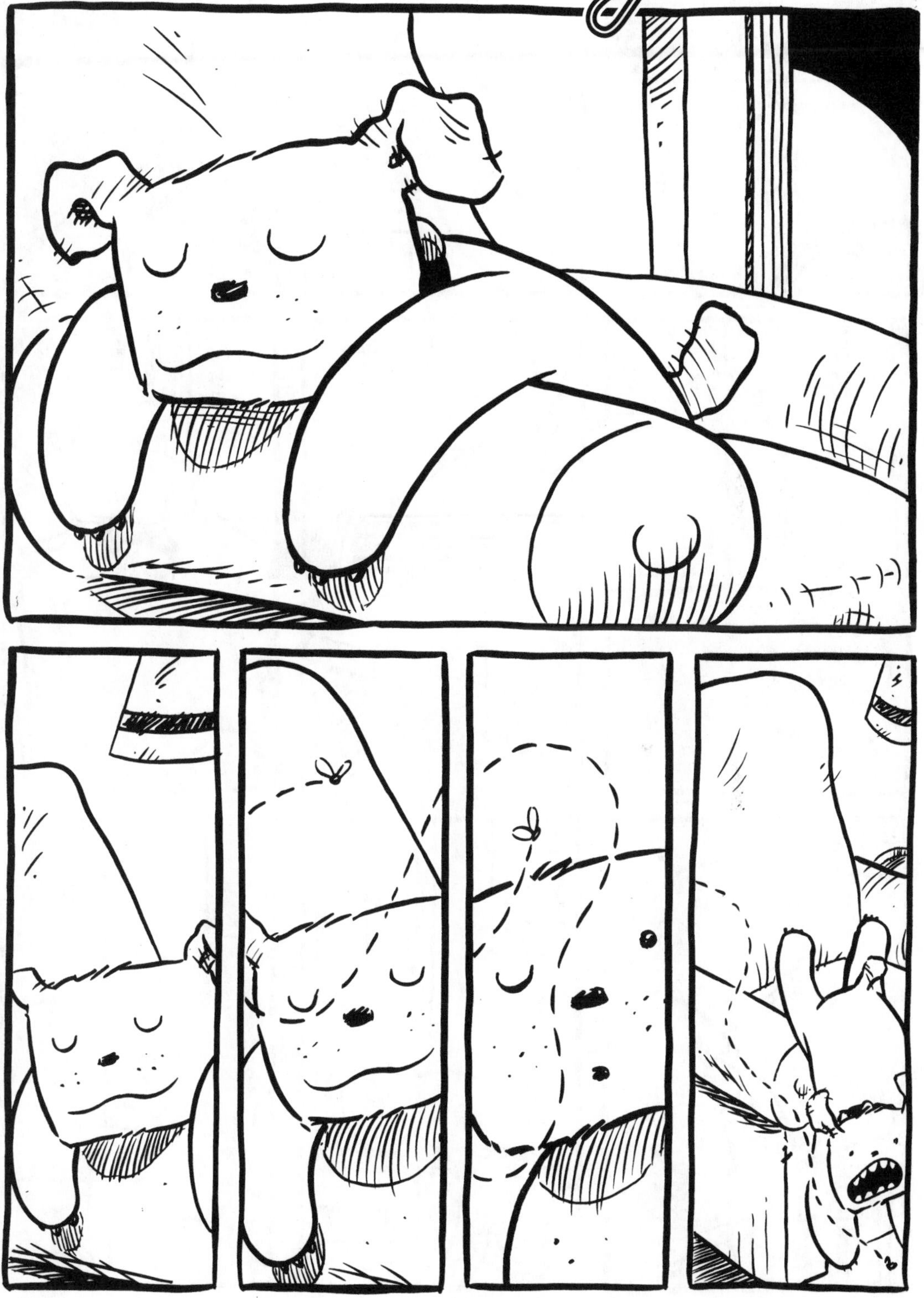

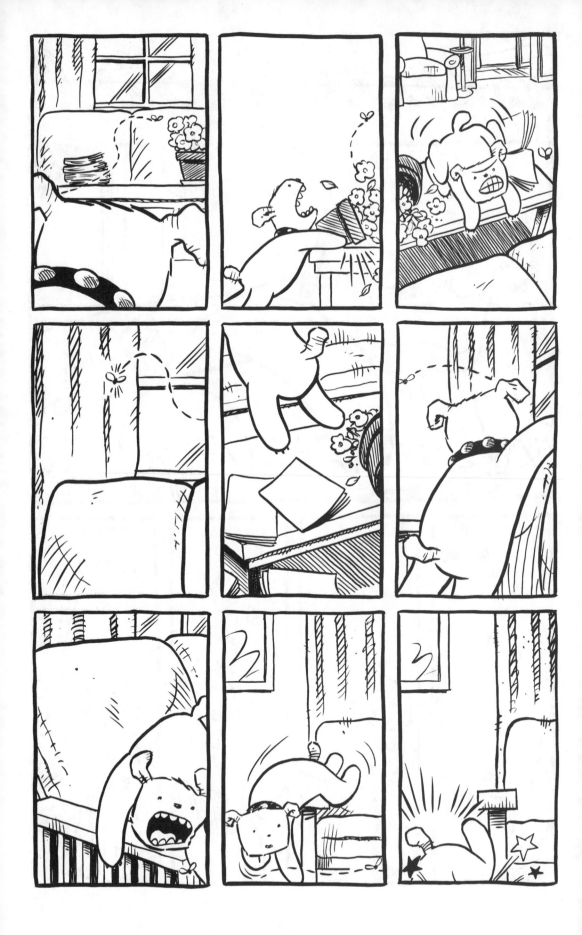

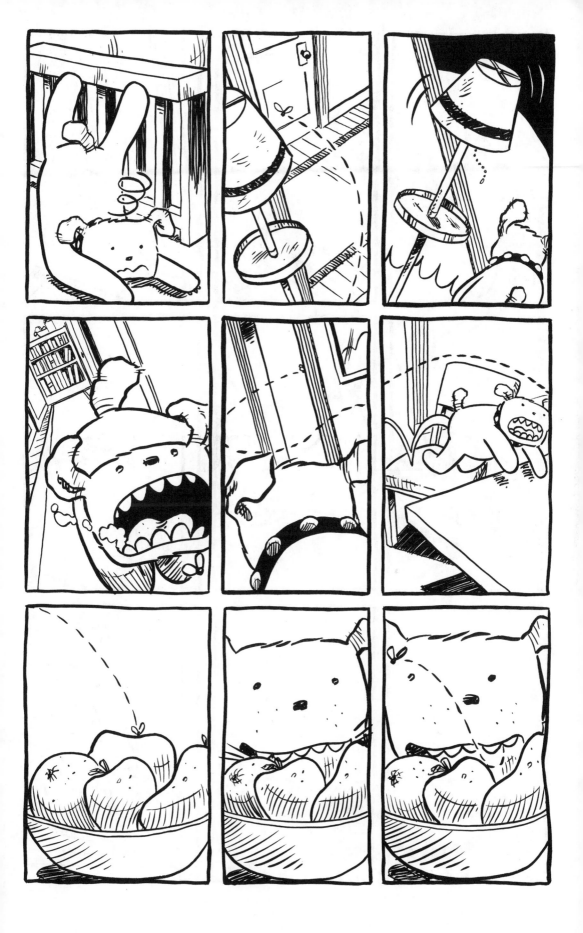

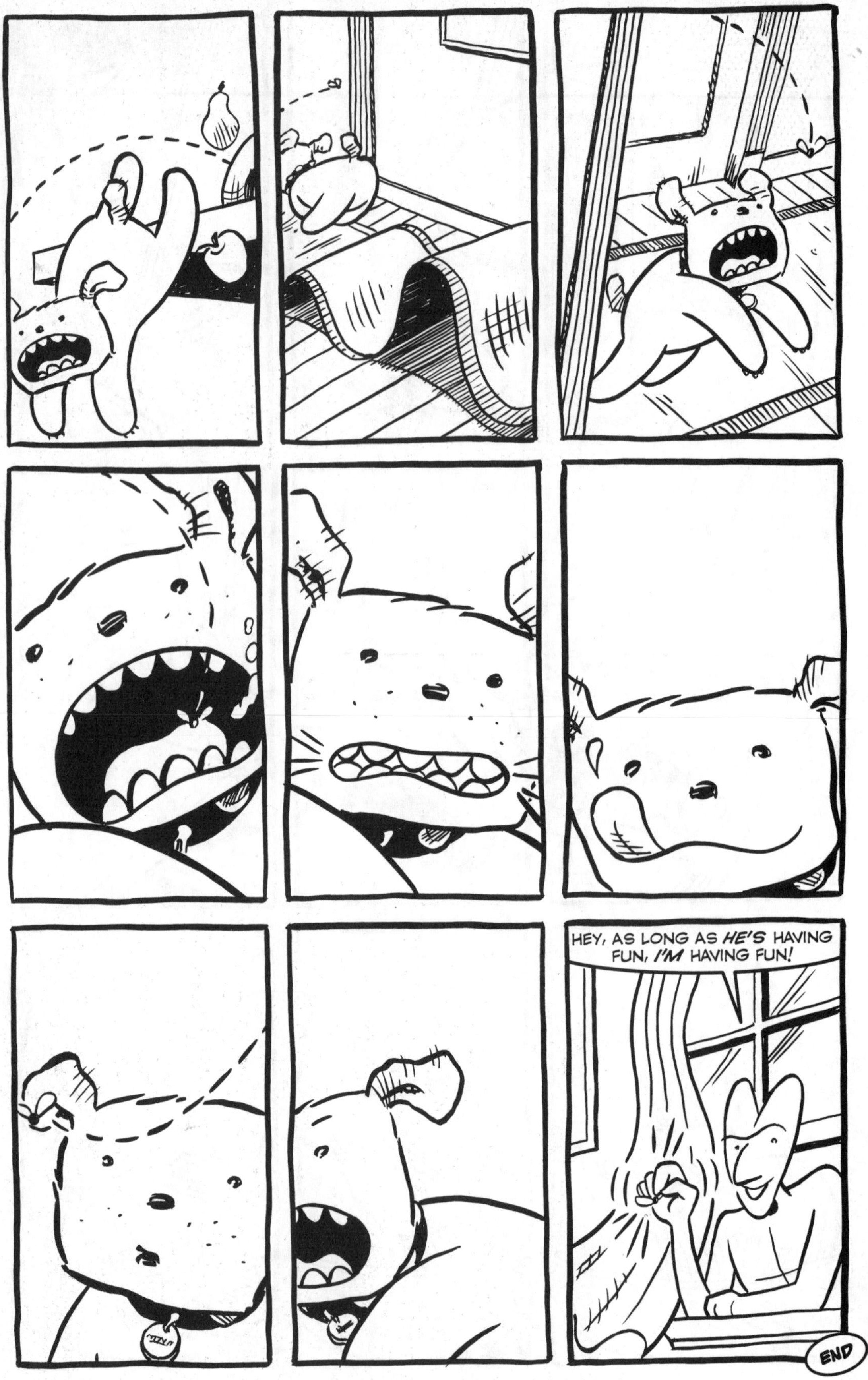
HEY, AS LONG AS *HE'S* HAVING FUN, *I'M* HAVING FUN!
END

electric girl issue ④

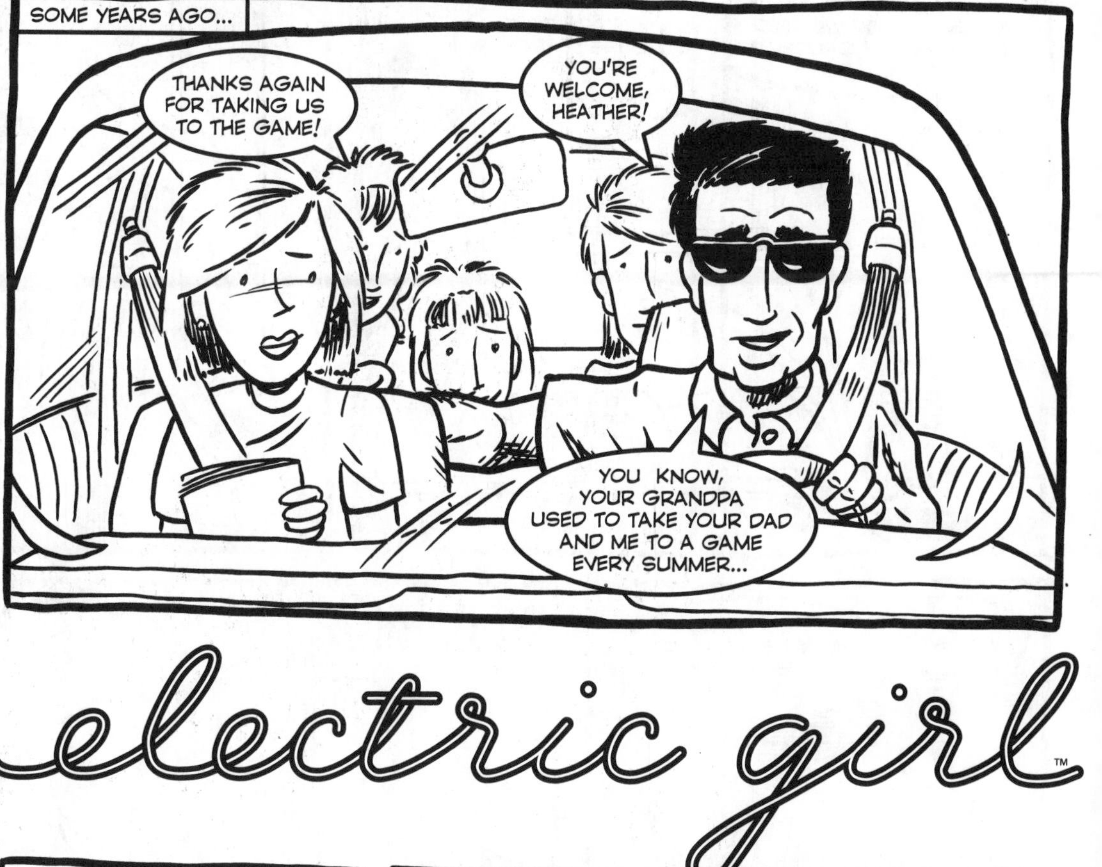
SOME YEARS AGO...
THANKS AGAIN FOR TAKING US TO THE GAME!
YOU'RE WELCOME, HEATHER!
YOU KNOW, YOUR GRANDPA USED TO TAKE YOUR DAD AND ME TO A GAME EVERY SUMMER...

electric girl™

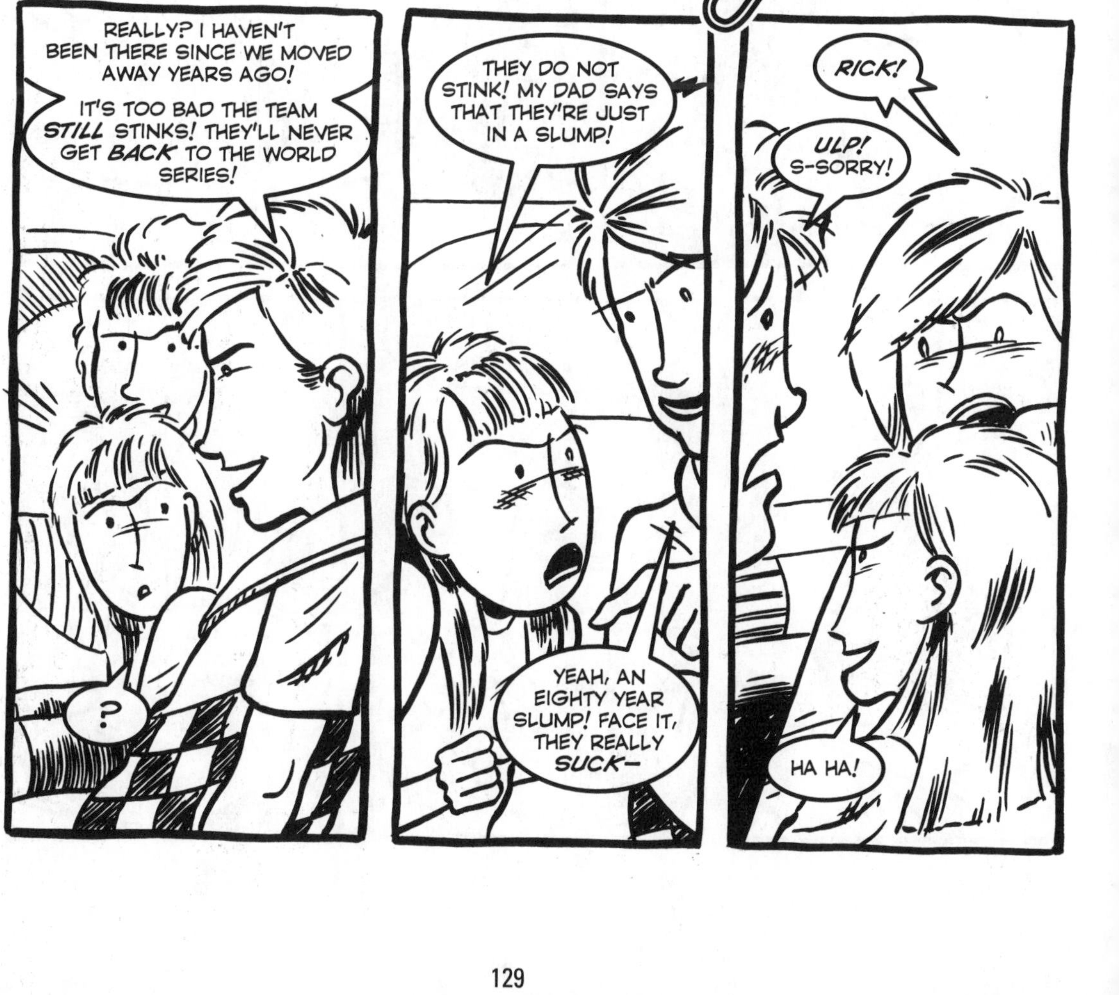
REALLY? I HAVEN'T BEEN THERE SINCE WE MOVED AWAY YEARS AGO!
IT'S TOO BAD THE TEAM STILL STINKS! THEY'LL NEVER GET BACK TO THE WORLD SERIES!
?
THEY DO NOT STINK! MY DAD SAYS THAT THEY'RE JUST IN A SLUMP!
YEAH, AN EIGHTY YEAR SLUMP! FACE IT, THEY REALLY SUCK–
RICK!
ULP! S-SORRY!
HA HA!

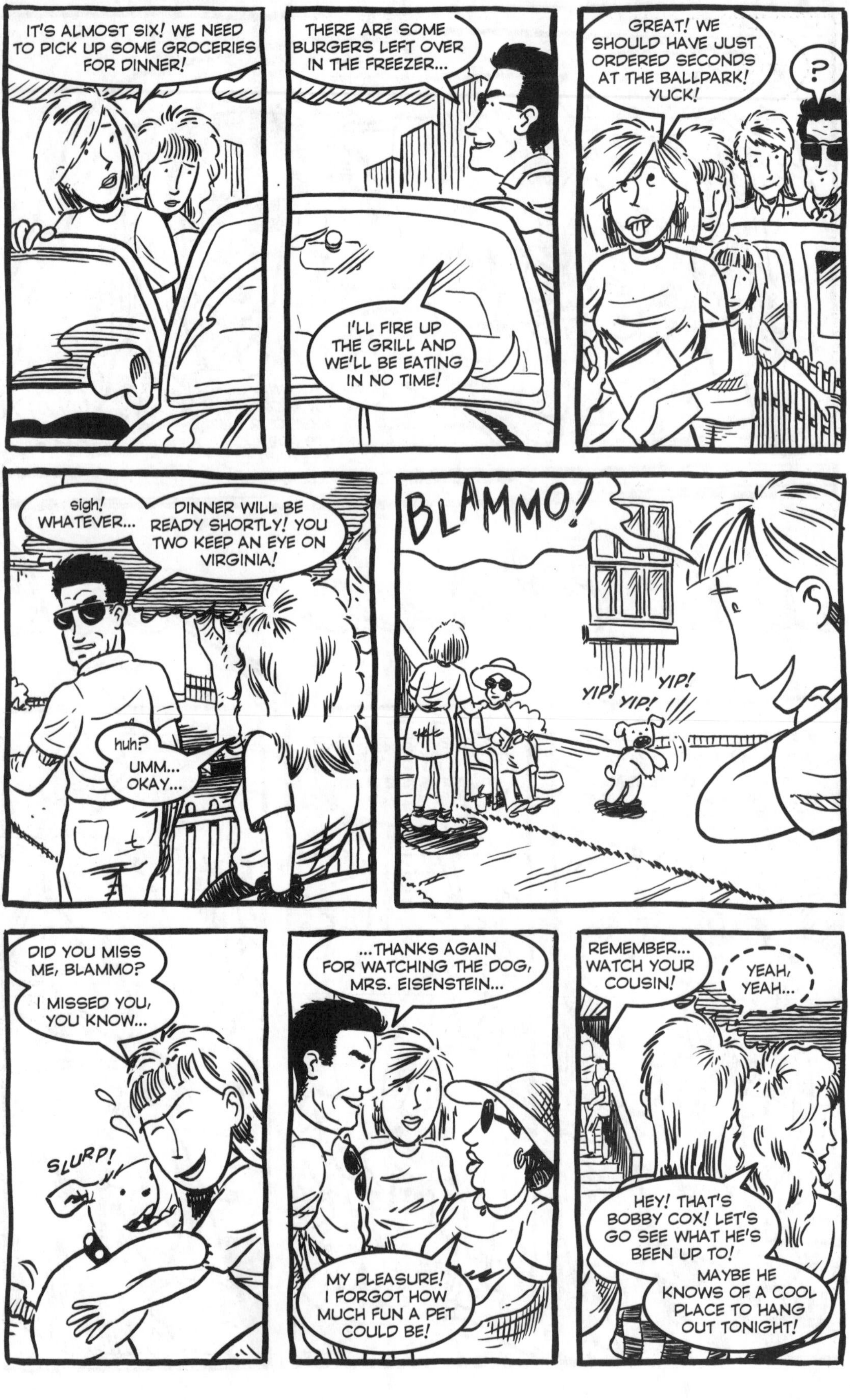

IT'S ALMOST SIX! WE NEED TO PICK UP SOME GROCERIES FOR DINNER!
THERE ARE SOME BURGERS LEFT OVER IN THE FREEZER...
I'LL FIRE UP THE GRILL AND WE'LL BE EATING IN NO TIME!
GREAT! WE SHOULD HAVE JUST ORDERED SECONDS AT THE BALLPARK! YUCK!
?
sigh! WHATEVER...
DINNER WILL BE READY SHORTLY! YOU TWO KEEP AN EYE ON VIRGINIA!
huh? UMM... OKAY...
BLAMMO!
YIP! YIP! YIP!
DID YOU MISS ME, BLAMMO?
I MISSED YOU, YOU KNOW...
SLURP!
...THANKS AGAIN FOR WATCHING THE DOG, MRS. EISENSTEIN...
MY PLEASURE! I FORGOT HOW MUCH FUN A PET COULD BE!
REMEMBER... WATCH YOUR COUSIN!
YEAH, YEAH...
HEY! THAT'S BOBBY COX! LET'S GO SEE WHAT HE'S BEEN UP TO!
MAYBE HE KNOWS OF A COOL PLACE TO HANG OUT TONIGHT!

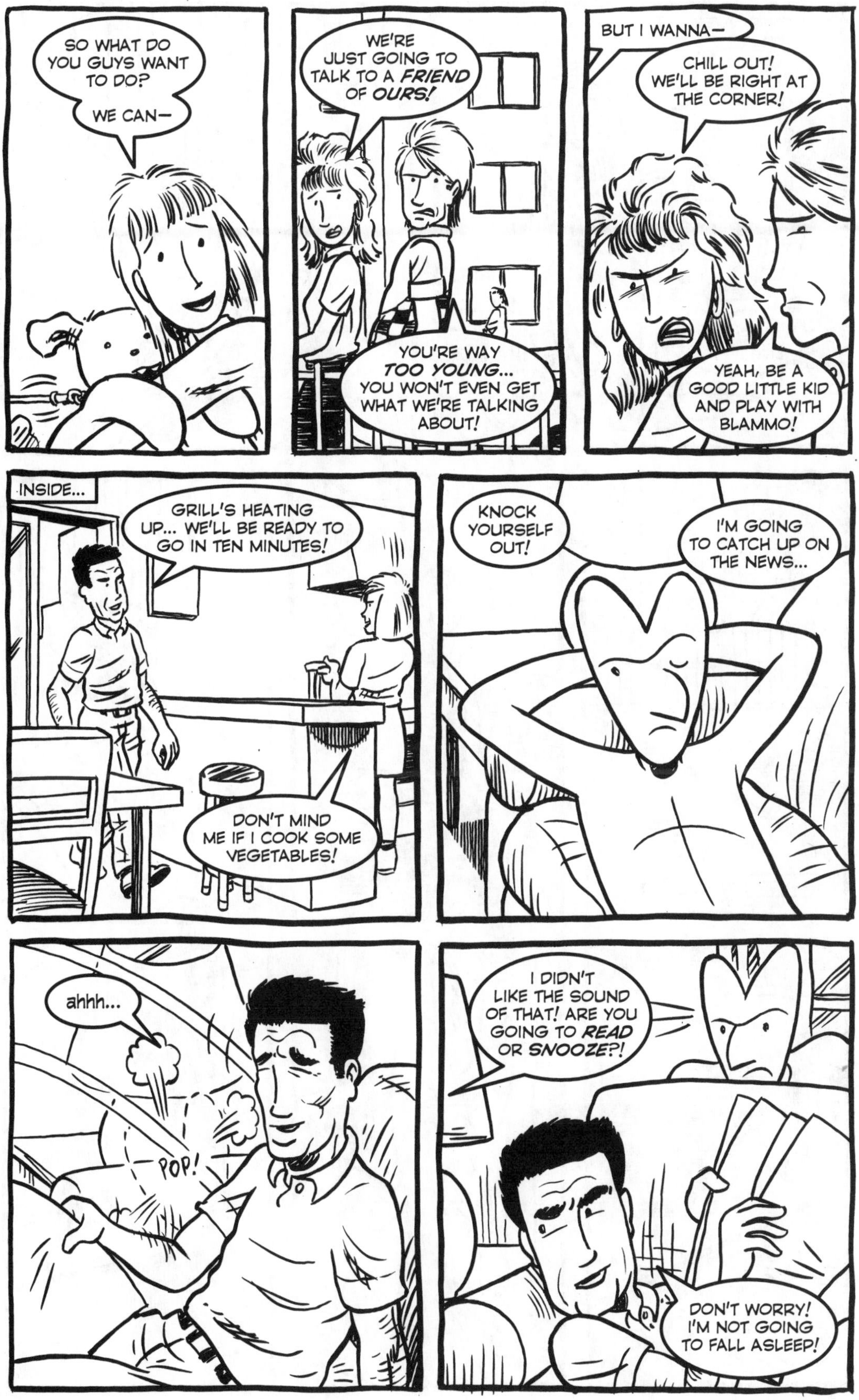
SO WHAT DO YOU GUYS WANT TO DO?
WE CAN—
WE'RE JUST GOING TO TALK TO A *FRIEND* OF *OURS!*
YOU'RE WAY ***TOO YOUNG...*** YOU WON'T EVEN GET WHAT WE'RE TALKING ABOUT!
BUT I WANNA—
CHILL OUT! WE'LL BE RIGHT AT THE CORNER!
YEAH, BE A GOOD LITTLE KID AND PLAY WITH BLAMMO!
INSIDE...
GRILL'S HEATING UP... WE'LL BE READY TO GO IN TEN MINUTES!
DON'T MIND ME IF I COOK SOME VEGETABLES!
KNOCK YOURSELF OUT!
I'M GOING TO CATCH UP ON THE NEWS...
ahhh...
POP!
I DIDN'T LIKE THE SOUND OF THAT! ARE YOU GOING TO *READ* OR *SNOOZE?!*
DON'T WORRY! I'M NOT GOING TO FALL ASLEEP!

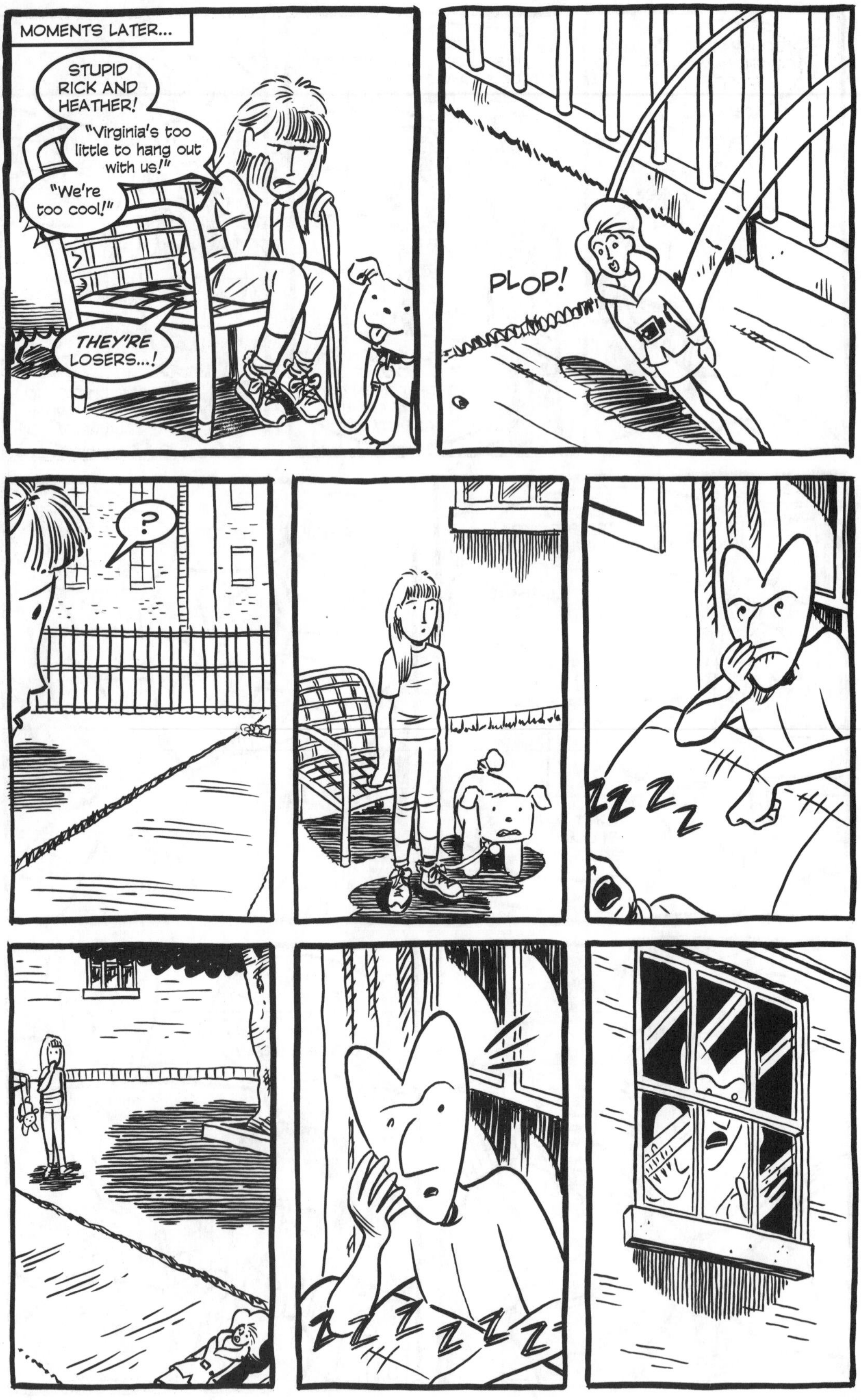
MOMENTS LATER...
STUPID RICK AND HEATHER!
"Virginia's too little to hang out with us!"
"We're too cool!"
THEY'RE LOSERS...!
PLOP!
?
ZZZZ
ZZZZZZZ

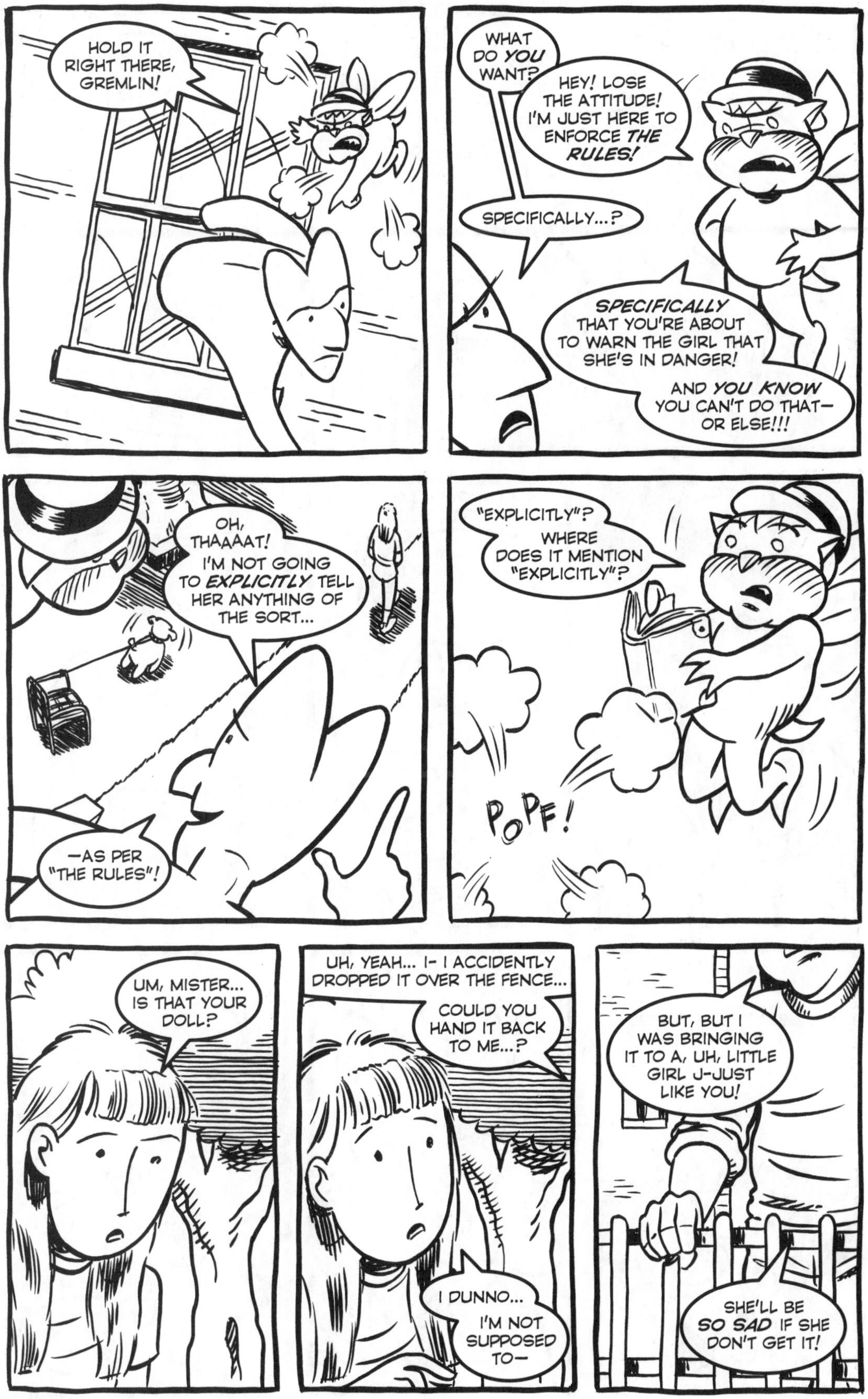
HOLD IT RIGHT THERE, GREMLIN!
WHAT DO YOU WANT?
HEY! LOSE THE ATTITUDE! I'M JUST HERE TO ENFORCE THE RULES!
SPECIFICALLY...?
SPECIFICALLY THAT YOU'RE ABOUT TO WARN THE GIRL THAT SHE'S IN DANGER!
AND YOU KNOW YOU CAN'T DO THAT— OR ELSE!!!
OH, THAAAAT! I'M NOT GOING TO EXPLICITLY TELL HER ANYTHING OF THE SORT...
—AS PER "THE RULES"!
"EXPLICITLY"? WHERE DOES IT MENTION "EXPLICITLY"?
POPF!
UM, MISTER... IS THAT YOUR DOLL?
UH, YEAH... I- I ACCIDENTLY DROPPED IT OVER THE FENCE...
COULD YOU HAND IT BACK TO ME...?
I DUNNO... I'M NOT SUPPOSED TO—
BUT, BUT I WAS BRINGING IT TO A, UH, LITTLE GIRL J-JUST LIKE YOU!
SHE'LL BE SO SAD IF SHE DON'T GET IT!

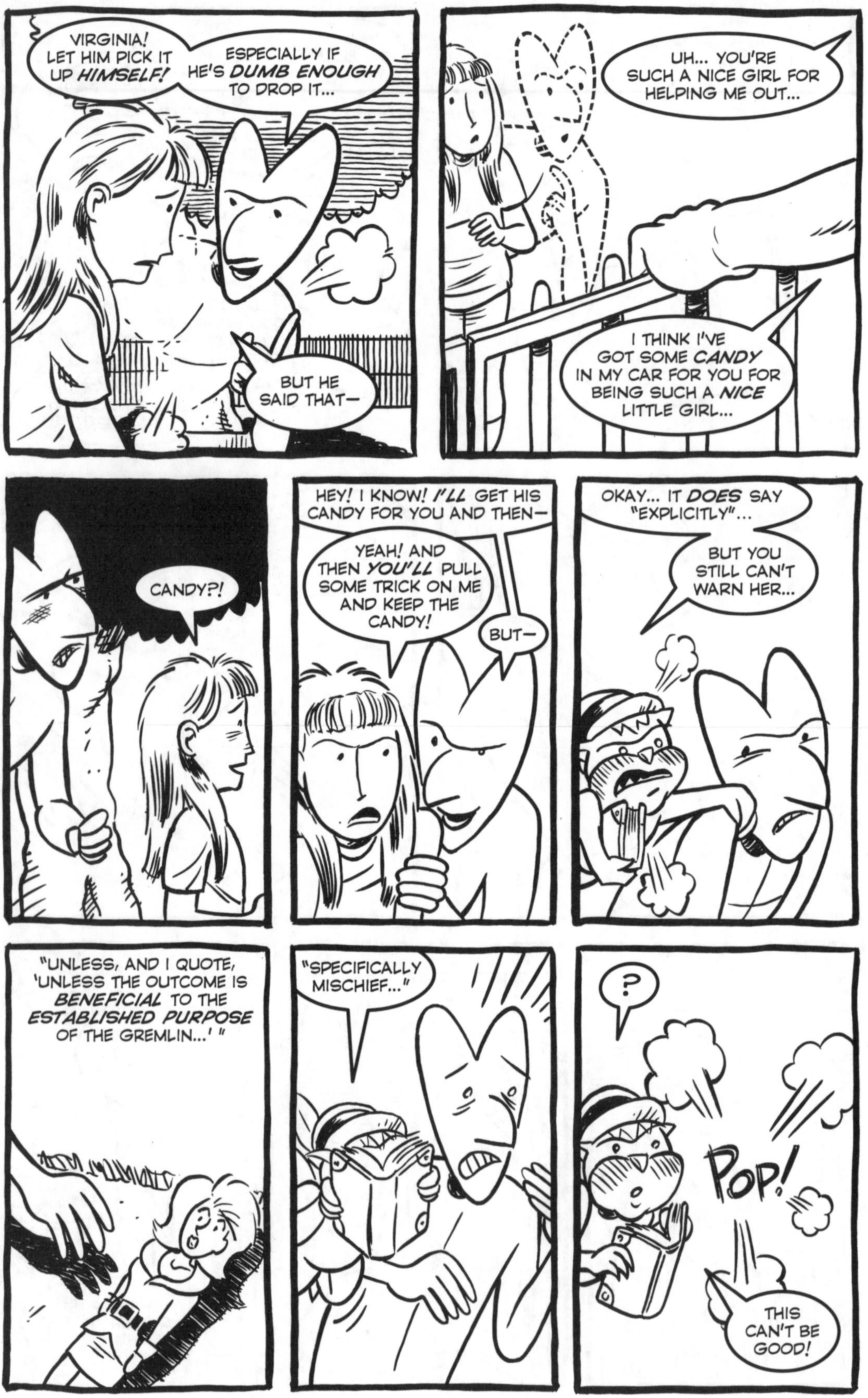
VIRGINIA! LET HIM PICK IT UP *HIMSELF!*
ESPECIALLY IF HE'S *DUMB ENOUGH* TO DROP IT...
BUT HE SAID THAT—
UH... YOU'RE SUCH A NICE GIRL FOR HELPING ME OUT...
I THINK I'VE GOT SOME *CANDY* IN MY CAR FOR YOU FOR BEING SUCH A *NICE* LITTLE GIRL...
CANDY?!
HEY! I KNOW! *I'LL* GET HIS CANDY FOR YOU AND THEN—
YEAH! AND THEN *YOU'LL* PULL SOME TRICK ON ME AND KEEP THE CANDY!
BUT—
OKAY... IT *DOES* SAY "EXPLICITLY"...
BUT YOU STILL CAN'T WARN HER...
"UNLESS, AND I QUOTE, 'UNLESS THE OUTCOME IS *BENEFICIAL* TO THE *ESTABLISHED PURPOSE* OF THE GREMLIN...' "
"SPECIFICALLY MISCHIEF..."
?
POP!
THIS CAN'T BE GOOD!

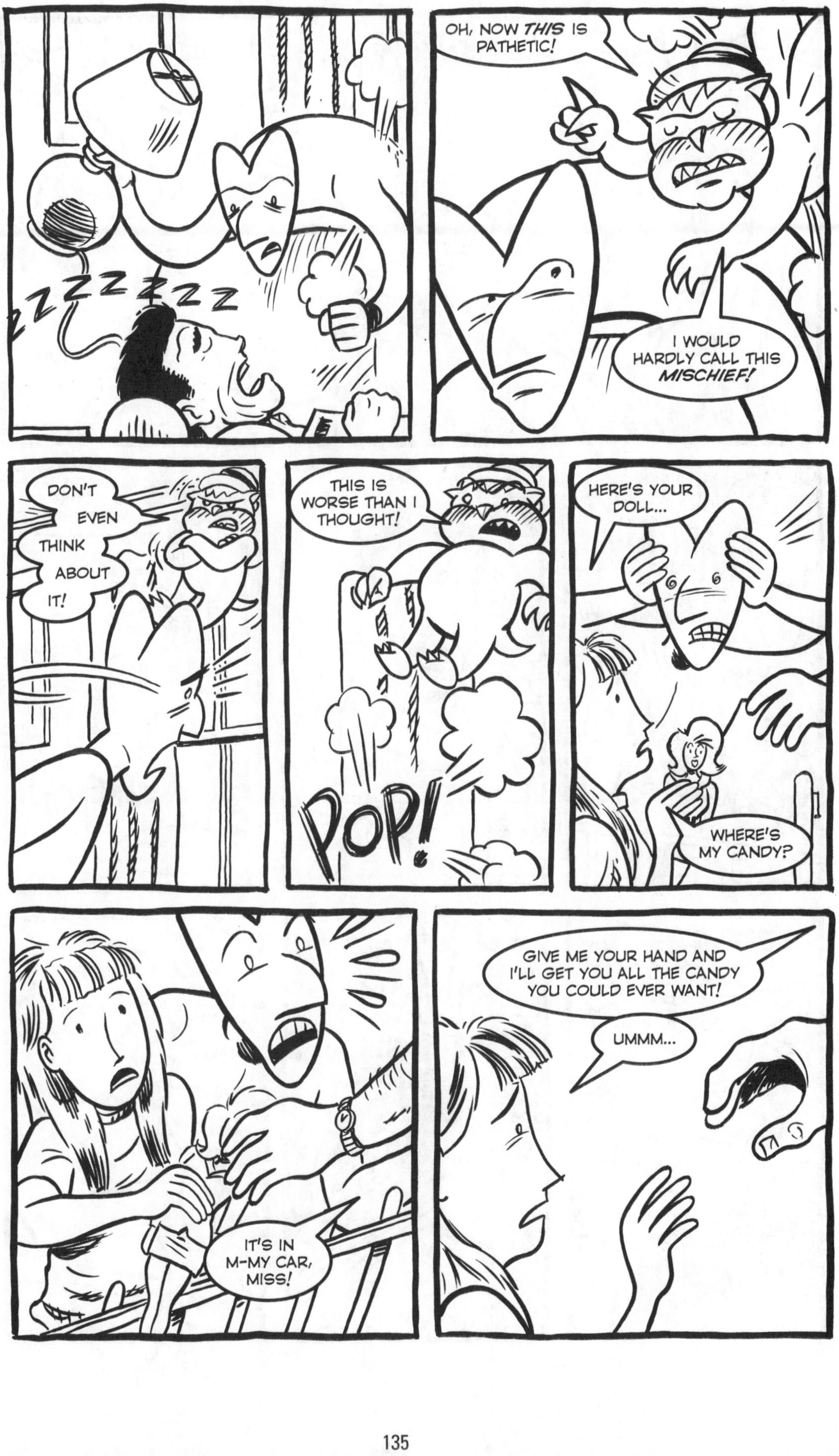
ZZZZZZZZZZ
OH, NOW *THIS* IS PATHETIC!
I WOULD HARDLY CALL THIS *MISCHIEF!*
DON'T EVEN THINK ABOUT IT!
THIS IS WORSE THAN I THOUGHT!
POP!
HERE'S YOUR DOLL...
WHERE'S MY CANDY?
IT'S IN M-MY CAR, MISS!
GIVE ME YOUR HAND AND I'LL GET YOU ALL THE CANDY YOU COULD EVER WANT!
UMMM...

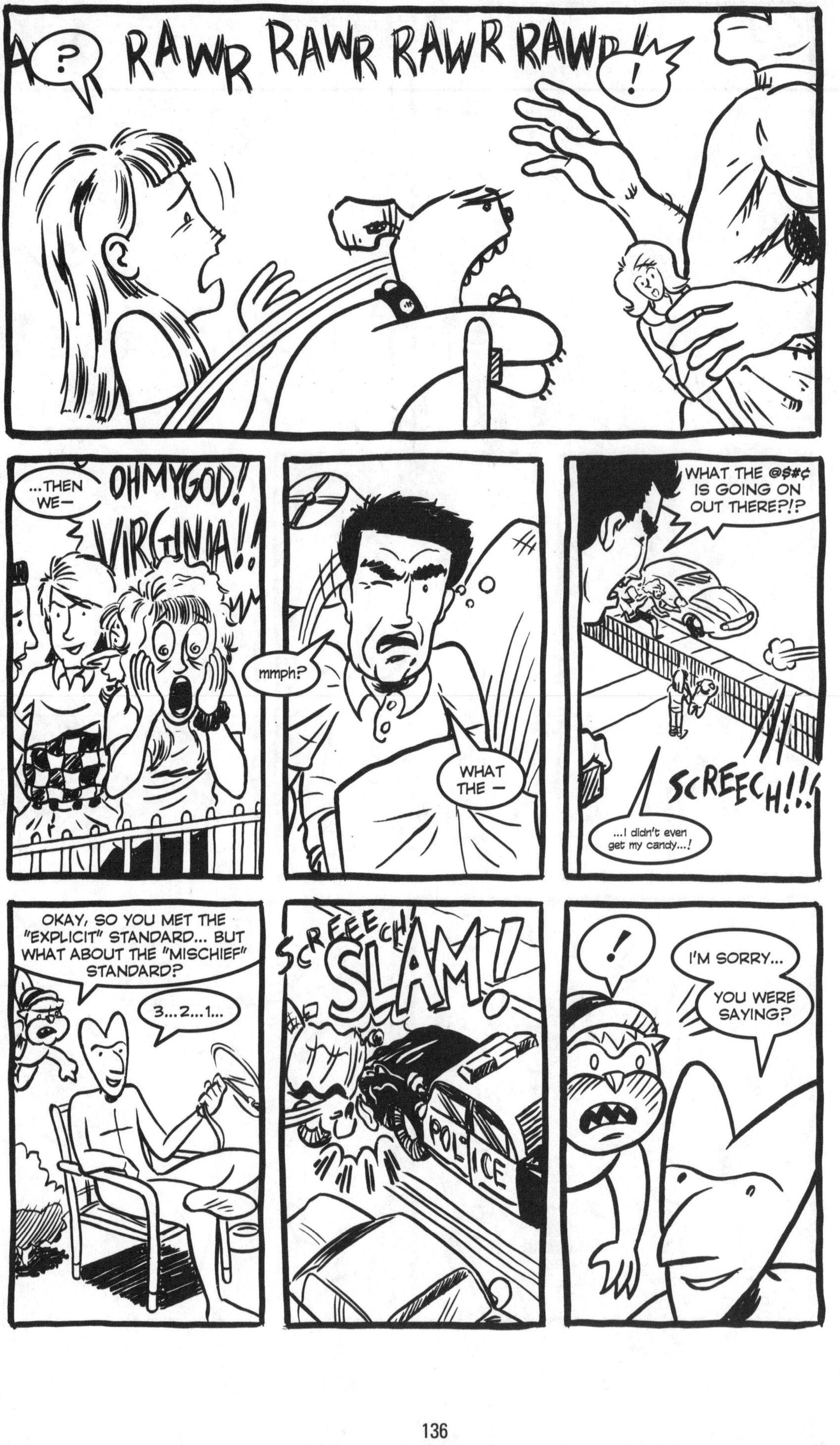
?
RAWR RAWR RAWR RAWR!
!
...THEN WE—
OHMYGOD! VIRGINIA!!
mmph?
WHAT THE —
WHAT THE @$#¢ IS GOING ON OUT THERE?!?
SCREECH!!!
...I didn't even get my candy...!
OKAY, SO YOU MET THE "EXPLICIT" STANDARD... BUT WHAT ABOUT THE "MISCHIEF" STANDARD?
3...2...1...
SCREEECH!
SLAM!
POLICE
!
I'M SORRY...
YOU WERE SAYING?

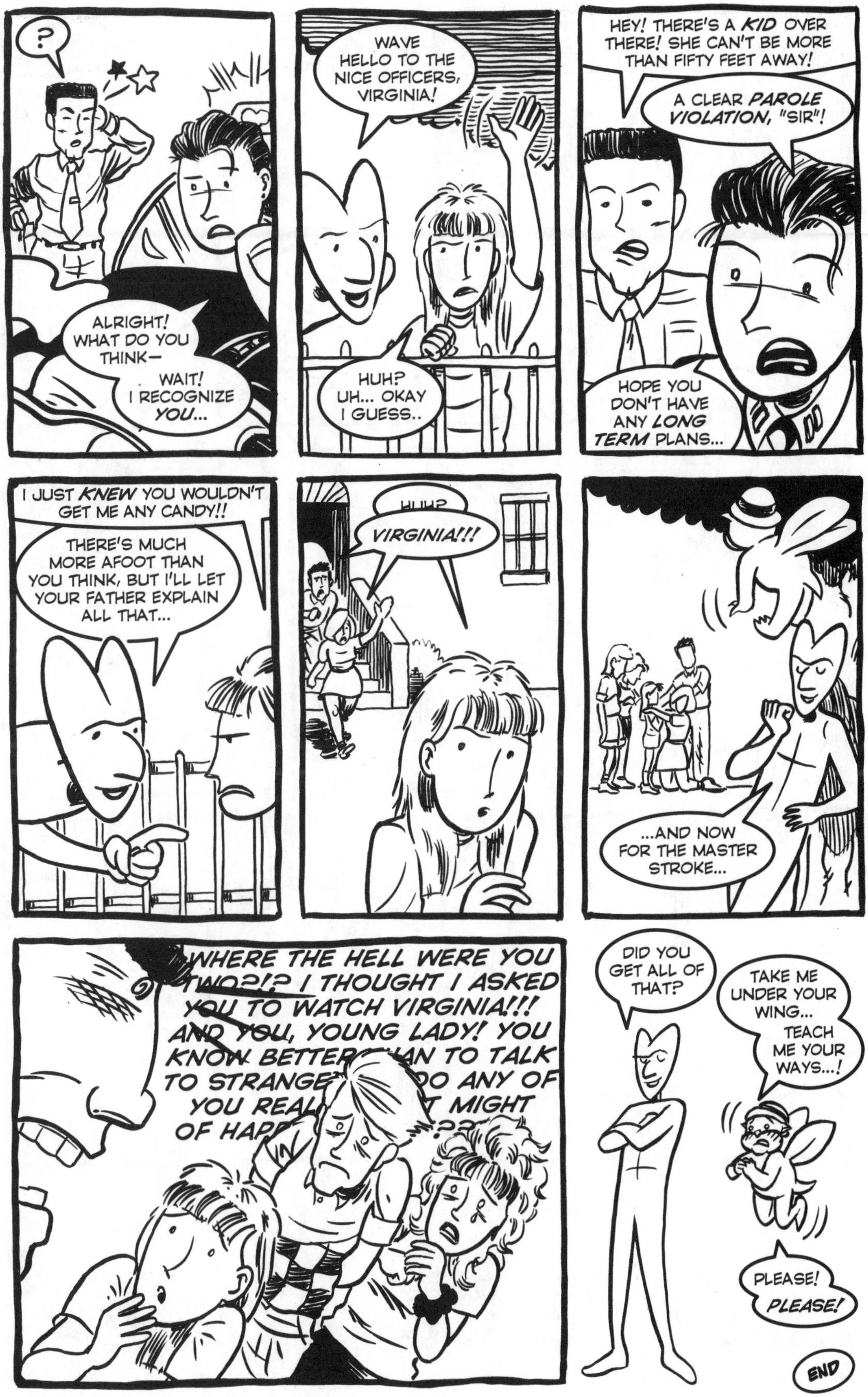
?
ALRIGHT! WHAT DO YOU THINK—
WAIT! I RECOGNIZE YOU...
WAVE HELLO TO THE NICE OFFICERS, VIRGINIA!
HUH? UH... OKAY I GUESS..
HEY! THERE'S A KID OVER THERE! SHE CAN'T BE MORE THAN FIFTY FEET AWAY!
A CLEAR PAROLE VIOLATION, "SIR"!
HOPE YOU DON'T HAVE ANY LONG TERM PLANS...
I JUST KNEW YOU WOULDN'T GET ME ANY CANDY!!
THERE'S MUCH MORE AFOOT THAN YOU THINK, BUT I'LL LET YOUR FATHER EXPLAIN ALL THAT...
VIRGINIA!!!
...AND NOW FOR THE MASTER STROKE...
WHERE THE HELL WERE YOU TWO?!? I THOUGHT I ASKED YOU TO WATCH VIRGINIA!!! AND YOU, YOUNG LADY! YOU KNOW BETTER THAN TO TALK TO STRANGE DO ANY OF YOU REAL MIGHT OF HAP
DID YOU GET ALL OF THAT?
TAKE ME UNDER YOUR WING...
TEACH ME YOUR WAYS...!
PLEASE! PLEASE!
END

...AND TODAY IS GOING TO BE A HOT ONE WITH THE HUMIDITY REACHING OVER 90%! SUMMER'S ARRIVING EARLY THIS YEAR!
HMMPH! LAST NIGHT THEY WERE PREDICTING RAIN!
SO WHAT ELSE IS—
HEY!
WILL SOMEONE TURN THE AIR CONDITIONER ON?!?
I'M DYING IN HERE!!!

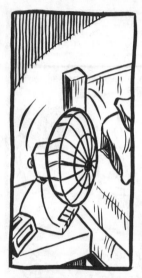

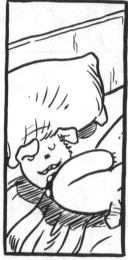

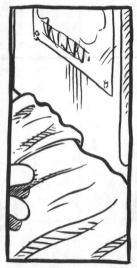

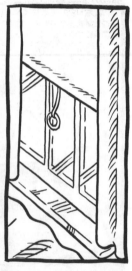

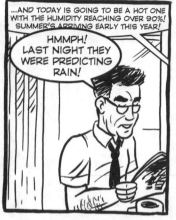

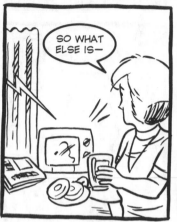

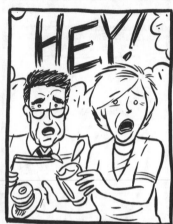

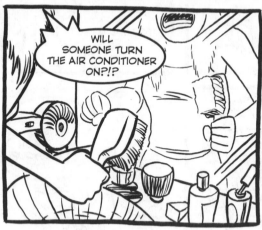

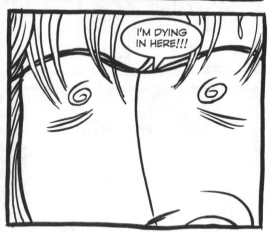

electric girl™

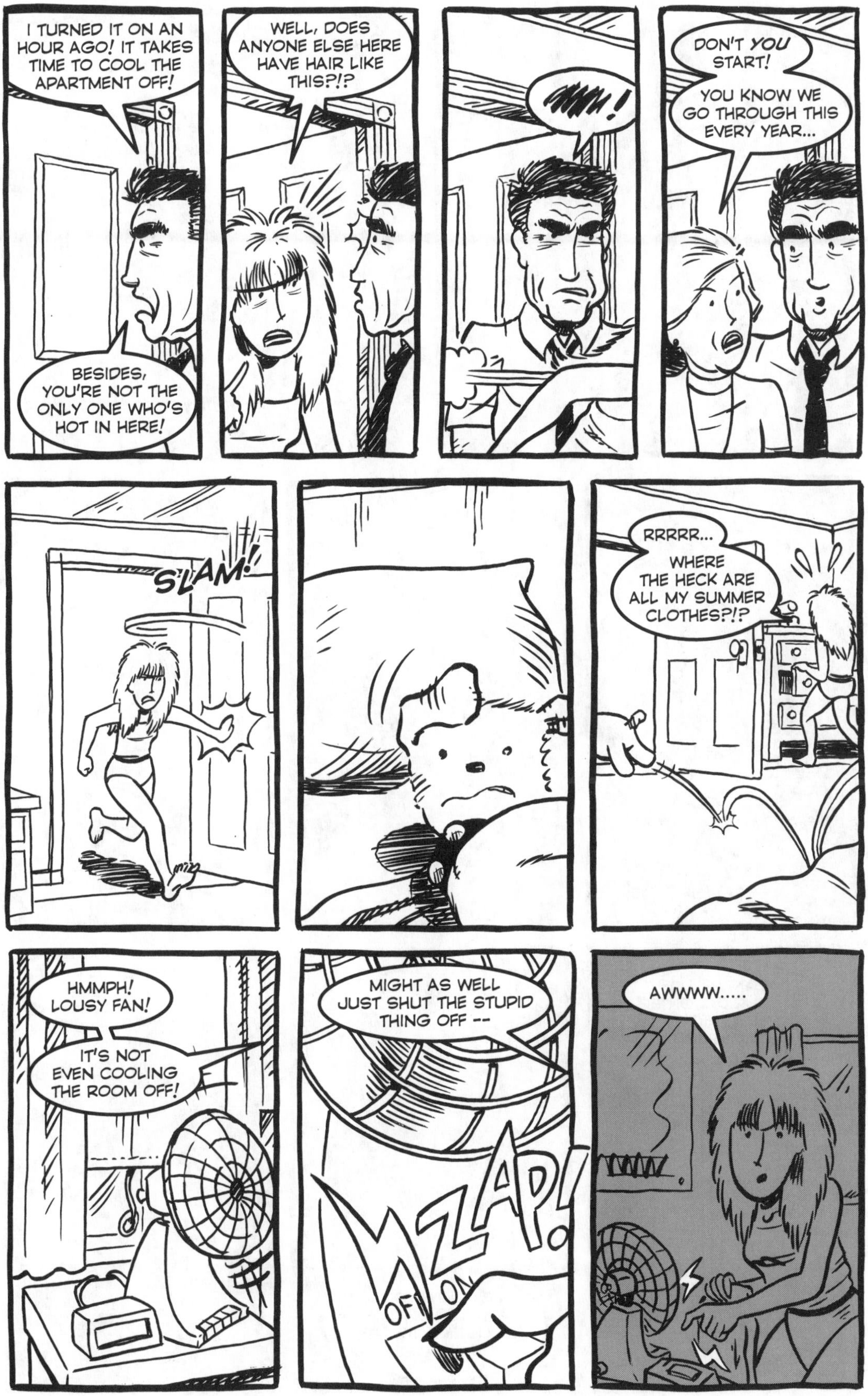
I TURNED IT ON AN HOUR AGO! IT TAKES TIME TO COOL THE APARTMENT OFF!
BESIDES, YOU'RE NOT THE ONLY ONE WHO'S HOT IN HERE!
WELL, DOES ANYONE ELSE HERE HAVE HAIR LIKE THIS?!?
DON'T YOU START!
YOU KNOW WE GO THROUGH THIS EVERY YEAR...
SLAM!
RRRRR...
WHERE THE HECK ARE ALL MY SUMMER CLOTHES?!?
HMMPH! LOUSY FAN!
IT'S NOT EVEN COOLING THE ROOM OFF!
MIGHT AS WELL JUST SHUT THE STUPID THING OFF --
ZAP!
OFF ON
AWWWW.....

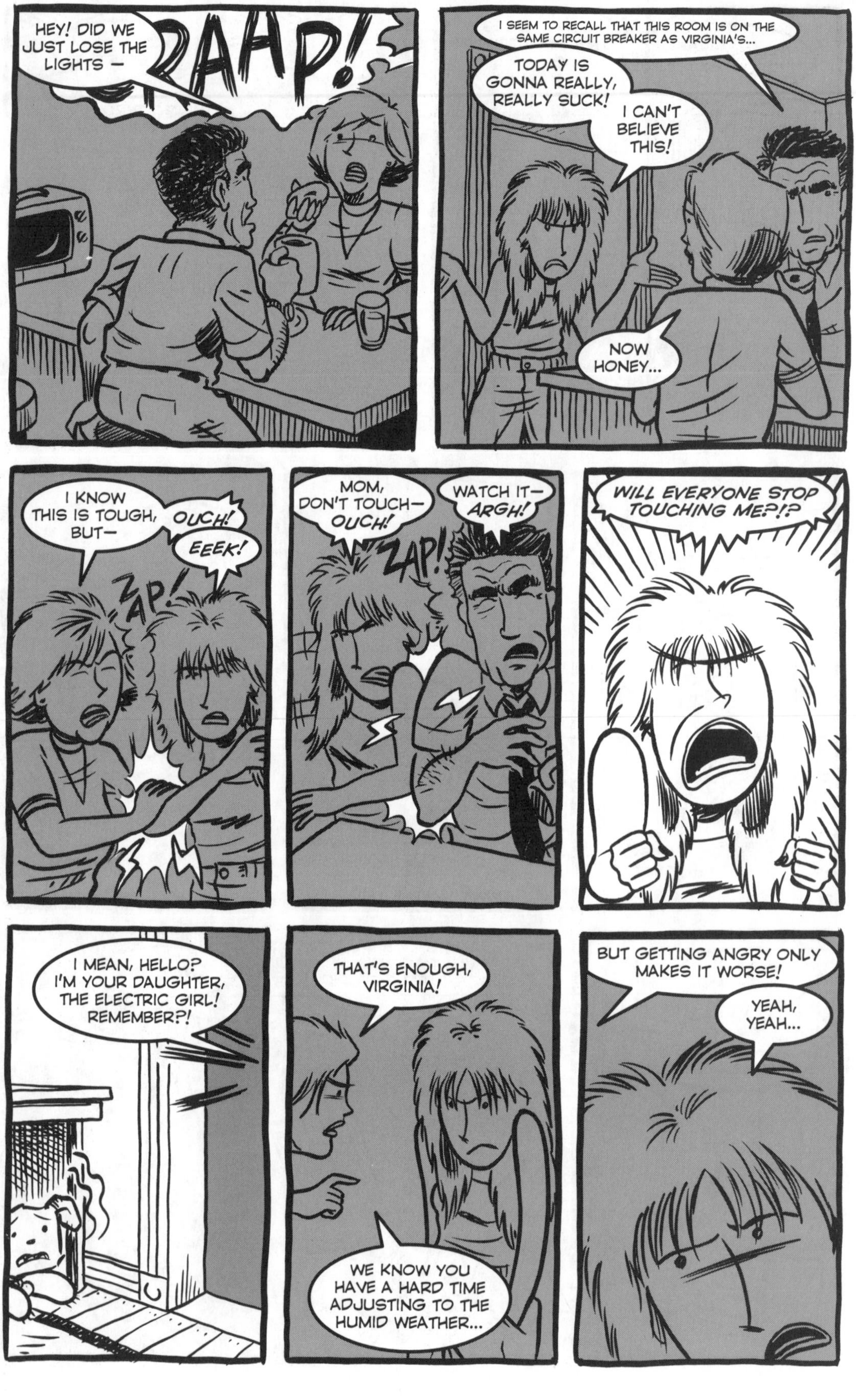

HEY! DID WE JUST LOSE THE LIGHTS —
ZAAP!
I SEEM TO RECALL THAT THIS ROOM IS ON THE SAME CIRCUIT BREAKER AS VIRGINIA'S...
TODAY IS GONNA REALLY, REALLY SUCK!
I CAN'T BELIEVE THIS!
NOW HONEY...
I KNOW THIS IS TOUGH, BUT—
OUCH!
EEEK!
ZAP!
MOM, DON'T TOUCH— OUCH!
WATCH IT— ARGH!
ZAP!
WILL EVERYONE STOP TOUCHING ME?!?
I MEAN, HELLO? I'M YOUR DAUGHTER, THE ELECTRIC GIRL! REMEMBER?!
THAT'S ENOUGH, VIRGINIA!
WE KNOW YOU HAVE A HARD TIME ADJUSTING TO THE HUMID WEATHER...
BUT GETTING ANGRY ONLY MAKES IT WORSE!
YEAH, YEAH...

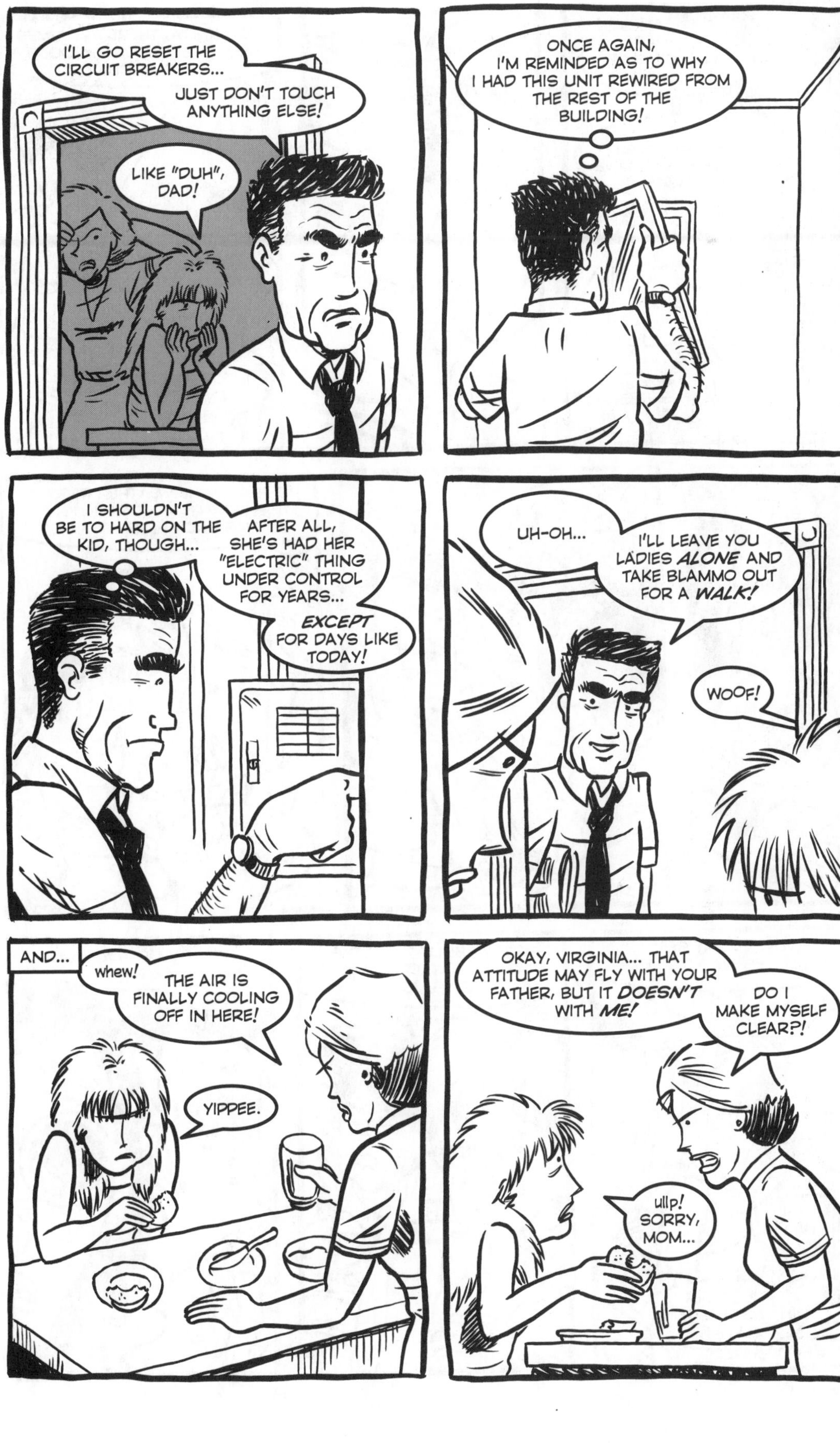
I'LL GO RESET THE CIRCUIT BREAKERS...
JUST DON'T TOUCH ANYTHING ELSE!
LIKE "DUH", DAD!
ONCE AGAIN, I'M REMINDED AS TO WHY I HAD THIS UNIT REWIRED FROM THE REST OF THE BUILDING!
I SHOULDN'T BE TO HARD ON THE KID, THOUGH...
AFTER ALL, SHE'S HAD HER "ELECTRIC" THING UNDER CONTROL FOR YEARS...
EXCEPT FOR DAYS LIKE TODAY!
UH-OH...
I'LL LEAVE YOU LADIES ALONE AND TAKE BLAMMO OUT FOR A WALK!
WOOF!
AND...
whew!
THE AIR IS FINALLY COOLING OFF IN HERE!
YIPPEE.
OKAY, VIRGINIA... THAT ATTITUDE MAY FLY WITH YOUR FATHER, BUT IT DOESN'T WITH ME!
DO I MAKE MYSELF CLEAR?!
ullp! SORRY, MOM...

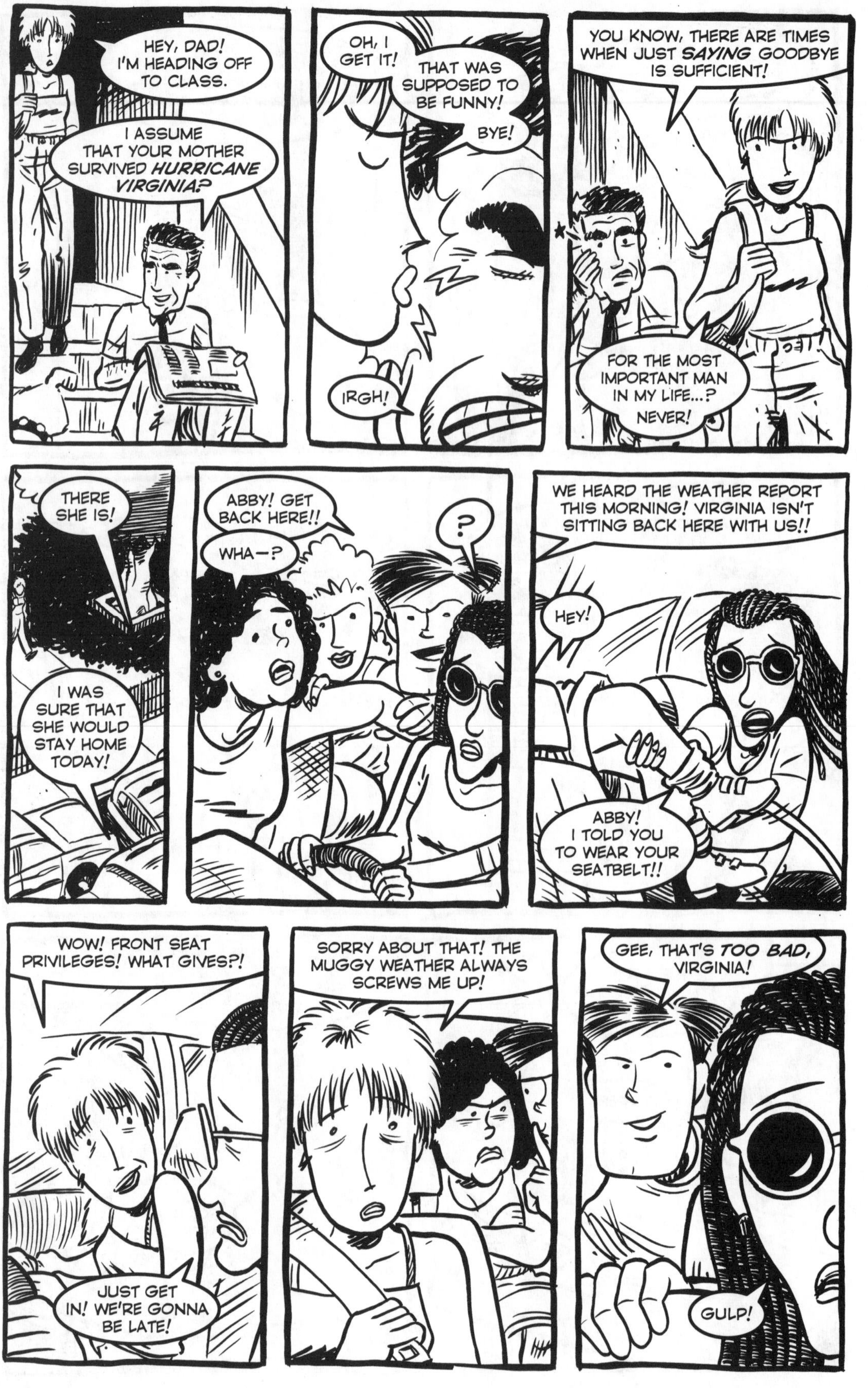
HEY, DAD! I'M HEADING OFF TO CLASS.
I ASSUME THAT YOUR MOTHER SURVIVED HURRICANE VIRGINIA?
OH, I GET IT!
THAT WAS SUPPOSED TO BE FUNNY!
BYE!
IRGH!
YOU KNOW, THERE ARE TIMES WHEN JUST SAYING GOODBYE IS SUFFICIENT!
FOR THE MOST IMPORTANT MAN IN MY LIFE...?
NEVER!
THERE SHE IS!
I WAS SURE THAT SHE WOULD STAY HOME TODAY!
ABBY! GET BACK HERE!!
WHA—?
?
WE HEARD THE WEATHER REPORT THIS MORNING! VIRGINIA ISN'T SITTING BACK HERE WITH US!!
HEY!
ABBY! I TOLD YOU TO WEAR YOUR SEATBELT!!
WOW! FRONT SEAT PRIVILEGES! WHAT GIVES?!
JUST GET IN! WE'RE GONNA BE LATE!
SORRY ABOUT THAT! THE MUGGY WEATHER ALWAYS SCREWS ME UP!
GEE, THAT'S TOO BAD, VIRGINIA!
GULP!

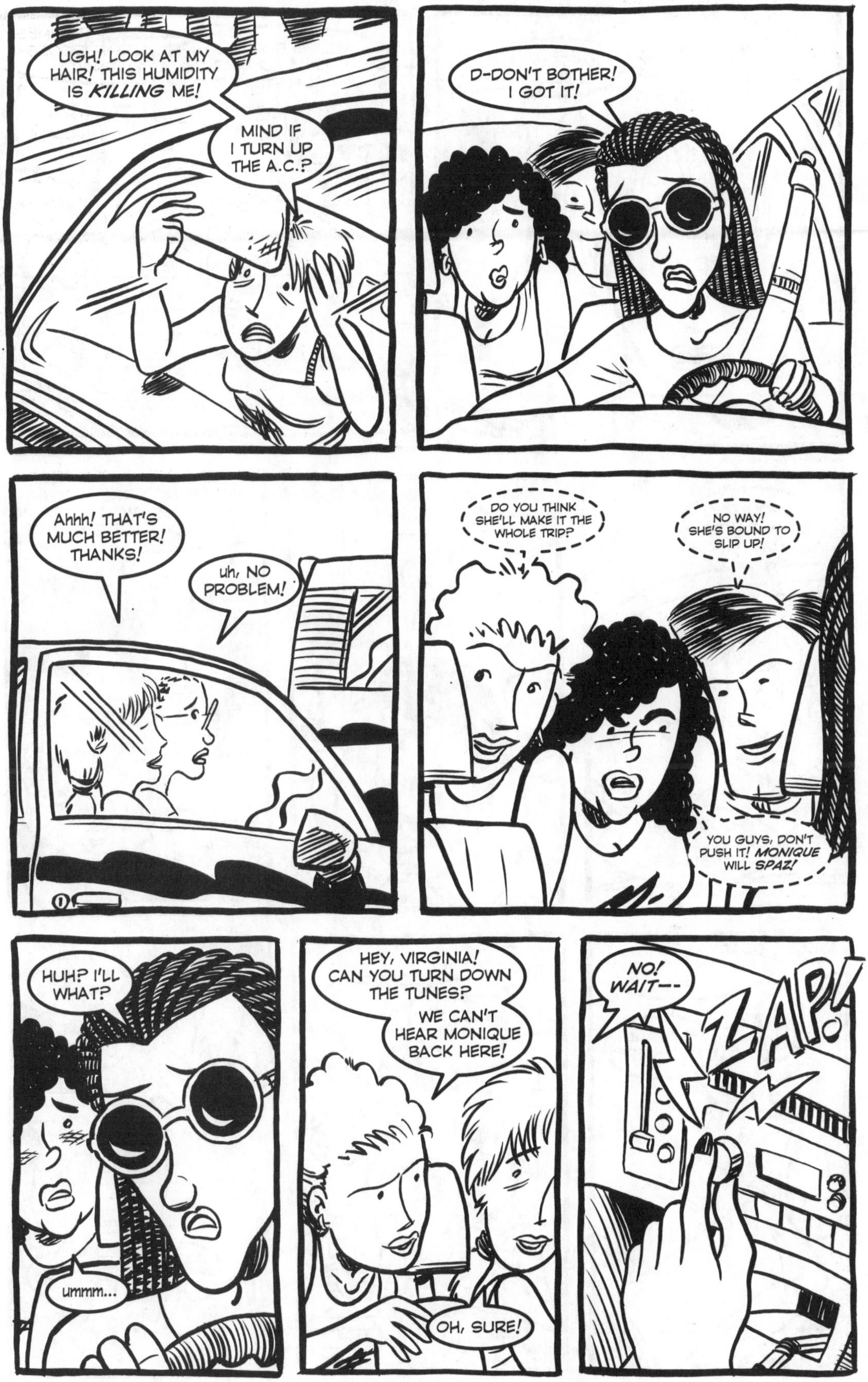
UGH! LOOK AT MY HAIR! THIS HUMIDITY IS *KILLING* ME!
MIND IF I TURN UP THE A.C.?
D-DON'T BOTHER! I GOT IT!
Ahhh! THAT'S MUCH BETTER! THANKS!
uh, NO PROBLEM!
DO YOU THINK SHE'LL MAKE IT THE WHOLE TRIP?
NO WAY! SHE'S BOUND TO SLIP UP!
YOU GUYS, DON'T PUSH IT! *MONIQUE* WILL *SPAZ!*
HUH? I'LL WHAT?
ummm...
HEY, VIRGINIA! CAN YOU TURN DOWN THE TUNES?
WE CAN'T HEAR MONIQUE BACK HERE!
OH, SURE!
NO! WAIT--
ZAP!

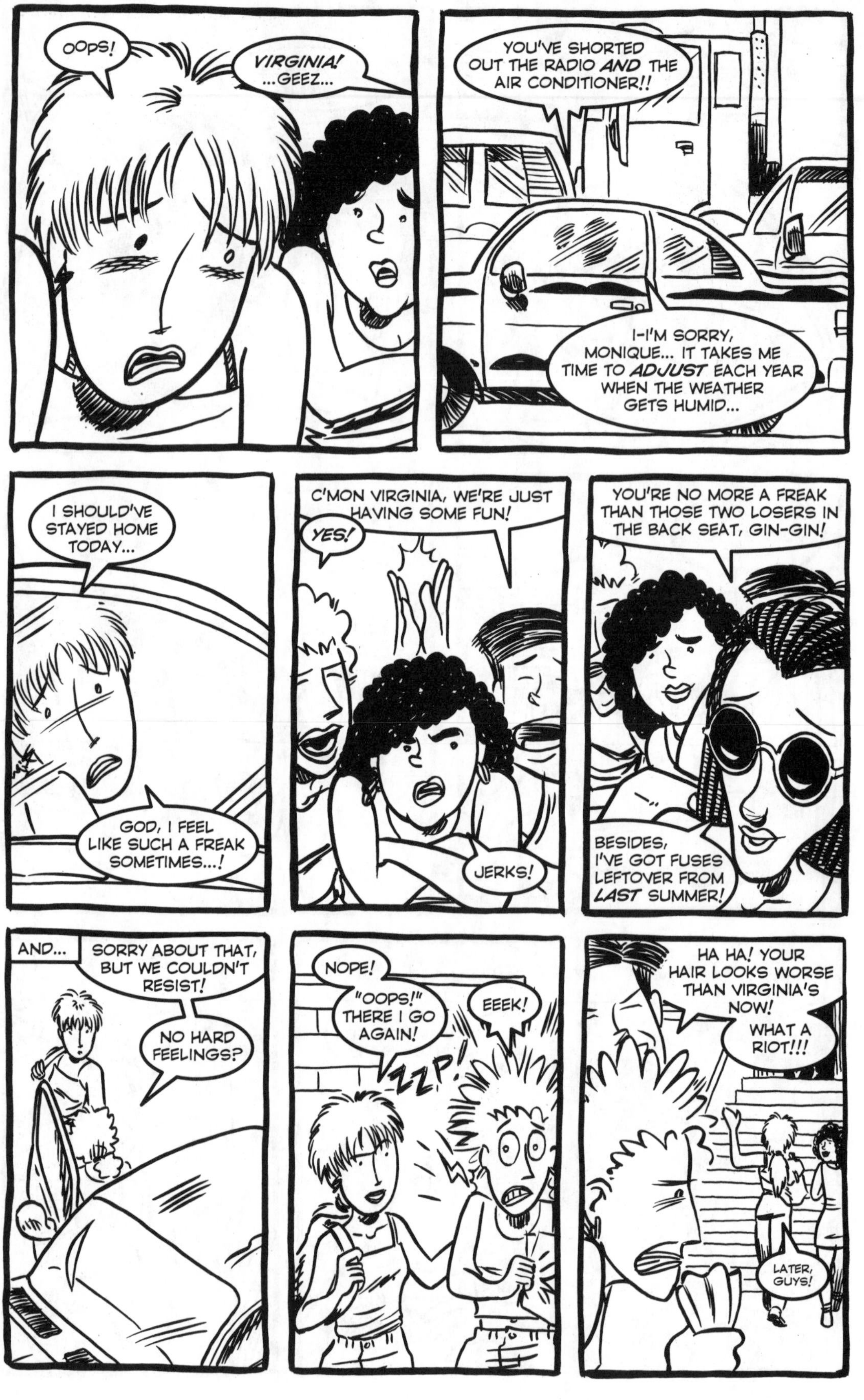

OOPS!
VIRGINIA! ...GEEZ...
YOU'VE SHORTED OUT THE RADIO AND THE AIR CONDITIONER!!
I-I'M SORRY, MONIQUE... IT TAKES ME TIME TO ADJUST EACH YEAR WHEN THE WEATHER GETS HUMID...
I SHOULD'VE STAYED HOME TODAY...
GOD, I FEEL LIKE SUCH A FREAK SOMETIMES...!
C'MON VIRGINIA, WE'RE JUST HAVING SOME FUN!
YES!
JERKS!
YOU'RE NO MORE A FREAK THAN THOSE TWO LOSERS IN THE BACK SEAT, GIN-GIN!
BESIDES, I'VE GOT FUSES LEFTOVER FROM LAST SUMMER!
AND...
SORRY ABOUT THAT, BUT WE COULDN'T RESIST!
NO HARD FEELINGS?
NOPE!
"OOPS!" THERE I GO AGAIN!
EEEK!
ZZP!
HA HA! YOUR HAIR LOOKS WORSE THAN VIRGINIA'S NOW!
WHAT A RIOT!!!
LATER, GUYS!

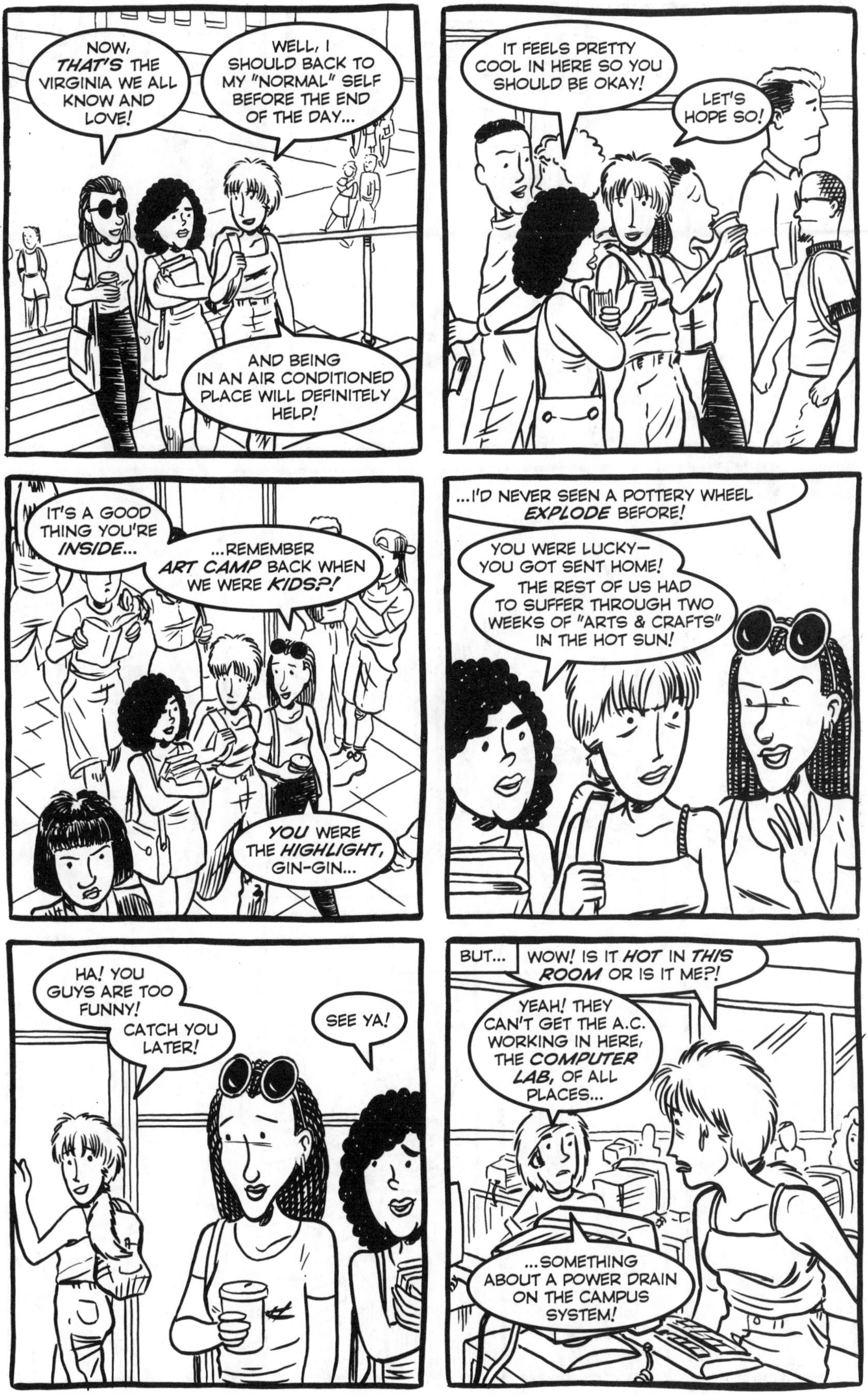
NOW, THAT'S THE VIRGINIA WE ALL KNOW AND LOVE!
WELL, I SHOULD BACK TO MY "NORMAL" SELF BEFORE THE END OF THE DAY...
AND BEING IN AN AIR CONDITIONED PLACE WILL DEFINITELY HELP!
IT FEELS PRETTY COOL IN HERE SO YOU SHOULD BE OKAY!
LET'S HOPE SO!
IT'S A GOOD THING YOU'RE INSIDE...
...REMEMBER ART CAMP BACK WHEN WE WERE KIDS?!
YOU WERE THE HIGHLIGHT, GIN-GIN...
...I'D NEVER SEEN A POTTERY WHEEL EXPLODE BEFORE!
YOU WERE LUCKY— YOU GOT SENT HOME!
THE REST OF US HAD TO SUFFER THROUGH TWO WEEKS OF "ARTS & CRAFTS" IN THE HOT SUN!
HA! YOU GUYS ARE TOO FUNNY!
CATCH YOU LATER!
SEE YA!
BUT...
WOW! IS IT HOT IN THIS ROOM OR IS IT ME?!
YEAH! THEY CAN'T GET THE A.C. WORKING IN HERE, THE COMPUTER LAB, OF ALL PLACES...
...SOMETHING ABOUT A POWER DRAIN ON THE CAMPUS SYSTEM!

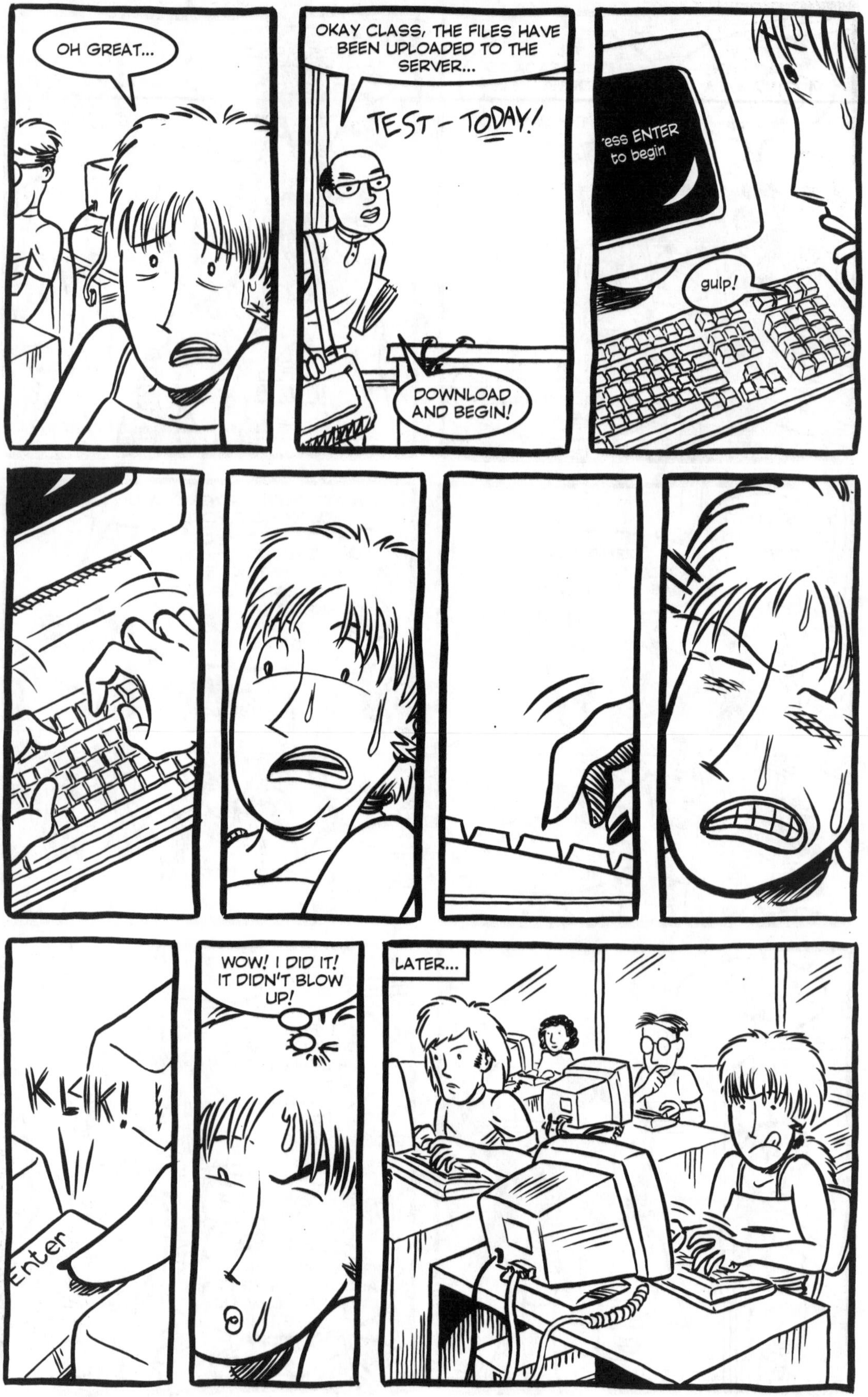

OH GREAT...
OKAY CLASS, THE FILES HAVE BEEN UPLOADED TO THE SERVER...
TEST - TODAY!
DOWNLOAD AND BEGIN!
'ess ENTER to begin
gulp!
KLIK!
Enter
WOW! I DID IT! IT DIDN'T BLOW UP!
LATER...

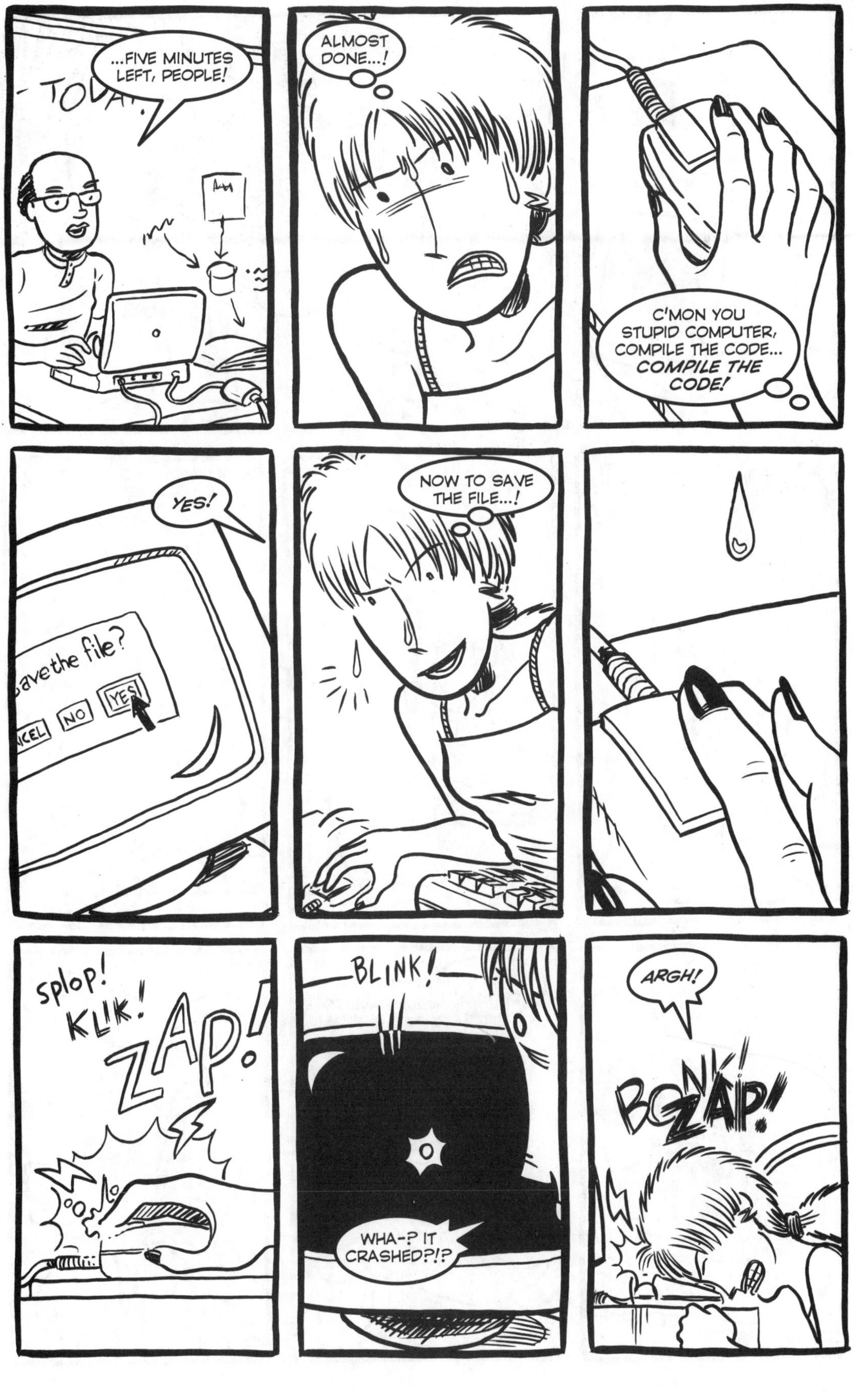

...FIVE MINUTES LEFT, PEOPLE!
ALMOST DONE...!
C'MON YOU STUPID COMPUTER, COMPILE THE CODE... COMPILE THE CODE!
YES!
save the file?
NCEL
NO
YES
NOW TO SAVE THE FILE...!
splop!
KLIK!
ZAP!
BLINK!
WHA-? IT CRASHED?!?
ARGH!
BONK!
ZAP!

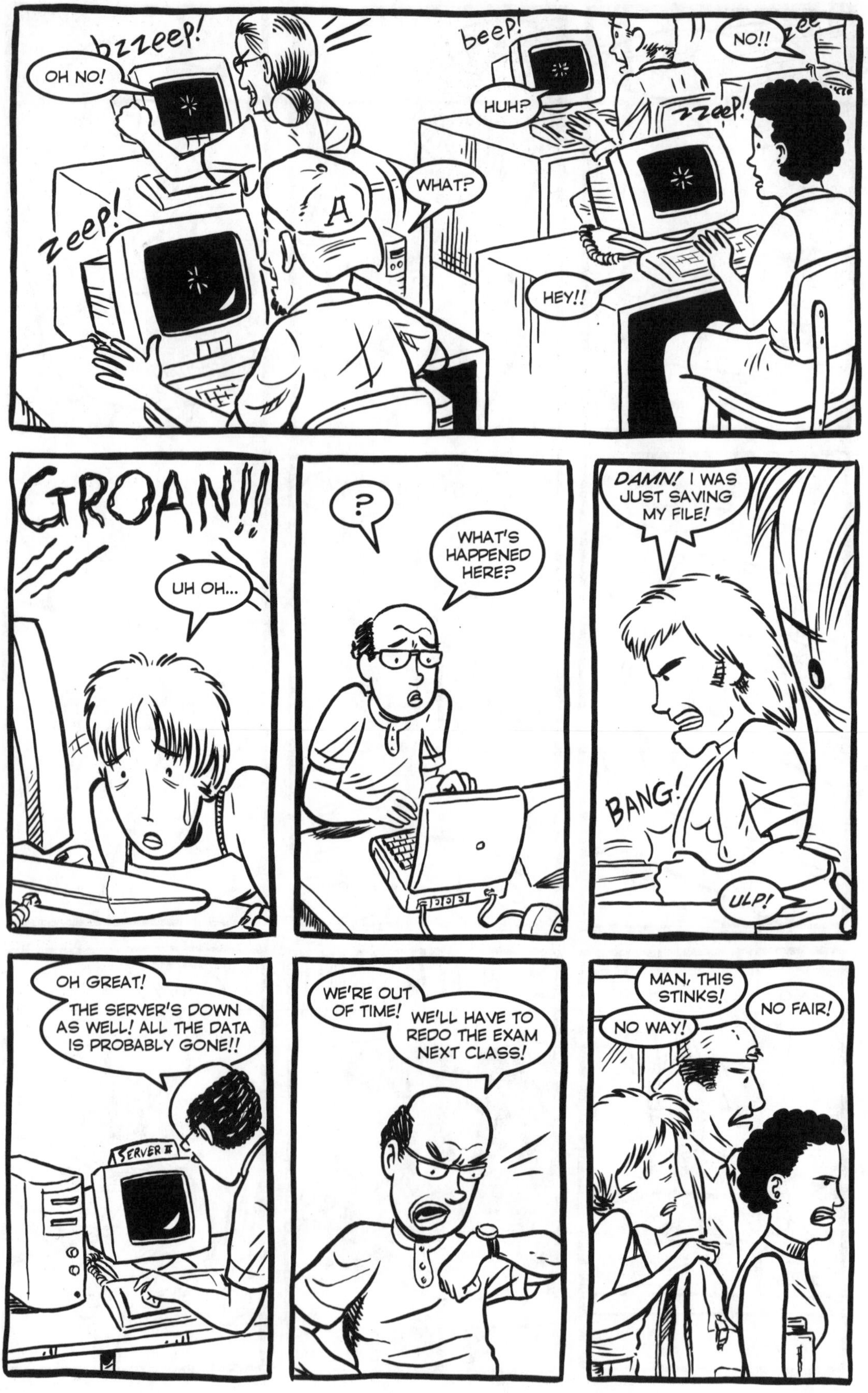
bzzeep!
OH NO!
beep!
HUH?
NO!!
zzeep!
zeep!
WHAT?
HEY!!
GROAN!!
UH OH...
?
WHAT'S HAPPENED HERE?
DAMN! I WAS JUST SAVING MY FILE!
BANG!
ULP!
OH GREAT!
THE SERVER'S DOWN AS WELL! ALL THE DATA IS PROBABLY GONE!!
SERVER
WE'RE OUT OF TIME!
WE'LL HAVE TO REDO THE EXAM NEXT CLASS!
MAN, THIS STINKS!
NO WAY!
NO FAIR!

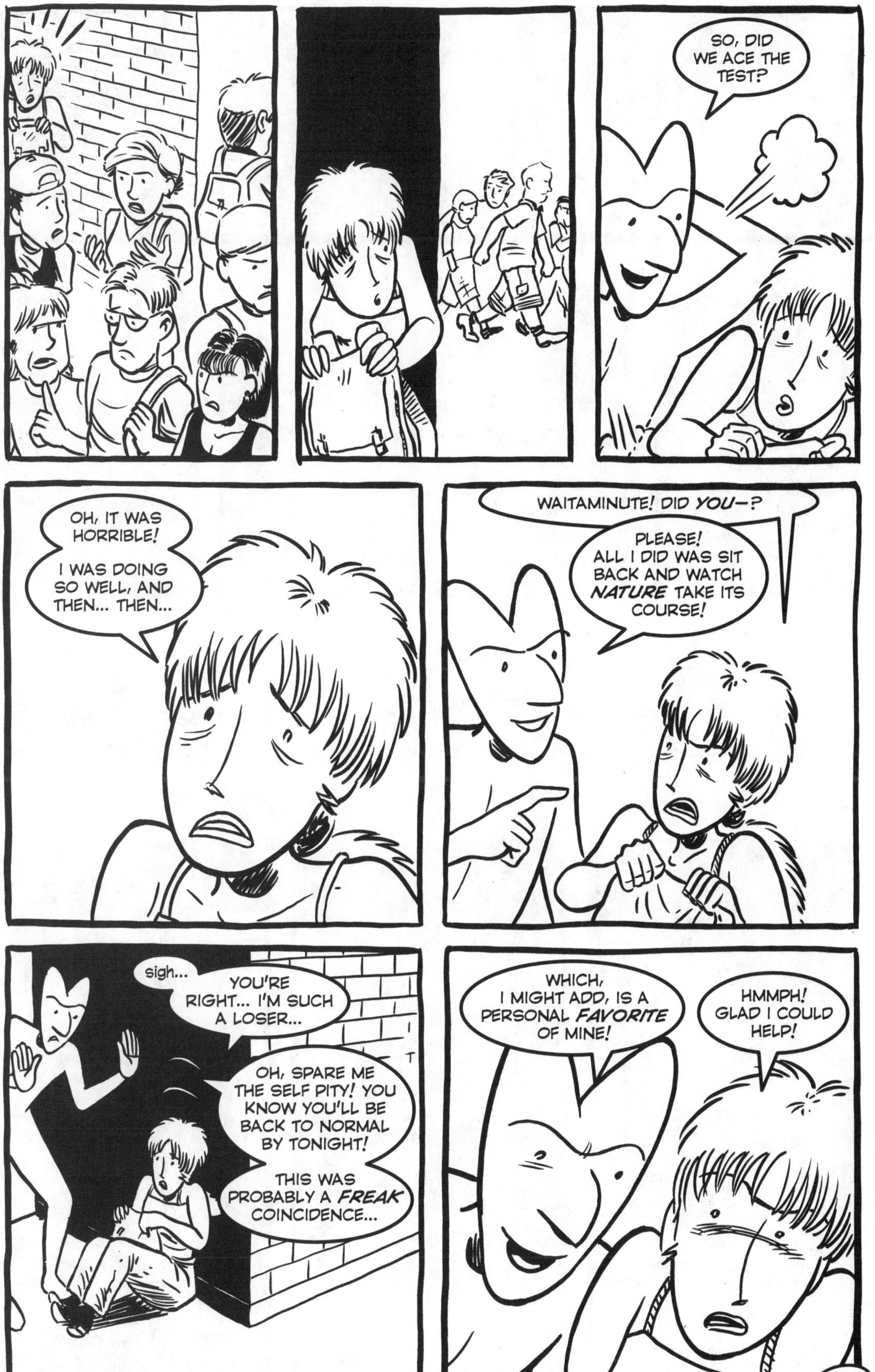
SO, DID WE ACE THE TEST?
OH, IT WAS HORRIBLE!
I WAS DOING SO WELL, AND THEN... THEN...
WAITAMINUTE! DID *YOU*—?
PLEASE! ALL I DID WAS SIT BACK AND WATCH *NATURE* TAKE ITS COURSE!
sigh...
YOU'RE RIGHT... I'M SUCH A LOSER...
OH, SPARE ME THE SELF PITY! YOU KNOW YOU'LL BE BACK TO NORMAL BY TONIGHT!
THIS WAS PROBABLY A *FREAK* COINCIDENCE...
WHICH, I MIGHT ADD, IS A PERSONAL *FAVORITE* OF MINE!
HMMPH! GLAD I COULD HELP!
END

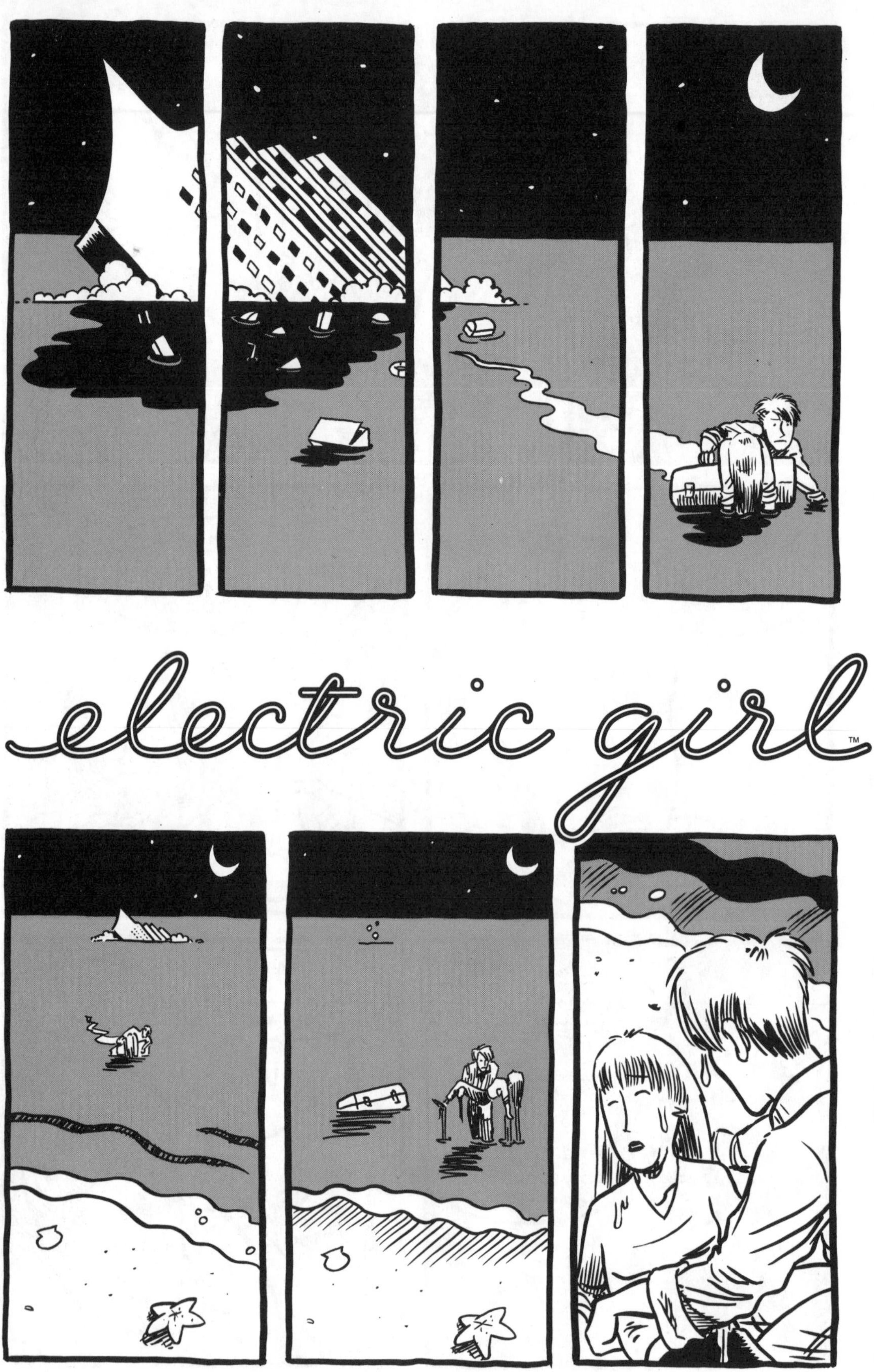
electric girl™

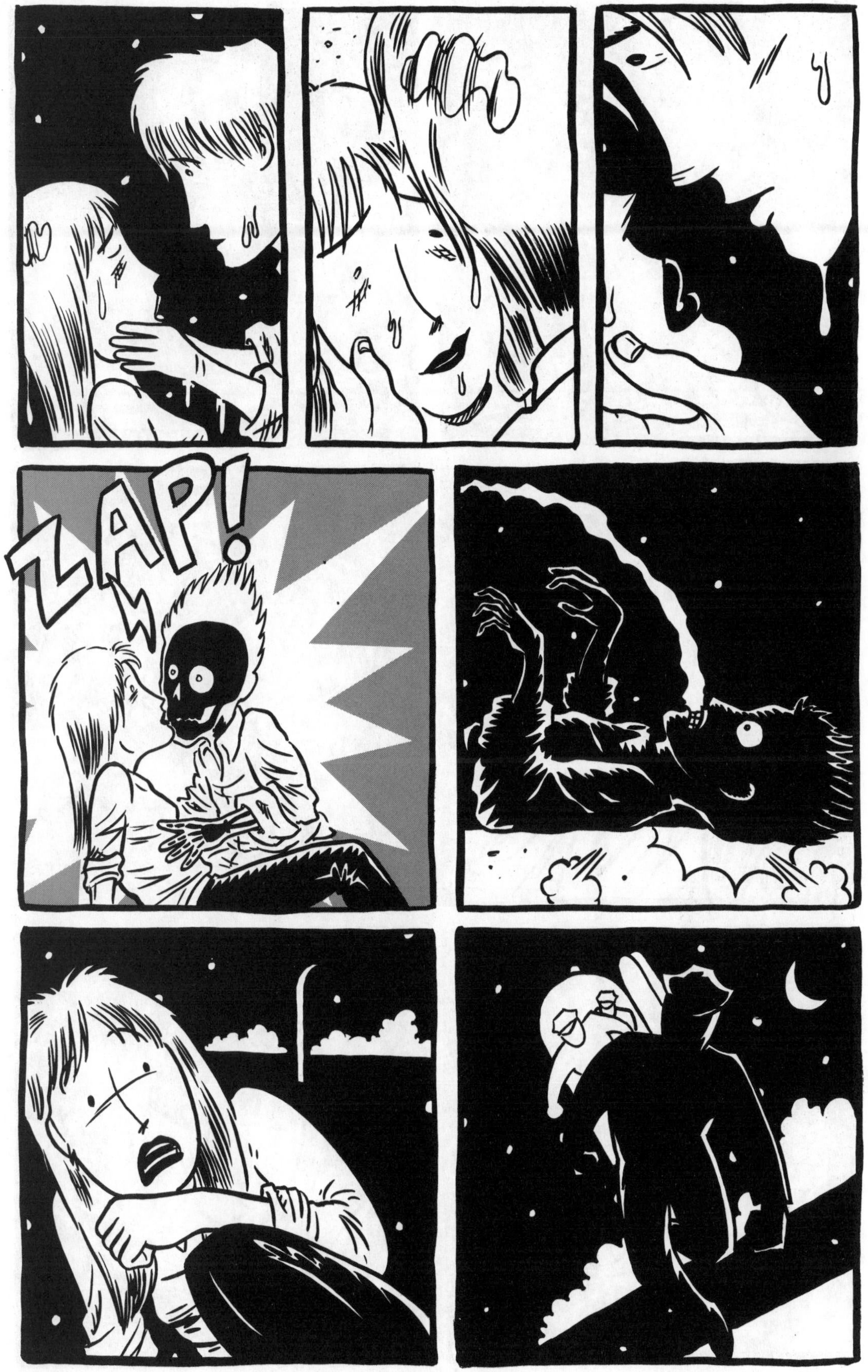
ZAP!

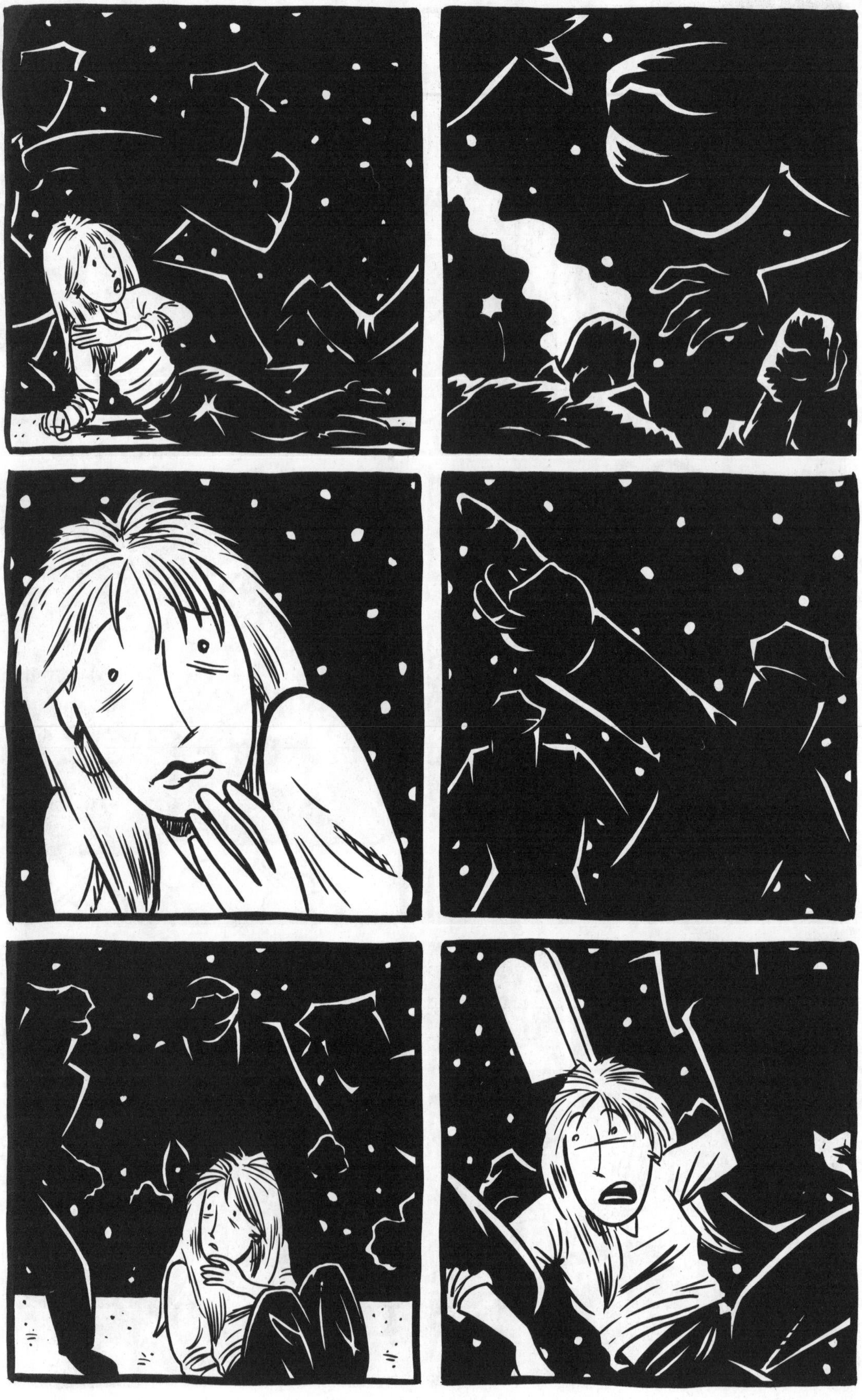

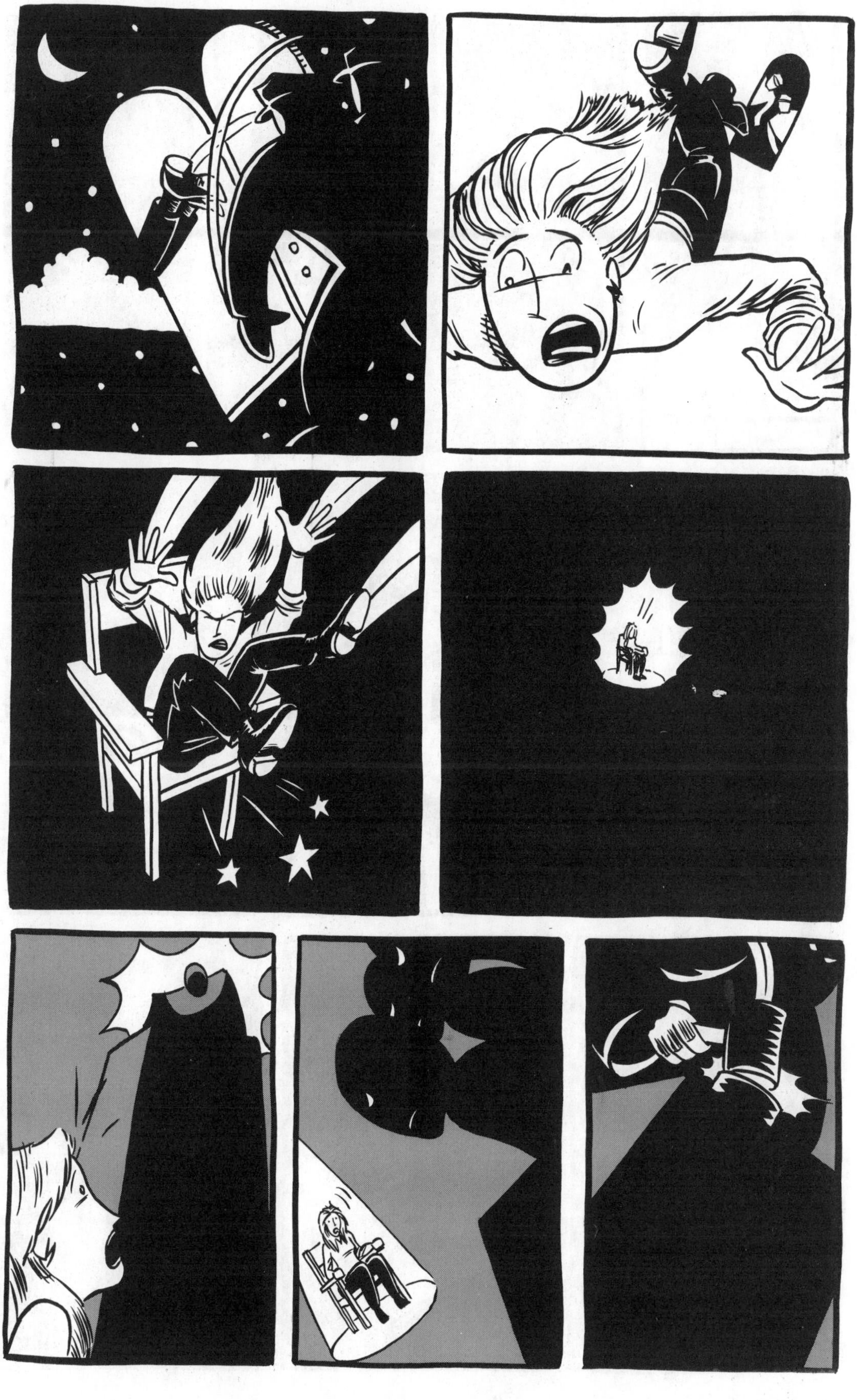

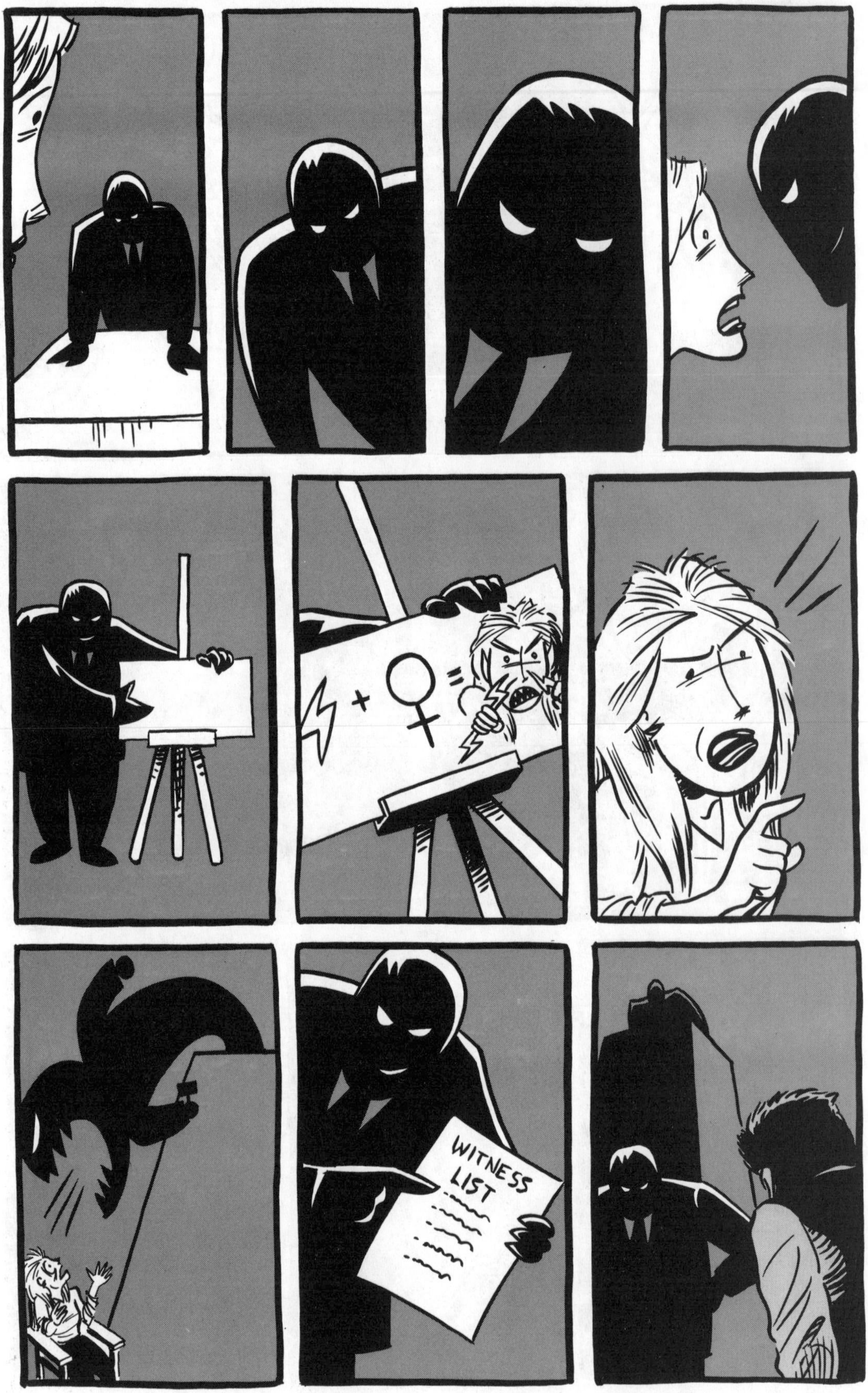
WITNESS LIST

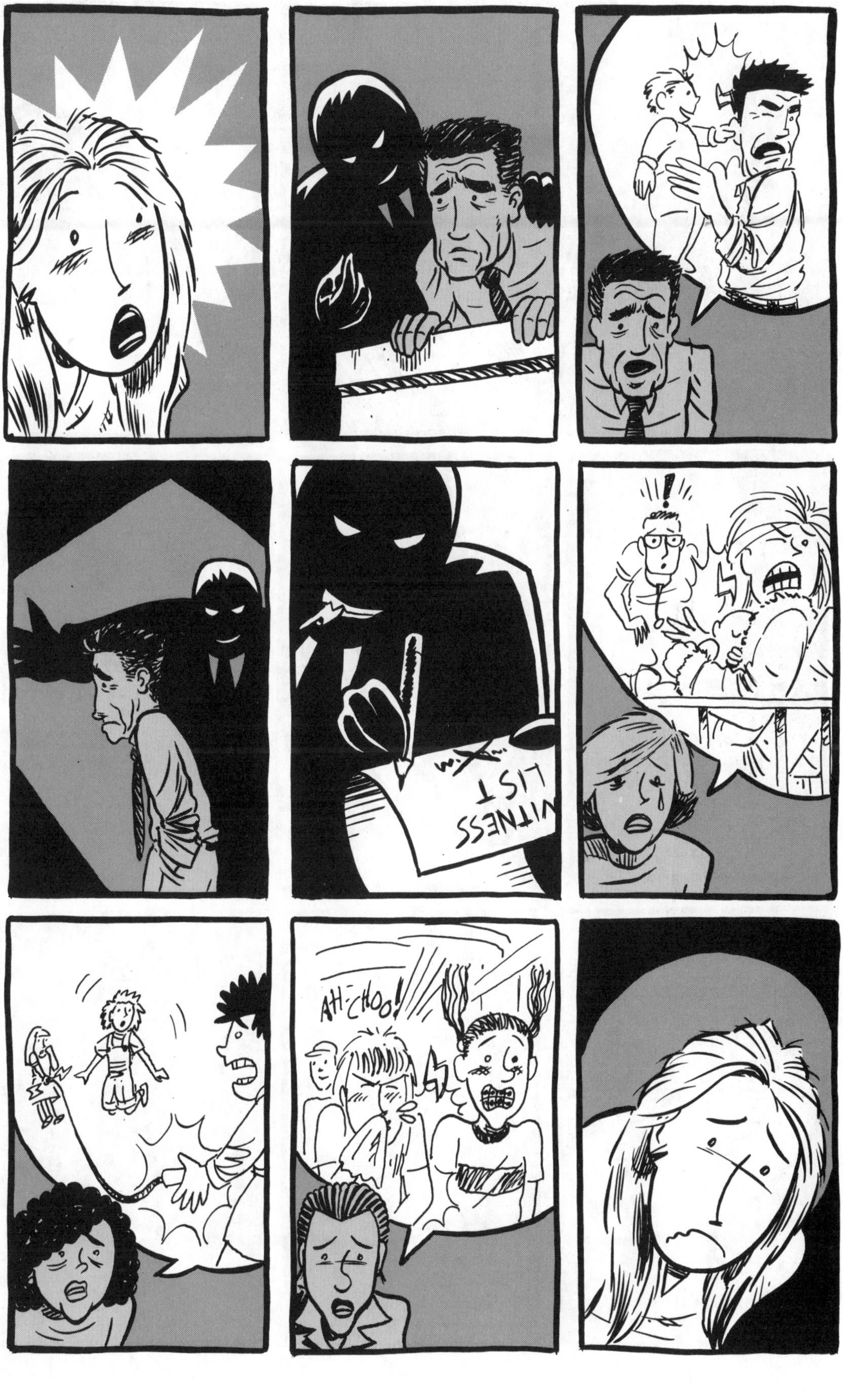
WITNESS LIST
AH-CHOO!

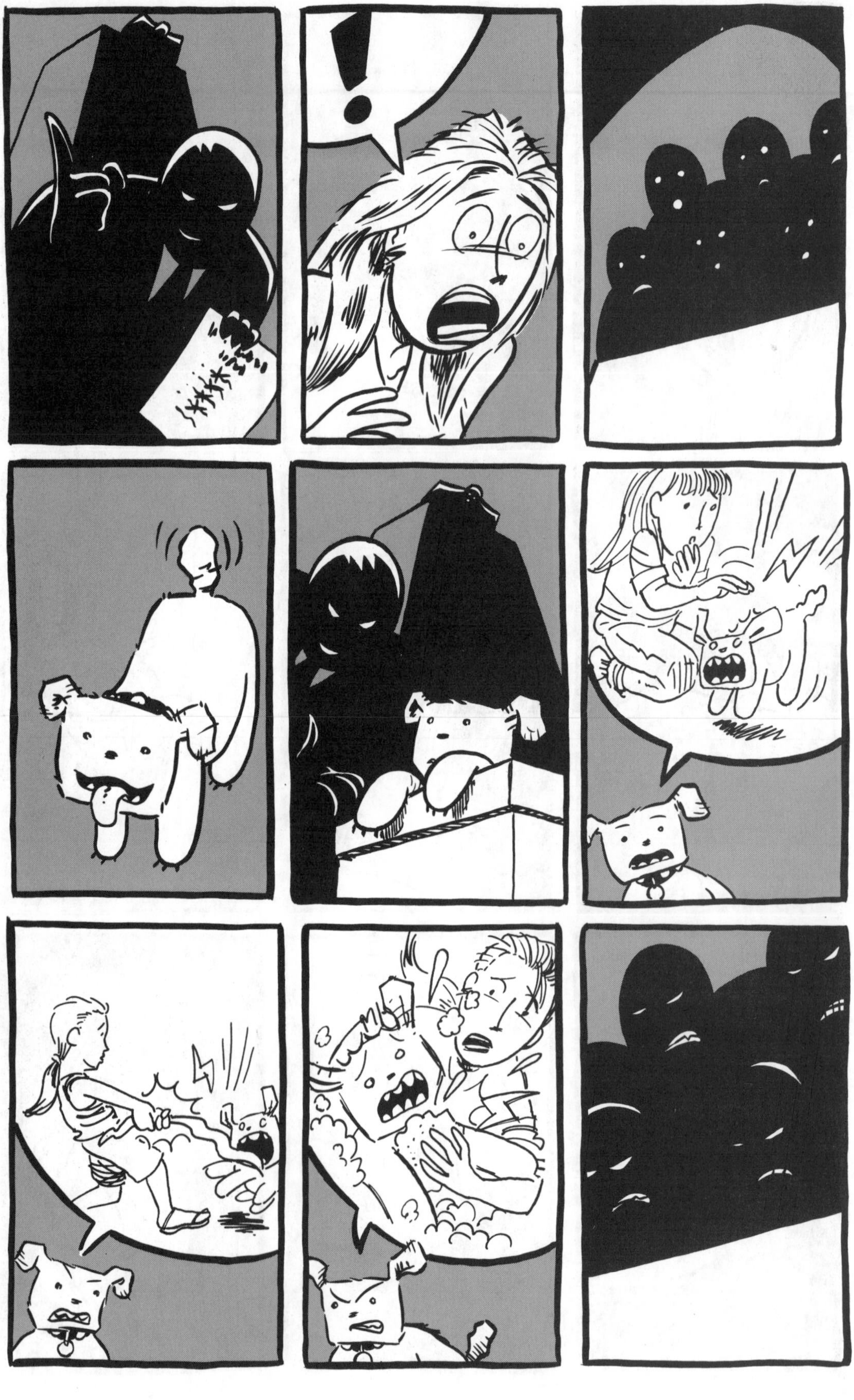
!

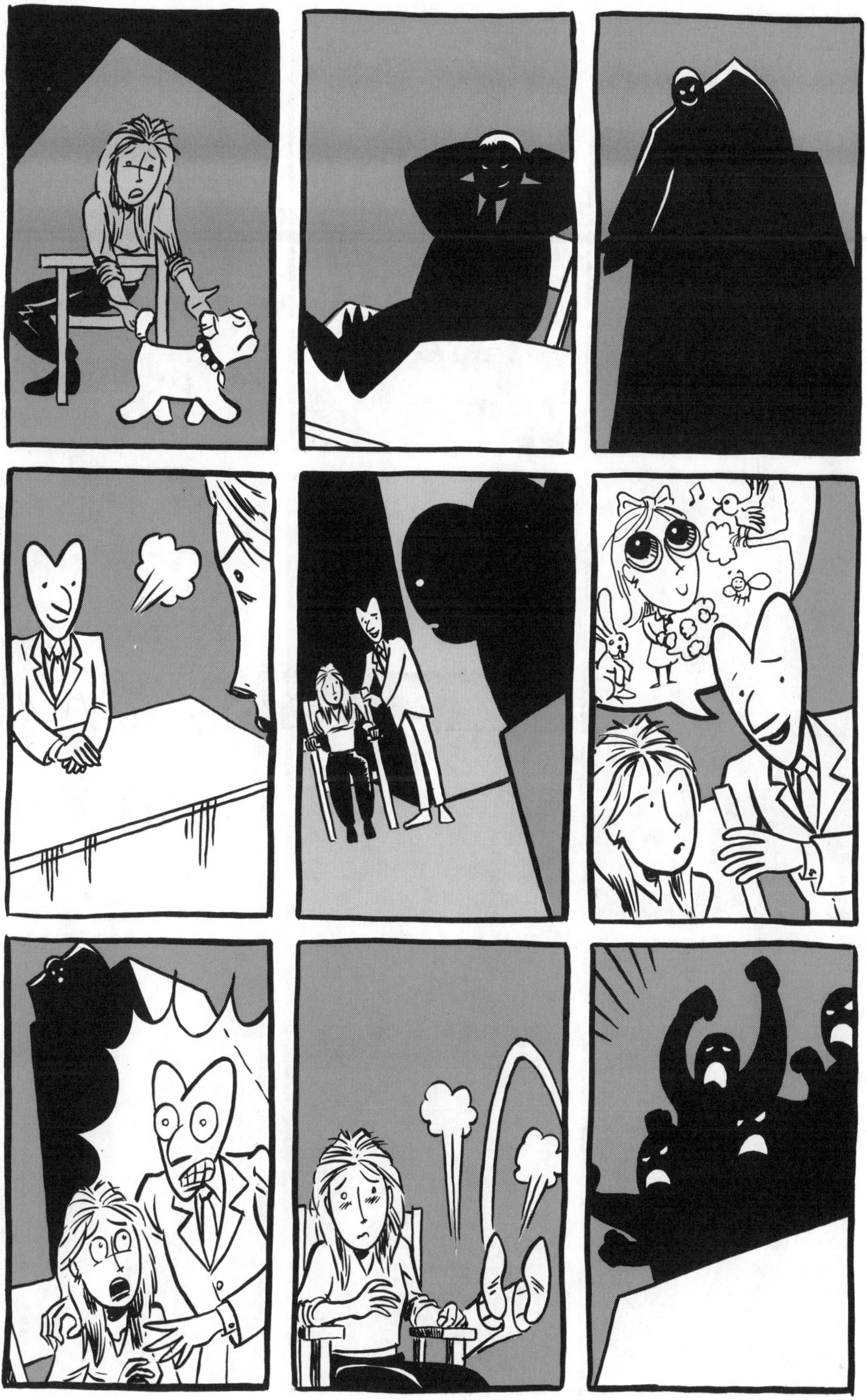

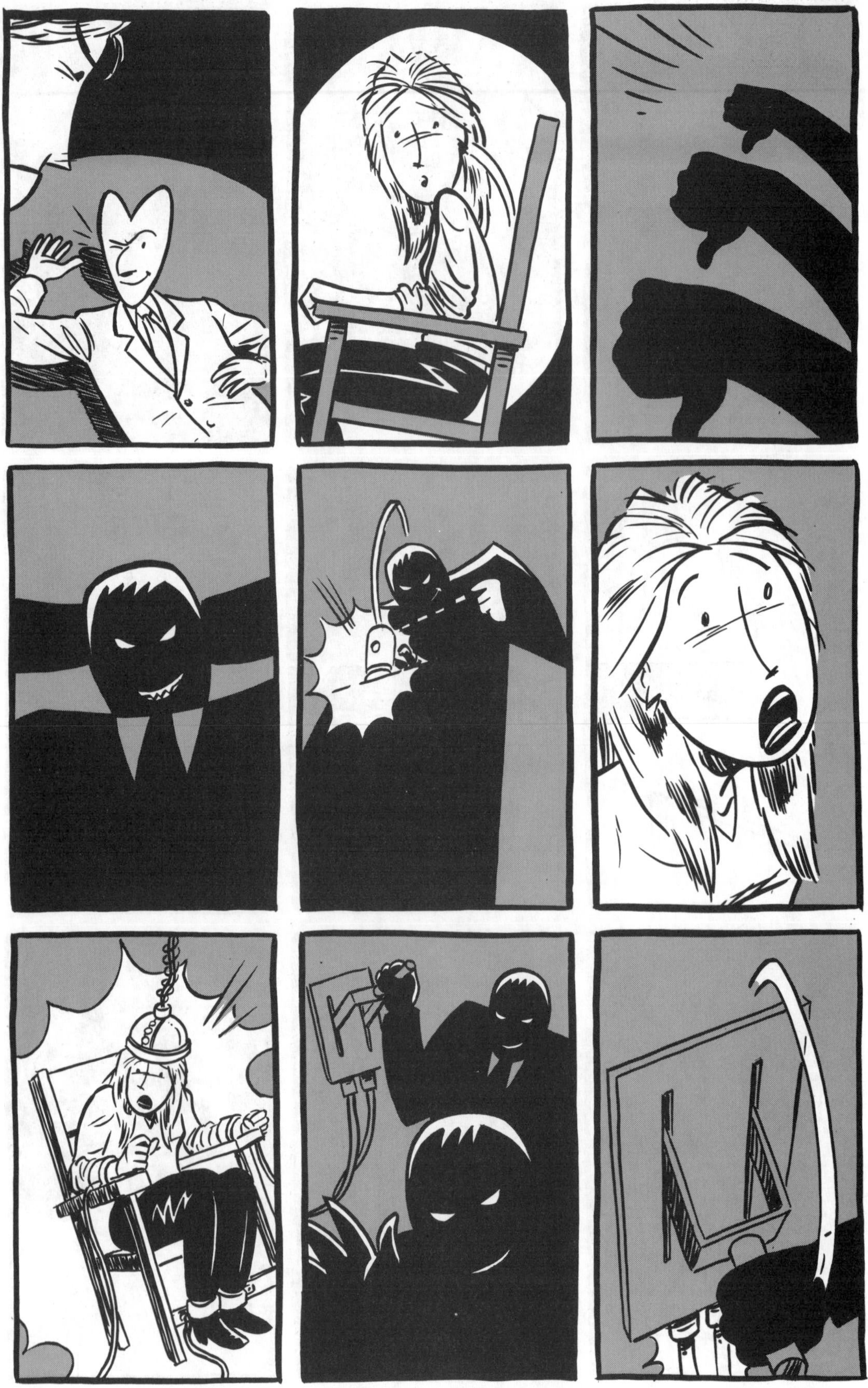

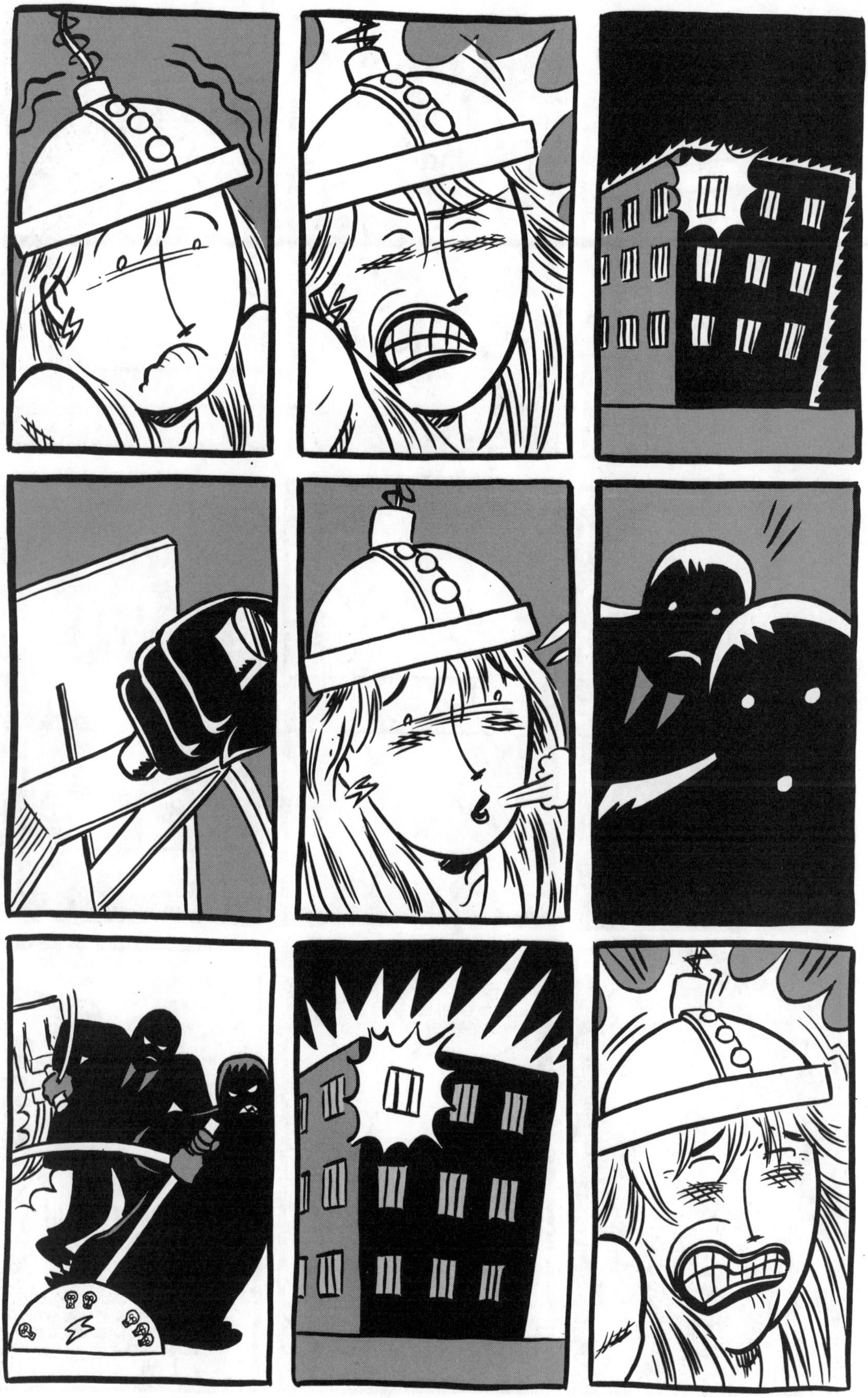

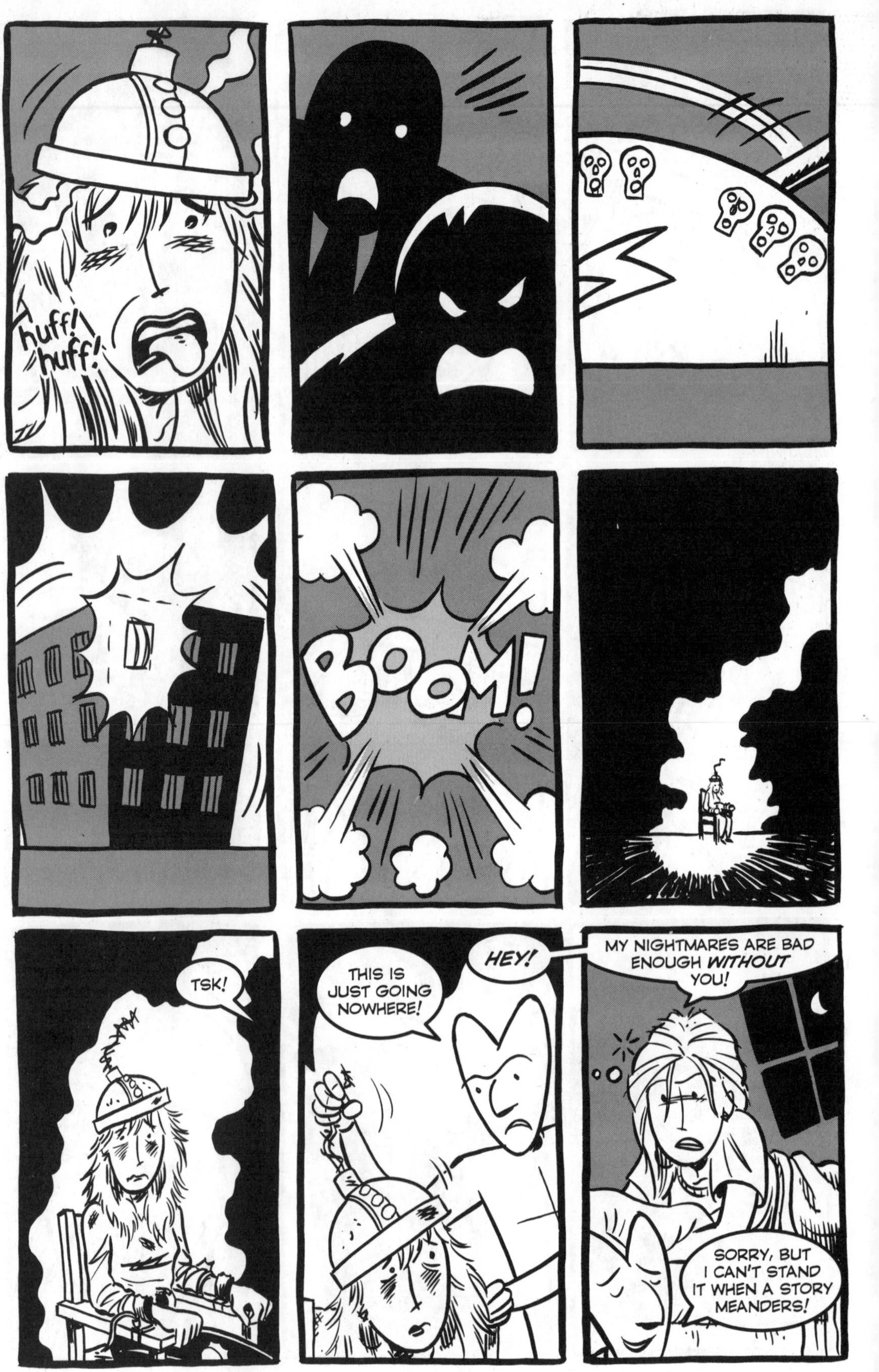
huff! huff!
BOOM!
TSK!
THIS IS JUST GOING NOWHERE!
HEY!
MY NIGHTMARES ARE BAD ENOUGH WITHOUT YOU!
SORRY, BUT I CAN'T STAND IT WHEN A STORY MEANDERS!

cover gallery

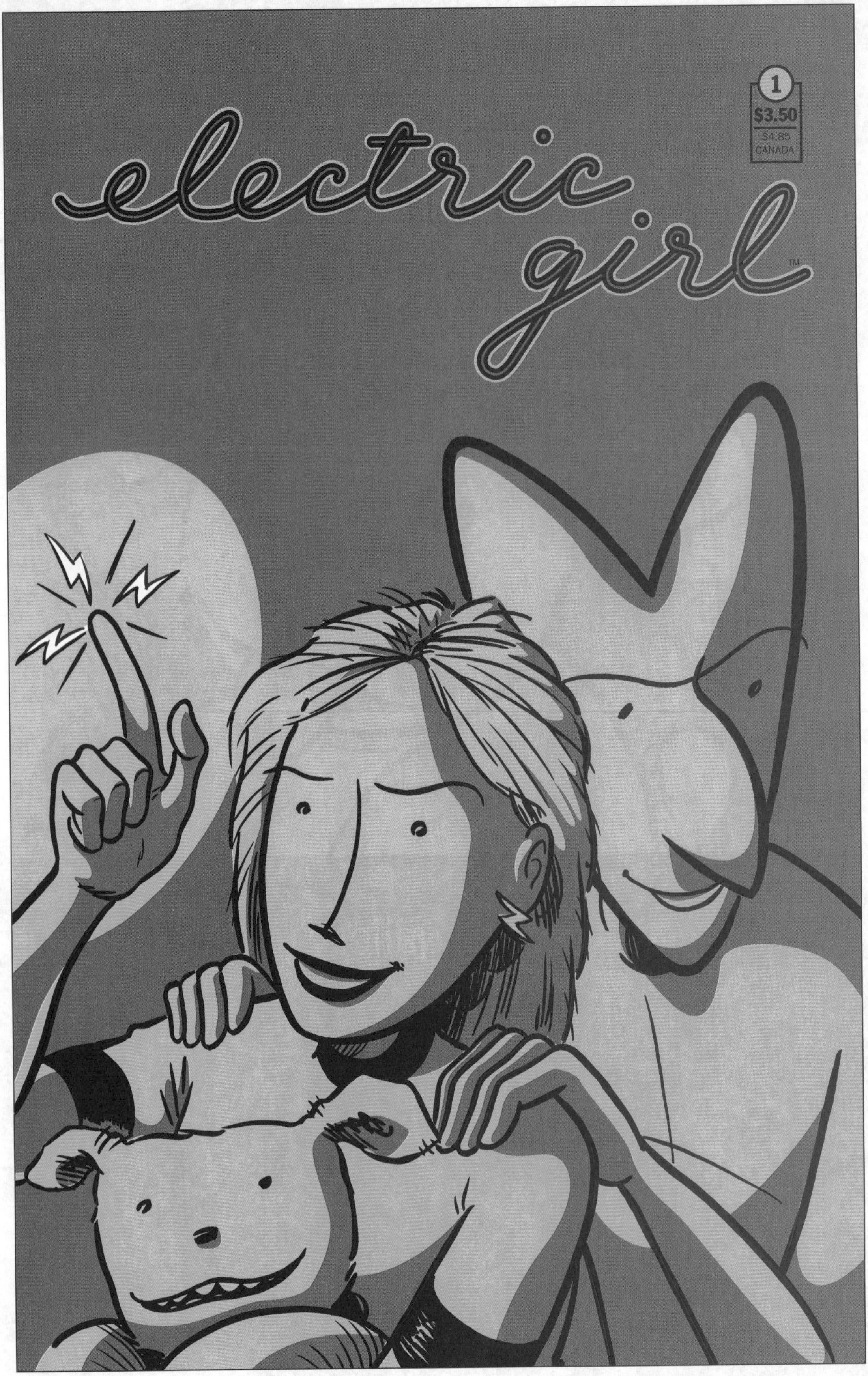

1
$3.50
$4.85 CANADA
electric girl™

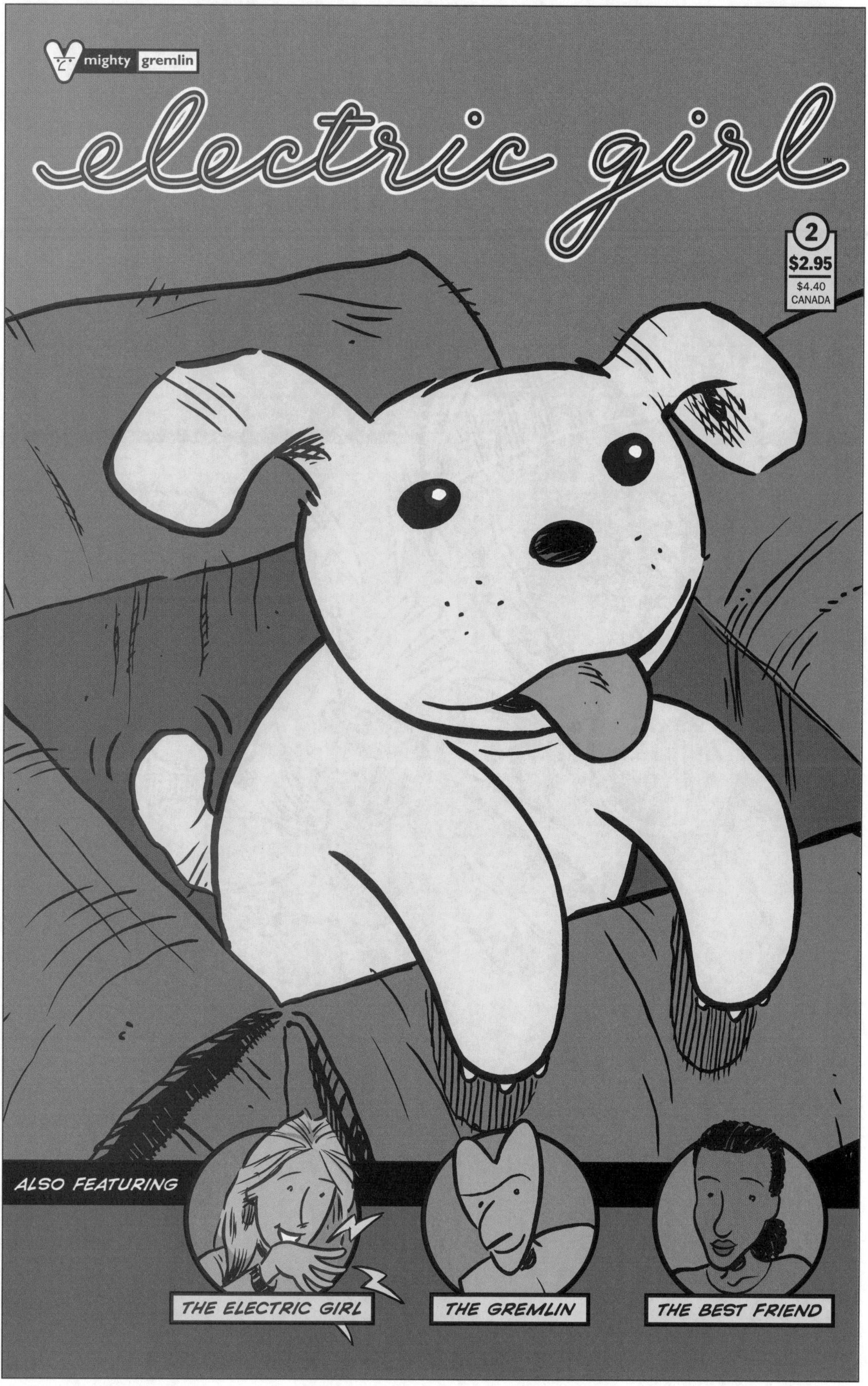
mighty gremlin
electric girl™
2
$2.95
$4.40 CANADA
ALSO FEATURING
THE ELECTRIC GIRL
THE GREMLIN
THE BEST FRIEND

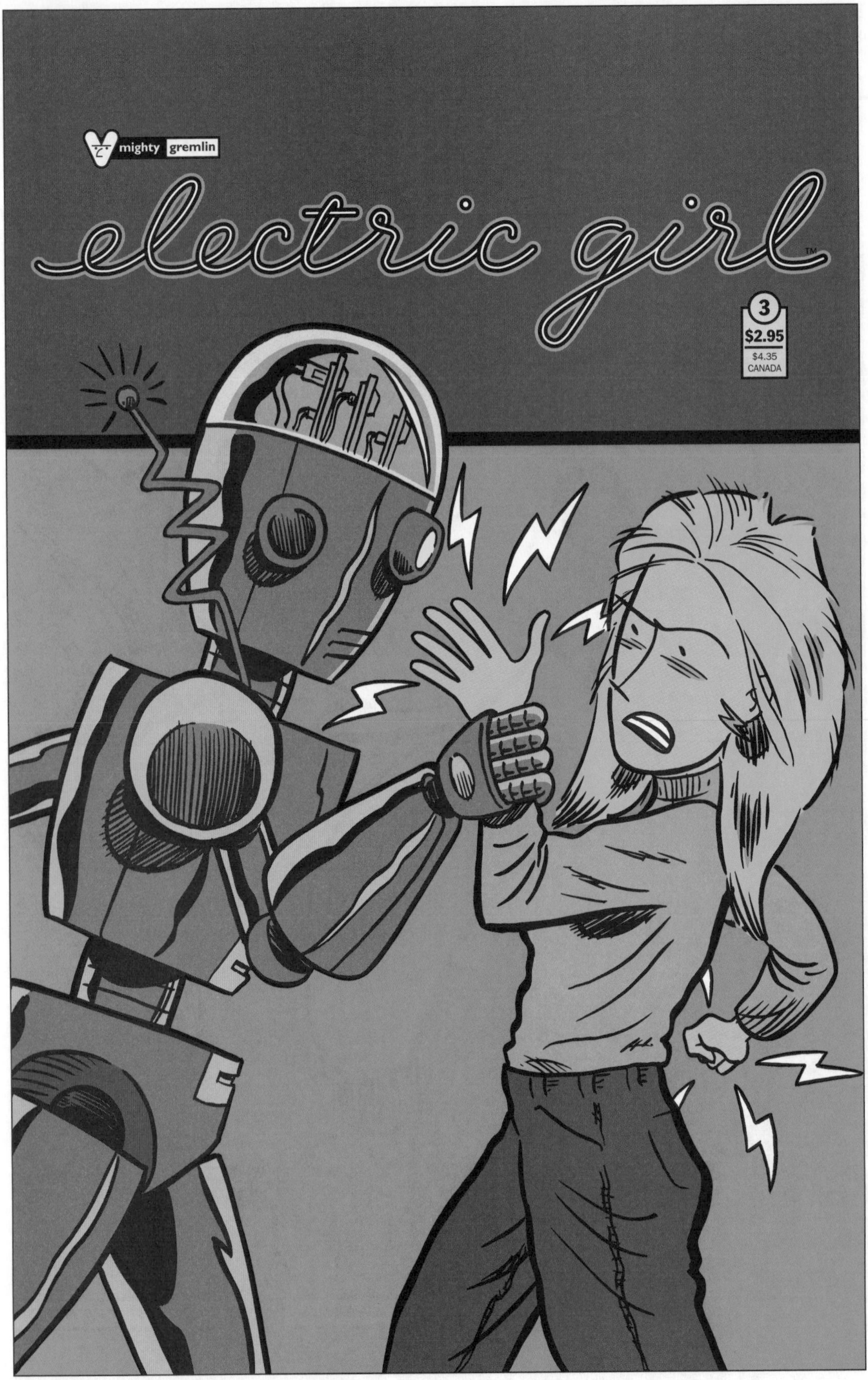

mighty gremlin
electric girl™
3
$2.95
$4.35 CANADA

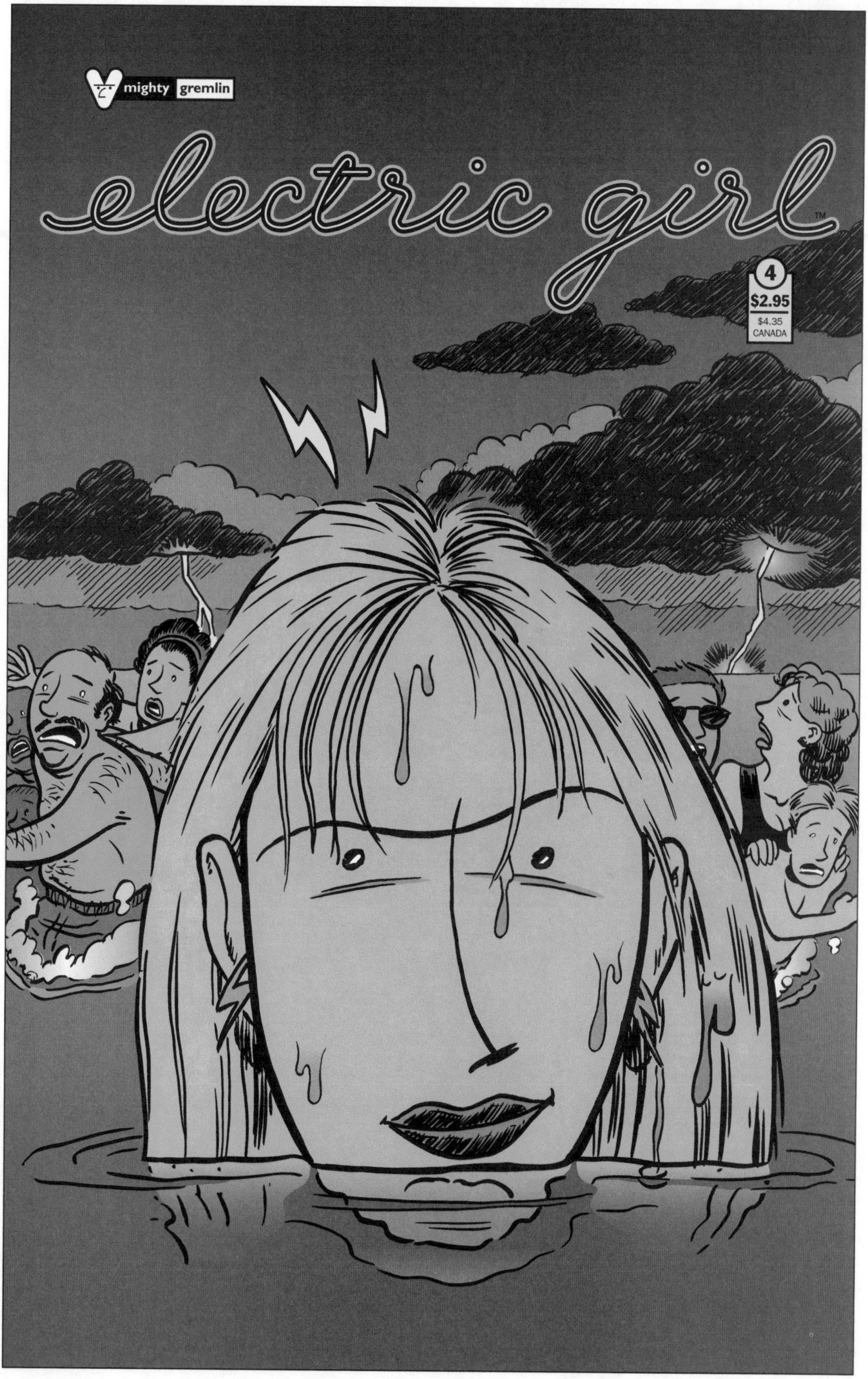
mighty gremlin
electric girl™
4
$2.95
$4.35 CANADA

Michael Brennan was born in the coastal town of Gloucester, MA, where he developed an aversion to both the ocean and seafood. He attended Massachusetts College of Art where he received his BFA with a concentration in Illustration.

In 1990, Michael started on the pre-cursor to **Electric Girl** in the form of a comic strip. After rejections from all the major syndicates, he retooled the concept in his spare time and the first issue of the **Electric Girl** comic book was published in 1998.

Mike's work has received critical recognition since the first printing of **Electric Girl Volume 1,** when he was nominated for an Eisner Award – one of the comic book industry's highest honors – in 2001. **EGv1** has also been named to the "Popular Paperbacks for Young Adults 2002" list by the Young Adult Library Services Association. (a division of the American Library Association)